CREATION
CHRIST AND CULTURE

Photo: Church of Scotland

T. F. TORRANCE

CREATION CHRIST AND CULTURE

Studies in Honour of
T. F. TORRANCE

Edited by
RICHARD W. A. McKINNEY

T. & T. CLARK LTD.
38 GEORGE STREET, EDINBURGH

PRINTED IN SCOTLAND BY
MORRISON AND GIBB LIMITED
EDINBURGH AND LONDON
FOR

T. & T. CLARK LTD., EDINBURGH

0 567 01019 8

FIRST PRINTED 1976

Preface

For more than twenty-five years Professor Torrance has been teaching the innumerable students who have flocked to New College, Edinburgh, from all over Scotland and, indeed, from all over the world. His influence during this period, on the successive generations of students who have come to study and do research at Edinburgh, has been considerable and more than matches that of his many famous predecessors and contemporaries at New College. Those who have entered into his lecture theatre, his seminar room or his study have benefited immensely from the experience. There they have encountered challenge and insight, encouragement and provocation. There, irrespective of their own particular views, they have learnt to admire and respect an eminent and learned theologian.

Professor Torrance has, throughout his career, won esteem as a theologian, as a teacher and as a man. As a theologian: because of his immense erudition within the fields of historical, philosophical and systematic theology and, indeed, in areas beyond the narrower confines of these disciplines. His great facility in being able to draw upon huge resources of learning and, in so doing, to shed imaginative light upon old problems or to make new connections between issues leaves all who have studied under him, or read his many publications, very much in his debt. As a teacher: because of his great willingness to expose himself to his students, seeking to provoke dialogue and create debate. Once we had learnt not to be overawed by his intimidating presence and learning, then those of us who were his students (especially the backbenchers'!) profited immensely from the opportunity to question and be questioned by a fine teacher. As a man: because of his great humanity and concern for others, and of his willingness to spend time, no matter how busy he was, with students who had problems or difficulties of any sort. Above all, because of his impressive faith which permeates everything that he does. It is fitting and proper that this *Festschrift* should appear in the year that Professor Torrance has been called by the Church of Scotland to be its Moderator.

These essays are contributed by a group of theologians drawn from different countries, confessions, disciplines and interests. This fact, in itself, symbolizes both the universality of the respect for Professor Torrance and the ecumenical breadth of his own interests and influence. The theme of the volume, *Creation, Christ and Culture*, has tried to take up some of his own concerns while, at the same time, making some positive contribution to the manifold tasks of contemporary critical theology. It is with respect, gratitude and admiration that we offer this *Festschrift* to Professor Torrance. With it we also echo what is an appropriately ecumenical hope: *multos faustos annos*.

In the preparation of this volume I made the initial translation of the essays contributed by Professor Moltmann and Professor Jüngel. They have both, however, corrected and emended these translations. I am grateful to Professor Yuill, until recently Professor of German at Nottingham, and to Mr John Slattery of the German department, for help in translating some difficult passages. I am also grateful to my colleague Dr Graham Davies for notes on some Hebrew terms used in Professor Moltmann's essay.

RICHARD W. A. MCKINNEY

Department of Theology,
University of Nottingham.

Contents

1 Covenant and Canon in the Old Testament

by R. E. CLEMENTS

That the Bible is divided between two Testaments, or 'covenants', provides the most basic of all the structural classifications of its contents, and at the same time offers one of the simplest and most widely used hermeneutical guides towards its interpretation. The correlation of an Old Covenant with a New Covenant has served as the most intelligible and useful way of recognizing the essential unity of the Bible within what is an evident element of disunity and discontinuity. It has been a natural outworking of this within the wide spectrum of Christian theology that the concept of covenant should provide it with a thematic framework with which to approach the Bible. The great variety of narratives, prophecies, laws, instructions and letters which go to make up the contents of the Bible, and which emanate from widely separated times and situations can be given a measure of theological perspective, and be set in some kind of relationship to each other by means of the particular covenant to which they can be referred. This is so even though many of its writings do not explicitly refer to either one of these two covenants, since the structure of the canon dictates which of them is the point of primary reference. For the Christian therefore the concept of covenant must be regarded as the foremost of a number of such concepts by which the theological, as distinct from the purely literary or historical, value and meaning of the Bible are to be understood. So far as the New Testament is concerned it is certain that the interpretation of the events surrounding the death and resurrection of Jesus of Nazareth as constitutive of a new covenant, with its consequence in a new understanding of the people of God, has arisen as a direct reflection of the fact that these events were seen to bear a unique relationship to the Old Testament. It was because this literature was already understood to point to a covenant between God and his people Israel that its application to a new series of events gave rise to the understanding that these new events constituted a new covenant. A quite primary interest attaches therefore to our obtaining some recognition of why the totality of the literature of the Old Testament came to be regarded as bearing witness to an 'old covenant' between God and his people Israel. It may be hoped that to be clear about the way in which this happened may shed some light upon its consequences for the interpretation of the Old Testament as a whole. To achieve this may hopefully serve as some small bridge between the historical-critical study of the Old Testament and the larger concerns of a Christian theology which is conscious of its biblical foundations.

At first glance the presentation of this issue as though it constituted a problem may appear strange, since it will be obvious that the prominence of the concept of covenant for the Old Testament is related to the prominence of the work of Moses and of the revelation of God on Mount Sinai which are evident in its writings. Yet in fact the issue cannot be neatly solved in this way for a number of reasons. In the first place the question of priority emerges with the recognition that, from a literary-historical viewpoint, it is precisely the importance that was attached to the Sinai event as the institution of a covenant between God and Israel that has led to such a large collection of laws, regulations and instructions being ascribed to it. Historically they certainly did not all originate here, but rather have had a diverse multiplicity of origins which can never be tracked down except in a very sketchy and incomplete way. Furthermore, as we look at the main streams of source material in the Pentateuch, it becomes plain that it is the latest strata of material which are most replete with laws and regulations which they ascribe to the revelation on Sinai. From occupying a relatively small and modest place in the earliest of the Pentateuchal narrative sources, J, the revelation on Sinai has come to occupy a very substantial place in the latest of the narrative sources, P, and thereafter an even larger mass of instruction and laws has been added, almost exclusively as a further extension of the revelation at Sinai. Why has all this happened, and why has Sinai come to enjoy this overriding significance?

A further point emerges here since the covenant between God and Israel made at Sinai is not the only historical point at which the concept of covenant is brought into play in the Old Testament to describe the relationship between them. There is a tradition of a covenant made with Abraham (Gen. 15 and 17) and of a promise made to David (2 Sam. 7), which could be described as a covenant in 2 Sam. 23:5. Even more striking and noteworthy is the fact that in P, the latest of the narrative sources of the Pentateuch, what took place on Sinai is not called a covenant, and this term is reserved for the promise made to Abraham regarding the greatness destined for his descendants (Gen. 17:2 ff.). Nonetheless in the way in which final shape has been given to the Pentateuch it is the event which occurred on Sinai, interpreted as the making of a covenant, which provides the necessary central point of focus for the entire work. As a result of this the effects of such an interpretation are evident throughout the whole of the Old Testament.

This leads us to yet another fact which has become clearer in the light of the extensive, and ultimately very productive, research into the use of the term *berith*—'covenant' in the Old Testament. This is that, although in a wide range of contexts, both sacred and profane, the term is certainly quite old, it was not used in the earliest sources to describe the Sinai event, except in a relatively minor way (Exod. 34:10).[1] It is the Deuteronomic literature of the seventh and sixth centuries B.C. which has given the term a new meaning and currency as the key concept by which the relationship between God and Israel is to be understood. It was only at a particular point in the history of Israel that the notion of covenant was appealed to as the most appropriate way of describing the nature of its relationship to God, even though such a description certainly had antecedents. This is the conclusion reached by L. Perlitt in his vitally important study *Bundestheologie im Alten Testament*,[2] to which we shall have occasion to refer again later. The actual usage of the Hebrew term *berith* therefore is not in any way uniformly spread throughout the literature of the Pentateuch, nor that of the Old Testament more widely, but is heavily concentrated in the book of Deuteronomy and the literature which has been directly influenced by this, namely the history of Joshua–2 Kings and the book of Jeremiah. We can therefore broadly recognize that the Deuteronomic covenant theology represents a kind of apex in the understanding of covenant in the Old Testament. In the Priestly Document, P, and the history of the Chronicler the term is used very differently and in wide areas of the prophetic books the term is not used at all. Certainly we may admit with W. Eichrodt that 'even where the covenant is not explicitly mentioned the spiritual premisses of a covenant relationship with God are manifestly present',[3] but this is not true to anything like the extent that Eichrodt claims. In wide areas of the Old Testament we can see that it is the way in which the material has been redacted, and even more prominently, the manner of its incorporation into the canon which has invested it with a covenant reference. This is

[1] The importance of this collection of cultic laws and regulations in the J account of the Sinai revelation, and its part in the emergence of its distinctive interpretation as covenant, is argued by F.-E. Wilms, *Das jahwistische Bundesbuch in Exodus 34* (Studien zum Alten und Neuen Testament XXXII), Munich, 1973, and J. Halbe, *Das Privilegrecht Jahwes. Ex. 34, 10–26. Gestalt und Wesen, Herkunft und Wirken in vordeuteronomischer Zeit* (FRLANT 114), Göttingen, 1975.

[2] L. Perlitt, *Bundestheologie im Alten Testament* (WMANT 36), Neukirchen-Vluyn, 1969, esp. pp. 54–128.

[3] W. Eichrodt, *Old Testament Theology*, Vol. I, (Eng. tr. by J. A. Baker), London, 1961, pp. 36 f.

undoubtedly particularly noticeable in the case of the prophetic writings of the Old Testament, where a broad categorization of the work of the pre-exilic prophets in relation to the Sinai covenant emerged, which was not explicitly present in the sayings of the prophets themselves. This gives rise to the main thesis of this essay: that it is the process of the formation of the Old Testament scriptures into a sacred canon which has done most to relate them to a concept of covenant, and that it is the Sinai-Horeb covenant which is consistently the point to which this reference is made. Canonization has evidently been a process in which the key concept of covenant has played a decisive role.

Since the twentieth century has witnessed the currency of three widely adopted hypotheses to explain the importance of the concept of covenant in the Old Testament it may be in order to reflect upon these. The first of these we may call the social-anthropological theory which has become best associated with the name of Max Weber,[1] although that of J. Pedersen[2] must certainly be set alongside his. This claims that in the type of social structure which we find attested of the Israelite tribes before the formation of a territorial state under David the institution of covenant, or oath, was fundamental to the stability and harmony of society. It extended the obligations of peace, trust and understanding beyond the natural ties of kinship. All of this is undoubtedly true, and can call for little dissent, but it fails to explain the reason for the use of the concept in so distinctive a way by Israel. In particular it fails to show why it was the God-man aspect of the relationship which became of paramount importance to Israel's interpretation of covenant, when its ordinary usage stressed the lateral relationships between man and man. It is precisely its distinctive use to describe the God-man relationship that we are concerned to understand. Furthermore it also calls for some fuller explanation if we are to know why Israel retained, or resorted back to, the concept of covenant after the formation of the state, when its social structure no longer required it. The difficulty is solved very simply and neatly by Eichrodt in postulating that 'Moses, taking over a concept of long standing in secular life, based the worship of Yahweh on a covenant agreement'.[3] Yet this is to introduce a historical hypothesis to explain a theological one, and in general we must recognize that there is virtually no evidence in favour of it, and much that is against. From a historical viewpoint our knowledge of what actually took place on Mount Sinai is obscure in the extreme, but more relevantly we should note that our earliest accounts of what

[1] M. Weber, *Gesammelte Aufsätze zur Religionssoziologie, III, Das Antike Judentum*, 1921.

[2] J. Pedersen, *Der Eid bei den Semiten*, Strassburg, 1914.

[3] W. Eichrodt, *op. cit.*, p. 37.

took place there stress most emphatically its significance as a moment of divine revelation when a theophany took place. The J account does mention the word *berith* in Exod. 34:10, and many have seen the account of the meal eaten by the elders of Israel in the presence of God in Exod. 24:11, as either intentionally an act of covenant agreement, or at least capable of being interpreted in this way.[1] Whether this is so or not, it is unlikely that this account goes back to the earliest stage of the Sinai tradition, and in any case it is an example of a relationship of a much less clearly defined nature than we are concerned to explain. To this extent it matters little whether we call it a *berith*-covenant or not, for it was certainly very much less than was later taken to be implicit in the relationship established on Sinai. The most we can conclude is that the tradition of what took place on Mount Sinai may early on have come to speak of it as a *berith* in a relatively minor way, and that this contributed to a much fuller and more distinctive interpretation of this term by the Deuteronomic literature.

The second of the hypotheses which have been given wide currency in an attempt to explain the importance of the concept of covenant to the Old Testament is that of the tribal amphictyony, understood as equivalent to a tribal federation. The thesis that before the formation of the monarchic state in the Saul-David era Israel was an amphictyony of twelve tribes goes back originally to a suggestion by A. Alt, which has been extensively worked out and developed by M. Noth.[2] Its merits and weaknesses have been examined and re-examined so much in the past decade that it would be out of place to attempt to do so again.[3] All that concerns us in the present context is the recognition of its hypothetical nature, and the fact that an amphictyony in itself does not necessarily imply that its members recognized their relationship to constitute some form of covenant agreement. As an explanation of at least some aspects of the life of Israel in the pre-state period the thesis of an amphictyony has a continuing value until it can be replaced by a more adequate account of Israel's structure. However, this certainly does not encourage any endorsement of the numerous derivative hypotheses which have been built upon it, and which have led to the use of the supposed existence of an amphictyonic covenant community to explain a wide variety

[1] Cf. D. J. McCarthy, *Treaty and Covenant* (Analecta Biblica 21), Rome, 1963, p. 10: 'A handclasp or a meal in common may constitute a covenant.'

[2] A. Alt, 'Israel, politische Geschichte', *Die Religion in Geschichte und Gegenwart*, 2nd ed., Bd. III, 1929, pp. 438 f.; M. Noth, *Das System der Zwölf Stämme Israels* (BWANT IV: 1), Stuttgart, 1930, rep. Darmstadt, 1966.

[3] A useful summary of criticisms is provided by A. Mayes, *Israel in the Period of the Judges* (S.B.T. Second Series 29), London, 1974; G. Fohrer, 'Altes Testament—"Amphiktyonie"—Bund?', *Studien zur alttestamentliche Theologie und Geschichte* (BZAW 115), Berlin, 1969, pp. 84–119.

of features in later Israel which came to make use of the idea of covenant. As a consequence the attempt to make the amphictyony the source of the major elements of the Deuteronomic covenant theology, as advocated for example by G. Ernest Wright,[1] must be regarded as totally unsubstantiated. Whatever features Deuteronomy has drawn from a historical knowledge of Israel's life before the introduction of the monarchy, there is nothing to uphold the contention that this was the source of its covenant theology. On the contrary, it becomes plain from the main contents of this covenant theology that this must be ruled out.

The third of the recent hypotheses which has been employed to an almost alarming extent in an attempt to explain the importance which the Old Testament attaches to the concept of covenant is that of a borrowing and adaptation from ancient Near Eastern Vassal-Treaties.[2] So widespread in fact has been the enthusiastic adoption of this hypothesis by some groups of Old Testament scholars that the very extent to which such a borrowing has been regarded as evident in so many different parts of the Old Testament has inevitably aroused suspicion and rejection. I have already dealt with the question of whether such an Israelite adoption of the form of Vassal-Treaties can be detected in parts of the prophetic literature, and have opposed such an idea, in my book *Prophecy and Tradition*.[3] No doubt to be too firmly insistent that the Old Testament has remained totally unaffected by the form of such treaties runs the same risk on the negative side as is demonstrated on the positive side by those who assert such a view, namely, that too much is built upon too limited and uncertain a range of evidence. It may indeed be that the Deuteronomic covenant theology has drawn in some limited measure upon the known patterns and language of statecraft in the seventh century B.C. in shaping its own ideas and language. If so then this borrowing provides one of a number of influential factors in creating a distinctive cluster of Deuteronomic religious ideas. It was certainly not the determining influence, nor in any way a very decisive one. Rather the major formative elements in the growth and formulation of the covenant theology of the Old Testament generally, and of the Deuteronomic movement in particular, must be seen to lie in the unique historical and religious situation in which Israel found itself at the end of the eighth century B.C., and in the years that immediately followed. Threatened within by a mixed inheritance of religious syncretism, oppressive monarchic rule and popular attachment to

[1] G. Ernest Wright, 'Deuteronomy', *Interpreter's Bible*, Vol. II, New York–Nashville, 1953, pp. 309 ff.

[2] Cf. especially G. E. Mendenhall, 'Covenant', *Interpreter's Dictionary of the Bible*, Vol. I, New York–Nashville, 1962, cols. 714–723.

[3] R. E. Clements, *Prophecy and Tradition*, Oxford, 1975, pp. 15–23.

an amoral cultus, and from outside by the restraints of Assyrian suzerainty, Judah faced an uncertain future. It was the ardent conviction of the Deuteronomic movement that Judah would, and could, survive as the heir of Israel, only by a renewed obedience and loyalty to Yahweh its God. It is in this unique context of political and religious crisis that the language of covenant came to be introduced and developed in a distinctive way as a suitable means of expressing the privileges and demands of Israel-Judah's relationship to Yahweh.[1] Certainly this covenant theology was not developed entirely *de novo*, but out of features already current in the religious traditions of the nation. Nevertheless what the Deuteronomic movement made of such a covenant theology is the important thing, and in this it is very clear that it was essentially a new creation. The term 'covenant' has certainly not previously been employed in the distinctive way that the Deuteronomists now affirmed, and this is the decisive factor.[2]

Overall we can see that it is the Deuteronomic movement which has established a clear-cut and highly significant theological proposition around the term *berith*, and has given this a prominent place in the Old Testament. More than this, however, it is the spiritual heirs of these Deuteronomists who have intruded the notion of covenant so firmly and deeply into the religious life of Israel that it has exercised a formative influence in shaping the Old Testament canon. Ultimately the notion of covenant has affected the existence, structure and interpretation of the canon as a whole, so as to make it into a literature which bears witness in all its parts to the covenant between Israel and God. We can usefully proceed therefore to consider what the essential features were of this Deuteronomic covenant theology, and by what paths of literary redaction the final canon has been reached.

There are three features regarding this covenant theology which stand out very strikingly, and which lend to it a theological character of a unique kind. These concern its relationship to Israel as a nation, to the land of Canaan as God's supreme gift to it, and to a written collection of laws and instructions described as *torah*. All three features have been passed on from this Deuteronomic nucleus to the Old Testament as a whole, thereby making it a 'covenant literature'—an Old Testament. As regards the origin of each of them, it is clear from the researches of Perlitt that they did not emerge all together in one single movement, but over a period of time so that the very word *berith* is more prominent in the later Deuteronomic writings than in the earlier. Nevertheless the details

1 The character and development of this theology is set out very clearly by L. Perlitt in the work cited above p. 3, n. 2.

2 Even W. Eichrodt, *op. cit.*, p. 53, admits that the Deuteronomic development occasioned 'a slight shift in the concept of the *b^{e}rīt*'.

of this need not concern us here since it is the final product that has contributed so heavily to the structure and understanding of the canon.

That Yahweh made his covenant with the entire nation of Israel, prior to the introduction of the monarchy and the subsequent division into two kingdoms, is asserted by the affirmation that this covenant was made in Horeb when 'all Israel' was present: 'Yahweh our God made a covenant with us in Horeb. Not with our fathers did Yahweh make this covenant, but with us, who are all of us here alive this day' (Deut. 5:2–3). Because this covenant was made with the entire nation (Heb. *goy*) of Israel, the Deuteronomic literature rigidly refrains from speaking of the divided kingdoms as constituting two *goyim*, rather they are the 'two houses of Israel'. The supreme benefit which Yahweh conferred upon this covenant nation was the gift of the land of Canaan, which is pictured as a kind of *summum bonum*, a supreme good and the source of all other wealth and prosperity. Conversely the supreme evil which threatens Israel if it should prove to be disobedient to the covenant is to be thrown out of this land: 'Therefore you shall keep his statutes and his commandments, which I command you this day, that it may go well with you, and with your children after you, and that you may prolong your days in the land which Yahweh your God gives you forever' (Deut. 4:40; cf. v. 26).

Existence as a nation and living on the land which God gave to their fathers are regarded as making up the 'salvation', or 'blessedness', of Israel affirmed in the covenant with Yahweh. That already much of the land had been lost in the eighth century as a result of the Assyrian incursions into Israel's affairs was clearly known to the Deuteronomists, as was also the fact that a substantial part of old Israel had disappeared with the downfall of the Northern Kingdom in 721 B.C. Nevertheless Judah remained as the surviving part of the nation with possession of a significant part of the land. This fact is of the utmost importance in connection with the much discussed question whether the Deuteronomic covenant theology is predominantly a theology of grace or of legalism. We must unhesitatingly insist on the former, for initially the Deuteronomic movement addressed itself to a people living within the sphere of divine salvation, but warning them that they could lose this with all its benefits if they proved disobedient to the covenant demands of God. It is this dimension of the Deuteronomic covenant theology which is linked so closely to its third main feature namely that its demands have been revealed and externalized in a written *torah*, which constitutes a 'book of the covenant' (2 Kings 23:3). This is simply an abbreviated description of 'the words of this covenant that were written in this book'. However so close is the identification between the idea of the covenant and the form of a written *torah* that obedience to the covenant and to the written *torah* become indistinguishable (cf. Jer. 11:1–8).

In origin the Hebrew word *torah* denotes some kind of religious, and predominantly priestly, instruction so that its adoption by the Deuteronomists undoubtedly lent to it a greatly extended meaning. They themselves defined it as made up of 'commandments, testimonies and statutes' (Deut. 4:44; cf. 2 Kings 23:3), thereby giving it a pronouncedly legal and ethical connotation which it certainly had not previously had. Within the Deuteronomic writings there is a substantial body of historical narrative tradition, so that this also came to be regarded as *torah*, and later the Deuteronomists extended it still further to relate it to prophecies and the prophetic writings (so especially 2 Kings 17:13). From this basis it became eventually a term of sufficient breadth for it to be used to describe the contents of the entire Old Testament. It is this point that most concerns us in the present essay. When we ask the question 'What is the literature of the Old Testament?', the unequivocal answer which that literature itself gives to us is 'The *torah* of the covenant between Yahweh and Israel'. This is neither because of the general pervasiveness of the idea of covenant within Israelite religion, since the term is not all that frequent, nor because of the general suitability of the term *torah* to describe the contents of the Old Testament, since this is not the case. The Old Testament can be described as *torah* only by a great extension of the original meaning of the term. It is the process of the formation of the Old Testament into a canon which has made possible its general characterization as *torah*, and this has become possible because this process of canonization has given a central focus to the tradition of Yahweh's covenant with Israel at Sinai-Horeb.

That the process of the formation of a written canon of scripture really begins with the book of Deuteronomy and the acceptance of a significant part of this as the basis of Josiah's reform in 621 B.C. has been accepted in virtually every modern study of the origin of the Old Testament canon. What has not been so clear until the emergence of a redaction-critical approach to the study of the Pentateuch has been the rather strange way in which this canonical book of Deuteronomy was incorporated with JEP to form the substantial basis of our canonical Pentateuch. The failure to recognize this is a weakness in the otherwise very useful and constructive book *Torah and Canon*[1] by J. A. Sanders. He starts from the recognition that the characterization of the Old Testament as *torah* is a process that belongs in parallel to its structure as a canon. Yet he traces this process basically to an understanding of the meaning of the word

[1] J. A. Sanders, *Torah and Canon*, Philadelphia, 1972.

torah itself as containing both kerygma and didache—divine revelation in the form of historical narrative and demands which define the response that man must make to this in the form of law. This is no doubt true enough, yet it fails to make clear that what binds these two things together and provides each of them with a certain content and range of meaning is the notion of covenant. The Pentateuch was seen to be *torah* because it is a literature relating to the covenant between Yahweh and Israel. In consequence of this the *torah* is rooted in a real history and is closely bound up with the two realities which form a central part of this history so far as the Old Testament is concerned: Israel's existence as a nation and its possession of the land of Canaan. We cannot understand the Old Testament satisfactorily if we fail to take account of these things, as the recent book by W. D. Davies *The Gospel and the Land*[1] reminds us. That the Old Testament canon was understood as the *torah* given by Yahweh to Israel, with its primary revelation at Sinai, can only be explained theologically on the basis of the concomitant belief that a covenant existed between them. It is the connection made by Deuteronomy between covenant and *torah* which provided the basis for the subsequent characterization of the entire Pentateuch as *torah*, and for regarding this as the core of the Old Testament. Such a connection between *torah* and covenant gave to the former term an eschatological dimension, since the understanding of how the covenant was to be realized was set within a context of hope. The wider effects of this are to be seen in the differing patterns of interpretation which emerged in Judaism and Christianity. Whereas the latter placed greatest stress upon the eschatological factor, the former saw *torah* as predominantly a timeless and ahistorical reality. What is clear is that the element of eschatological hope is very prominent in the Old Testament literature and has entered deeply into the formation of the canon. This is revealed by a proper regard for the way in which the original nucleus of the canon in the book of Deuteronomy was redacted and extended in the subsequent formation of the Old Testament.

Most significant of all in this respect is the fact that, although the book of Deuteronomy is of an earlier date than the Pentateuchal source P, it was only combined to form the Pentateuch as the last of the four main source strata. Hence we have a work which is structured JEP (basically Genesis to Numbers) with D (Deuteronomy). The book of Deuteronomy was added last, although it was not the latest to be written, but was, by common consent of scholars, the first to be regarded as canonical. It is this last major step of Pentateuchal redaction which has made the whole into a canonical

[1] W. D. Davies, *The Gospel and the Land. Early Christianity and Jewish Territorial Doctrine*, Berkeley–Los Angeles–London, 1974.

work and which has carried over the Deuteronomic conception of a canonical *torah* to the whole. Sanders is certainly wrong when he states so categorically: 'Most of the legal material in the Pentateuch was contributed by P' (*op. cit.*, pp. 35–6). The distinctively 'legal' conception of the Pentateuch was contributed by Deuteronomy, or more precisely by the redactor who combined Deuteronomy with JEP. Subsequent to this, some substantial 'Deuteronomistic' redactions were made to the earlier (JEP) account of the revelation at Sinai, the most notable of which is the inclusion of the Decalogue at Exodus 20:2–17. Such a redaction was certainly not theologically neutral, as has sometimes been maintained,[1] but was a most decisive step in investing the literature of the Pentateuch with the authority of Yahweh's covenant and *torah* revealed at Horeb-Sinai.

This theological aspect of the redaction history of the Pentateuch is all the more revealing because of its connection with the formation of a collection of canonical prophecies and prophetic writings. I have already touched upon this in my book *Prophecy and Tradition*[2] so that it may be sufficient to look again at some of the facts dealt with there in greater detail. The reason why the book of Deuteronomy was not combined earlier with the older JE material of the Pentateuch, as was at one time almost universally accepted among Pentateuchal critics, is because it was instead incorporated into the Former Prophets (Joshua to 2 Kings). It was also closely associated with an early collection of written prophecies which now forms the central core of our Latter Prophets. This is significant in two directions for, as far as the Old Testament canon is concerned, it shows that a collection of canonical prophecies was being formed long before the first part of the canon, the Law or *torah*, was completed. Theologically however, it is also significant for its shows that the existence of a canonical *torah* in Deuteronomy was being understood directly in relation to the eschatological hope of the prophets. This centred most of all upon the hope of the restoration of Israel by its return to its land and its recovery of nationhood. Gradually such a hope was postponed under the years of Persian domination, and with this a new interest in the *torah* of the covenant emerged. As a result law and eschatology came to provide the basic theological foundations within which Judaism developed in the closing years of the Old Testament period. By the time of the emergence of the earliest Christian community their mutual inter-relationships provided an accepted frame of reference within which the Old Testament literature as a whole could be interpreted. A very instructive example of this is to be seen in Paul's appeal to a number of passages from the Pentateuch in

[1] Cf. M. Noth, *A History of Pentateuchal Traditions* (Eng. tr. by B. W. Anderson), Eaglewood Cliffs, 1972, pp. 250 ff.

[2] R. E. Clements, *op. cit.*, pp. 41–57.

I Corinthians 10:1–11: 'Now these things happened to them as a warning, but they were written down for our instruction, upon whom the end of the ages has come' (v. 11). Here two striking features of an Old Testament hermeneutic appear. The first of these is that the historical narratives contained in the Pentateuch are *torah*, and so they are understood as *tupoi*—'examples' (1 Cor. 10:6). The meaning of events is found in their expression of God's law and man's response to it. In this case it is the inevitability of divine judgment upon human idolatry and moral laxity. Much more striking and unexpected, however, is the assertion that the recording of these examples is for a future age, those upon whom 'the end of the ages has come'. Here in a very brief collection of Old Testament passages the two foundations of a hermeneutical understanding are firmly in evidence: law and eschatology. The Old Testament is not just law, or *torah*, but law set within a very distinctive perspective of eschatology. This is all the more noteworthy here because the passages cited are from the Pentateuch (Exod. 32:4, 6; Num. 25:1–18; 21:5–6; 16:41, 49), the very kernel of the *torah*. Whether Judaism, with its emphasis upon the Old Testament as law, has been more faithful to the inner canonical structure of its writings than has the Christian Church, with its central stress upon the element of eschatological promise contained in them, cannot be discussed here. What we can notice, however, is that both categories of interpretation are embedded in the structure of the Old Testament canon itself, and this is so because they are both related to a common interlocking factor—the concept of a divine covenant between God and Israel made at Sinai.

2 The New Creation in I Enoch

by MATTHEW BLACK

Although the idea of a New Creation has a classic place in Jewish apocalyptic literature, the actual expression itself is extremely rare. It occurs, in an eschatological context and referring to the creation anew of the heavenly bodies, in the opening verse of the (Ethiopic) *Astronomical Book of Enoch*: Ch. 72:1 'The Book of the courses of the luminaries of the heaven . . . which Uriel . . . showed me; and he showed me all their laws . . . unto eternity, till the New Creation (*geḇer ḥadis*) is completed, which lasts forever'. Although this particular verse has, unfortunately, not survived in the very substantial extant portions of the Aramaic astronomical Enoch,[1] there is no reason to doubt its authenticity or its pre-Christian date, now guaranteed by the Aramaic discoveries.[2]

A similar expression occurs at 1 QH xiii.11, 12 where the subject of the hymn (which is only fragmentarily preserved) appears to be the works of God in creation and His capacity 'to create new things' (*liḇᵉro' ḥaḏašoṯ*). The context, however, seems to be concerned with the primordial rather than with the eschatological creative activity of God. A closer parallel to 1 En. 72:1 occurs at 1 QS iv.22 ff. where the context is again eschatological, although, in this case, the writer is thinking, not of a cosmic or heavenly 'new creation' but of a 'new creation' in the world of mankind. The Hebrew expression used, lit., 'the making of the new' (*ʿᵃsoṯ ḥaḏaša*) is virtually identical with that used by the Ethiopic translator at 1 En. 72:1. The contextual setting reads: '. . . He (God) will give the upright insight . . . and to them *belongs all the glory of Adam*. And there shall be no more wickedness. Until now the spirits of truth and wickedness strive within the heart of man . . . For God has set them in agreed parts *until the decreed End* (cf. verse 20, *the decreed Judgment*) *and the New Creation* (*ʿasoṯ ḥaḏaša*).'[3]

[1] See J. T. Milik, 'Problèmes de la Littérature Hénochique à la Lumière des Fragments Araméens de Qumran', in *H.Th.R.* 64, 1971, p. 338.

[2] The 4Q Aramaic astronomical fragments are variously dated by Milik to the end of the third or the beginning of the second and to the first century B.C., e.g., 'Henastr^{b} est copié en écriture hérodienne classique, donc du tournant de notre ère'. (*ibid.*)

[3] See my *Scrolls and Christian Origins*, Edinburgh, 1962, p. 133. I have italicized the special features associated, in Hebrew tradition, with the 'new creation'.

In his commentary on 1 En. 72:1[1] R. H. Charles draws attention to a parallel and possible source in the Zoroastrian Yasts, xiii.57–8,[2] where it is stated that 'the stars, the moon, the sun and the endless lights . . . move around in their far-revolving circle for ever till they come to the time of the good restoration of the world'. If this means the restoration or renewal of the cosmos, it may well be the source (as Charles maintains) of the Jewish apocalyptic idea. The Zoroastrian author appears to be thinking in purely astronomical terms; and this may also be true of the Jewish writer too in this opening verse of his astronomical book. As we shall see, however, in all other passages where the New Creation is mentioned or implied in I Enoch the apocalyptist is always thinking, like the author of 1 QS, in terms of *a second Genesis*, a new creation which embraces the Universe and mankind.

The more immediate source of the idea, and perhaps even of the expression, in Hebrew tradition is obviously Second Isaiah, at Is. 43:19 ('Behold I do a new thing (*'oseh ḥaḏaša*)'), but more especially Is. 65:17 ff. and 66:22 (cf. also Ps. 102:26). Indeed, the one passage Is. 65:17 ff., is the Hebrew *locus classicus* for this idea, and might well be held to warrant most of the later tradition in the Apocrypha and Pseudepigrapha and rabbinical sources.[3]

'. . . the former troubles are forgotten . . .
For behold, I create
new heavens and a new earth . . .
Rejoice and be filled with delight,
you boundless realms which I create . . .' (NEB)

Is. 66:22 reads:

'For, as the new heavens and the new earth
which I am making shall endure in my sight,
says the Lord,
so shall your race and your name endure . . .' (NEB)

In both these passages one notes the integral connection of the cosmic and human aspects of the New Creation.

[1] *The Book of Enoch*, Oxford, 1912, p. 151.

[2] *Sacred Scriptures of the East*, ed. F. Max Müller, Vol. XXIII, the *Zend-Avesta*, p. 194. I have not found any reference to this idea in R. C. Zaehner's comprehensive study of the Zoroastrian theology of creation, *Zurvan: A Zoroastrian Dilemma*, Oxford, 1955, pp. 133 ff., 196 ff.

[3] Cf. Sanday and Headlam, *Romans*, Edinburgh, 1900, pp. 210 ff., G. Dalman, *Words of Jesus*, Edinburgh, 1902, pp. 177 ff. See my *Scrolls and Christian Origins*, p. 135. Passages noted by Dalman are Jub. 1:29, Baruch 32:6, 2 Esdr. 7:25, Targum Deut. 32:1 (Jerusalem Targum), Deut. 32:12 (Onk.), Mic. 7:14, Hab. 3:2, T. B. Sanh. 92b, 97b, etc.

Such passages as Is. 65:17 ff. can easily be mistaken for apocalyptic; and it is sometimes difficult to decide where prophecy ends and apocalyptic begins. Thus J. D. Smart's understanding of Is. 65:17 seems to assume that it is an apocalyptic passage: he writes 'The eschatological framework of Second Isaiah's thought here comes fully into view once more . . . Already in ch. 51:6 he had seen the old heavens and the old earth vanishing like smoke . . . Now he envisages a new creation, a universal new beginning.'[1] There is undoubtedly an apocalyptic element in the writings of Isaiah: Is. 24–7, while coming from a different strata of the 'Isaiah' tradition, is usually regarded as the earliest apocalypse, though, in fact, even these chapters are closer in content to the later prophecy of the Old Testament than to Daniel or I Enoch.[2] Is. 65:17 ff. is on the edge of apocalyptic prophecy but seems still best regarded as the product of the prophetic (and poetic) imagination of a post-exilic writer inspired by the splendid vision of Israel's future opened up by the Return from Captivity. The 'new heavens and the new earth' do mean the miraculous transformation by Jahweh of the exiles' world, but Claus Westermann is probably right in insisting that 'The words "I create anew the heavens and the earth" do not imply that heaven and earth are to be destroyed and in their place a new heaven and a new earth created—this is apocalyptic, Rev. 21:1; II Peter 3:13, and the addition in Is. 66:22. Instead the world, designated as "heaven and earth", is to be miraculously renewed'.[3]

When we contrast the prophetic vision of Second Isaiah with I Enoch and with the later apocalypses etc., which Is. 65:17 ff. has inspired, what we seem mostly to find is a tendency to literalization of poetic imagery. The 'New Creation' at 1 En. 72:1 is certainly to be so understood; and nowhere does this become more evident than in the climactic vision of a new heaven in the *Apocalypse of Weeks* (1 En. 91:16).

The *Apocalypse of Weeks* and the *Dream-Visions of Enoch* (1 En. 83 ff.) give us two closely related apocalyptic accounts of universal history, beginning, in the first case, with the generation of Enoch, in the second with Creation itself. History is divided into phases or periods, within the classic time-scale of the Seventy Periods ('Weeks') of Hebrew historiography, familiar in the Daniel

[1] *History and Theology in Second Isaiah: A Commentary on Is. 35, 40–66*, London, 1967, p. 280.

[2] Cf. M. Hengel, *Judaism and Hellenism*, London, 1974, Vol. I, p. 180.

[3] *Isaiah 40–66: A Commentary*, London, 1969, p. 408. What Westermann means by 'the addition in Is. 66:22' is not clear to me, but if he is referring to the whole of verse 22, then the inclusion of this verse in the category of 'apocalyptic' shows how easily 'prophecy' shades off into the new prophecy, 'apocalyptic'.

Apocalypse, but appearing also elsewhere in apocalyptic literature.[1] As a linear and, as it were, progressive time-scale, beginning with the drama of creation and proceeding through the progressive phases of history to the climactic events of the Judgment and New Creation, it stands in striking contrast, as something distinctively Hebraic, to the cyclic notions of time in other cultures, Greek and Oriental.[2]

The context of 1 En. 91:16 is that of the Last Judgment in the Ninth and Tenth Weeks. The Eighth Week is given over to an account of the victory of the righteous, 'by the sword', and the rebuilding of the Temple (described in the Aramaic text as 'the Temple (Palace) of the Kingdom of the Great One'): the allusions are unmistakably to the victories of the Maccabees and the restoration of the Temple service in 165 B.C. In the Ninth Week (verse 14) the author passes from historical allusion to apocalyptic prediction: there is to be revealed the Great Judgment, and this is to take place in two stages, first, *for all the children of men* (so 4Q Aram. Eth., for the whole world). It is, therefore, to be a universal Judgment; and all the works of the wicked are to vanish from the whole earth. The wicked themselves will be cast into the Pit (Gehenna) (Eth., and the world shall be written down for destruction), and all mankind will then look to the path of righteousness. The second stage of Judgment takes place in the Tenth Week, in the seventh part; it is to be 'an eternal judgment' (Eth., 'the great eternal judgment') 'in which He (God) will execute vengeance amongst the angels'. The last reference is clearly to the fallen or apostate angels, the Watchers of the earlier *Book of the Watchers*.[3]

Then follows the prediction of the New Creation, also in the Tenth or Final Week (1 En. 91:16). At this point the Aramaic text is relatively well preserved, and, apart from a few unimportant variations, agrees with the Ethiopic version.

'And the first heaven shall pass away (Eth., 'shall depart and pass away'), and a new heaven shall appear, and all the powers of the heavens shall shine and rise for all eternity, with sevenfold brightness (Eth., 'shall give sevenfold light').'[4]

[1] Cf. 1 En. 10:12; Jubilees 5:10; Testament of Levi 16–17; Dan. 9:24 ff. For the possible origin of this 'time-scale' in a Qumran *Book of the Periods* (*of History*), see Milik, *op. cit*., pp. 356 ff. That this traditional 70-period historiography has influenced Lk 3:23–38, as Milik claims (*ibid*.), is possible (70 generations from Enoch as at En. 10:12 and 1 En. 91), but that Matthew's genealogy has also been so influenced (Milik, *ibid*.) is less convincing.

[2] Cf. M. Hengel, *Judaism and Hellenism*, London, 1974, pp. 181 ff. For the cyclic notion of history, consult especially S. L. Jaki, *Science and Creation: From eternal cycles to an oscillating Universe*, Edinburgh, 1974.

[3] See Milik, *op. cit*., pp. 333 ff.

[4] See my article, 'The Fragments of the Aramaic Enoch from Qumran', in *La Littérature juive entre Tenach et Mischna*, ed. W. C. van Unnik, Leiden, 1974, p. 25.

The apocalyptic writer is drawing his ideas and phrases from Is. 30:26: 'The moon shall shine with a brightness like the sun's, and the sun with seven times his wonted brightness, seven days' light in one, on the day when the Lord binds up the broken limbs of his people and heals their wounds' (NEB). All this is poetic imagery of the ancient prophet to describe the glorious approach of the Lord's salvation; it is like the related image of the same prophet-poet that the light of the heavenly bodies would become superfluous because God Himself would illumine the world, and, in particular, the Holy City (cf. Is. 60:19; 24:23; Rev. 21:22 ff.). It is not denied that the imagery in the *Apocalypse of Weeks* may not have the same force: verse 17 reads:

> 'And thereafter there will be many weeks and there shall be no end to all their number for ever, and all shall be in righteousness (Eth., . . . and all shall be in goodness and righteousness and sin shall no more be mentioned forever)'.

The interest of the Jewish writer is throughout concerned with salvation, here the salvation of mankind; so that the vivid imagery of a New Creation, where the heavenly bodies will give sevenfold brightness, is also a prophetic way of underlining the glory of God's salvation. At the same time, it seems equally undeniable that 1 Enoch is here depicting a totally new cosmic dimension of God's creative work, the newly created heaven at the End of Time.

This verse 16 bears a striking resemblance to Rev. 21:1[b] [*καὶ εἶδον οὐρανὸν καινὸν καὶ γῆν καινήν.*] *ὁ γὰρ πρῶτος οὐρανὸς καὶ ἡ πρώτη γῆ ἀπῆλθαν*. The first part, 1a, is clearly echoing Is. 65:17a where the LXX has *ἔσται γὰρ ὁ οὐρανὸς καινὸς καὶ ἡ γῆ καινή* . . . but the second part, 1b, is practically verbatim 4Q Aram. En. (except for the change in tense necessitated by the context in Revelation): 'And the first heaven shall pass away (Eth. 'shall depart and pass away')'. An equally striking difference between Rev. 21:1 and 1 En. 91:16 is the omission of any mention in the latter of a new or transformed earth. This is an integral element in the Isaianic prophecy in its *Heilsgeschichte* setting, which Revelation follows by bringing the ideal Jerusalem down from heaven to earth. This omission in 1 Enoch could be very significant. At Ch. 104:2, in a characteristic piece of apocalyptic paraenesis (fortunately preserved in Greek)[1] there is again no mention of a transformed earth. The idea is here implicit that the faithful righteous will pass directly into the transformed heaven. The 'gates of heaven' will be open to receive the righteous, who have suffered humiliation and affliction in this life; and they are 'to shine as the lights of heaven', to have 'joy as the angels' and be 'companions of the hosts of heaven'. Here we have

[1] See *Apocalypsis Henochi Graece*, ed. M. Black, Leiden, 1970, pp. 42 ff.

an eschatology and doctrine of the after-life strongly reminiscent of that familiar in the Qumran writings (and at Lk. 20:35 ff.).[1] The apparent assumption at 1 En. 91:16 is not that the earth will be transformed with the heavens, but that a new heaven will appear and become the abode of the righteous forever.

A generation and less ago priority of place and importance for this idea would probably have been given to 1 En. 45:5 which reads (in Charles's translation of the Ethiopic):

'And I will transform the heaven and make it an eternal blessing
 and light,
And I will transform the earth and make it a blessing:
And I will cause Mine elect one(s) to dwell upon it:
But the sinners and evil-doers will not set foot thereon.'

In view of the complete absence of the section on the Parables (Chs. 37–71) from the Aramaic Enoch, and the late date of composition, which we may now be obliged to assign to them, we cannot be certain that this midrashic treatment of Is. 65:17 was not written or inspired by Christian ideas.[2]

In the *Apocalypse of Dreams* (or *Dream-Visions*), which is also substantially preserved in Aramaic, there is no mention of a New Creation (of the heavens or the earth) but in the closing visions of the Last Judgment and in its sequel in the 'zoomorphic' vision of the new people of God, there are several important features which make it relevant for our enquiry; for, if its most recent interpreter is correct, it speaks of a second Eden and a new Adam.

As in the *Apocalypse of Weeks* the Last Judgment takes place in two stages, but in this case judgment falls firstly on the apostate angels (the 'stars') and on the seventy 'angel shepherds', then secondly on the 'blinded sheep', i.e., the guilty Israelites who are also, like the fallen angels, cast into the fiery abyss.

This is followed by the post-judgment vision of the new people of God, Gentiles as well as Israelites: it is described by Charles as 'The New Jerusalem, the Conversion of the surviving Gentiles, the Resurrection of the Righteous, the Messiah'.[3]

Verses 28–9 describe the rebuilding of a new House for the sheep 'greater and loftier than the first'—clearly a reference back to the

[1] See *The Scrolls and Christian Origins*, pp. 139 ff.

[2] Cf. Milik, *op. cit.*, pp. 373 ff. The Parables may be a late composition, but at the same time may also have utilized older material: these verses could come from a pre-Christian Jewish apocalypse. But they are not in the same class of evidence as the other parts of 1 Enoch which have been shown to be pre-Christian by the 4Q Aram. Enoch fragments. See further my forthcoming contribution to the W. D. Davies *Festschrift*, 'The Throne-Theophany Prophetic Commission and the Son of Man'.

[3] *op. cit.*, p. 214.

First Temple. As in the *Apocalypse of Weeks*, the writer is thinking of the restored Temple of the Maccabaean period, though this may also, no doubt, be held to imply the creation of a new Jerusalem. In the same zoomorphic language as the earlier visions, verses 30–3 describe the assembling of the 'beasts of the field' and 'the birds of heaven', who have been described in verse 30 as doing homage to the sheep, i.e., Israel. The ingathering of the Gentiles within the new Israel is clearly meant.[1] Verse 33 speaks of all the sheep who had been destroyed and dispersed assembling in the new House; and this is interpreted by Charles to mean that the righteous dead as well as the dispersed Israel are to arise and take their place among the new people of God (cf. Dan. 12:2).

How are we to interpret the symbolism of the White Bull (and white bulls) of verses 37–72? Traditionally the White Bull has been identified as 'the Messiah' and 'all their generation who were transformed into white bulls' as the new people of God. Recently, however, Milik has argued that the symbolism of this last vision corresponds to that of the opening Dream-vision, where the White Bull is Adam: the White Bull of En. 90:37 is the New Adam and the 'white bulls' symbolize his descendants, the new race of mankind: 'L'ère finale ne sera qu'une reprise, entièrement parfaite cette fois, de l'ère primordiale. Le "taureau blanc" de 90, 37 est de toute évidence le nouvel Adam (Adam-taureau blanc, 85, 3), mais plus glorieux que le premier, car "ses cornes sont grandes". Tout comme le progéniture d'Adam était faite de "taureaux blancs" (85, 8–10), de même les contemporains du second Adam deviendront "tous des taureaux blancs" (90, 38).'[2]

The messianic understanding of the White Bull symbolism probably goes back to R. H. Charles. It is the 'prophetic Messiah' who is here described, and yet 'not really the prophetic Messiah; for he has absolutely no function to perform, as he does not appear till the world's history is finally closed'.[3] It is true, Charles does recognize that the intention of the author was to describe the conditions of a restored Eden: on verse 38 ('. . . and they all became white bulls') he comments: 'All the members of the Kingdom are transformed: the white bull (i.e., the Messiah) into a great animal, and the sheep, beasts and birds into white bulls or oxen. Thus mankind is restored to the primitive righteousness of Eden, i.e., Adam was symbolised by a white bull.'

It may be argued that Milik is reading too much into the parallelism

[1] Cf. Mic. 4:6, 7 and J. Jeremias, *Jesus' Promise to the Nations* (Studies in Biblical Theology, No. 24), London, 1958, pp. 61, 65, n. 2.

[2] Milik, 'Problèmes de la Littérature Hénochique à la Lumière des Fragments Araméens de Qumrân', *H.Th.R.* 64, 1971, p. 359.

[3] *op. cit.*, p. 215; cf. also F. Martin, *Le Livre d'Hénoch*, Paris, 1906, p. 235.

of the symbolism of Ch. 90 with that at Ch. 85 (Adam as the first White Bull). At Ch. 89 Noah is also described by this image. On the other hand, the eschatology of 1 QS iv.23, cited above, supports the view that the vision refers to a second Genesis and a new Eden with a Second Adam. The eschatological pattern at 1 QS is the same familiar one of the Last (Decreed) Judgment, accompanied by the restoration of the Glory of Adam ('. . . to them—the new Israel—belongs all the glory of Adam . . .') and followed by the New Creation.

A further parallel occurs at CD iii.18–20 where 'all the glory of Adam' is to belong to those who 'hold by' or 'adhere to' the 'sure House in Israel': '(. . . God in his marvellous mysteries made expiation for their sins and forgave their transgression); and He built for them a sure House in Israel, the like of which has never stood before or since. Those who adhere to it are destined for eternal life (*ḥayyē neṣaḥ*) *and all the glory of Adam is theirs*, just as God has established through Ezekiel the Prophet . . .' The context points unequivocally to the expectation of a New House in a New Temple in Israel, which the Bene Zadok will inherit—a new and everlasting Temple, where its priestly servants will enjoy everlasting life and have restored the lost image and glory of Adam.[1] Here is an even closer parallel to 1 En. 90:29, 37.

At verse 38 Milik accepts the excellent conjecture of Dillmann of an original Hebrew R'EM 'buffalo', where the Ethiopic has nagar = ῥῆμα, 'word', only postulating an Aramaic R'EMA: 'Le successeur du Taureau blanc eschatologique sera "une buffle qui a sur sa tête de grandes cornes noires", 90, 38. . . . Notre écrivain apocalyptique n'a voulu exprimer que la puissance accrue de ce patriarche eschatologique. Il laisse deviner que l'histoire nouvelle se poursuivra dans ce sens ascensionnel au cours des générations successives d'hommes de plus en plus glorieux et parfaits, en net contraste donc avec l'histoire antérieure, caractérisée par la séquence descendante: taureaux—veaux—brebis, entourées d'animaux et d'oiseaux nocifs.'[2] There is nothing, in my opinion, in the text to justify this theory that the descendants of the Second Adam are to become more 'glorious and perfect' than their predecessors. It is true, the 'buffalo' has 'large black horns', but the first 'white bull' has also 'large horns', and, if anything, the colour black would suggest a declension rather than the *sens ascensionnel* of Milik's theory. In the second dream-vision, Cain and Abel are symbolized by two bulls, one black, the other red (Ch. 85.30 ff.): clearly black here stands for 'evil', the opposite of 'white'

[1] For the *ḥayyē neṣaḥ* (eternal life), cf. my *Scrolls and Christian Origins*, p. 139 and for the restored 'glory of Adam', my commentary on *Romans* (New Century Bible), London, 1973, pp. 66 ff.

[2] Milik, *Litter. Hénochique*, p. 359 ff.

for 'purity'; and 'red' signifies the blood of martyrdom. Similarly elsewhere 'black' is used in this pejorative sense, e.g., 'the wild, black boar' at 89.12, signifying Esau. A pejorative sense, however, is clearly impossible in the context of 90.38, where the Lord is said to rejoice over all the oxen.[1] Could the imagery here not bear another meaning? At 89.9 the three sons of Noah, Shem, Ham and Japhet, are symbolized by the three colours: Shem is a white bull, Ham a black bull and Japhet a red bull. It is no doubt arguable that we have again the same pejorative meanings for 'black' and 'red' as in the second vision, but the explanation of Beer in Kautzsch[2] seems more reasonable: 'White, red and black here, differently from 85.3, signify the three different skin-pigments of the three races: Semites (white), Japhites (red) and Hamites (black).' Is it too fanciful to see in the symbol of the buffalo with the huge black horns a reference to the black descendants of Ham, now brought within the new human family, like the Gentiles? The buffalo with 'the huge black horns' may be, in the author's mind (as Milik thinks), the first of the eschatological patriarchs, but one from the South, Egypt and the Nile valley, Nubia or Ethiopia.

[1] Cf. Charles, pp. 216 ff. 'I cannot understand the epithet "black" here. It seems wrong.'

[2] *Die Apokryphen und Pseudepigraphen des Alten Testaments*, Tübingen, 1900, Bd. II, p. 291.

3 Creation, Wisdom and Christ

by R. S. BARBOUR

It is on all counts a remarkable state of affairs that the prophet Jesus of Nazareth should within thirty years of his death have become worshipped as the Lord of all, the divine being who was in the beginning with God and through whom the worlds were made—remarkable, but not without a few distant parallels in the many-coloured religious scene of the Graeco-Roman world of the first century A.D. It is even more remarkable that millions of presumably intelligent people are today still prepared to make the same confession and to believe that a meaning can be attached to it. Our concern here is with that part of the early Christian confessions which acknowledged Christ as the one through whom all things came into being. The aim of this paper is not to throw any new light on the origins of that conviction, or to expound its precise meaning in the various forms in which it appears in the New Testament, but simply to point to one aspect of it in particular, concerned with the Divine Wisdom, and to ask whether its implications have been fully explored. In order to do this it will be necessary first to summarize some of the forces which appear to have been at work in the development of the idea and then to relate these to certain New Testament emphases.

I. *Wisdom and Creation*

When Constantine dedicated his great church to the Wisdom of the Uncreated Word he was summing up a long process of theology and worship. But it seems clear enough that in the centuries before Constantine and the Council of Nicaea—as indeed subsequently—the Uncreated Word played a much greater part in Christian theology than did the Divine Wisdom. Occasionally, as in the theology of Theophilus of Antioch, the Divine Wisdom found a prominent place alongside the Word, but in Theophilus it was identified not with Christ but with the Spirit.[1] Later it came in some quarters to be connected with the Church.[2] But for the most part,

[1] Theophil. *ad Autol.*, 2, 15.

[2] J. Daniélou, *A History of Early Christian Doctrine*, vol. I, *The Theology of Jewish Christianity*, London, 1964, pp. 311 ff.

in the early centuries, it was the Word rather than the Wisdom of God which was thought of as active in Creation. In origin the two ideas are closely linked, and in some passages in Scripture and the Fathers they are barely distinguishable; but the nuances of meaning of 'Word' and 'Wisdom' are likely to be rarely quite the same; and there is something to be said for asking the question about Christ as the agent of creation in this form: 'What is meant by the assertion that Christ is the *Wisdom* of God through which the world was made?'—as well as in the more familiar form suggested by John 1:3. There is historical justification for doing this; in a number of places in the literature of Judaism God's Wisdom is his agent in creation, whereas the Word has no explicit creative functions in Palestinian Judaism, and apart from the Prologue of John 'creation through the Word' is not found as a Christological expression in earliest Christianity.[1] Thus we should probably not look for a hypostasized or personified 'Word' of God as the background for the Word of the Johannine Prologue, and it may be true that the genealogy of the Logos has still to be found.[2] But it seems safe to say that the figure of Wisdom is likely to be as prominent in that genealogy as any other known to us. True, she lost her importance after a time; in Rabbinic Judaism 'Wisdom surrendered her cosmic functions . . . to the Torah'[3], in Philo she surrendered them, for the most part, to the Logos, and in Christianity she surrendered them to Christ. But she stands behind all these, in some sense at least, and her somewhat disreputable connections with Levantine goddesses and with later gnostic speculations should not be allowed to obscure her continued importance for us today. The Wisdom tradition in Judaism is a highly complex phenomenon to which a good deal of attention has been paid in recent years.[4] Here I can only point in summary fashion to a few of its features which are of relevance for our theme.

But first, a familiar point should be alluded to in passing. There is of course the closest connection in the New Testament between the assertion that Christ is the agent or mediator of creation and the assertion that he is the agent of redemption; creation and new creation belong together. Indeed it is arguable that it was mainly the conviction of his primacy in redemption that led to the parallel

[1] H. F. Weiss, *Untersuchungen zur Kosmologie des hellenistischen und palästinischen Judentums* (TU 97), Berlin, 1966, p. 310.

[2] H. Conzelmann in *The Future of our Religious Past* (ed. James M. Robinson), London, 1971, p. 243. Greek (mainly Stoic) influences must not of course be excluded from consideration here.

[3] Weiss, *op. cit.*, p. 289, as quoted in M. Hengel, *Judaism and Hellenism*, London, 1974, I, p. 171.

[4] See especially H. Ringgren, *Word and Wisdom*, Lund, 1947; W. McKane, *Proverbs*, London, 1969; G. von Rad, *Weisheit in Israel*, Neukirchen, 1970; B. L. Mack, *Logos und Sophia*, Göttingen, 1973.

assertion of his primacy in creation (we shall return to this). At the same time—and for reasons which we cannot enter into in detail here—it will not do simply to say that Christ's mediatorship in creation is an inference from his mediatorship in redemption. Wisdom-theology has certainly played an important part in the development of the former idea.

The earlier stages of the Wisdom-tradition cannot concern us here. Later, when Wisdom appears in Job, Proverbs, Sirach and Baruch as a divine being distinguishable from God and existing before the creation of the world we have to notice in the first place that this is the language of poetry and (in some sense) of myth being used to express not only how things were in the beginning but how they are, and how they ought to be.[1] The interest is theological, soteriological and sometimes also cosmological. There is probably no better case in the literature of Judaism for a study of the interrelation of what would nowadays be called 'myth' and what would nowadays be called 'metaphysics' than the figure of Wisdom; such a study, by illuminating the intentions of the authors concerned in describing Wisdom's part in creation, could hardly fail to throw some light on the similar Christian assertions about Christ. Among others, the following motifs appear to be relevant:

(1) The idea of Wisdom implies the desire to understand, and this appears in two main contexts. First there is the desire to be assured of the position of Israel or of the righteous within God's purposes, and to link this to God's whole plan for the world and thus 'die Soteriologie kosmologisch zu verankern'.[2] This and other factors lead, especially in Sirach and the Wisdom of Solomon, to the working out of 'a tremendous scheme of world history and saving history'[3]—which remains impressive even when some of the cosmopolitan and universal implications of Wisdom-thought are narrowed down through the identification of Wisdom with the Torah (Sirach 23) and the restriction of her gifts to Israel. Thus one main theological function of the idea of Wisdom is that of overcoming the meaninglessness of contemporary history and fear of a hostile world. God's Wisdom, which is hidden, can nevertheless be revealed to men. This theme is taken up in a number of ways in the New Testament.

Second, there is an urge to understand nature and the cosmos as a system, an urge foreign to Israel in its earlier days, which represents

[1] '. . . in the O.T. Wisdom is a means of expressing the Divine Immanence in Creation and also the Divine Activity in morality and knowledge, in short what we may call the Redemptive activity of God:

For whoso finds me finds life. . . .
All who hate me love death. (Prov. 8:35a, 36).'

W. D. Davies, *Paul and Rabbinic Judaism* (2nd edn), London, 1955, p. 168.

[2] B. L. Mack, *op. cit.*, p. 106.

[3] G. von Rad, *Old Testament Theology*, Edinburgh, 1962, I, p. 445.

a movement of an almost rationalistic kind. As with the prophet of the exile and the Priestly Document, the belief in Yahweh demands that his activity in bringing a saving knowledge to his people and his activity in creation be related, or even identified; but the method of the relation or identification is quite different in the Wisdom literature from those in prophetic and priestly authors.[1] But all three stand for the conviction that ultimately soteriology and cosmology cannot be divorced.

(2) Closely connected with the foregoing is the point so frequently made in modern books on Judaism, that the idea of Wisdom was a means of bridging the gap between a transcendent God and an evil world. Wisdom is hidden with God, yet also available to man. This function of Wisdom can be expressed, and was expressed, in a number of different contexts and different ways: the Divine Wisdom is a cosmic entity, yet present also in Israel and in the individual Israelite; it is a metaphysical entity, or a mythical entity, but also a recognizable moral characteristic of human beings; it is hidden from all created things, but it is also to fear the Lord and to depart from evil (Job 28).[2] There are of course many actions or qualities which can be ascribed both to God and to men in Hebrew thought: righteousness, holiness, uprightness, truth. These can form a bridge of sorts between God and man, but none of them is personified or hypostasized in that metaphysical-mythical way which enables the human mind and imagination to pass from God to man without confounding the two or dividing the one 'substance' of Wisdom in the process. Perhaps the clearest example of this is to be found in Wisdom 7:22–8:1. Once more, the analogy with New Testament assertions about Christ (and patristic doctrines of His Person) hardly needs to be pointed out. What needs further investigation than it has yet received is precisely the way in which the mythical and poetical imagination of the Wisdom writers has made possible a type of thought, or even vision, which is an important antecedent of the New Testament creeds and confessions.

(3) This leads to a comment on the personification of Wisdom in the Wisdom literature. Recent investigation has made ever clearer that Jewish Wisdom-thought or speculation owes a large debt to Egyptian ideas about Maat and especially Isis—as no doubt to Greek and other ideas also—but has effectively subordinated such ideas to the central demands of the Yahwistic faith.[3] Thus we have

[1] Von Rad expresses the contrast vividly: *ibid.*, p. 450.

[2] Even if Job 28:28 is a later addition to the poem, as most scholars think, it is still witness to the way in which the metaphysical and the ethical aspects of Wisdom can be placed side by side without any sense of incongruity. Cf. Wisd. 9:4; 'Give me the wisdom that sits by thy throne', and many other passages.

[3] W. L. Knox, 'The Divine Wisdom', JTS XXXVIII, 1937, pp. 230–7; *St. Paul and the Church of the Gentiles*, Cambridge, 1939; H. Conzelmann, 'Die Mutter

what may be called a 'fluctuating personification' of Wisdom in the Jewish literature, in which the personification makes possible the building of the imaginative bridge between God and man, while the moral and metaphysical connotations of the very word Wisdom—Ḥokmah, against the background of faith in Yahweh, make any kind of idolatry or polytheism out of the question. Christian theology and metaphysics have often failed to acknowledge the service rendered to them by the mythical element, and its usefulness for the imagination, in this hinterland of Christology.

The personification, or partial personification, of Wisdom in Hellenistic Judaism raises an interesting series of questions relating to creation and causation. Creation, in the Jewish framework of thought, belongs to God alone. Causation, at least in the sense of the initiation of motion, in the normal Greek framework of thought belongs to the soul: in the words of Iamblichus, which no doubt sum up a very widespread conviction of the Greek-speaking world at the turn of our era, 'the essence of the soul is bodyless, uncreated entirely, and indestructible, having its being and life by itself, self-moving throughout, and *the beginning of nature and all motion*'.[1] It would go beyond the evidence to suggest that in the first century A.D. efficient causation (in Aristotelian terms) could only be thought of in terms of action by the soul or by a personal being; but such a statement would be close to the truth. The only initiators of actions and of things (objects which have form), we might also say, are God and the soul; and where that or something like it is true difficulties arise both with regard to creation and with regard to causation. The difficulty with creation is that the soul's activity in initiating action or imposing form on matter (and this applies to God or to the world-soul, as in the *Timaeus* and Middle Platonism, as well as to other souls) always implies a pre-existing 'matter' to be activated or formed. Such 'matter' is itself eternal and therefore divine (as Erwin Rohde put it: 'Wer unter den Griechen unsterblich sagt, sagt Gott'[2]), and may in consequence be thought of as a second God; it was against this kind of danger that the doctrine of *creatio ex nihilo* eventually took shape.[3] The difficulty, or one of the difficulties, arising with regard to causation in this frame of reference concerns the giving of a plausible account of everyday processes in the natural

der Weisheit' in ed. E. Dinkler, *Zeit und Geschichte*, *Festschrift R. Bultmann*, Tübingen, 1964, pp. 225–34; (English in ed. J. M. Robinson, *The Future of our Religious Past*, London, 1971, pp. 230–43); B. L. Mack, *op. cit.*, esp. pp. 34–42.

[1] Quoted in A. Ehrhardt, *The Beginning*, Manchester, 1968, p. 190. Italics mine.

[2] E. Rohde, *Psyche* (7th edn), Tübingen, 1921, II, p. 2 (Eng. trans., London, 1925, p. 253).

[3] See especially H. F. Weiss, *Untersuchungen zur Kosmologie des hellenistischen und palästinischen Judentums* (TU 97), Berlin, 1966, Teil I, Weltbildung und Weltschöpfung.

world. To adopt a different form of causation-language for a moment, God and the soul make excellent primary causes, but leave no room for an adequate statement of secondary causes. That too is of course an exaggeration; but I think it cannot be denied that the difficulty was present.

The idea of the Divine Wisdom contained resources for dealing with both of these difficulties, even if those resources were never fully utilized. For, with regard to creation, the Divine Wisdom partakes of the Divine power without having to be thought of as an independent soul or unmoved mover, an entity over against another entity, namely an equally ultimate 'matter'; the problem of the *creatio ex nihilo* is not thereby solved, but we have the basis for an understanding of the Divine action in creating and upholding the world without necessarily postulating a metaphysical dualism between the mover and the moved, the *poioun* and the *paschon*, the God/soul and matter, on the one hand, or falling into pantheism on the other.

Equally, with regard to causation, it is possible to conceive of the Divine Wisdom entering into the hearts of men and ordering all things well (Wisd. 7:27, 8:1) without having to deny the operation of secondary causes or suppose that in everything God is the only real agent. The Divine Wisdom is also a concept with some potentiality for meeting some of the problems of the one and the many: 'Though she is but one, she can do all things, and while remaining in herself, she renews all things' (*ibid.*). There is here at least the beginning of a possibility of understanding the Divine action both in human beings and in the natural world in such a way that God upholds all, yet is not the only genuine agent. The ramifications of this with regard to the problem of evil are beyond our scope here.

(4) In his wisdom God created the world (Prov. 3:19, etc.), and he gives wisdom to men (2:6, etc.). Many metaphors and similes describe this nature and activity of Wisdom. She can be both the master-workman (Prov. 8:30—if that is the correct translation)[1]—the *demiourgos* or *technitis* (Wisd. 7:22; 8:6, cf. 8:5)—and the pattern or blueprint of creation.[2] She is light and a reflection of eternal light (Wisd. 7:26), she is a tree—the tree of paradise, no doubt—she is food and drink (Sirach 24), etc. She is also of course identified with God's Word and with God's Law (Sirach 24:23,

[1] M. Hengel, *Judaism and Hellenism*, London, 1974, p. 153, and others argue for the meaning 'favourite child'.

[2] That this is implied in Prov. 8:22 and Job 28 (and in Col. 1:16) was shown by A. Feuillet in a memorable article: 'La Création de l'Univers "dans le Christ" d'après l'Epître aux Colossiens (1:16a)', *New Testament Studies* 12, Oct. 1965, pp. 1–9.

Wisd. 9:1 f.). Sometimes her femininity can be described quite sensuously (Prov. 9:1–6), at others it is entirely incidental. The general point to be made about this language is simply this, that in most of the passages referred to we have, in Conzelmann's language,[1] not myth but reflective mythology, that is the adopting and adapting of mythical material to serve as the material for theology. I am well aware that the only basis for such a judgment must be sought in exegetical work, and here must simply assert again that the material found in the Wisdom tradition of Judaism must be taken seriously as theological material of importance, *inter alia*, for Christology.

(5) Philo in speaking of Wisdom prefers the language of birth and motherhood to that of craftsmanship and construction.[2] Wisdom is mother of the *kosmos* (which is the *monos kai agapetos aisthetos huios*), of the Logos, and of the High Priest, who puts on the *kosmos* as a garment. Some of the functions of Wisdom in creation, as depicted in the earlier literature, tend to pass in Philo to the Logos or to other entities.[3] It is at first sight tempting to suppose that the shift from emphasis on Wisdom to emphasis on the Logos has to do with the greater degree of philosophical or metaphysical interest in Philo, but that does not appear to be the case. Wisdom in Philo is closely connected with the term *dynamis*, as Hegermann's treatment makes clear, and here perhaps lies an area where further research is urgently needed; comparison and contrast with the conception of divine power in the New Testament, and especially in Colossians and Ephesians, would be instructive.

The other general feature of Philo's thought which demands mention here is his ability, by means of allegory and in other ways, to move to and fro between the universal and the particular, the collective and the individual, the cosmic and the psychological. Here again, if less strikingly than in the case of the other authors cited, the idea of Wisdom assists these processes through its capacity for carrying many different kinds of connotation.

(6) We should briefly note the 'typology of Wisdom' established by one of the most recent writers on the subject, B. L. Mack. He distinguishes the near Wisdom, the hidden Wisdom and the disappeared (verschwundene) Wisdom, and argues that the first has the closest links with Egyptian mythology, while the second and third are primarily the creations of Jewish thought. He traces a develop-

[1] *op. cit.* (English edn), p. 232.

[2] Philo is ample source for a life-time's study on his own. I draw here briefly on the work of H. Hegermann, *Die Vorstellung vom Schöpfungsmittler im hellenistischen Judentum und Urchristentum* (TU 82), Berlin, 1961, H. F. Weiss, *op. cit.*, and B. L. Mack, *op. cit.*

[3] Cf. Weiss, *op. cit.*, pp. 209–11; Mack, *op. cit.*, pp. 145 f., and the passages from Philo there cited. Philo can however still refer to Wisdom as the power or entity δι᾽ ἧς τὰ ὅλα ἦλθεν εἰς γένεσιν.

ment, accompanied by influences from Egyptian mythology and Greek philosophy, from Job and Sirach to the Wisdom of Solomon and Philo. Mack's treatment makes clear yet again how the figure of Wisdom, sometimes conceived mythologically, sometimes rather theologically or philosophically, contributes to the solving of problems which will recur later, of course in different forms, in the Christological controversies of the early Church. His typology of 'near' and 'hidden' cuts across more traditional ways of classifying the ideas concerned, but for that very reason throws new light on the theological functions of that material.

(7) Finally, the figure of Wisdom has the closest connections with ideas and speculations in pre-Christian Judaism concerning an Urmensch or Primal Man, concerning Adam, and (according to some views) the Son of Man. Bultmann and others have connected the 'Urmensch-myth' with the 'Wisdom-myth'. But it is very doubtful whether there was a pre-Christian 'Urmensch-myth' of the type posited by Bultmann, nor is it clear that there was a single 'Wisdom myth' rather than a variety of Wisdom myths and speculations. In any case, the most recent scholarship supports the view that the Wisdom material can be investigated on its own as an area distinct from the 'Primal Man' and Adam speculations,[1] and what further justifies us in leaving these latter aside is that while they are very relevant to questions concerning pre-existence, they do not for the most part directly impinge on the idea of creation through an agent (whether Wisdom or Christ). It is different with the Logos and the Spirit. But they too must be left aside here.

II. *Wisdom, Creation and Christ*

What are we to make of the material so cursorily surveyed in relation to the New Testament assertion of the creation of all things through Christ?

(1) Our first assertion concerned the function of Wisdom in assuring man of his place, and of the reality and activity of God, in a world that threatened to be purposeless or meaningless; and in answering his questions about the created order. That the early Christians found this assurance in Christ needs no stressing. What is important here is of course that in Christ they found the revelation of God's hidden Wisdom, active from the beginning of all things, and so found a continuity between creation and redemption, or a line leading back from redemption to creation, which made it impossible to conceive of salvation in gnostic terms as rescue from a wholly evil or hostile world. I have already abjured the task of trying to decide by what process or processes they came to this

[1] Cf. the authors cited in Mack, *op. cit.*, p. 18.

conviction, but one or two comments are necessary here. W. D. Davies argued that Paul regarded the person and teaching of Jesus as the New Torah, and that since the Torah had already been identified in Judaism with the Wisdom of God and thought of as pre-existent and active in creation it was natural for Paul to think of Jesus in the same way.[1] Whether that be correct or not, it seems certain that the identification of Christ with Wisdom was also made, perhaps for other reasons, by other Christians contemporary with Paul;[2] and it is likely that we should see the process taking place on a wider front of thought and confession than Davies postulated for Paul.

One example of this 'wider front' is of particular importance for our purpose. The use of phrases like 'through our Lord Jesus Christ', employing the preposition *dia* with the genitive case, has been plausibly associated with early Christian worship.[3] It is through Christ that all the blessings of salvation and new life have been won; in worship this truth is both realized and celebrated.[4] Similar *dia*-phrases are of course also used in those passages in the New Testament which speak of the function of Christ in creation: notably I Cor. 8:6; Col. 1:16; Heb. 1:2 f. and John 1:3. I Cor. 8:6 is certainly the earliest of these passages, and it has often been supposed to reflect the context of worship or confession, and indeed to be a quotation of a pre-Pauline creed or hymn. Whether it is a quotation or not,[5] there can be little doubt that the closing phrase—*hemeis di' autou*, referring to Christ—describes the new life, the new creation, and especially the new orientation towards God (*hemeis eis auton*, earlier in the verse) brought about by Christ. Does *ta panta* in the phrase *di' hou ta panta* then refer simply to the whole event of the *new* creation, as it appears to do in passages like II Cor. 5:18? Or to one

[1] W. D. Davies, *op. cit.*, pp. 147–76.

[2] It is often said that the identification was pre-Pauline; e.g. R. G. Hamerton-Kelly, *Pre-existence, Wisdom and the Son of Man*, Cambridge, 1973, p. 148: '... the pre-Pauline Church identified the risen Christ with the pre-existent Logos/Wisdom/Anthropos, and themselves with Christ.' But apart from the fact that everything seems to be identified with everything else here, have we really any justification for calling this pre-Pauline? If Paul was converted soon after the Resurrection, he had few predecessors but many contemporaries in matters of this kind.

[3] W. Kramer, *Christ, Lord, Son of God*, London, 1966, pp. 84–90.

[4] The celebration of the blessings of salvation by means of such language was a second stage, according to Kramer (*loc. cit.*); the appeal to the Lord's present power was primary.

[5] W. Thüsing, *Per Christum in Deum*, Münster, 1969, p. 225, supposes rather that it is a 'von Paulus selbst geprägter und in seiner Predigt und Unterweisung öfter gebrauchter Kernsatz', and this view seems preferable. The fact that the use of prepositions in this verse recalls Stoic formulations (cf. J. Dupont, *Gnosis*, Louvain and Paris (2nd edn), 1960, pp. 335–45) need not tell against this view.

aspect of the whole relationship between God and man, as appears to be the case in I Cor. 9:12? Or does it include a reference to the creation as such (as the phrase *ex hou ta panta* earlier in the verse very well might do) and does it in effect here mean 'the totality of things', as it certainly does in Colossians and Ephesians (cf. Col. 1:17, 20; Eph. 1:10, 23; 4:6)? The correct conclusion on this matter appears to have been reached by Thüsing: in this verse 'Paulus denkt entsprechend seiner sonstigen Verkündigung zuerst an die Mittlerschaft Christi im Heilsgeschehen; er denkt diese Mittlerschaft aber so universal, dass sie sich notwendig auch auf die Schöpfung ausdehnen muss, schon weil Schöpfung und Heilsgeschehen für ihn ein untrennbares Ganzes bilden.'[1] The reference to creation, perhaps implicit or secondary in I Cor. 8:6, becomes explicit in the *dia*-formulations of Col. 1:16, Heb. 1:2 f. and John 1:3, and the influence of the Jewish Wisdom-theology on all these passages is universally recognized.

It might thus seem that it was in worship, in the experience of the renewal of the whole of life in the Spirit or in Christ, that the earliest Christians came to focus their thoughts on the mediatorship of Christ in Creation. Through Him they had been born anew, through Him there was a new creation; but the agent of the new creation must be none other than the agent of the first creation, namely the Wisdom of God. That may well be true; but whatever its *Sitz im Leben* their thought must have proceeded on a still broader front than those indicated in the last two paragraphs. On the one hand, other ideas related to that of Wisdom (Christ as *eikon*, Christ as *arche* of creation, Christ as primal man) have played their part—although none of these (except possibly *arche*) directly asserts the active or creative mediatorship of Christ in creation. On the other hand, the whole eschatological context of early Christianity, with its sense of fulfilment of God's purposes and of the universal Lordship of Christ, must have provided some impetus for the assertion of the primacy and the activity of Christ in creation: eschatology, as has often been said in different ways in recent years, led back to protology.[2] (This is one of the least pleasant ways of saying it, but one cannot deny that the jargon is convenient.) But there is something more behind all that. In his study of the idea of pre-existence in the New Testament R. G. Hamerton-Kelly puts forward the view that 'the history of the idea of pre-existence in the synoptic tradition begins . . . with the experi-

[1] *op. cit.*, p. 229. Cf. Kramer, *op. cit.*, pp. 94–9; E. Schweizer, *Lordship and Discipleship*, London, 1960, p. 102.

[2] 'The starting-point for the connection of the Christ with creation is to be found in the understanding of the redeemer as the goal of all history', Chr. Maurer, 'Die Begründung der Herrschaft Christi über die Mächte nach Kolosser 1, 15–20', *Wort und Dienst* NF4, 1955, pp. 79–93. Cf. W. Pannenberg, *Jesus, God and Man*, London, 1968, pp. 390 ff.

ence of the sovereignly active grace of God in the historical Jesus'.[1] If, as he and others have argued, Jesus' words and deeds were indeed accepted during his lifetime as bringing God's sovereign grace into the very lives of ordinary men, that may or may not have carried with it some implications about the pre-existence of the one who so spoke and acted; but if those very words and deeds which brought God's astonishing grace into the lives of men also corresponded, strangely, with what ordinary men considered to be natural, normal and right, and in accordance with the true constitution of things, then we have the basis for something less questionable and no less arresting. This man, it might have been said, not only brings the marvellous newness and freshness of God's coming Kingdom (already mysteriously present); he also brings the original, primal, rightness of things, which any man who is really human can recognize, into focus once more. In Him the old and the new become one without confusion and without separation; and that is the secret of the Kingdom. It is also God's Wisdom embodied in a man; and it is the reason why, in due course, He will appear to His followers celebrating His triumph after His Resurrection as the one through whom are all things—redemption and creation too.

I am not of course asking anyone to believe that that is precisely how any eye-witnesses of the life of Jesus in Galilee and Judaea actually saw things. I am suggesting that there is, in the records of His ministry, material which can be interpreted in that way; and that, whatever the actual process by which the earliest Christians came to a belief in the mediatorship of Christ in creation, there was here the foundation for that total sense of security in God which had been one main object of the Wisdom theology of the Jewish people in the period immediately preceding the coming of Christ. There was of course ample precedent in Judaism for the belief that the last things would be as the first;[2] what is new with Christianity is the realization that because the last things were upon them, and were what they were, therefore the first things must have been thus also—*dia Christou.*

When that had happened, many more or less mythological ideas, of diverse origin, could be used to establish the fact that this was a new creation corresponding to, and redressing the wrongs of, the old; indeed, some such ideas may have been present in the ministry, and the mind, of Jesus himself. The cultic celebration of the renewal of creation, especially at the autumnal festival, is a much-disputed topic, but it is at least possible to say that it may have played a part here.

[1] *op. cit.*, p. 89, Hamerton-Kelly argues that already in the theology of Q Christ as 'Wisdom's last envoy' and Son of Man is thought of as pre-existent.

[2] A convenient summary of some of the material is found in N. A. Dahl, 'Christ, Creation and the Church', *The Background of the N.T. and its Eschatology*, ed. W. D. Davies and D. Daube, Cambridge, 1956, pp. 422–43.

The link between exodus and creation, and the thought of a new creation, certainly did. Ancient Hebrew cosmology and cosmogony, relation to the deep (*tehom*), the primal ocean, the centre of the earth (identified especially with Jerusalem, with the temple and the foundation-stone in the temple), the cosmic mountain in the north, and other topics, have certainly left traces in the New Testament. But the extent to which they have influenced the thought of the mediatorship of Christ in creation is hard to assess.[1] Nor is any of them likely to have much direct impact on present-day searchers for truth who cannot see anything relevant in such ancient cosmologies. For the moment we must content ourselves with concluding that, just as Wisdom was conceived as addressing men very personally and entering into their lives, but also as being the very foundation or basic principle on which the world was built, so it was with Christ. But we still can hardly see how it could be true that the Jesus who had addressed men and the principle on which the world was built could be found to be one and the same.

(2) Our second point, different only in emphasis from the first, concerned the role of Wisdom in bridging the gap between God and the world. We hardly need to trace any of the many ways in which this theme appears in the New Testament: it is obvious that the presence of Jesus is indeed a tabernacling of the Divine Wisdom or Logos with men (John 1:14). One point, however, may claim our particular attention.

In a number of passages in the Wisdom literature (Wisd. Sol. 13:1–9 is a good example) the Wisdom which comes from God and which He alone can bestow is contrasted with human wisdom which is really foolishness. (The particular theme in the passage referred to is the activity of God in creation; Paul takes up a very similar line of thought, perhaps under the influence of this passage, in Romans 1 and 2). The whole theme takes wing in the New Testament: 'I thank thee, Father, Lord of heaven and earth, that thou hast hidden these things from the wise and understanding and revealed them to babes' (Matt. 11:25, cf. Luke 10:21, in a perikope where the influence of Wisdom-thought is evident): 'Has not God made foolish the wisdom of the world? For since, in the wisdom of God, the world did not know God through wisdom, it pleased God through the folly of what we preach to save those who believe . . . Yet among the mature we do impart wisdom . . . a secret and hidden wisdom of God, which God decreed before the ages for our glorification' (I Cor. 1:20 f.; 2:6 f.). In a sinful world, wisdom has become foolishness and foolishness looks like wisdom. Whatever the words of Jesus just quoted

[1] A useful exposition of these and similar themes is to be found in Thomas Fawcett, *Hebrew Myth and Christian Gospel*, London, 1973, although some of his assertions about mythical themes in the Gospels must be treated with reserve.

may refer to (the antecedent of the words 'these things' is quite unclear, and probably understood differently by Matthew and by Luke), the 'folly of what we preach' for Paul is the Cross and the crucified Messiah; God's response, it may be said, to the terrible weight and power of man's sin, but also, it seems, that 'which God decreed before the ages for our glorification'. (I do not have in mind here the problem of God's decree, supralapsarian or postlapsarian, but rather the question of the relation between creation and redemption or new creation, as it is expressed in Wisdom-terminology).

On the one hand, God's Wisdom in creation, the beauty and order of the world which he has made together with the majesty of his purposes in history, has been distorted by men and concealed from them; it is therefore the work of his Wisdom to reassert his original purpose and restore that which has been distorted or destroyed. There is a continuity, expressed in many ways in the New Testament, between the old creation and the new. On the other hand, the work of redemption is God's unforeseen, unexpected and wholly new response to man's disobedience. That men should die and be resurrected was not unexpected in Judaism; that God Himself should in some sense do so was totally unexpected and there is nothing in the order of creation that points towards it. Christ in His death and resurrection is the supreme example of God's strange Wisdom, the foolishness of God which is wiser than men. But Christ as the head of the first creation, He through whom all things were made, is also and in another sense the supreme example of God's Wisdom; and the two are not easy to hold together. The difficulty comes out in many contexts and in many ways; one instance is seen in the Christ-hymn of Phil. 2:6–11, where we have to comprehend the relation between the being 'in the form of God' of v. 6 and the 'high exaltation' (*hyperhypsosen*—was it even higher than before?) of v. 9 (creation of course is not directly in mind here). Another instance, again with specific reference to Christ Himself, can be seen in the Christ-hymn of Col. 1, if it is true that in that hymn cosmological ideas current in Hellenistic Judaism have been employed to describe the cosmic reference of the Christian eschatology and soteriology. The problem then is, as formulated by Hegermann: 'Wie kann das All, das *par nature* schon den Schöpfungsmittler zur *kephale tou somatos* hatte, überhaupt einer Erlösung bedürftig sein, und wie kann der Schöpfungsmittler zu seiner kosmischen Hauptstellung, die er *par nature* ewig innehat, in der Zeit kraft göttlicher Erwählung erhöht werden?'[1]

[1] *op. cit.*, p. 106. The phrase *par nature* refers to a quotation from P. Benoit, who, understanding the first part of the hymn in a literal cosmological sense, maintains that 'der Schöpfungsmittler das All "porte en lui par nature en tant qu'il est le Fils, l'*eikon*" ' (see *Revue Biblique* 63, 1956).

Formulated in very general and less sharp terms, the question is 'in what senses is the new creation the completion or restoration of the old, and in what senses is it the reversal of the old? And how can we hold the two together?' To turn to another aspect of it: does Jesus bring the completion or fulfilment of the Mosaic Law, or does He bring its cancellation? (We must bear in mind here that the cosmic nature of the Torah was already a current idea). And again to another aspect of it: is Jesus of Nazareth, as portrayed for us in the Gospels, essentially the earthly appearance of the Divine Wisdom or Logos, which was in the beginning, and about which we know in other ways, or must we seek 'in the historical and resurrected Jesus himself the power in which the world intrinsically coheres'?[1] That may seem a different question from those just mentioned; but it is at all events very closely related to them. It is easy in one sense (if you accept the presuppositions involved) to see in the cosmic Christ of, say, the Colossian hymn 'the power in which the world intrinsically coheres'; it is less easy to see that same power in the historical and resurrected Jesus. For it is in the history—by which I here mean the ministry, the death and the resurrection—that the new thing which God does, and the *discontinuity* between the old and the new, are most easily and most often seen; while it is in the 'metaphysics', the theological truth of the creation and preservation and redemption of the world through Christ, that the *continuity* is most often observed. Of course the distinction is artificial and absurd; what are the death and resurrection, which here appear in the first half of our disjunction, if they are not the redemption, which here appears in the second? Nevertheless, the disjunction just stated does, I believe, represent a recurring and enfeebling tendency in Christian thought; and if God's Wisdom in the Word of the Cross, which seems to be foolishness, can be thought together with the 'mythical' truth of Christ as the Wisdom of God in creation, that will have a part to play not only in holding together creation and redemption but in maintaining the identity of the Jesus of history and the Christ of faith. It ought also to have a part to play in any attempted solution of the problem of evil—although I do not want to argue that the Word of the Cross *per se* offers any solution of that problem. In any case, the idea of Wisdom has a flexibility which should aid us in thinking through the whole question of the relation of creation and redemption.

The last two paragraphs have raised questions and not provided answers. But to ask the question about the Wisdom of God in creation and in redemption is again seen to involve asking the question about Jesus in his historical manifestation—just as it is also to seek the answer to the question about the gulf between the Creator and his fallen world.

[1] W. Pannenberg, *op. cit.*, p. 394.

(3) My third point above concerned the personification of Wisdom, and the effect of that personification on ideas of creation. A human figure is not at first sight a suitable candidate for presentation in the garb of the Divine Wisdom. Wisdom, I suggested, formed a bridge between a transcendent God and the world of human affairs precisely because it could be conceived both as an aspect of God's being and power and as a characteristic of men without blurring the distinction between the two, and at the same time could be personified in a manner which gave it living reality. But it cannot easily be said of a man either that he 'is a reflection of eternal light' and an image of God's goodness, or that he 'passes into holy souls and makes them friends of God, and prophets' (Wisd. 7:26 f.). In fact, Judaism was prepared to say things not unlike the former about Adam; but that was partly because he too had become a mythical or ideal figure. The real difficulty, however, lies elsewhere. We can speak of Wisdom as being with God, and in men, without dividing the substance of Wisdom; but as soon as we say that Wisdom became man, or that the Logos became flesh, we introduce a conceptual distinction between the Wisdom that was in the beginning, and is and ever shall be, and the human existence which was also Wisdom but was not in the beginning. It could almost be said that the whole history of Christology is the history of attempts, often unsuccessful, to hold together these two aspects of the one Person. From the angle of the role of Christ in creation the difficulty can be presented in this way: how can He be both creator and created? To wrestle with these matters is beyond me; but it is here if anywhere that the bridge between God and man, between the holy Lord and His creation, has in fact to be built. Perhaps the pondering of a paradox will help us a little: only the Creator can create His own creatureliness, and only He who has done this can be seen at the deepest level to be the Creator; for the only truly creative and sovereign act visible to man is the act of self-abnegation in love—nothing else represents unconquerable power. Something of that insight, as it seems to me, lies behind the New Testament assertion that it is Christ crucified and exalted through whom all things were made. But if so—and we shall return to this—our understanding of the truth of creation through Christ is again seen to depend on our understanding of the Gospel story, and our understanding of the Divinity upon our understanding of the humanity and the history of the Word or Wisdom made flesh.

But of course to speak of the Divine Wisdom (or Word) as personified and to speak of it as incarnate are two very different things, and it may seem as if in the last paragraph I have moved illegitimately from the one to the other. The point however is that the movement must be made, and the question is how it should be made. Some deal with the problem by moving from incarnation to creation or from eschatology and the Lordship of Christ to creation, and not vice versa (as we have already noticed); Barth's doctrine of the primacy of the covenant with man over creation itself[1] and Pannenberg's derivation of the place of Christ in creation from the summation of all things in Christ (Eph. 1:9 f.)[2] are examples of this. Again, these issues are far beyond our scope here; but the thought of the Wisdom of God in salvation and in creation, with its emphasis on His delight in all created things and in the resourcefulness of the Creator within the processes of evolution, may have its part to play in relating the concept of creation more vividly both to incarnation and to eschatology, and in making it comprehensible to modern minds how there can be such a thing as a 'creative power' behind the phenomena of the universe and how such a power could possibly be 'personified' or in any sense personal.

One of the things at issue here is one of the greatest obstacles to the intellectual reception of the Christian faith for many contemporary minds: the anthropocentricity of Christianity's understanding of the universe and the necessary ontological primacy of the personal (or so it would appear) in any Christian theology and philosophy.[3] The possibility that sentient and intelligent life exists on countless other planets only reinforces the difficulty. It would be foolhardy to suggest that ancient ideas about the Wisdom of God in creation have anything directly to contribute to our questions here; but perhaps enough has been said to suggest that there may be a real if indirect contribution to be made.

(4) The fourth point in the previous section was no more than a brief allusion to some of the images used in the Jewish literature, together with the assertion that these must be treated not merely as picturesque mythology but as serious 'mytho-*logy*'. To explore this would be a subject on its own. But it is surprising how many of the functions of Wisdom in the books referred to find their fulfilment in the account of the ministry of Jesus, especially in its Johannine form:

[1] E.g., *Church Dogmatics* IV.1, Edinburgh, 1956, p. 53: 'But if Jesus Christ is the content and form of the first and eternal Word of God, then that means further that the beginning of all things, of the being of all men and of the whole world, even the divine willing of creation, is preceded by God's covenant with man as its basis and purpose.'

[2] *loc. cit.*

[3] On anthropocentricity the difficulty that people feel today was stated very clearly by Stuart Hampshire in a recent radio programme (*Listener*, 15 May 1975, p. 640): 'In the great historical religions . . . human beings are placed at the centre of the universe, so that the drama of the universe takes place around them and is arranged for their benefit. Although it is true that mere size—the contrast between a meson and a medium-sized person—is not in itself greatly significant, the picture that one carries of the universe as a whole really is significant, because the historical Semitic religions . . . really do picture human beings as standing at the centre. Once you lose that picture, everything changes.'

'in John, Jesus is personified Wisdom'.[1] Beyond this, which is concerned mainly with Jesus' heavenly origin and revelation of God's will, his address to men in the first person (like Isis, and Wisdom), his instruction, his gathering of disciples, etc., the language of the Jewish books which describe Wisdom in connection with the creation of the natural world points us in another direction. The presence of Wisdom 'covering the earth like a mist . . . in the waves of the sea, in the whole earth . . . like a palm tree in Engedi and like rose plants in Jericho' (I quote from Sirach 23—much else could be quoted) can be linked (and there is some historical basis for this) with the Christian awareness of Christ's presence throughout his creation—a theme of so-called mystical theology, from Ephrem in the east to Columba in the west, which we today must somehow urgently recover. The possibility of such a recovery is there in the vastly increased knowledge of the natural world which science has brought and the new opportunities of learning about it which television and other methods of education have made possible. Now we wait for the flame of wonder to be relit. The thought of Christ as the Wisdom of God in creation has its vital part to play here; and the words of Jesus in the Gospel are not irrelevant at this point, because sparrows and lilies are precisely what we are talking about.

(5) and (6) The brief comments about Philo, and about a modern categorization of types of Wisdom, under these headings above need no corresponding comment here—except perhaps to recall that the use of the imagery of motherhood in Philo, and the influence of the figures of Isis, Astarte and others, have tended to disappear in Christianity, or have been transferred from Christ to the Virgin Mary. Indeed, the poor reception that Sophia has had from Christian theology in the past must be largely due to the fact that she is female. Perhaps we shall be able to think more clearly about such things when we have got over some of our current difficulties about the relations between male and female.

Most of the material in section II of this paper has pointed to the need for looking again at the records of Jesus of Nazareth with the thought of the Divine Wisdom in our minds. To that we now turn.

III. *Wisdom, Creation and Jesus*

The presence of Wisdom-theology and Wisdom-Christology in all four Gospels has been the subject of a good deal of discussion in recent years.[2] Useful as this work is, it does not for the most part

[1] R. E. Brown, *The Gospel according to John*, Anchor Bible, London, 1971, CXXV. Brown gives an excellent summary of Wisdom motifs in John: *ibid.*, CXXII–CXXV. Cf. pp. 521–3.

[2] See especially Felix Christ, *Jesus Sophia*, Zürich, 1970; M. Jack Suggs

bear directly on the question which now faces us: what light can the records of Jesus throw on the meaning of the assertion that through him the worlds were made?

I can only offer a few hints and guesses. Theology has often been content simply to hoist before men the miracle of God's condescension in the Incarnation, and allow that to do its work unaided. Quite rightly so: from the Christ-hymn of Philippians 2 and the Epistle to Diognetus[1] down to our own times it has been enough to say 'Lo! Within a manger lies He who built the starry skies.' But sometimes the attempt has been made to press further, and to state in what ways the creative power, which is seemingly abnegated in the Incarnation, is nevertheless also expressed in it.

I take first the teaching of Jesus. In an oft-quoted passage at the beginning of his book on the parables C. H. Dodd wrote:

> There is a reason for this realism of the parables of Jesus. It arises from a conviction that there is no mere analogy, but an inward affinity, between the natural order and the spiritual order; or as we might put it in the language of the parables themselves, the Kingdom of God is intrinsically *like* the processes of nature and of the daily life of men. Jesus therefore did not feel the need of making up artificial illustrations for the truths He wanted to teach. He found them ready-made by the maker of man and nature. That human life, including the religious life, is a part of nature is distinctly stated in the well-known passage beginning 'Consider the fowls of the air . . .' (Matt. 7:26, 30; Luke 12:24–8). Since nature and supernature are one order, you can take any part of that order and find in it illumination for other parts. Thus the falling of rain is a religious thing, for it is God who makes the rain to fall on the just and the unjust . . . and the love of God is present in the natural affection of a father for his scapegrace son. This sense of the divineness of the natural order is the major premiss of all the parables.[2]

Dodd's language about the natural order and the spiritual order invites the use of his exposition in support of some form of natural theology[3] (notice how he begins by asserting an affinity between the two orders, and then slides into asserting their identity); and no

---

Wisdom, Christology and Law in Matthew's Gospel, Harvard, 1970; R. G. Hamerton-Kelly, *op. cit.*; J. M. Robinson, *op. cit.*, pp. 84–130.

[1] *The Epistle to Diognetus*, chap. VII, is one of the most beautiful statements of this truth in early Christian literature.

[2] *The Parables of the Kingdom*, London, 1935, pp. 21 f.

[3] This is the concern of W. D. Davies, who quotes this passage from Dodd, *Paul and Rabbinic Judaism*, London, 1955, pp. 174 f.

doubt there is an affinity between most uses of the Wisdom theme and natural theology. But our concern here is rather different. It is to assert that the existence of the parables, like the existence of Jesus who spoke them, is in a real sense the presence of the Kingdom. In what real sense? At least in this, that the Wisdom of God in creation, which made and upholds the world as it is, here continues to address, convict and uphold men and women who have lost sight of it—or think they have, until the exercize of their 'natural' reason brings them back into view of it again. This is how the world is, says Jesus—sometimes it is the natural world, sometimes the world of human affairs, sometimes both—and he speaks, not as one for whom the sinfulness of men or the apparent indifference of natural processes constitute a problem, but as it were from God's side, calling for something that is beyond men's anxious questions about the nature of God's purposes; something that is, as was said above, at the same time both profound, natural and utterly new. This is the creative Wisdom of God in action, summoning men and women to a prodigality and recklessness of love which is somehow also exhibited in the prodigality and recklessness of nature's processes (a modern comment, that, but in line as I believe with the main thrust of Jesus' teaching here); summoning them to that openness to the future which some recent theologians have seen as at the heart of the idea of creation; summoning them to see that God's rule is both among them and not yet present, for the fact that the world is God's and is good is not a *semel factum* but a *semper fieri* or perhaps a *hodie fieri* and a *cras fieri*.

Such generalities are a poor substitute for exegesis. But what I have tried to say about the parables can also be said about much of Jesus' other teaching. 'The moral teaching of Jesus insists upon the original will of the Creator, and just in this way it is the revelation of the will of God for the last days, in which the Kingdom of God is proclaimed on earth.'[1]

It is in line with this that Jesus speaks of evil not as a problem but as an enemy to be overcome, as chaos is overcome by the divine power in the creation myths. His miracles are relevant here, again precisely as the works of God's Wisdom, both restoring and renewing all things. As Professor Torrance has put it, 'In the whole life, death and resurrection of Jesus God Himself was directly at work affirming as good what He had made and making good His own Word in the creation of the world. That is what was involved in every act of mercy and healing in which the commanding fiat of the Creator was

[1] N. A. Dahl, *op. cit.*, p. 442. Dahl here adds a reference to H. J. Schoeps' article '*Restitutio principii*, as the basis of the *Nova Lex Jesu*', *Journal of Biblical Literature*, 1947, pp. 453–64. Schoeps refers especially to Jesus' teaching on marriage and divorce.

found on the lips of Jesus.'[1] In all this, as it seems to me, it is important to think not only of the Word of God with all its connotations of power in action, but also of the Wisdom of God, with its connotations of a hidden yet single and indeed flexible plan, of accommodation to what man himself can grasp and display, of accommodation to all the dislocations that man causes, yet also of a purpose and a way of working that are far beyond anything that man could conceive unaided.

There are of course other more obvious points of contact between the Wisdom-tradition and the picture of Jesus in the Gospels. Some of them have been dealt with in the studies alluded to at the beginning of this section—Jesus' 'Wisdom sayings' for example, his apophthegmata, and those passages in which he is presented as speaking in the guise of Wisdom herself, or as Wisdom's 'last envoy'. He appears, too, in a garb very like that of the righteous man of the Wisdom literature in whom Wisdom dwells (see for example Wisdom of Solomon 2 and 3, and the echoes thereof in the Passion narrative especially in its Matthean form). But these perhaps do not carry us much further along our particular road of enquiry. When we turn, however, to the death and resurrection of Christ so many possible lines of thought leap into the mind that only silence is possible—qualified, perhaps, by a single observation. Whatever else we do, we must not fly to a too-easy relating of the particular process of disintegration and revivification which took place in the death and resurrection of the body of the Lord with the constant processes of disintegration and revivification in which created existence consists. It is all too easy, for example, to find some kind of principle of sacrifice and renewal, of 'death and resurrection', running right through the universe, and to link that in a facile way with the death and resurrection of Christ. But on the other hand, to deny any effective relationship is to destroy the whole conception of the Wisdom of God in creation and in Christ (and of course to destroy much more as well).[2]

[1] *God and Rationality*, London, 1971, p. 143. Cf. p. 150 f. John 5:17–20 is a profound theological comment on this theme, less often alluded to than it might be in discussions about creation. Jesus' healings on the sabbath link creation and new creation (as in Rabbinic Judaism the sabbath links the two: Strack-Billerbeck, *Kommentar*, IV, p. 839 f.; cf. also Hengel, *op. cit.*, I, pp. 166 ff. on Hellenistic Judaism).

[2] One possible line of thought here is suggested by Prof. John Macquarrie's interpretation of creativity as 'letting be'. Love also is 'letting be', and so is sacrifice, and the death of Christ, which can thus be subsumed under the same category of thought as the act of creation: 'Creation, reconciliation, and consummation are not separate acts but only distinguishable aspects of one awe-inspiring movement of God—his love or letting-be, whereby he confers, sustains, and perfects the being of the creatures' (Macquarrie, *Principles of Christian Theology*, London, 1966, p. 247). The question with all such lines of thought must

There for the moment our hints and guesses must come to an end. In the circumstances, a *Zusammenfassung* hardly seems desirable, even if it were possible. Professor Torrance, to whom these thoughts come with admiration and gratitude, has been a valiant fighter for a theology which will not yield to the false dualisms of the past and yet will maintain the transcendence and the glory of God as the origin and the goal of all life. The ancient mythology and theology of Wisdom are not entirely irrelevant to that aim. If Christ is indeed the creative Wisdom of God incarnate, what does that tell us about *being* and *act* in the doctrine of God; about *knowing* and *being*, and all the epistemological problems to which twentieth century theological flesh is heir; about Christology, and the human as well as divine wisdom in the mind of Christ (against Apollinarian tendencies); about the relation between *Spirit* and *matter* (or mass/energy or whatever else we should call it) in the light of modern cosmologies? These questions stand before us now as always.

always be: how far do they *disclose* an underlying unity in diverse material, and how far do they *impose* an artificial unity in the course of the mind's continuing effort to simplify and organize?

4 'Logos, Image, Son': Some Models and Paradigms in Early Christology

by ALASDAIR HERON

The dialogue between theology and the natural sciences to which T. F. Torrance has been such a notable contributor has opened up many avenues of fruitful investigation for theology. Not the least significant of these is the study of method—not chiefly the experimental method for which modern science is properly renowned, but rather the method of interpretation, the rationale of the advance towards a more comprehensive understanding of a subject. Although this is often overlooked, no doubt because of the hidden(?) influence of positivist or reductionist assumptions—assumptions which, followed consistently, would demote science to mere technology, and with equal facility relegate theology to the realm of *belles lettres* —the heart of the scientific enterprise cannot adequately be defined simply in terms of prediction and control (appropriate though such definition is for central aspects of the experimental method) but must also be recognized to involve *the sustained attempt to make sense* of the matter under investigation. In this attempt, modern science has been quite astoundingly successful: it has in fact virtually replaced such time-honoured disciplines as philosophy and law as the dominant non-theological feature of the intellectual scene—a substitution none the less significant because theology (and not only theology) has not yet succeeded in coming to terms with it in the same way as it once did with philosophy and law. The natural sciences present today the instance *par excellence* of the endeavour of the human mind to grasp and understand reality. As such, they offer to cast fresh light on other areas of enquiry as well by revealing more clearly at least some central aspects of the method which this endeavour applies.

This essay is concerned with one such aspect: the use of models and paradigms in the process of interpretation; and with one line of theological development which leads from the Logos christology of the Apologists to later orthodoxy. Here, the reflections of modern times on the method of scientific interpretation and the development of scientific understanding supply categories which are helpful for making sense of developments in theology as well. First our use of 'model' and 'paradigm' must be explained; then we shall study in some detail the operation of the Logos paradigm in its heyday; lastly we shall touch more briefly on the emergence of alternative paradigms, such as Image and Son, in the third and fourth centuries. We shall thus be concentrating selectively on one very narrow line of theological development; the same principles can, however, be observed in all sorts of theological and non-theological enquiry. Needless to say, the question of the rightness or wrongness of any such development, or of the validity or invalidity of its conclusion, cannot be settled simply by analysing it in this way; but such analysis, in so far as it helps to clarify the meaning of the development, is also of the first relevance for those questions as well.

Models and Paradigms

In the broadest sense, a model is any picture, analogy or metaphor which is used to grasp and describe anything we may be attempting to understand. It may be as simple and concrete as an illustration drawn from everyday experience ('atoms are like billiard balls') or as complex and abstract as a sophisticated mathematical formula. Either way, it helps to 'make sense' of the subject under study and provides a working tool by which it may be grasped. The discovery and use of such models rests ultimately on our capacity to recognize or suspect resemblances between *this*, which is strange or new or unexplained, and *that*, which is already familiar: this capacity, difficult though it is to explain or justify, is a foundation of human rationality itself, and underlies not only our highest speculations but also (and in very much the same way) our most elementary acts of recognition or comprehension.

By its very nature, however, the development and application of a model is a tentative and provisional enterprise. A suspected resemblance may turn out to be delusory; or it may transpire that, though genuine enough, it does not shed much light. Even if the resemblance turns out to be real and illuminating, the model must still be used in a way that leaves open the possibility that important differences may yet emerge between it and the *interpretandum*: otherwise there is a risk that the model will so dominate the stage as to impede further discovery. Because of this essential gap between the model and that which it enables us to grasp, the case may even arise where two *prima facie* irreconcilable models must be used together to describe the same phenomenon—light, for example, behaves in some respects like a series of waves, but in others like a stream of particles: the two models have to be used together, even though they seem to rule each other out. A model is always *only* a model, not the thing itself.

In spite of this apparent inadequacy, however, the (conscious or unconscious) use of models is essential to the expansion of knowledge. We cannot but work towards the comprehension of the unknown from the starting-point of the known, and using the patterns, categories and images which we already have. This does not mean that no new knowledge, properly speaking, can be gained at all: the boundaries between the known and the unknown are not static and immutable. But in the dynamic movement of the expansion of knowledge, we find ourselves always on a shifting frontier, where we must continually reach out with the help of what is already available in order to touch and make sense of what lies beyond. The necessity and the inadequacy of models alike reflect and are ultimately grounded in the nature of this movement. (The inability of any fundamentally static theory of knowledge and truth, whether of a Platonic or a positivist type, to give a convincing account of genuine discovery reflects and is ultimately grounded in its *failure* to recognize the nature of this movement.)

In the development of knowledge in any field, models may be used in a number of different ways. For our purposes it will serve to indicate three of those, each corresponding to a different stage. The boundaries between them are fluid, but a broad distinction may still be made.

(1) A model may serve to crystallize and focus a particular insight: a pattern, for example, is seen in the *data* or object being studied which reminds us of one already familiar, and so offers the possibility of making sense of what up till then had not made sense. In the metaphors made famous by Bishop Ramsey, 'the penny drops, the light dawns'. A model thus discovered is heuristic; it 'discloses' something of the nature of the object and opens up a path into it. It gives us, so to speak, a place to stand on and look around, a centre about which the previously unknown and uncomprehended (or misapprehended) begins to take a shape we can understand. As such, it represents a break through to discovery, a promise of recognition, a beginning of comprehension.

(2) Given that a model discovered in this way proves reliable enough to be retained, there ensues a complex process of refinement and clarification. This may be deliberate and conscious, but it need not be so: in much learning and consolidation of insights it is in fact a matter of unconscious assimilation and modification. Whether consciously or unconsciously, the adequacies and inadequacies of the model are probed until it becomes clearer just how far it can be relied on as a guide to the nature of the *interpretandum.* Nor is that all: where, as frequently is the case, more than one model is being employed, these may interact in a process of mutual limitation and transformation, resulting in a more complex combined model which

is more adequate than either of the original models on its own. The emphasis at this stage is thus on the development and refinement of the model: it is still heuristic, but in a rather different sense from that described under (1). No longer does the model simply focus a sudden insight; rather, it is being applied, tested and corrected in order to achieve a more reliable, stable and comprehensive grasp.

In connection with this kind of interaction of models in a continuing process of consolidation it is useful to distinguish between that model which at any particular point occupies the centre of attention and any others which are also present, but filling a secondary role or even being modified and altered by the central, dominant one. Such a dominant, controlling model is a paradigm: it largely determines the overall picture, and other models are given their place and even on occasion their meaning in terms of it. This paradigmatic status, however, is no more absolute or immutable than the status of any model. A model may serve for a time as the paradigm, and then subsequently be relegated as the enquiry moves on and another model takes on its paradigmatic role. At the same time, any useful contribution made by the erstwhile paradigm during its hour of glory need not be lost when it is dethroned: it can be carried over into the new paradigm, which thus takes on something of the colour of its predecessor. On a purely superficial analysis, this might appear inconsistent, but it is justified by the fact that all models, including paradigms, are *only* models, and are used, modified and disposed of according to their usefulness as interpretative tools. The carrying-over of elements of the meaning of one paradigm to another which would not on its own possess them is simply a further reflection of the nature of models themselves.

(3) As a result of the process sketched under (2), a more or less stable final or provisionally final model may be worked out and accepted as a broadly adequate and reliable overall picture of the *interpretandum*. It then becomes a sort of map, a means of conceptualization, a shorthand description: the effective terminus of the line of investigation. Those models which attain this dignity become virtually inbuilt elements of the system of knowledge to which they belong. They do not thereby cease to be models; but, having survived the long and dangerous road from initial insight(s) through various tests and challenges, modifications and refinements, they are reckoned to have proved themselves so far as that is possible. They then become recognized discoveries rather than part of the process of discovery, established rather than provisional and tentative. This does not locate them permanently in a haven of peace where the chill winds of challenge can no more blow bitterly upon them; but the challenge is more likely to come from the raising of entirely new questions in an entirely new horizon than

from a questioning of their validity in their own terms. In this sense, many of the doctrines of classical theology—the *homoousios* of Nicaea, the 'one person in two natures' of Chalcedon, the doctrine of the Trinity as formulated in the *Athanasianum*, for example—may be regarded as relatively stable final models.

Much recent theological discussion of models has concentrated on the first and last of these ways of using them, dealing either with models and discovery, or with the model-character of conciliar and similar definitions. In such discussions, it has chiefly been the logical status of theological statements which has been at issue. But the intermediate stage, which involves the dynamics of continuing reflection and enquiry, of experimentation with models and the interaction between them, of the expanding of horizons in order provisionally to integrate as much as possible of what needs to be said in a unified grasp—all this has its own special interest as revealing the rationale of theological enquiry in a way which exclusive concentration on the (more instantaneous) beginning or (more static) conclusion of a line of investigation cannot do. It is accordingly with this intermediate stage, with the development of models and the use and modification of particular paradigms, that we shall now be concerned.

The Logos Paradigm

The high point of the Logos christology was of course in the second half of the second century, when it was most clearly articulated by four of the Apologists—Justin, Athenagoras, Tatian and Theophilus. No doubt other contemporaries whose works are wholly or partly lost may also have used it, and certainly other, slightly later writers, such as Irenaeus and Tertullian, show the influence of one or another of these four in their own theologies. Nevertheless, there is plenty of material to occupy us in the surviving work of this group: indeed, there is more than enough, and we must bracket off two areas of enquiry as lying outside our scope here.

First, there is the as yet unresolved question of where exactly this Logos christology came from. These four, in spite of various divergences, all appear to be very much on the same wavelength; and it is a different wavelength from those of earlier writers who speak of the Logos, and in particular from those of Philo on the one hand and of the Fourth Gospel on the other, to say nothing of such fragmentary references as Ignatius' enigmatic description of Christ as 'the Logos coming forth out of silence' (*Magn.* 8:2). Philo, the Johannine tradition, and the lines of thought reflected in Ignatius all lie in the background, as does the considerable speculation on the Logos in Stoic thought, and subsequently in Middle Platonism. But neither separately nor together do these fully explain the thought of Justin and the others, though that thought cannot be understood apart from this extensive background. We must leave aside the problem of the precise relationship between the background and the Apologists themselves, and concentrate rather on the shape of their own Logos theory.

Second, we shall also exclude from our central analysis several key aspects of the Logos model as used by the Apologists themselves, though this is not because these are not important—rather the reverse: they are foundational to the Logos christology, but are peripheral to our chief subject here. Justin in particular used the idea of the Logos to link the truth incarnate in Christ with, on the one hand, the truth grasped by philosophers even before Christ *I Apol.* 5:4; 46:2 ff.; *II Apol.* 10:1 ff.), and, on the other, with the *logos spermatikos* which is the basis of rationality in human beings (*I Apol.* 32:8; 46:2; *II Apol.* 13:3 ff.). Similarly, Tatian interprets Joh. 1:5 to mean that the Logos is 'the light of God' as opposed to the darkness, which 'is the soul without understanding' (*Oratio ad Graecos* 13), while Theophilus describes the Logos at creation as 'shining like a lamp to illuminate what is under heaven' (*Ad Autolycum* II 13; cf. also II 15, where God, his Word and his Wisdom are symbolized by the first three days of creation, and man, 'who needs their light', is represented by the making of the lights on the fourth day). The Logos has to do with the divine rationality, with created rationality, and with the illumination of the latter by the former. By the same token, he is linked as a matter of course with the creation of the world itself (Justin, *I Apol.* 64:5; *II Apol.* 6:3; *Dial.* 61–2; Athenagoras, *Legatio* 4:2; 6:2; 10:1 ff.; Tatian, *Ad Graec.* 5; 7; Theophilus, *Ad Autol.* I 7; II 10; 18; 22). In this connection, he is identified simultaneously with the divine Sophia, or Wisdom (Justin, *Dial.* 61; cf. 62; Athenagoras, *Leg.* 10:4; Theophilus, *Ad Autol.* II 10—though Theophilus more often distinguishes the Sophia from the Logos, making it the third in the divine 'triad' and so in effect equating it with the Spirit: *Ad Autol.* II 15; 18) and with the *arche* or 'beginning' of all created reality (Justin, *Dial.* 62; Tatian, *Ad Graec.* 5; Theophilus, *Ad Autol.* II 10; cf. I 2). This double identification is based on Prov. 8:22 ('The Lord created me the beginning of his ways') which is spoken by the divine Wisdom, and came to be a key christological text in the early church. The connection of the Logos with rationality and revelation on the one hand and with creation and cosmogony on the other, a connection which the Apologists took over from earlier theories of the Logos, was an essential presupposition for the articulation of their Logos christology. It is accordingly also presupposed in the following analysis; but while we shall touch on aspects of it, we must in general concentrate more narrowly on the way in which the Logos model, given this background, was used to fix more precisely the status of Christ and his relation to God.

A way into this question is offered by the fact that both Athenagoras and Theophilus find it possible to use the Logos to explain, indeed to demythologize their description of Christ as 'Son of God':

> Let no one think it stupid of me to say that God has a Son. For we do not think of God the Father or of the Son in the way of the poets, who weave their myths by showing the gods as no better than men. But the Son of God is his Logos in idea and in actuality (Athenagoras, *Leg.* 10:2). What else is the 'voice' (*sc.* of God, heard by Adam in Paradise) but the Logos of God, who is also his Son? Not in the way that the poets and mythmakers describe sons of the gods being begotten by intercourse, but as the Truth describes the Logos who is for ever within the heart of God . . . This, God begot as his spoken Logos . . . (Theophilus, *Ad Autol.* II 22).

Christ is not to be thought of as 'Son of God' in the way that pagans might imagine, picking up from their own familiar legends the idea of an all-too-human 'divine begetting'. Rather, it is as God's Logos, his rationality and word, that he is of God and from God. The point may appear to us an elementary, even a banal one; and no doubt to some extent it is. Nevertheless, it points to the facts that the description 'Son of God' was one which needed to be interpreted, and that the Logos model offered itself as a means of such interpretation. Justin too is aware of the need to clarify the description of Christ as 'Son':

> Having it written in the memoirs of the apostles that he is Son of God, and saying that he is Son, we recognise that he is, and that he came forth from the Father by the Father's power and will before all the things that were made; and he is also called Wisdom and Day and Sunrise and Sword and Stone and Rod . . . (*Dial.* 100).

While the term Logos is not used here, we are clearly moving in the same circle of ideas: 'Son' points to a kind of 'coming forth' from God, and the Logos model could be and was used to clarify this 'coming forth' not merely as a convenient *ad hominem* refutation of pagan conceptions of 'divine begetting', but because at a more profound level it supplied a way of understanding what it meant to talk of a 'Son of God' at all.

This more profound application of the Logos model is reflected in the Apologists' linking of the Logos with the ideas of 'Son', 'Firstborn' and 'begetting'. So for Justin, the Logos is 'the first offspring of God' (*I Apol.* 21:1), 'the first Power after the Father and Lord and God of all' (*I Apol.* 32:10), 'the Firstborn' (*I Apol.* 33:6; 46:2; 63:13), or even straightforwardly 'Son' (*I Apol.* 32:10; 63:4; *II Apol.* 6:3) or 'Only-begotten' (*Dial.* 105: here Justin states that Christ is 'Only-begotten . . . being begotten from him in a special way as Logos and Power'; cf. also the application of the Logos model in *Dial.* 61, to which we come below. This model is thus also present in the *Dialogue*, though not so prominent as in the *Apologies*—which underlines its fundamental importance for Justin). Similarly, Athenagoras says that 'the Logos is recognized as Son' (*Leg.* 18:2) and that 'we confess God and the Logos (as) Son' (*Leg.* 24:2), as well as offering his demythologization of 'Son' by means of Logos (*Leg.* 10:2, quoted above). Theophilus, as we have seen, also gives this interpretation (*Ad Autol.* II 22, quoted above), and Tatian too calls the Logos 'Firstborn' (*Ad Graec.* 5) and describes the Father as 'having begotten him' (*Ad Graec.* 7).

Just how deeply anchored this understanding of the Logos was in the minds of the Apologists can be seen in a point which Justin emphasizes repeatedly, and which the other three would no doubt have been happy to accept as well. Not only is the Logos 'Son' and 'Firstborn'; it is precisely *because* he is the Logos that Christ is properly 'Son of God'. So Justin speaks of 'his Son, who alone is properly called "Son", the Logos' (*II Apol.* 6:3), and insists:

> The Son of God, who is called Jesus, even if he were merely an ordinary man, would be worthy to be called 'Son of God' for his wisdom . . . But in a unique way, quite apart from ordinary begetting, we say that he was begotten from God as his Logos (*I Apol.* 22:1–2).

Again, 'Jesus Christ alone was properly begotten as Son of God, being his Logos and Firstborn and Power' (*I Apol.* 23:2); 'Jesus is the Christ because he is the Son and Apostle of God, being formerly his Logos' (*I Apol.* 63:10); 'he was the Only-begotten of the Father of all, being uniquely begotten from him as Logos and Power, and later became man through the Virgin' (*Dial.* 105). Logos here is not only being *associated* with the ideas of sonship and begetting; it is being used to *explain* them, and so to explain who Christ really is.

What is in fact happening here is that of two available models, 'Son' and 'Logos', the former is being subordinated to the latter and understood in terms of it. Thus 'Logos' has become a paradigm, gathering to itself the various associations and connotations of 'Son', and in the gathering, interpreting and reinterpreting them, and so at the same time offering a basis for them. To see how far this process went, we must move on to other aspects of these models. 'Son' suggests on the one hand a kind of 'begetting' or 'bringing forth', and on the other a special relationship of similarity and distinction between parent and offspring. The Logos paradigm supplied ways of interpreting both themes, but in each it ran into difficulties which could only be resolved when it ceased to be *the* paradigmatic model.

The 'begetting of the Son' is interpreted by means of the Logos model as an event analogous to that in which a rational mind (*logos*) expresses itself in a rational word (*logos*). The Logos as God's 'Word' is in a sense his 'Son', and the 'begetting' of the Logos is the act by which God 'speaks' him or 'sends him forth'. The apologists generally simply presuppose this complex of ideas—they were in a position to assume that their readers knew what they meant—but they do on occasion spell it out. So Justin instructs Trypho:

> In the beginning, before all the creatures, God begot a certain rational Power from himself, which is sometimes called by the Holy Spirit the Glory of the Lord, sometimes Son, sometimes Wisdom, sometimes Angel, sometimes God, sometimes Lord and Logos . . . He is entitled to all these names because he serves the will of the Father, and because he was begotten from the Father by the Father's choice. But do we not observe something of the kind even in ourselves? When we utter a word, we 'beget' the word . . . (*Dial.* 61).

The same analogy is used by Tatian (*Ad Graecos* 5), and hinted at, though less directly, by Athenagoras (*Leg.* 10:2–3). The clearest statement of all, however, is given by Theophilus. He draws on the distinction, established by the Stoics, between the *logos endiathetos*, or 'inner word', broadly equivalent to 'mind' or 'thought', and the *logos prophorikos*, or 'word borne forth', that is, the 'spoken word':

> . . . the Truth describes the Logos who is for ever within (*endiathetos*) the heart of God. Before anything came to be, God had him as his counsellor, for he is God's own Mind and Understanding. When God willed to make what he had decided upon, he begot this Logos as coming forth (*prophorikos*), 'the Firstborn of all creation' (Col. 1: 15) . . . (*Ad Autol.* II 22; cf. also II 10).

This statement of Theophilus' underlines two highly significant implications of this use of the Logos model. The 'begetting' of the Logos is linked directly to the creation of the universe; and it involves a transition for the Logos himself from being 'within' God to being distinct from God. Here in fact we have the Achilles' heel of the model, so we must dwell a little on these points.

The other three, like Theophilus, all combine the thought of a sort of two-stage history of the Logos himself with that of his emergence for the purpose of creation. So Justin calls him 'the Logos who was with God before all the things that were made, and was begotten when in the beginning God created and ordered all things through him' (*II Apol.* 6:3). Athenagoras is similar:

> . . . I shall explain briefly what 'Son' (*pais*) means. He is the first offspring of the Father, not as if he had come into being (for God, who is eternal Mind, had from the beginning his Logos in himself, being eternally rational (*logikos*)), but . . . as having come forth to give form and reality to everything material (*Leg.* 10:3).

The same pattern of thought is also in Tatian:

> God was 'in the beginning' (*arche*), but we have learned that the 'beginning' is the power of the Logos. For the Master of all, being himself the reality of everything (*hypostasis tou pantos*), was in one sense alone, in that the creation had not yet taken place. In so far however as he himself was all power, and the reality of things visible and invisible, everything was with him. With him also, through his rational (*logikos*) power, there existed also the Logos, who was in him. And by his will, the Logos leapt forth from his simplicity; and the Logos, not coming forth in vain, became the Firstborn work of the Father: him we know as the beginning (*arche*) of the cosmos (*Ad Graec.* 5).

Tatian's thought here is particularly complex, and we shall return to it later. At this point, what is important is that he, like the others, identifies the 'birth' of the Logos, not as a simple coming into existence, but as the movement of the Logos out of God in order to create the universe. Neither he nor any of the others goes more fully into the precise manner of this movement or attempts to locate it more exactly but the main thrust of their thought is faithfully reflected by Tertullian when he adds the clarification that it was when God said 'Let there be light!' that the 'complete birth of the Word' occurred and the Word 'was made Son of God' (*Adversus Praxean* 7). The primacy of the Logos model over that of Son could not be more complete: 'Son' describes a second stage in the history of the Logos, a stage preceded by the Logos' previous history in which he was Logos alone. And the transition to this second stage is made necessary by the creation of the world, of which the Logos/Son is the *arche*.

These implications of the paradigmatic application of the Logos model, harmless though they might appear, raise serious difficulties. To speak of the Logos as 'coming forth' from God, and so as 'becoming Son of God' seems to suggest some kind of change in the Logos himself. The ambivalence of the Logos concept, with its double reference to 'mind' and 'word', partly conceals this suggestion; but it cannot eliminate it, for the suggestion flows from that very ambivalence. By the same token, the nature of the continuity between the two stages in the history of the Logos remains problematic, and for the same reasons. Similarly, to link his 'being begotten' with the creation of the universe does indeed serve the purpose of connecting him with God the Creator, and of subordinating the existence of all other reality to his being; but it also ties him in his status as Logos/ Son to the whole of created reality as its *arche*, as the mediating principle between God and everything else. The 'Son of God' thus becomes a link in a descending chain of reality which leads from God at one end to the world we know at the other. Thus while he can still be called 'God' (Justin, *I Apol.* 63:13; *Dial.* 48; 61; Athenagoras, *Leg.* 10:5; Theophilus, *Ad Autol.* II 22), he can also be described as 'the Firstborn *work* of the Father' (Tatian, *Ad Graecos* 5). This does not mean that Tatian is a proto-Arian, or significantly opposed to the other three. Rather, all four are accurately reflecting the one or the other side of the fundamentally ambivalent Logos paradigm. (The drive of the thought of all four, had they been faced with the question, would certainly have been in a Nicene rather than an Arian direction. It is no accident that one of the earliest and most vitriolic post-Nicea attacks on Arianism came from Marcellus of Ancyra, whose christology represents the anachronistic—and not entirely helpful—persistence into the fourth century of a virtually unadulterated Logos paradigm. Nevertheless, the possibility of Arianism is inbuilt in that ambivalence, even though authentically Arian conclusions could only be reached by letting the two sides of the model fall apart, so establishing (as Arius did: cf. Athanasius, *Contra Ar.* I 5) a radical disjunction between the Wisdom or Logos of God and the created Wisdom/Logos/Son. Such a radical disjunction is utterly foreign to the thought and intention of the Apologists, but they could not, within the horizon of the Logos paradigm, set up any adequate defences against it.)

For the Apologists, however, this ambivalence did not appear to be a problem, and for at least three reasons. First, their use of the paradigm depended on its double-sidedness, so that their attention was focused on its positive usefulness rather than on any possible negative features. Second, it was only with the passing of time, and finally with the emergence of Arius himself, that the extent of the difficulties could be grasped. That grasp depended in its turn on the recognition of a radical qualitative difference between God and all that is not God—a difference which the hierarchical pattern of thought of the second and third centuries did not perceive with the same intensity. The Apologists, like most of their second and third century contemporaries and followers, were broadly content with the chain: God-Logos-Logos/Son-creation, and the problem of where precisely the line was to be drawn between God and not-God did not exercise them in the way that it was to trouble Arian and Nicene alike a century and a half later. (Arius accordingly deserves more credit than he is usually given for raising this question in all its sharpness, and so acting as the irritant who drove the church to greater clarity on the matter, and indeed to an understanding of the transcendence of God closer to Biblical than to Hellenistic patterns of thought!) Third, the difficulty which they did see in the Logos paradigm was a different one: how to preserve the integrity and unchangeability of God the Father himself? Talk of God's 'sending forth his Logos' seemed to them to threaten, not a possible change in the Logos, but, much more seriously, a change in God. This accordingly became the target of their efforts to clarify and modify the model; but the result is, on the whole, to intensify the difficulties we have already noted in regard to the status and integrity of the Logos. This brings us to the second main theme signalled above: the question of the similarity and distinction between God and the Logos, and the Apologists' attempts to maintain the unchangeability of God throughout.

The application of the Logos model as a paradigm obviously assumes the possibility of a clear distinction between God and the Logos/Son. The distinction is emphasized particularly by Justin: the 'rational Power' begotten by God in the beginning (*Dial.* 61) is also he to whom God says, 'Let us make man' (Gen. 1:26), and therefore 'numerically distinct, with his own rational being' (*Dial.* 62). Later in the work, he goes into the question more fully, rejecting any idea that this Power is simply a sort of radiation like light, without substantial reality or subsistence of its own:

> I have already briefly explained that this Power . . . is not merely nominally reckoned (*sc.* as distinct) in the same way as the light of the sun, but rather is a numerically distinct reality; for I said that this Power was begotten from the Father, though not by separation, as if the being of the Father were divided up . . . (*Dial.* 128).

While Justin makes a special point of this, none of the others would have been any more willing than he to tolerate the kind of dynamic monarchianism which he is ruling out here in his discussion with Trypho. But if the Logos/Son is, as the application of the paradigm implies and Justin here makes explicit, a distinct reality over against the Father, this leads to a dilemma. Either he is something or someone entirely different from God, or he is in some sense a separated part of God himself. In the first case, his relationship to God becomes problematic; in the second, God himself must have undergone change and alteration of his own being in order to produce him. The first alternative leads to the problems we have already noted as inherent in the transition from Logos to Logos/Son as postulated by the Apologists; but as we have also seen, their use of the model attempted to circumvent the difficulty by stressing the continuity of the Logos himself through that transition. Hence, for example, Athenagoras' insistence that the Logos 'did not come into being' when he 'came forth', 'for God, who is eternal mind, had from the beginning his Logos in himself, being eternally rational' (*Leg.* 10:3). It was accordingly the second horn of the dilemma which drew their attention, for they were equally unwilling to accept it. How then could the 'coming forth' of the divine Logos be understood in a way that would not make him an emerging and self-separating part of God? Athenagoras himself offers no answer to this, but the other three all grapple with it. Theophilus sees the difficulty, but offers the least successful answer:

> When God willed to make what he had decided upon, he begot this Logos as coming-forth, 'the Firstborn of all creation', without thereby depriving himself of the Logos. Rather he begot the Logos and remained with the Logos in permanent communion . . . So the Logos is God, having come to be (*pephukos*) from God . . . (*Ad Autol.* II. 22).

While this statement is one that could hardly be faulted, even from the standpoint of later orthodoxy—for it points impeccably both to the origin of the Logos in God, and to the subsequent communion of the Logos with God—it does not really deal with the problem which Theophilus has recognized and indicated with his reference to 'deprivation'. If the Logos is first 'in God' and then 'comes forth', it must appear that something has changed in God himself, that God no longer has the Logos 'in himself'. To this problem, it is no very satisfactory answer to say that the Logos and God remain in 'communion': that is a subsequent matter entirely.

Justin and Tatian, however, attempted to go further into the matter. In *Dial.* 128, partly quoted above, Justin insists that though the process of 'begetting' produces a reality numerically distinct from the Father, it is not a kind of cutting up or division of the Father's own being (*ousia*): this cannot be, because 'everything which is divided and cut up is no longer the same as it was before'. He then offers the analogy of fires kindled from a fire: 'these we see as distinct, yet that from which many others can be kindled is not lessened, but remains the same' (*ibid.*). Here, he is summarizing what he had said earlier in using both the image of fire and that of the uttering of a word in order to explain God's 'begetting' of 'a certain rational Power from himself':

> Do we not observe something similar to this happening even in ourselves? For when we speak out a word, we beget the word. We do not speak it out by separation (*apotome*) of a sort that would

> lessen the *logos* within ourselves. In the same way with fire, we see another fire being kindled without any lessening of that from which it was kindled: that remains the same as it was, and what was kindled from it appears equally as itself, but has not lessened that from which it was taken (*Dial.* 61).

Thus God's own being is not changed or lessened by the production of the Logos/Son, any more than our own minds are changed or lessened by the expression of our thoughts in words. The inner Logos remains unaltered, though the external Logos/Son is 'kindled' from it as a fire is kindled from another fire. So Justin hopes to preserve God's own being from reduction or division in the 'begetting' of the Logos as Son. This would however seem to impale him firmly once more on the first horn of the dilemma: in what sense is the 'spoken Logos' the same as the 'thought Logos'? Is he not rather a separate and distinct reality which only properly begins to exist when it is 'spoken' or 'begotten'? Neither the ambivalence of the Logos concept nor the image of the two fires can really deal satisfactorily with this problem: rather, they conceal the difficulty by glossing over the transition which is involved, implying that there is a basic continuity between the two stages, but failing to explicate that continuity further.

It is against the background of these difficulties that Tatian's even more complex application of the Logos paradigm must be seen; for he gathers up Justin's ideas from *Dial.* 61 but attempts to push a stage further. His account is notoriously obscure, but the broad pattern of his thought can be traced in a fairly straightforward way. (The same pattern is also in Tertullian, *Adv. Praxean* 5 ff.: he appears to be dependent on Tatian, but develops the ideas with greater clarity.) Tatian presents it as follows:

> God was 'in the beginning'; but we have learned that the 'beginning' is the power of the Logos (*logou dynamis*). For the Master of all, being himself the reality (*hypostasis*) of everything, was in one sense alone, in that the creation had not yet taken place. In so far however as he himself was all power (*dynamis*) and the reality (*hypostasis*) of things visible and invisible, everything was (*sc.* already) with him. With him also, through his rational power (*logike dynamis*), there came to be the Logos, who was in him. And by his will, the Logos leapt forth from his simplicity (*haplotes*); and the Logos, not coming forth in vain, became the Firstborn work of the Father: him we know as the beginning of the world. He came to be by unfolding (*merismos*), not by separation (*apokope*). For that which is separated (*apotmethen*) is removed from its origin; but that which is unfolded (*meristhen*) takes up its own place in the pattern (*oikonomia*), yet does not make that

from which it was taken any the less. For just as many fires are lit from a single torch, yet the light of the first torch is not lessened by the kindling of many torches, so too the Logos in coming forth from the power (*dynamis*) of the Father did not make his parent to be without the Logos (*alogos*). I myself, too, am speaking, and you are listening; yet of course in addressing you I do not become empty of my *logos* by the transmission of my *logos*. My aim is rather, through the sending forth of my own voice, to structure the unstructured material which is in you (*sc.* in your mind)—just as the Logos was begotten in the beginning, and in turn brought about our making . . . (*Ad Graecos* 5).

Here, in effect, a four-stage pattern is unfolded. First, there is God himself, existing alone, before all things. Second, however, this aloneness includes within itself the *potential* (*dynamis* as opposed to *energeia*) of everything else that will be, for God is the ground of being (*hypostasis*) of everything else: this potential is labelled 'power of the Logos' or equally 'rational power', and is understood to be the rational capacity of God himself. Third, as an expression and realization of that power, there is *also*, in God, the Logos himself: his being is thus distinguishable from that of the 'power of the Logos', as Tatian remarks later: 'The heavenly Logos came into being (*gegonos*) as Spirit from the Father and as Logos from the rational power (*logike dynamis*)' (*Ad Graec.* 7). Fourth, this Logos 'comes forth' out of the 'simplicity' of God, not by a process of separation, but rather by one of unfolding, of opening out what is already there implicit in God. This 'coming forth' leads to the creation of the universe, of which the Logos himself is the 'beginning'. (The complexity of this pattern is somewhat obscured by the fact that Tatian does not advance beyond Justin's analogies of thought and spoken word, and of fires kindled from a fire. Those two-stage pictures are not of course intended by him to illustrate the whole pattern, but only the 'unfolding without separation'. Tertullian, following Tatian in *Adv. Praxean* 5 ff., makes the four stages clearer by characterizing them as: first, God himself; second, the divine *ratio*, or rational capacity; third, the unspoken divine *sermo*, or word—in other words, the thought; and fourth, the spoken *sermo*.)

The aim of this exceedingly complicated analysis, which results in a considerable complexification of the originally relatively simple Logos model, is to ensure not only that the integrity of God is not harmed by the production of the Logos, but also that the permanence and continuity in being of the Logos himself will be guaranteed, and in a way which will allow both for his distinctness from God and for his being 'in God' as well as 'out of God'. This is why the distinction between the 'power of the Logos' and the Logos himself is central for Tatian. The 'power of the Logos' is constitutive of the being of God, but it is not altered or diminished by the bringing into being of that which is its expression. The existence of the Logos in God does not alter the 'power of the Logos'; nor, equally, does the 'coming forth' of the Logos out of God. Thus God himself remains unaltered throughout. At the same time, the Logos as distinct from the 'power of the Logos' does not only come to be when he is 'sent forth': he is already in God himself, so that there is no hiatus in his being, and even his 'coming forth' is an articulation of what is already there, not the breaking away into separation. Thus Tatian seeks to avoid both horns of the dilemma, and to establish the distinct reality of the Logos without either making him entirely different from God, or making God's own being divisible and changeable.

This escape from the dilemma inbuilt in the use of the Logos paradigm has however been bought at the price of the virtual disintegration of the paradigm itself. In place of the straightforward two-stage model—*logos* as mind and as spoken word—we now have three stages—rational capacity, unspoken thought, spoken word. This has been done in order to avoid the difficulties of the two-stage pattern; but the difficulties are still there, only pushed one stage further back. What relation obtains between rational capacity on the one hand and unspoken thought on the other? And how far is there a genuine continuity between unspoken thought and spoken word? The Logos model on its own cannot satisfactorily answer those questions, or establish either the similarity between the Father and the Logos, or the continuity of the Logos himself through his being 'sent forth'. Thus Tatian's handling of the model reflects an awareness of its inadequacies resulting in the attempt to modify it; but the result is the attenuation of the meaning of the model itself. This is in effect the end of the road for the Logos paradigm: the point has been reached where the modifications demanded by the process of enquiry and reflection demand its replacement by other models and paradigms which will more adequately cope with those difficulties, and give a more satisfactory account of the relation of the Logos or Son to the Father, and of his being over against the things that have come into being through him.

Alternative Paradigms—Image and Son

Space permits here only the briefest mention of two particularly important alternative paradigms which emerged in the third century as a means of coping with the problems we have noted in the Apologists' handling of the Logos model. These problems gather round the questions of the relation of the Logos to the Father, and of his status in regard to creation, and are symbolized most clearly in the fact that the sonship of the Logos is understood by Justin and the others as a function of his 'coming forth' to create the universe. Later theology was to depart from them precisely at this point, and to seek in the Son model a more fundamental paradigm than Logos, carrying it back to interpret the ultimate relationship to the Father, and using it at the same time to establish the radical distinction between the Son and everything created. It was assisted in this by the introduction of other models and paradigms as well, most notably that of Image. We may therefore select first of all Origen's combination of the paradigms of Son and Image to develop his concept of 'eternal generation'; and secondly Dionysius of Rome's reiteration of the Son paradigm to distinguish Christ from the creatures.

When Origen came to summarize his christology in *De Principiis* (I 2), he started by defining Christ, not as the Logos, but as 'the only-begotten Son of God' (I 2:1), whom he goes on to identify as 'the Wisdom of God, existing substantially' (I 2:2). Further this Wisdom is co-eternal with God himself:

> Who . . . can suppose or feel that God the Father ever existed, even for a moment of time, without having generated this Wisdom? For in that case he must say either that God was unable to generate Wisdom before he produced her, so that he afterwards called into being her who formerly did not exist, or that he possessed the power indeed, but . . . was unwilling to use it; both of which . . . are alike absurd and impious . . . Wherefore we have always held that God is the Father of his only-begotten Son, who was born indeed of him, and derives from him what he is, but without any beginning . . . (I 2:2).

Obviously, we are not here in a totally different world from that of the Apologists. They too could call the Logos 'the Wisdom of God', as they could call him 'Son'. The difference is that these titles were given by them to the *spoken* Logos: with Origen, they are fundamental descriptions of an eternal reality, not of a second stage in the being of that reality. The point is underlined by Origen's quite explicit demotion of the title 'Logos' in I 2:3: the Son and Wisdom 'is called the Logos' because he is 'as it were the interpreter of the secrets of the mind (*sc.* of God).' Thus the roles of 'Logos' and 'Son' have been reversed: 'Son' names what he really is, 'Logos' describes a particular function. That Origen can make this radical shift in perspective is not only because of the negative argument just quoted from I 2:2, important though that certainly was for him, but because, unlike the Apologists, he has found a way of interpreting 'Son' so that it can describe a permanent status rather than a stage in development:

> Human thought cannot apprehend how the unbegotten God becomes the Father of the only-begotten Son. For it is an eternal and ceaseless generation, as radiance is generated from light. He is the radiance of the eternal light, the unblemished mirror of the activity of God, and the image of his goodness . . . he is the only one who is by nature a Son, and is therefore called 'only-begotten' (I 2:4–5).

So the complex paradigm of Son/Image moves into the forefront while the older Logos paradigm is relegated to the sidelines. As a result, the difficulties of the continuity and integrity of the Logos and of his permanent status in relation to God are disposed of: Christ is the enduring reflection of God, and as such, is also 'Son of God'. At the same time, this new paradigm leaves the integrity of God untouched, so that that concern of the Logos christology is also maintained, and arguably more successfully than by the Apologists. This is not to say that there are no problems remaining with Origen's theory. It is still markedly subordinationist, nor, given Origen's concomitant doctrine of an eternal creation, does it serve entirely adequately to distinguish between the Son and the creatures. Nevertheless, it represents a notable advance through the replacement of the Logos paradigm by that of Son/Image.

Very little later, the somewhat more pedestrian Dionysius of Rome was to apply the paradigm of Son to distinguish between 'begetting' and 'making', and so to break away from the risk of potential Arianism which we have seen is inbuilt in the Logos paradigm. Tatian could describe the spoken Logos as 'the Firstborn *work* of the Father', and so long as 'Son' meant simply 'spoken Logos' it could not help to distinguish between his status and that of other things which have been made. Once, however, 'Son' is taken to have a more ultimate reference to the permanent and fundamental status of him who is Son of God, it can be applied for this purpose; and this is how Dionysius uses it in his *Letter against the Sabellians*, addressed with diplomatic tact to the church in Alexandria, but really intended for the edification of Bishop Dionysius:

> . . . one must censure those who hold the Son to be a work, and consider that the Lord has come into being, as one of the things which really came to be; whereas the divine oracles witness to a generation suitable to him and appropriate, but not to any fashioning or making. A blasphemy is it then, not ordinary but the greatest, to say that the Lord is in any sense a handiwork. For if he came to be Son, once he was not; but he was always . . . In many passages of the divine oracles is the Son said to be 'begotten', but nowhere to have 'come into being' . . .

'Son', taken in this sense, can no longer be equated with 'Firstborn work': rather it excludes such an equation.

Thus the difficulties arising with the Logos paradigm came to be dealt with piecemeal in the third century through the substitution of the paradigm of Son or Son/Image. That shift then came to be decisive in the fourth century, as one telling instance illustrates. In his *Letter to the Church at Caesarea* after the Council of Nicea, Eusebius quotes both the creed which he claims to have presented at the Council, and the actual Nicene formula. The christological section of his creed runs:

> And in one Lord Jesus Christ, the Word of God, God of God, Light of Light, Life of Life, Only-begotten Son, Firstborn of all creation, begotten of the Father before all ages, through whom also all things came to be . . .

Everything here fits in with the horizon that we have seen in the Apologists. Christ is primarily 'Word of God', secondarily, 'Only-begotten Son, Firstborn of all creation, begotten of the Father before all ages'. Admittedly, Eusebius had also added the formula 'the Father truly Father, the Son truly Son'; but the thrust of the main paragraph runs counter to that, though Eusebius, who was not noted for his clear thinking, was probably quite unaware of the tension between the two approaches. Essentially, his creed follows the line of thought of the Apologists, and is still dominated by the Logos paradigm. This is not to say that he himself was a conscious follower of the Apologists: that mantle belongs more properly to Marcellus of Ancyra, who understood the implications of the Logos theology, and its ultimate intention, in a way that Eusebius was incapable of doing. But it witnesses to the fact that Eusebius, and doubtless many others, especially in the East, were still trapped in the Logos paradigm with all its potential dangers. This is the main reason why Eusebius and others found it difficult or impossible to see what was wrong with Arius' views. But the Council of Nicea itself in its own formula departed from the pattern of Eusebius' in precisely this respect:

> And in one Lord Jesus Christ, Only-begotten of the Father, that is, of the substance of the Father, God of God, Light of Light, true God of true God, begotten, not made, *homoousios* with the Father, through whom all things were made . . .

The new emphasis here is precisely on the *Sonship* of Christ: he is primarily 'Only-begotten' and, 'begotten, not made'. This is why on the one hand he is *homoousios* with the Father, and on the other radically distinct from everything created. Hence too the elimination of such phrases as 'Firstborn of all creation' and the transposition of the first reference to 'begetting' to the beginning of the paragraph, away from association with creation. So the same motives which had led Origen and Dionysius in the third century to depart from the Logos paradigm and substitute those of Image and Son brought the Council of Nicea to do the same. And in the long and bitter years of controversy which followed, the thought of the defenders of Nicene orthodoxy was continually to circle around the images of 'Son', 'Image' and the like, thus once more underlining the shift in horizon which had taken place from the time of the Apologists.

This is not to say, however, that the efforts of the Apologists were misguided or that their successors simply rejected them. Their development of the Logos model was an essential stage in the working-out of a coherent christology, even though it was only a stage in a journey and not a final terminus. It supplied a kind of scaffolding to help in the construction of the building, even though the scaffolding itself eventually needs to be dismantled when its work is done. And much of what was worked out with the help of the Logos paradigm eventually came to be integrated in the new paradigm of Son. It had helped, for example, to demythologize the concept of Son itself, and so to pave the way for its further use even in ways which transcended the boundaries of the Logos paradigm. It offered a way of thinking of Christ as the eternal mind or thought of God; and this was picked up and carried on—for instance in Origen's concept of the eternally-begotten Wisdom, which includes all that the Apologists were attempting to express in speaking of the Logos in God. It helped to formulate an understanding of Christ as the one in and through whom the universe was made; and this too was retained and integrated in subsequent christology. And in these and similar areas, the Logos model was still retained, and Christ continued to be described as the Logos, even though this was now modified by the new paradigm which also coped with the difficulties on which the Logos model foundered when made paradigmatic by itself. Thus its temporary paradigmatic status enabled it to make a lasting contribution to the development of christology, even though eventually other paradigms came to replace it. In this respect the dynamics of theological enquiry, involving the use of various models, their refinement and modification, the domination of paradigms and their eventual replacement, follow the same kind of pattern as may be observed in the most various fields of investigation, and in particular in the development and application of models and paradigms in scientific study. There is a wide field here awaiting further exploration: this scratching of the surface is offered as a tribute to one who has opened innumerable horizons for his students and colleagues.

5 Some Comments on the Background and Influence of Augustine's *Lex Aeterna* Doctrine

by DIETRICH RITSCHL

'*Natura ius est*'—law is natural, or rooted in nature. This statement of Augustine[1] directs our attention to a major problem in western culture, that of ascertaining the *foundation of law.* Augustine gave to western culture its way of approaching the problems of organizing social life with respect both to human relations and to men's relation to God, and he did this largely by creating a synthesis of Christian beliefs with Greek and Roman reflections upon *physis* and *nomos.* Thus he arrived at some highly influential but troublesome views concerning the world's creator and world order. In his doctrines of God and creation and of man's relation to both he combined Plato's and Aristotle's *idealism* regarding the eternal good, the virtues and natural law with *voluntaristic* ideas drawn especially from the later Roman Stoics. The result was that Augustine bequeathed to the western world two basically incompatible views of natural law.

Later theologians, notably Thomas Aquinas,[2] understood Augustine to have preferred the idealistic (realistic) interpretation. It was Duns Scotus who, for philosophical reasons, revived Augustine's notion that God is not bound to a pre-established set of laws, not even ones which are intrinsic to or identical with his own divine self, but that he is able to *decree* by an act of will what constitutes law. In its subsequent development, natural law theory continues to display this bifurcation. The voluntarist view runs through medieval nominalism to Hobbes and Rousseau, the idealist view through medieval realism to Grotius and Leibniz. The movement from medieval 'sacred state' to the modern 'social state', so to speak,

[1] Literally 'Law is "by nature"'. In this passage (*De diversis quaestionibus*, LXXXIII, 31), Augustine is distinguishing natural law (*natura*), which is not engendered by opinion but implanted by an 'innate force', from (1) customary law (*consuetudine*, developed through custom or usage) and (2) written legislation (*ius lege*). Cp. also Cicero, *Rhetorica* II, 53.

[2] *Summa Theologica*, I–II, 90–108, esp.: 91.1; 91.2; 91.3; 93.1 (on 'Whether the eternal law is a supreme exemplar existing in God?'); 93.2; 93.3 (on 'Whether every law is derived from the eternal law?'); 95.2. Augustine is Thomas' constant conversational partner in the development of his doctrine of natural law.

brought no change in the basic question concerning natural law and positive law, namely, the question dealt with in the nominalist-realist controversy. Thus a question pertaining to the (philosophical) understanding of God in relation to man strongly influenced, one might say tyrannized, jurisprudence from late antiquity to the present. For this ancient theological problem shows up not only in Roman Catholic Thomistic thought, all the way to *Humanae vitae*; it also reveals its presence painfully, though in secularized dress, in the Nürnberg trials, the writing of the U.N. Charter, and in new legislation in Italy, West Germany, and even in the U.S.S.R. and Japan. Contemporary philosophy of law[1] either continues to struggle with the classical issues, or else lightly shrugs them off, admitting thereby that the quest for the foundation of law is unanswered still.

In theology, the underlying problem is expressed in the form of a quest for ethical criteria. Here too, the debate on natural law has not reached a conclusion. After the controversy between Barth and Brunner in the thirties and the dramatic struggle over 'orders of creation' (dramatic because of the direct implications for the theological-ethical evaluation of the Nazi regime), we continue to be perturbed by a deeply rooted vagueness about natural law.[2] It suffices to mention the total absence of a Christian consensus on issues traditionally 'solved' by referring to natural law, such as war, capital punishment, the function of the state in relation to the church. In regard to church-state issues we might mention specifically the complications connected with the Lutheran doctrine of the two realms, and the differences between Eastern Orthodox and Western Christian views as they arise within the World Council of Churches. Christians—theologians in particular—have presented an enormous problem to western culture and to mankind in general, and there is little justification for declaring the debate closed merely because some of the theological presuppositions of the past are no longer ours.

I contend that in addition to the idealist-voluntarist problem,

[1] For a representative selection, cf.: R. Pound, *An Introduction to the Philosophy of Law*, Yale Univ. Press, 1922, 8th ed. 1966, pp. 9–21, 114 f.; P. Vinogradoff, *Common Sense in Law*, Oxford Univ. Press, 1959, Ch. IX; H. L. A. Hart, *The Concept of Law*, Oxford Univ. Press, 1961, pp. 181 ff., esp. pp. 189–95; Sidney Hook, ed., *Law and Philosophy*, New York Univ. Press, 1964, Part II; Lon L. Fuller, *The Law in Quest of Itself*, Northwestern Univ. Press, 1940 (and Beacon Press paperback, 1966), Ch. I, and *The Morality of Law*, Yale Univ. Press, 1964 (2nd ed. 1969), esp. Ch. III; W. Maihofer, ed., *Naturrecht oder Rechtspositivismus*, Darmstadt, 1966 (includes a bibliography of publications from 1945–60); Felix E. Oppenheim, *Moral Principles in Political Philosophy*, Random House, 1968.

[2] For two attempts at overcoming the difficulties, see Douglas Sturm, 'Naturalism, Historicism and Christian Ethics'; 'Toward a Christian Doctrine of Natural Law', in *New Theology No. 2*, Marty and Peerman, eds., The Macmillan Co. (paperback), 1965, pp. 77–96, and John Macquarrie, *Three Issues in Ethics*, Harper & Row, 1970, Ch. 4.

Augustine made certain other mistakes which still have their effect upon us. For one thing, although he rediscovered aspects of the Apostle Paul's understanding of grace, he certainly misunderstood the passages in Romans 1 and 2 which allegedly refer to natural theology and natural law. Also, his indebtedness to Manichaeism prevented his conceiving of any direct application of the Christian doctrine of justification to the formation of social structures in general, and thus he failed to see that the juridical aspects of justification can be exemplary for an understanding of the function of *iustitia* in human relations.[1] Looking for common ground on which Christians and non-Christians can be united, he turned instead to the 'natural manifestation' of God's eternal law, i.e., to natural law. Finally, I submit the thesis that the origin of this complex of problems was in Augustine's *concept of God*,[2] and that it is there that we must look for the source of our present difficulties regarding the foundation of law, in jurisprudence, and regarding the quest for ethical criteria, in theology and in political science. In short: had it not been for Augustine's Neo-Platonic understanding of God, which influenced fifteen hundred years of thought in the west, western jurisprudence and political theory, as well as theological ethics, would have been spared a great number of problems.

Despite the fascination of the jurisprudential questions, limitations of space decree that the rest of this essay be devoted primarily to discussion of issues in theological ethics (especially in Augustine's thought), and to the pertinent background in Greek philosophy. As the next step, it will be well to introduce some basic distinctions.

I. *Some General Clarifications*

The following four sets of distinctions should be kept in mind, it seems to me, lest one confuse the various ways in which natural law[3] can be conceived.

(1) The underlying notion of *nature* may be given different

[1] Cf. Markus Barth, *Rechtfertigung*, Zürich, 1969 (*Theol. Studien* 30).

[2] Cf. my analysis and the bibliographical references in *Memory and Hope*, New York, Macmillan and Co., 1967, pp. 105–15, 124–32.

[3] For a general orientation, see *New Catholic Encyclopedia* articles on 'Natural Law', 'Natural Law and Jurisprudence', 'Natural Law in Economics', and 'Natural Law in Political Thought'; the excellent study by Hans Welzel, *Naturrecht und materiales Gerechtigkeit*, Göttingen, 1951, 4th ed. 1962; and Erik Wolf, *Das Problem der Naturrechtslehre*, Karlsruhe, 1959. Raziel Abelson, in 'Unnatural Law' (in Sidney Hook, *op. cit.*, cf. footnote 1, page 64) makes much of the confusion regarding natural 'laws', 'rights', 'norms' and 'necessary conditions of justice' (which he prefers, p. 170), as though these distinctions had not already occupied the attention of the scholastic theologians of the Middle Ages and of the Renaissance in Spain.

meanings.[1] It will suffice to mention the following possibilities: Nature may be understood as 'essence', as 'original status' (*Ur-Ordnung*), as genuineness/perfection (Aristotle's *entelecheia*), as 'causality', as reason, as idea. The notion of nature is many-faceted, but in general the intention is quite clear to conceive it as in some sense 'rational' or 'logical', i.e., not arbitrary or chaotic or incoherent.[2] If there is any one element which the various doctrines of natural law have in common with regard to their notions of 'nature', it is the idea of an underlying unity in things, carrying with it also the applicability of at least a minimum of basic ground rules. We may add that the history of natural law concepts reveals a common presupposition that 'nature' is that which in itself exhibits no 'progress' but only the persistence or recurrence of the structures of the past. There are exceptions to this last observation, however, e.g. in Thomas Aquinas' distinction between the unchangeable 'first principles' and other items of natural law which may possibly change.[3]

(2) Another set of distinctions concerns the question of where that which functions as 'nature' in natural law is *located*. It seems that there are four possible locations: (a) in God (thus Plato, Aristotle, Augustine, Thomas); (b) in the *kosmos* (thus e.g. the Stoics); (c) in man or human institutions; and (d) in the 'nature of a situation', i.e., in the limitations put upon man by his environment, the impact of the past upon the present, in such limiting specifics as age, health, sex, knowledge, ignorance, fallibility. Combinations of these four basic locations are of course possible and it is here that difficulties have arisen in natural law theories in the past. Moreover, the word 'location' has been used here to express the idea of a fixed and necessary relation between that in which nature is located, on the one hand, and whatever actual content we give to natural law, on the other. When the location is in God, then the authority of God appears to be placed behind, and used to justify, such things as the inquisition, the crusades, and other forms of warfare. Augustine's and Thomas' doctrines of man and the church permitted such justifications. One wonders about the divine authorization of a Roman Catholic moral theology in which, for instance, abortion is treated so strictly—I think rightly so—while rather more ready justification is found for capital punishment and, even though limitedly, for war.

[1] Erik Wolf, *op. cit.*, pp. 21–93, lists nine concepts of nature: nature as 'individuality', 'originality', 'genuineness', 'causality', 'ideal nature', 'creatureliness', 'reality', 'vitality', and 'restoration'.

[2] Even Duns Scotus, e.g., in reducing 'original ideas' to their bare minimum of unchangeable existence, insists on 'logics' or logical coherence, with respect also to God's mode of making decisions.

[3] *Summa Theologica*, I–II, 94.5.

(3) Directly connected with the question of the location of 'nature' is the problem of its *recognizability* as a norm. One can accept the validity of natural laws but restrict the possibility of recognizing them as normative to only a part of mankind,[1] or to only a part of their content.[2] This distinction is of considerable importance, as a comparison between, for instance, the Roman Stoics and William of Ockham would readily show.

(4) There are different *contexts of thought* in which the search for a *norm* may lead toward natural law concepts. Norms may be sought in juridical contexts (in relation to positive law), in philosophical contexts (e.g., in reflection on 'values'), in relation to socio-political questions, and, of course, in theological ethics.

II. *Developments Prior to Augustine*

Historians have drawn attention to the fact that to the Greeks, the idea of law was connected either with eternal-rational truths or with the spontaneous, vital expression of will power. But 'will' never achieved equal rank with 'reason' in Greek thought. Linguistic evidence shows that there was no single word for 'will' in early Greek culture, indicating a lack of any clear-cut or comprehensive notion of it; at best, it was looked upon as the organ which executes what knowledge or reason dictates.

Comment should also be made on the relation between law (*nomos*) and nature (*physis*) in Greek thought. While Heraclitus, e.g., thought of a unity of nature and law, the later sceptical reflections of the Sophists led to a separation of the two. But the decay of the Greek city-states and the increasingly chaotic Greek political situation, while causing or reinforcing scepticism in some minds, occasioned in others a search for a universally valid and applicable foundation of law. A broader and more lasting theoretical basis was needed than the various systems of positive law could provide. Some law or set of laws in the form of ground rules and basic norms became necessary, such as Aristotle had in mind when he spoke of what is *physei dikaion*, right by nature or naturally righteous.[3]

[1] E.g., in Plato's *Republic* only those who 'know' are capable of governing the (ignorant) masses of society; cf. also the parallel distinction between knowers and non-knowers in Gnosticism later.

[2] Thomas Aquinas, *Summa Theologica*, I–II, 93.2: 'Every knowledge of truth is a kind of reflection and participation of the eternal law, which is the unchangeable truth, as Augustine says. Now all men know the truth to a certain extent, at least as to the common principles of the natural law. As to the other truths, they partake of the knowledge of truth, some more, some less; and in this respect they know the eternal law in a greater or lesser degree.' And, 'Although each one knows the eternal law according to his own capacity, in the way explained above, yet none can comprehend it, for it cannot be made perfectly known by its effects'.

[3] *Nicomachean Ethics*, V, 10; *Rhetoric*, I, 13; *passim*.

Parallel with this development, a more philosophical or intellectual reflection on traditional notions of virtue led to a form of what might be called quasi-natural law, i.e., the concept of a positive law which was to be based upon natural and necessary virtues. Whether what is thus *nomo dikaion* (right by law) is truly *natural* law or whether it is really positive law posing as natural and universal, is a matter of debate. The tendency to claim universality may be related to the fact that the themes of intellectual reflection in classical Greece were drawn originally from Greek religion, and the religious *Weltanschauung* directs thought towards a grounding of morality in the nature of things, or in something transcending purely human convention or contrivance. Natural law concepts, and especially reflections concerning the virtues, must be seen against this background. To recognize this fact is perhaps also to understand better how natural law could be affirmed later by Christian thinkers on explicitly religious grounds. But at this point it may also be well to call attention to what may be the most vulnerable aspect of all natural law theories. They are open to the charge that they involve a *petitio principii*; that is, that they claim to discover in 'nature' elements which are 'there' only because they have already been included in the original conception or definition of nature, although they were in fact derived from elsewhere (from the contemporary culture, from religious belief).

It may seem strange that although the sharp distinction between *physis* and *nomos* arose in Greek philosophy, it was the Greeks who gave the concept of natural law to western culture. The fact is that the recognition of a tension between law and nature arose out of the awareness of the early Greeks that man is by nature inclined to dislike and fight with his fellowman, and that to declare man *metron hapanton* (the measure of all things) is an act of *hybris*. The norms by which human life, individual and communal, is to be regulated must come from somewhere outside or beyond man himself. The whole philosophical development from the Sophists to Plato by which the ancient notions about the cosmos, man and the gods were demythologized actually ended in revitalizing something of that very mythological tradition by means of the idea that the gods established laws, or that eternally true laws are in themselves of divine character. It is at this point that the dominant rationalism of Greek ethics appears, for in order to grasp the eternal truths concerning moral virtues, man needs *episteme*, knowledge which includes insight and reflection. Here is one of the central features of the whole complex which we call natural law. Plato[1] was certain that the object and content of *episteme* is identical with the *Ideas* and that things in the cosmos participate in (by *metexis*) and copy (by *mimesis*) these

[1] E.g. in the *Theaetetus*.

eternal ideas. The soul has access to the ideas of goodness and righteousness by employing its rational powers, supported by self-restraint as a personal virtue. We can also easily understand the temptation to make use of all these thoughts for an exposition of a Christian *Weltanschauung*: are not man's evil inclinations, the necessity for divine regulation, the possibility of knowledge of eternally valid truths and virtues, as expressed in Platonic philosophy, all congruent with the Bible? This is certainly what appealed to the Christian apologists of the second century, and also in some measure to Augustine.

An additional complication—but also an enrichment—was provided by Aristotle. Whereas Plato had advocated some form of *chorismos*, i.e. of separation or 'gap' between the world of ideas and the natural world of things (at least in his middle period, e.g. the *Republic* and the *Phaedo*), it was Aristotle who transformed this structure into a system of teleological metaphysics. The ideas are now immanent in things, thus permitting the unity of *hyle* and *eidos*, of form and appearance. This redefined nature presents another 'temptation' for later Christian theology, notably for Thomas Aquinas. The 'energy' of nature is in fact the highest and best actualization of what is possible. Nature is basically good, friendly, and admirably intelligent, constantly performing processes with optimal end-results; nature has 'its own intent'. Augustine's and later concepts of natural law are certainly more directly akin to Platonic and Stoic doctrines than to Aristotle's, but the Platonic, Stoic and neo-Platonic natural law tradition which reached medieval thinkers, and in part also Augustine, already included Aristotelian modifications of the Stoics' and Plato's thoughts.

It is true, however, that the western history of natural law[1] basically begins with the Stoa. But textbooks of the history of philosophy have at times exaggerated the difference between Stoicism, Platonism and the rest of Greek philosophy. There are strong Platonic overtones in early Stoic reflections on natural law. And Aristotle, it must not be forgotten, understood himself to be a Platonist, at least in the sense of a constructive interpreter. Nevertheless, there are, of course, specifically Stoic features which cannot be found in this form in the rest of Greek philosophy, e.g. the optimism concerning the ability of *all* men to grasp the *logos* of the *kosmos* by virtue of the fact that every man is believed to have or

[1] The development in the Eastern Church has recently been described by Father Stanley S. Harakas, 'The Natural Law Teaching of the Eastern Orthodox Church', in *New Theology* No. 2, Marty and Peerman eds., the Macmillan Co. (paperback), 1965, pp. 122–33. His assessment of the Augustinian and Western concept of the *lex aeterna* as 'an objective body outside the will of God', however, is coloured by a one-sided and textbook-like knowledge.

possess part of this *logos* in himself. Another addition to basically Platonic thoughts is the Stoic emphasis on the importance of man's will. Individual Stoic ethics is based upon man's belief both in a paradisic ideal in pre-historic times, and the necessity of becoming part of the causal nexus of the things and occurrences all of which may be indications or manifestations of the cosmic fate, the *heimarmene*. Reflections on causality and the ontic structures of the cosmos coincide, at least theoretically, with reflections on man's moral duties. Physics and ethics no longer are enemies or unrelated realms of human reflection but have become twin-brothers. There is, however, an ambiguity on this point. The Stoic philosophers set out to demonstrate the universal impact of *world*-reason, of the eternal law of nature, but they ended up by referring to *man*'s nature. This ambiguity reappears in later Christian reflections when at times the eternal will and law of God is the referent in natural-law statements, and at others it is human nature, its possibilities and limitations. (For example, in what sense is birth control against natural law? Is it against the will of God who created the ordered nature of the world and of mankind or against an element in human nature *per se*, specifically the procreative function?) The Stoic differentiation between *lex aeterna* and *lex naturalis* does some justice, at least terminologically, to this duality. Moreover, the Stoics taught that man's conscience is itself part of world-reason, a *lumen naturae*, a light, and a 'bridge', so to speak, between the general and the particular, between the *lex aeterna* and the individual moral behaviour according to the *lex naturalis*. All human laws, the *lex humana*, must reasonably be in accordance with the *lex naturalis*, which in turn is the expression of the *lex aeterna*. This is the well-known Stoic schema which we find again in Augustine, and following him, in Thomas.

This mature development of natural law concepts, as we find it in Cicero, Seneca and Marcus Aurelius, is also mirrored in Justinian's *Corpus Juris*. For the later Roman lawyers it served as a bridge between the *ius civile* of the Roman citizens and the *ius gentium* of the rest of mankind.[1] The church, too, was quick to accept the concept of an eternal and natural law as a proper expression of God's universal lordship. In addition to some passages in the later parts of the New Testament, early Christian documents show familiarity with natural law philosophies. In the year 96, I Clement praises in a long chapter (20) the 'harmonious', 'peaceful' regularity of natural events and seasons, 'at his command and never with a deviation', and Ch. 24 compares the resurrection with the coming and passing of day and night and the growth and decay of plants. All of this is, in truly Stoic fashion, ascribed to the divine will and

[1] *Corpus Juris, Digest*, I, 1, 9, *passim.*

predestination of him whose true nature is unsearchable. The Apologists, including Tertullian, continued to expound these theories and applied them to moral behaviour as well as to the formulation of some common denominator between Christians and non-Christians. The theologians of the second and third centuries, with the notable exception of Irenaeus, agreed in their belief that, despite the fall of man, all men have access to a basic knowledge of God's eternal, world-ordering laws. The Apologists' tendency to identify the *lex naturalis* with the *lex Christi* of course posed the question whether Christian faith is 'natural' or by grace, but this dilemma was neither seen nor solved until Augustine, in utilizing Tertullian's rather vague concept of illumination, attempted a more thorough answer. The result was a strong separation between Christians and non-Christians.

This brief survey would be incomplete if one of the finest aspects of Greek, and especially Stoic, natural law were omitted: the *respect for man.* It is lamentable that Augustine and the later church, while uncritically accepting the theoretical structure of Stoic natural theology, did not really take seriously this very concrete outgrowth of Stoic thought. Why must Seneca's sentence *homo est sacra res homini* necessarily be in competition with the Christians' belief that their *sacra res* is God in the man Jesus? The Apologists of the second century did agree in principle with this Stoic respect for one's fellow-man. The Latin fathers, including Augustine, it must be admitted, also knew that love towards one's neighbour is connected with the insight that man is made in the *imago Dei.* But of much greater influence in the church were the general Stoic and Platonic views of the oneness of the cosmos as well as of the hierarchical structure of levels of being and of values. These general views reappeared in the church and led to a theological sanctioning of the Roman political order (and the empire as a whole) as well as to a rationale for the hierarchy of the ecclesiastical structure. For many centuries the church was unwilling to sacrifice these two ideals but violated in a thousand forms the ethical demand to respect the life of one's fellowman. The crusades, the inquisition, the persecution of Jews, would have horrified a true Stoic philosopher of natural law. The irony is that the church argued on the basis of natural law in providing rationales for these crimes. If there is any historical demonstration for the vicious circle of the *petitio principii* which is at the root of the logic of an ethic informed by natural law, this is it.

III. *Augustine's* lex aeterna *Doctrine*

Historical reflections on natural law have often focused on the so-called secularization of natural law concepts at the time of later nominalism, the Reformation, Grotius, Hobbes and Pufendorf. Indeed, it is interesting that theologians have prepared the way for a jurisprudence and a theory of the state which operated with a *lex aeterna*—without-God, as it were. But of greater interest, at least in the context of our present question, is the fact that Platonic and Stoic concepts of natural law, of the world-*nous*, of cosmic reason, concepts of Greek philosophy and religious cosmologies of antiquity, have been *transferred to the God of the Bible*. This shift developed, as we have seen, over a period of several centuries, but it was perfected and presented in more or less systematic form by Augustine. The second shift in the development of natural law, to the 'secular' theories of the Renaissance, appears more understandable in the light of this prior importation of philosophical ideas into theological thought.

Augustine's position on natural law is part of the larger picture of his doctrines of God, of the world and of man. Some Stoic ideas helped to prepare the ground for Christian other-worldliness, and Plotinus' *Enneads* had been very influential in providing the conceptual framework for the ideal of reaching ever higher levels of spiritual and intellectual spheres, thus leaving behind the world with its problems. The two influences converge in Augustine who accepted from the later Stoa the emphasis on the human will and from Plato and neo-Platonism the vision of ideas, according to which a timeless God had created the world and in harmony with which he would govern and redeem it.[1] But while man, who consists of both body and soul, has access to and at least a partial share in absolute truth, he also lives in the world, and a fallen world at that. Here several problems arose for theology, not all of which were solved by Augustine. The question concerning the origin of the soul was left unanswered, as were questions about how the body and soul interact (e.g., the question of how sensation occurs). The problem of the recognizability of absolute truth (by fallen man) was solved with the doctrine of illumination, but solved only for believers, not for all men. It is clear, however, that man is located at the point of contact between the absoluteness of God and the transitoriness of creation. Although the 'contact' itself was destroyed by the Fall, Augustine claims that God nevertheless makes manifest his eternal law within the realm of creation. This then is a restatement of the ancient idea of the existence and relevance of natural law, valid for all men. The obvious conflict with Augustine's view of the fallenness of man is bracketed, as it were. The semi-pelagian climate of post-Augustinian theology did not call for an exploration of this problem, but it is worth remembering that the impact of Augustine's radical concept

[1] These influences can readily be seen, e.g., in *De trinitate*, *De civitate Dei*, and *De duabus animabus*.

of the Fall at the time of the Reformation brought into question the notion of the recognizability of eternal or natural laws.

Not merely the results but also the actual unfolding of Augustine's natural law concept presented some theological problems. In accepting Cicero's[1] concept of *lex aeterna* he faced the question of how to build into his theology the pagan concept of *heimarmene, fatum.* This was an integral part of the Stoic notion of eternal laws. Augustine transformed the Stoic *fatum* into 'orders of creation' and connected them with his understanding of predestination. One must assume that he truly believed this to be a theologically permissible adaptation. But in fact this is the very point at which time and again in the history of theology insoluble problems have arisen. By transferring the laws of world order into, and by ultimately identifying them with God, how can it be avoided that God be used as a means of 'explaining (and justifying) the world'?

The *lex aeterna* is to Augustine the sum of the *rationes aeternae* from which are derived, by the very nature of God's creation and activity of preservation, the *rationes seminales causales* of the various things and orders in the cosmos. Also derived from this is the *lex rationis* which is the natural law. It is written into the hearts of men (Rom. 2:14) basically in the form of the 'golden rule' (Matt. 7:12).[2] This law, residing in man's heart or conscience as he grows up and develops reasoning power, is not identical with the *lex Christi* since the latter is seen by Augustine as belonging to the area of God's 'positive' law (i.e., given by revelation) which is not recognizable in creation. The difference between natural law as an outgrowth of or derivation from the *lex aeterna* on the one hand, and God's positive law on the other, is correlated in Augustine's understanding with the fact that there are two sources of knowledge of the law: creation and the Bible.

The following scheme could perhaps clarify these interconnections although it should be kept in mind that Augustine's thoughts do not lend themselves to clear systematizations.

The *lex aeterna* is the source of all righteousness, the origin of any and every kind of good law; it is indeed God's own reason and will. Derived from it is not only the *lex temporalis*, so to speak the 'incarnation' of the eternal law in the realm where everything is subject to time, but also the basic structure, the blueprint and ongoing source of life of all of creation. (Whether these *rationes seminales* reside in God and with them in embryo-form all of

[1] For Cicero's concept, cf. *De legibus*, I, 16; *De republica*, III, *passim*., *De natura deorum*, 1.15; but cf. also Augustine's criticism of the absence of predestination in Cicero, *De civ. Dei*, V, 1–10.

[2] *Ennarationes in Psalmos*, 57, 1; *De Ordine*, II, 8, 25; *Epistle*, 157, 15; and *passim.*

creation, is a complicated problem, in regard to which Thomas had difficulties in interpreting Augustine.) Only two sub-categories or forms of the *lex temporalis* are recognizable in creation: the law *in paradiso data*, as early and as old as Adam, and the law *naturaliter insita* which now dwells in every man's heart as the *lex cordis*. So far the scheme follows the Stoic tradition. But these two types of the *lex temporalis* are in need of interpretation by a third sub-category or form of God's eternal law 'incarnate' in time; the law which is *in litteris promulgata*. This is the juncture in Augustine's teaching on eternal and time-bound laws where the Bible decisively enters into the picture. The written law of God—this is undoubtedly what Augustine intends to say—is superior to and must interpret the other manifestations of God's eternal law, noticeable and recognizable in creation. Unfortunately, however, the situation is not as clear as

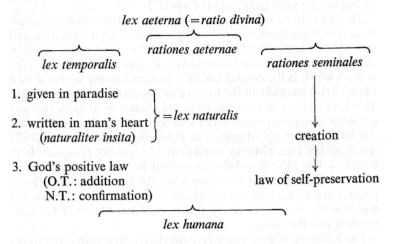

lex aeterna (=*ratio divina*)

rationes aeternae

lex temporalis | *rationes seminales*

1. given in paradise
2. written in man's heart (*naturaliter insita*) } = *lex naturalis* → creation → law of self-preservation
3. God's positive law (O.T.: addition N.T.: confirmation)

lex humana

might appear at first sight. First of all, the written law of God, and that is a positive law, is superior to natural law, not as to its origin but with regard to its recognizability. And secondly, although Augustine usually did not adhere to Tertullian's negative attitude towards the Old Testament, he did introduce a distinction between the Testaments with reference to the law contained in them. Sometimes he mentions the Old Testament in connection with or in addition to the first two types of the *lex temporalis*, i.e. to natural law, but in other places he uses Old Testament and New Testament passages indiscriminately to provide an account of what he calls the *lex veritatis*, which he views as a confirmation of other laws. He also suggests that the *lex Christi* is recognizable only by illumination (a doctrine later unfolded by Bonaventure) whereas he calls the *lex Mosis* a positive law which apparently can be understood by the power of reason alone. There appears to be a lack of clarity at this crucial point of Augustine's teaching and it is not surprising that the medieval church had difficulty in understanding him. It may well be that the difficulty resides not in Augustine but in the very attempt to utilize natural law concepts for Christian theology and ethics, or conversely, to utilize God as authority to validate natural laws. An insoluble problem seems to be created by the ambiguity concerning the interpretative function of the written word of God in relation to what man observes in nature and ascribes to God's creating and preserving activity.

It remains to be said that in addition to the temporal-natural law Augustine seems to refer to a *lex naturae* 'which has never been violated, and which is common to us with the beasts'.[1] This has to do with the physical limitations of our body and, in its positive content, appears as the law of self-preservation. Human laws, then, should be decreed in accordance with both the natural laws as interpreted by God's written (positive) law, and with the creational-natural limitations and conditions of man. It has been said,[2] however, that Augustine did not make conformity to natural law a condition for the validity of human law.

The crucial point in Augustine's teaching is his doctrine of God. The neo-Platonism of Victorinus and Ambrose permitted Augustine a doctrine of the creator-God who is free and at the same time lord over the creation. Augustine tries hard never to deviate from the thought that everything that is, and possibly can be, exists by an act of will of the creator. At the same time he asserted the freedom of human will, interpreting it as an expression of God's creativity in the world. Everything that is, including human beings, exists, so to speak, doubly: in 'world-reality' as well as in the mind of God. This existence 'in the art' (a truly Platonic thought) and mind of God precedes the temporal form of existence and also 'survives' it, as it were, since it continues in God's memory after it has ceased to exist in its temporal form. The essences of the temporal things within God are the *rationes*, reflections of his eternal and infinite *ratio* and perfection. They remain unchanged in God forever as archetypes and memories at the same time. The obvious occurrence of ongoing becoming within the world, of the creation of new things and beings, is explained by Augustine as an ongoing divine creativity known to God from before all time. The logical instrument for explaining the

[1] *De doctrina christiana*, I, 26, 27; quoted by Herbert A. Deane, *The Political and Social Ideas of St. Augustine*, Columbia Univ. Press, 1963, p. 87.

[2] Herbert A. Deane, *op. cit.*, p. 90: 'As far as I have been able to discover, in none of the works written during the remaining forty years of his life does Augustine ever state that positive law must conform to God's eternal law or to the law of nature if it is to be valid.' (The possible exception is a passage in the early work *De vera religione*.) Cf., however, *De libero arbitrio*, I, 6, 14.

connection between the eternal *rationes* and the becoming of finite things is the notion of *rationes seminales* or *causales*.[1] It expresses God's eternal responsibility for the existence and development of things and beings in creation and one should perhaps appreciate this basic theological intent. Later theology, including Protestant scholasticism, continued to operate with the concept of a *creatio continua*, 'playing down' the activity of man and other beings, and assigning to God ultimate responsibility and creativity. This doctrine of exemplarism, as it was called, would of course be meaningless if it merely referred to being and becoming and not to *order*. There is no becoming in creation without order. Consequently, the doctrine of the divine *rationes* is also a doctrine of divine orders, that is, of eternal law in its divinely willed and organic relation to natural law.

Utilizing the basic distinctions we introduced above in Part I, we can perhaps say that the problem with Augustine's doctrine of *lex aeterna* and natural law is three fold. Firstly, he uses a *concept of nature* which he has borrowed from Aristotle's physics and which is indiscriminately applied to everything in creation, physical, human and social entities alike, as though *everything* other than God could satisfactorily be described by the use of the categories essence/manifestation in time. One wonders whether such use of 'nature' does justice to the 'many natures of nature'. Secondly—and here we touch upon the heart of the logical and theological problem—Augustine 'locates' the sum of all being, beauty and order *in* God, but he wants to reconcile a timeless God with a transitory world. The results are unhappy for our understanding of God, the moral order, and the relation between the two. On the one hand, the timelessness of God carries over into a conception of a natural moral law with essentially unchanging content. On the other hand, certain aspects of humanly formulated morality tend to be read into the nature of God. This danger was noted earlier in the comments made about 'locating nature' in God. The observation can now be added that, perhaps because of the logically necessary and deductive way in which the individual propositions of a system of law are connected, a similar logically necessary and deducible relationship is posited between God and the moral order of creation. In fact, it seems to me that there are only three possible ways of linking a world law or the laws of nature to a concept of God:

(a) One can say that the law resides in God, that it is part of his very self. Creation then becomes, not a separate reality, but a function or operation of the divine being; the world is an emanation of God. (But since the world is manifold, the thought that it originally resided in God endangers the concept of the *simplicitas Dei*; this was Thomas' worry concerning Augustine.)

[1] E.g. *De Genesi ad litteram*, 6.5, 8; *De trinitate*, III.8, 13–14–15.

(b) One can say that the *lex aeterna* is, so to speak, prior to God so that God is bound to its rules. (This means that either his intellect and his will are separated, which was the danger in Thomas, as Duns Scotus saw it, or that the creator-god is merely a demiurge, the *lex aeterna* being the true God.)

(c) One can say that by the act of creation God 'passed on' to the cosmos the eternal law according to which creation now continues to unfold in a manner known to man since (at least part of) the divine law left its imprint in man's heart and reason. (This means that God is either no longer needed—as for example in Deism—or that he is understood pantheistically.)

Augustine operates with the first and the third of these possibilities. He did not consider as an option the christological interpretation attempted by Thomas Aquinas, who tended to identify the eternal *ratio* with the Word, the second person of the Trinity. It would be premature to regret this omission because a christological-trinitarian interpretation of the sum of all natural law is indeed not possible and so has not been achieved by Thomas either. I do not see more than the three possibilities listed. The christological is not a fourth option unless one would declare that which took place in Jesus Christ, what he 'stood for', did and suffered, to be *natural*, normative and 'normal'; but few writers in the church have ever attempted that. The *lex Christi* is not a sub-category or a normal manifestation of what is usual and normal in the order of the cosmos. Or in short, it is not 'natural' to love one's enemy and to honour the weak.

Thirdly, the problem with Augustine's *lex aeterna* doctrine is the question in what sense it can serve as a *norm* for ethics. We have already mentioned the ambiguities concerning the universality of a generally recognized natural law and the necessity of illumination of those who understand God's positive law in addition to what the rest of mankind understands.

In concluding these reflections on Augustine one may wonder whether the God he spoke of was perhaps defined in terms of a counter-force to chaos, of an eternal being over against the transitoriness of the world and the things in it, of order in contrast to disorder, and of eternal goodness as eternally distinct from the sin and evil he saw during his own lifetime. In favour of this suspicion there is the fact that Augustine's concept of grace is developed in contrast to his concept of sin and his understanding of the work of Christ in contradistinction to the fallen state of man.[1] His God, the location of eternal law, would then be the highest principle of order, developed in the theologian's mind as a counter-force to chaos and worshipped in the church as the source and goal of the believers'

[1] I have tried to show this in *Memory and Hope*, Ch. III (cf. above footnote 2, page 65).

beatific vision. Although one may regret his departure from a biblically oriented concept of God and lament the theoretically avoidable fusion of Stoic natural law with Christian neo-Platonism, one would do well to appreciate at least one major theological aim of Augustine. He did attempt to counterbalance the cosmic dualism of Manichaeism by affirming that creation is basically good because it is held together by him who also made it. The *lex aeterna* doctrine postulates this even if in the domain of anthropology and ecclesiology Augustine was unable to overcome his Manichaean heritage. But calling attention to this relative theological advantage will hardly reassure theological and other critics, including jurists, who have many reasons to view with regret and some distaste the fifteen hundred year history of natural law in the western world.

IV. *Concluding Remarks on Augustine's Influence*

Augustine left undecided the question whether God created the moral order of the world in accordance with what was right, or whether the created order is right because He willed it. It is well known that this question appeared again in various forms in later medieval philosophy and theology. To read the later issues back into Augustine would be an over-simplification and would not do justice to his own questions and conceptual apparatus. Augustine managed a combination of idealistic and voluntaristic interpretations of God and of the *lex aeterna* which worked reasonably well for his purposes. Yet the two interpretations stand side by side without being fully synthesized, and problems are left implicit in his thinking which in time led to difficulties. The idealistic-rationalistic strain tended to be linked with the timeless, other-worldly, static concepts of God, nature and law. Voluntarism was linked more with dynamic and temporalistic ways of thinking, with freedom and creativity. But since Augustine bequeathed an unstable combination of two basically incompatible interpretations of things, his successors have tended to pose choices between mutually exclusive alternatives: either absolutism and legalism in ethics, or relativism and arbitrariness; either a strict natural law basis for jurisprudence, or an amoral positivism; either the primacy of intellect or of will in God; either the good is prior to God, or it is whatever God (arbitrarily) wills. Such problems might have been avoided if Augustine had founded his ethics upon the idea of God as one who acts providentially and redemptively in history, an insight which is certainly present in his thought but which he failed to follow through consistently.

The trend of the discussion on natural law in early and high medieval times is clearly towards a theoretical investigation of man's ability to recognize eternal values and divine characteristics, and it was not until Scotus and Ockham that the basic theological question moved into the foreground. If one should not read Duns Scotus' formulation of the idealist-voluntarist issue back into Augustine, one should not read it into Thomas either. He too was more interested in the question of the recognizability of the eternal law and of its relation to human law rather than in the fundamental question to which Scotus drew attention. Thomas' teaching on natural law[1] is a combination of Augustine's influence with Aristotelian and ecclesiastical-canonical material. The history of the development up to Thomas, via Isidore and William of Auxerre, and summaries of Thomas' own teaching, can be found in many publications. For the context of our question it suffices to mention that Thomas fully accepted Augustine's concept of *lex aeterna* in formulating his understanding of the world law, but that in his understanding of natural law there is an added teleological dimension which permits him to think that *reason* is the agent by which an *end* is perceived, so that the knowledge of this end makes a natural law appear as a *directive*. Knowing 'the end of things' in the Aristotelian sense, within their natural-causal context, is a source of ethical directives. It is at this point that Thomas goes beyond Augustine. He not only teaches in great detail which beings know of and participate in the eternal world law, and to what extent; he also affirms that the teleological principle inherent in each thing is tending towards divinely intended goodness. This combination of being with values, of ontology with ethics, permits the transition from the recognition of things to the recognition of values. It is well known that in later centuries, notably in Hume and Kant, but also in analytic philosophy in the twentieth century, a sharp distinction has been made between is-sentences and ought-sentences. It has been argued that the knowledge of some thing or situation that *is*, does not by itself provide any basis for inference concerning what *ought* to be. Foregoing a discussion of this problem, we should at least notice that the most effective criticism of natural law, the charge that its advocates read into nature what they already know, runs parallel to the philosophical argument that is-sentences cannot be turned into ought-sentences. Thomas Aquinas invites both criticisms.

The decisive turn in the history of post-Augustinian natural law theories came with the two great Augustinians, Duns Scotus and William of Ockham. Scotus'[2] critical questions to Thomas are of

[1] For a helpful introduction, cf. Michael Strasser, 'Natural Law in the Teachings of St. Thomas Aquinas', in *Church-State Relations in Ecumenical Perspective*, Elwyn A. Smith, ed., Duquesne Univ. Press, 1966, pp. 152–75. See also Ernst Wolf, 'Zur Frage des Naturrechts bei Thomas von Aquin und bei Luther', in *Peregrinatio*, Munich, 1962, pp. 183–213.

[2] Cf. G. Stratenwerth, *Die Naturrechtslehre des Johannes Duns Scotus*, Göttingen, 1951.

lasting importance and are, in fact, theologically still unanswered. It is hard to understand why Thomas' teachings are at times today still utilized and advocated[1] as though Scotus had never dealt with them. Although I cannot discuss here the many valuable insights which are to be found in Scotus, I shall at least mention one or two issues in regard to which his thinking could be clarifying and fruitful. Christians have displayed a certain hesitation in accepting the Stoic emphasis on the oneness of mankind, since Stoic thought seems to slight the concrete, historical realities of persons and communities which are so important in the biblical perspective. Yet an atomistic individualism is just as unbiblical. I suggest that no adequate solution will be found to the problem, which is equally important to ethics and jurisprudence, as long as we depend upon natural law doctrine, for in this respect it displays the same inadequacies as the Stoicism from which it is so largely derived. Scotus points the way to a better solution. The philosophical apparatus with which he defined the individuality of a thing or situation provides a way of affirming human individuality without denying the oneness of humanity or lending support to modern individualism. I do not mean to suggest that he has presented answers to all our urgent problems. On the contrary, the perennial problem of ethics and jurisprudence, the task of concretization of general concepts or statements, was opened up wide in Scotus' teachings. But his intra-theological criticism of a thousand-year theological 'usurpation' of a problem of the philosophy of law deserves our attention. Scotus also discarded the concept of *lex aeterna*, or at least that version of it according to which it resided in God and provided unchanging ethical norms. In fact, I believe that his critical thoughts concerning eternal and natural law, God's goodness (*bonitas*) in himself and towards creation, and his teachings on human freedom and will, open up the historical dimensions of the foundation of human law.

To develop the thesis just stated, however, would be beyond the limits of this essay. Neither do I take it upon myself to suggest what jurists should contribute towards progress in the natural law debate and in search for the foundation of law. Theologians, I should like to submit, ought to focus on the following tasks:

(1) A reassessment of the doctrine of God in relation to traditional and contemporary concepts of nature. We need to come to an understanding of God in which he is seen as positively related to the natural world, to time and history, to novelty and creaturely freedom.

(2) An assessment of the anthropological implications of the fact

[1] E.g. H. A. Rommen, 'In Defense of Natural Law', in *Law and Philosophy*, ed. Sidney Hook, pp. 105–21.

that 'nature' can be changed, manipulated, that man's relation to nature is entering upon a new phase in history.

(3) An exploration of the reasons for concern about the oneness of mankind, and of ways of conceiving and speaking of it.

(4) An explication of the idea that Christian ethics, or better, the ethics of Christians, should serve as a catalyst and corrective to the humanisms or humane moralities of one's historical epoch, rather than as a set of standards to be imposed on all men.[1]

(5) A search, together with non-Christian humanists, for penultimate (i.e., time-bound but generally applicable) norms in interpersonal, social and international relations, such as are needed for physical and psychical survival and for unfolding the humanity of all men.[2]

(6) An investigation of the structural and functional differences between ethics and jurisprudence. Once greater clarity is achieved about the distinctive subject matter and method of each discipline, more constructive relations between them would be possible, and jurisprudence might finally be freed from some of the problems inherited from theology and ethics, such as the effects of the idealist-voluntarist muddle.

[1] John Macquarrie, *op. cit.*, p. 17, agrees with my harsh statements (in *Memory and Hope*, p. 190) concerning 'anonymous Christianity'. I have sympathy with his attempt to formulate thoughts on a humanity shared by all men and also with his emphasis on hope (pp. 131 ff.). This indeed seems to me to be the anchor for a Christian theological search for ethical norms, although I myself would like to stress the promise as the basis of hope more than does Macquarrie.

[2] H. L. A. Hart's search for a 'minimum content of natural law' is intriguing, *op. cit.*, pp. 189 ff. He defines what is 'natural' in terms of limitations shared by all men. This is no natural law in the classical sense, but it is an attempt to take seriously man's 'natural nature', without, however, deriving norms from these observations.

6 The Body of God's Presence: A Trinitarian Theory

by ROBERT W. JENSON

Preliminaries

Lest there be any initial misunderstanding, the following is not fundamental theology, only some bits of a particular locus. The soteriological question at theology's base is not whether or, directly, how God is present, but who God is. If there is any God, necessarily he is present to us—but whether this is good news or bad depends on which putative God that is. To have an 'I-Thou' relation to God may be to reside in hell, should the relation be with any of the gods one most hears of, including many of those touted—illicitly, to be sure—in Jesus' name.

Once it is settled which putative God we confess as in fact God, we do of course need discussion of where and when we may find him, or where and when he finds us. A doctrine of God's presence is not fundamental theology; but it is a necessary subsequent locus. I hope this essay may contribute some items.

The Phenomenon of the Body

I begin with five propositions about the phenomenon we evoke with the word 'body'. I do not claim that the five exhaustively describe the phenomenon; they merely describe it for my present need. The phenomenon in question is not, of course, the abstract givenness of masses in space, but the personal body.

First. The body is the *object-presence* of the person. Personal presence occurs always as address, as the word-event by which one person enters the reality of an other. This entrance may be destructive: it may initiate a mutual reality of lordship-and-slavery, and of struggle over who will be which. If it does not, it is because the address is such as to enable and solicit reply; i.e., because the one who enters grants himself as object also of the other's intention. Contrary to much of what has been said on the matter, authentic personal mutuality depends precisely on mutual self-objectification. If I address you, I make you my object. And if I do not seek to enslave you, I so address you as also to grant myself as your object. Of course, there is that treating of the other 'as a thing' which has been called 'objectification'; but what this consists in, is that I seek *so* to make you my object as to withhold my own self-objectification.

The total of possibilities, that I may grant myself as object for those I address, is 'my body'. The body is the self, as the describable and so intendable object of an other self. The body is the *available* self.

Second. The body is the object-presence of the person *also to himself*. Whether or not there is immediate self-consciousness (which I am inclined to deny), there surely is mediate self-consciousness as consciousness of my own body. This consciousness is, in my view, interpersonally mediated. In that you have me as your object, and in that you and I share a world in our communication, I also have myself as a worldly object. And in that I have myself as an object, I may address also myself: the word becomes my interior reality. Once again contrary to much of what has been said, the inner linguisticality of personal existence, its essential character as choice and hope and knowledge, depends upon the person's objectification in a society. This leads directly to my next point.

Third. The body is the *to-be-transcended* presence of the person. In that you can address me, and so exhort, enlighten, curse, bless or make promises to me, you are beyond me, speaking from a hope and clarity—or damnation and darkness—which is not mine and which your words open. And most remarkably, in that I also have myself as my object, I transcend *myself*, I am beyond myself as a describable object in the world; and so am not merely a describable object.

What I then am, is a specifically theological question. There is the transcendence which is the unalterability of the past; and there is the transcendence which is the freedom of the future. As non-object, I may be the one I *was* in the beginning, and still 'really' am in an eternity which is Persistence of the Beginning; or I may be the one I am not yet but will be in that eternity which is Triumph of the End. We will save time if I intrude the theological decision of the gospel. Then the lines above must read: '. . . which is *not yet* mine . . .', and '. . . I am *future to* myself as a describable object. . . .'

Just so, the body which is thus transcended, mediates the *past*. In that I give myself as body, I give the one I already am, I give the product of my deeds and sufferings to date. The only 'available self' is the so-far-achieved self. The body is the possibility of *re*cognition, the availability of continuity with the past.

In that you thus transcend me, you can be free from me; my address is not an incantation that fixes your reality. Just so, my address can itself be the word that in fact frees you: that opens futures not set by your past, that grants hopes and comforts you do not find in your—available, i.e., past—self. Just so, you can be free not only from but for me. And in that you and I share me as our object, your freedom for me is my freedom for myself. The occurrence of this shared freedom is 'spirit'.

Fourth. In that the body is the available person and mediates the past person, it is the person's *identifiability*. To address myself to one addressing me, I must be able to pick him out from the maelstrom of actuality. I may do this by merely pointing—to his body, not his spirit. In so far as the act of identification becomes linguistic, it occurs by, or depends upon, 'definite descriptions': 'the one who . . . and who . . . and who . . .' and so on until the 'Oh, that one' falls. The clauses after 'who' will either be descriptions of the person's bodily appearance or location, or biographical items, items of that past which the body mediates. Identification depends entirely on the body; a pure spirit would be—at least for all others—no one in particular and everyone in general.

Fifth. In so far as the possibilities of object-presence, which are the body, are realized, there occur what traditional sacramental theology helpfully calls *visible words*. In Reformation use, the pair to *visible words* is *audible words*, utterances in a language. A language is a sign-system with grammar: with syntax and semantic rules. Syntactic rules enable endless new combination of signs into the complex signs, sentences, that are the actual vehicles of communication. Semantic rules govern the grasp of signs on signed reality, and enable new signs to replace old ones as needed; in that languages have semantic rules, they can change and grow or shrink.

All signs are objects in the world: sounds, marks, movements, buildings, etc. But the power and adaptability which grammar gives the words of a language, is purchased by making their reality as objects in the world inessential to their function. A language's infinite ability to generate new sentences, and create and redefine old words, means that the next time 'the same thing' may be said by some quite different set of objects. Language is the home of spirit; but a person who was present only by utterances of language would withhold his objectivity.

In so far as in our communication we grant ourselves as objects, we make words not governed by grammar, and so not replaceable in their givenness as objects in the world: the individually unique word-objects that are works of art, and the signs of sign-systems without grammar, as the various touchings of a traditional society's social intercourse. The kiss, e.g., once given, we cannot decide to 'say the same thing in future' by some other gesture; for there is no way to make the needed definition. If we cease to kiss, the particular meaning of the kiss also ceases. No more can we replace even the most minor Moore marble with some other, or the bread and cup of the Eucharist with popcorn and soda-bottle. The totality of my visible addresses is my body's realization, its gesture, its act.

Gods and Their Revelations

As I am a creature, I may attempt to reveal myself to you in some purely 'spiritual', disembodied address. And we can at least imagine my success, by which I would become for you an ineffable being-in-general, and make you utterly my slave. Sartre's book on Genet is a rich and horrifying exposition of this possibility. But *God* cannot even be conceived as so revealing himself. God's revelation—for the moment, *any* God's revelation!—must be an embodied revelation, a grant of divine objectivity. A God's revelation must be both audible and visible words; religion cannot do without sacrament.

This is so because to be a God is to be in some fashion 'eternal', to be in some fashion the possibility that past and future make a whole. The address of God—for the moment, of any God!—is the possibility that remembrance may rhyme with hope, if only by dispensing from hope and fear together. It is the possibility that anticipation may vivify the past, if only by revealing life as the past's endless repetition. God is eternal: in his presence my present embraces and is embraced by the past which gives its content and the future which is its meaning.

The address of a God, therefore, must be spirit *and* body; it must be language and sacrament. It must open an infinite future; but it must rhyme that future with all the past. A disembodied, purely linguistic, communication, however it might occur, and whoever might be able so to speak, could not reveal God. God's presence must grant us an object, to be embodiment of the one who addresses us.

There is, of course, an objection. God, says all normal religion, has no body. Just so, the embodiment of God's presence, his self-objectification in his revelation, is both universal in religion and of most ambiguous status. Visible words are religion's most obtrusive feature, and its greatest embarrassment. For religion normally seeks in God the Transcendence of the Beginning, and so the eternity of the Beginning's Persistence, the eternity of changelessness. The presence of such a God is a *nunc stans*. Therefore it can only be represented by any object; for, whether it be their defect or their glory, all our objects change.

In normal religion, the objects which belong to revelation can each only momentarily embody the coherence of past and future; the divine objectifications are successive and interchangeable. If religious longing for God *himself* comes alive, it must leave such revelatory objectifications behind. If philosophical passion for truth simple comes alive, revelatory objectifications will be subjected to an hermeneutic of 'symbols' and *Vorstellungen.* At the higher stages, sacramental visibility becomes mere 'outward forms and ceremonies'.

Of course, since a God's revelation is (I have argued) essentially embodied, to leave revelation's objects behind is to leave revelation itself behind. But that is religion's normal path. For it, revelation is a mere starting point and impetus. God's self-communication is that which the higher stages of spiritual development break through, in order to possess God himself or be possessed by him, in order no longer to be separated by that outward space which the word posits. A normal revelation is a spring-board towards Ineffability.

The Embodiment of the Gospel's God

The gospel does not set us on this path. Since the person who is in the gospel God's revelation is also the content of the descriptions by which God is identified, the gospel allows no way to transcend the revelation while still grasping the identity of God. So religiously peculiar is this knitting of revelation and identification, that it may reasonably be questioned whether it is helpful to call what happens with Christ a 'revelation' at all. For the purposes of this essay, it seems helpful to me.

The gospel's prohibition of the attempt to transcend revelation is enforced equally by the Reformation's doctrine of justification by faith alone, and by the ancient church's creedal christology. The Reformation doctrine says of the gospel as *viva vox,* as address for and of God, that it is unconditional promise, i.e., that it can be challenged by no other or greater grasp of God. And the very purpose of the Nicene 'of one being with the Father', was to keep the religious from 'phantasizing that by their reflection they can transcend the life of the Son'.[1]

But if we cannot transcend the self-revelation of the gospel's God, then neither can we transcend his embodiment therein, the objectification he presents us. This means, e.g., that all attempts to abstract Jesus' meaning from his objective human reality, to abstract 'the Christ of faith' from 'the Jesus of history', are not merely exegetical mistakes, they are worship of another God than the God of the gospel. It means that all anti- or a-sacramentalism tends to idolatry, whether done in favour of moral earnestness, or by spiritual deprecation of externality, or by ceremonialist transformation of common liturgy into the occasion of mystic ascent.

The consequences for the specific doctrine of God are even more remarkable. At the Offertory of the Eucharist, e.g., we bring symbolic objects, with the prayer that God incorporate them into the very

[1] Gregory of Nyssa, *Against Eunomius,* PG 45, 833.

economy of his divine life. To what sort of God can such a prayer be made? The God of the gospel is one for whom self-revelation is not something he merely happens to do, so that if we confront the subject of revelation we find something other than the revelation. He does not merely have a word, he is his Word: the event of his self-communication is the event of his reality as God. Given God and we who are other than God, all religion admits that it depends on an act of divine self-communication; but the God of the gospel would be in communication even if we did not exist, or were cut off from him. It is clear that we are now speaking of God as the doctrine of the Trinity does.

It follows that the God of the gospel does not merely penultimately embody himself for certain purposes. He is the Word that he speaks, and the Word God speaks is embodied word. God has a body, in at least all the ways described above. Such an assertion is a shock to our inherited and built-in ontology, which treats body and spirit, object and subject, as two sorts of substantial reality, and classifies God as spirit. But that this way of thinking is still initially inevitable, does not make it true.

God's Body

Christianity must assert the embodiment of God. Traditional theology, at least in its popular versions, has handled this by describing a series of metaphysical additions. First there is God, who as such is permanently disembodied. This God is, in the second place, triune, which enables his right hypostasis not to know what his left hypostasis is doing: the Son can involve himself with embodiment, while the Father remains pure. Such involvement is required by God's will of grace; for we, to whom he wishes to be present, can apprehend no presence that is not also an object-presence—whether this inability is due to creaturehood or sin is disputed. Therefore the Son was united with the man Jesus, who does have a body; thus embodiment was added to God. On returning to God as Jesus, the Son took this body with him. But in the sacramental, 'visible', side of the gospel-proclamation, and especially in the bread and cup, God provides a substitute. Now there is, on the one hand, an object present to us; and on the other hand, there is somewhere and somehow the body of Christ. The task of sacramental theology is to explain yet a second addition: how Jesus' own body-object gets joined to the objects on the tables, or vice versa.

This description is, of course, a caricature; all theologians would object to it. The objections would mostly be of the sort that, as we say, 'break through' the stated pattern. But I think it fair to say that such subtleties have amounted to little in the consciousness of the community. We should consider whether the gospel's very real breakthrough in the apprehension of God may not mandate and enable a whole different doctrine of God's embodiment. I will attempt a doctrine whereby God is described as embodied in and of himself, and not merely by additive adaptation to us. I will assert of God the descriptions by which I have phenomenally specified 'body'. If someone says that 'body' calls for other phenomenal characters than my five, that some of these cannot be asserted of God, and that therefore we should not attribute 'body' to God, there are these possibilities: (1) these other phenomenal characters do after all fit God; (2) they do not, but whether then to speak of God's 'body' is a matter for semantic negotiation, with no substantive risk for either side; (3) they do not, but in the ensuing semantic negotiations, my opponent has a hidden agenda—'God *can't* have anything like a body'; (4) they do not, and so as to make it silly to speak of God's 'body', which defeats my project. I will make my attempt in three runs.

First. God is Word eternally in himself. Thus God addresses God, God *intends* God; i.e., God has God as descriptively knowable and specifiable; i.e., God is object for God. Just so, and only just so, he can be, if he chooses, an object for an other than himself—if that as which God intends himself, and that which he presents to our intention, are the same. That God reveals himself, means that an object which we intend as we seek to reply to God's promise, is the same object that God intends in the eternal immanent Conversation that he is. God is, also in his self-possession, free. If he chooses to have himself as an object that is also our object, that is how it is.

The promise that only God can make in fact sounds through our time; we are in fact addressed by a call that claims to come from him. This promise is made 'in Jesus' name', in the name of a body-person and our possible historic object. Just in that the promise is made in such a name, it is not the intrusion of some ineffable slave-master spirit, but of one who gives freedom. When we believe, Jesus provides the object of our intention. If the promise is true, if it is truly God's Word, Jesus is also the object of God's intention of himself: *as God turns to himself, he turns to Jesus the Nazarene*. He might have turned to himself as to some other personal object, but he does not. So—directly, without metaphysical pastings-together—Jesus, the body who walked in Palestine, is *unum ex trinitatis*.

All this, of course, is true only in the Resurrection. If Jesus were our historic object only, he would not be God's revelation. God is God of the living; his body is not a corpse. But if Jesus is our object as a living man, then he now speaks ever new to us; and must be a body also in that speaking. We come to 'the sacraments'.

If the gospel-promise is true, its occurrence is Jesus' presence. For what the gospel promises is a final community constituted by Jesus' final self-giving. The making and hearing of such a promise is itself an event of fellowship; final self-promise is already the act of love. Nor can the witness who speaks in Jesus' name be the subject of the promise, and so of the fellowship; for he, with death still before him, can make no final promises. The event of the speaking of the gospel is the event of Jesus' personal presence to those addressed. And in so far as the speaking of the gospel is necessarily, for reasons already discussed, embodied address, audible *and* visible words, this visibility is the risen Jesus' object-presence now to us, the present-tense body of the Lord.

Questions arise here about the man Jesus similar to those I am discussing about God: what sort of human existence is it, whose embodiment can be so described? The ancient quarrel between Lutheran and Reformed still remains to be overcome. But in this essay we are concerned with the visible words of sacraments as the embodiment of *God*; and to that point I may simply repeat myself. If God chooses to intend himself as those objects which make the present-tense body of Christ, then he so chooses. As God turns to himself, he turns to the loaf and cup passed round, the washing with water, and all our community's objectivity in the gospel. There he sees himself. That he does so is our salvation.

Second. To say that God has a body, is to say that God transcends also himself. There is in God beginning and goal, what is left behind and what is set ahead, past and future. God has himself as what he is free from, and just so free for. All the analysis and rhetoric of idealist and existentialist doctrines of human existence, fit God before they fit us. It was the idealist attempt to combine gospel-given insight into personhood, with the unquestioned dogma that God has no body, that displaced trinitarian language from God to us, and so created the existentialist rhetoric.

God leaves himself behind, and just so chooses and wins himself, for the goal that is his own free fulfilment. The event in which this happens, is the crucifixion and resurrection of Jesus. Self-transcendence is not so simple as some rhetoric supposes; Sartre's tortured and self-defeating analyses are closer to truth than most. Really to leave oneself behind is to die, to have one's body as corpse-body. To be beyond *then*, to look back *then*, is either to be deathless disembodied spirit, or to rise from the dead. To do either is to be God; the thing once done, others can be included. To be deathless disembodied spirit is to be Brahman; to bring off death and resurrection in one personal existence, is to be the Trinity.

The 'spiritualists' asked Luther: Would God let his body be pushed about on the table, and given over to all and sundry who come? The question is logically odd, of course. For to answer 'No', is to confess the sort of God who could have no body anyway. It is precisely in that the Eucharist, and all the sacramental reality of the gospel, enacts the giving-over of God's object-presence, and his assuming of lordship just thereby, that it can be God's true embodiment.

Third. God identifies himself by Jesus. This is the deepest and most quickly made statement of God's embodiment. In that God is self-transcendent person, the question 'Who am I?' is his question also, though the threat of puzzlement and failure is not. And in the inner linguisticality of his life, he answers, 'I am the one who raised the man Jesus from the dead'. That this is so, is the saving fact. That it has come to be so, is the saving work. This inner self-identification is God's very being. He might have been other than this affirmation of the man of our hope; that he is what he is, is the accomplishment of Jesus' life, death and resurrection.

If there has been a resurrection, then to the question 'Who is God?' we must answer, 'Whoever did that resurrection'. When we are being religiously usual, we identify God by our a priori religious needs, e.g., 'God is whoever is omnipotent, as I am not'. Then we seek additional information, e.g., on what terms he will share his omnipotence, from revelation. But if there has been a resurrection, also our identification of God is imposed and given, it belongs to revelation. Then the truth of our knowledge of God, is that he freely identifies himself in the same way that he lets us identify him. Then the fact of revelation is the fact of freely chosen and granted coincidence of the way we pick out God, and the way he picks himself out.

In the Great Prayer of the Eucharist, according to most ancient orders, the Narrative of Institution is followed by the 'Anamnesis'. In this prayer, we turn to God to recall before him the life, death and resurrection of the Lord, and to plead for fulfilment of the promises to which God in these events committed himself. The act is the service's most explicit obedience to the command that our thanksgiving shall be 'for remembrance' of Jesus. We remind God, in the style of much Old Testament and Jewish table- and Passover-prayer.

At this place in the service, this reminding is done not only with words, but also with the loaf and cup; for the Narrative has just made these the centre of all liturgical action. The prayer-book precisely states the situation: '. . . we . . . make here before thy divine Majesty, *with these thy holy gifts* (my emphasis), the memorial which thy Son hath willed us to make. . . .' We propose these objects to God, as those by which he shall remember his past acts and the commitment thereby entered, i.e., *by which he shall identify himself*. So, with respect to this aspect of 'body', the sacramental objects are the body of God. Indeed, I cannot refrain from transgressing the bounds of this essay to suggest: in that these objects remind God of Jesus, they are Jesus' body also.

A Trinitarian Theory

The bowdlerized version of standard theology understands God's embodiment as achieved by addition of Jesus' body to God. That God is triune is what makes such an anomaly possible. But God's triunity itself is antecedently conceived.

This sort of trinitarian theology represents, it seems to me, an odd sort of conceptual shift. The trinitarian formulas resulted in the first place from defence of God's embodiment against intrusion of an identification of God as the great Persistence, to whom embodiment is inappropriate. But the formulas once there, they were handled as given doctrine, and, I suggest, partly captured by the spirit of their old antagonist: they came to be taken as description of the inner arrangements of a pure reality of God pseudo-temporally prior to the Incarnation.

In the present attempt, God's embodiment is described by propositions that are themselves trinitarian propositions, evocations of the dynamics in which God is triune. Jesus, like every human creature, *is* a body. And he *is* the Second Hypostasis of God: the Confrontation of Jesus and his 'Father' and their common Future as Spirit, is the being of God. The distinction of the immanent and economic trinities should not be handled as a distinction of two realities: it rather establishes that the one triune Event *might* have happened otherwise than it does, e.g., so as not to be the Father's 'Yes' to a crucified brother of us.

Trinitarian theology is the attempt to say who God is, if the personal body Jesus is true God. It must then be so that, vice versa, trinitarian theology provides a *theory* of that embodiment itself. The present attempt is to start unpacking that theory.

7 The Relation of the Doctrines of the Incarnation and the Trinity

by D. M. MacKINNON

The aim of this paper is not historical; it does not follow the method classically illustrated in Lebreton's well-known study of the origins of the doctrine of the Trinity, still less to duplicate the excellent study recently published by my colleague in Cambridge Professor G. C. Stead.[1] What it seeks is perhaps nearer in style to Professor Moltmann's recent book *Der gekreuzigte Gott*.[2] That book is indeed a work that I greatly admire and I have recently had the privilege of discussing part of it with its author. But he would allow me to say that the main lines of what I venture to set out were more or less completely drawn before I read what he had written.

There are in Christian theology a certain number of unresolved problems which touch the very heart of its most fundamental concerns. I say unresolved problems; I might have said rather places where absolutely central issues are clearly at stake, where a whole number of questions seem almost to tumble into one another, and where at the same time, any sort of clarity seems more a matter of fitful vision, than of sustained perception.

There are few better introductions to the questions with which I wish to deal in this paper than a fragment from the notebooks of Gerard Manley Hopkins, belonging to the year of his tertianship:

> Why did the Son of God go thus forth from the Father not only in the eternal and intrinsic procession of the Trinity but also by an extrinsic and less than eternal, let us say an aeonian one? To give God glory and that by sacrifice . . . This sacrifice and this outward profession is a consequence and shadow of the procession of the Trinity, from which mystery sacrifice takes its rise; but of this I do not mean to write here. It is as if the blissful agony or stress of selving in God had forced out drops of sweat or blood, which drops were the world, or as if the lights lit at the festival

[1] *Theology*, 1974, pp. 508–17, 582–8.
[2] Munich, 1973; ET, London, 1974.

> of that 'peaceful Trinity' through some little cranny striking out lit up into being one 'cleave' out of the world of possible creatures. The sacrifice would be the Eucharist . . .[1]

If we were concerned with the interpretation of this very remarkable passage with full regard to its author, I should have to treat of the metaphysics and theology of Duns Scotus, and also of the elusive concept of the *aevum*, introduced by medieval theologians as a kind of middle term between temporal and eternal. But the passage is simply quoted as a point of departure. For surely it conveys with the sort of passion that one would expect from a considerable poet the way in which the two realities of the eternal God and the historical mission of the Incarnate play upon each other. If I may speak very loosely in a way that may seem offensive to the philosophical conscience, it is as if the still transcendence of God in his aseity suddenly became vibrant with the energy, the strain, the joy, the grief, the triumph and the failure of the ministry of Jesus and that ministry itself was found in all its tension and incompleteness to catch in a manner wholly unique the very being of the eternal. The language of my commentary may seem extravagant; certainly it has nothing of the grace of the original. But it is of a coincidence of opposites, an interpenetration of seemingly mutually alien realities that Hopkins writes. By this interpenetration both alike are illuminated.

What is clear is that the poet's meditation takes for granted the legitimacy of an *ontological* idiom in Christology. In his influential book *Die Christologie des neuen Testaments*,[2] Dr Oscar Cullmann insisted that the New Testament titles of Christ were to be construed *functionally*, and not *ontologically*. Where the Johannine self-designations, Light of the World, Bread of Life, Resurrection and Life, Way, Truth and Life etc. were concerned, Cullmann invoked the authority of an interesting monograph on the Johannine Christology[3] published a few years before his own book by Dom Jacques Dupont, O.S.B. For Cullmann the terms—*ontological* and *functional*—are correlatives; his use of the term *ontological* has little or nothing to do with the branch of philosophy called ontology, by Professor Peter Geach of the University of Leeds, for instance,[4] who in faithfulness to the tradition classically formulated in Aristotle's *Metaphysics*, spoke of it as that branch of philosophy concerned to give as comprehensive account as possible of certain concepts,

[1] *The Sermons and Devotional Writings of Gerard Manley Hopkins*, ed. by Christopher Devlin, London, 1967.

[2] Tübingen, 1957; ET, London, 1960.

[3] *Études sur la Christologie de St. Jean*, Paris, 1950.

[4] *Proceedings* of the Joint Session of the Aristotelian Society and Mind Association, 1951.

involved in discourse concerning any subject-matter whatsoever e.g. thing and quality, existence, truth, etc. Such enquiries indeed have great significance for theology, as mention of the conceptual apparatus involved in the Nicene and Chalcedonian definitions reminds us. But when Cullmann referred to *ontological* as distinct from *functional* Christological concepts, he was concerned to distinguish concepts by means of which Christ's work is articulated from concepts purposing to capture what the One is, who in them is incarnate.

The influence of Melanchthon's well-known dictum: *Hoc est Christum cognoscere, eius beneficia cognoscere* is here strong. For us to know Christ (including in this knowledge an ability to characterize what may be said of him, and not for instance of Hosea and Jeremiah, of Socrates, of the author of the 2nd Epistle to the Corinthians, of John Bunyan and John Henry Newman, of Dietrich Bonhoeffer and Franz Jägerstätter) is to know the rôle or rôles that is or are exclusively his. What he is apart from such rôle or rôles that help to define the order of his ministry, we do not know, nor need to know. Thus it would seem that the sort of deep theological enquiry undertaken by the late Bishop Frank Weston in his book *The One Christ*[1] would be disallowed as certainly sterile and arguably invalid *ab initio.*

Verbum supernum prodiens,
Nec Patris linquens dexteram
(St Thomas Aquinas)

It may be said that even thus to pose the question of the relation of the Word incarnate to the Word through whom the entire created order is sustained in being is to be precipitated into every sort of metaphysical bewilderment, and those especially concerning the relations of the temporal to the eternal. Yet according to Dr Alec Vidler, the late Professor C. E. Raven regarded Weston's book as the greatest Christological work in English of this century, and this in spite of the deep differences that separated the two men over such issues as the 'Kikuyu controversy', and the missionary bishop's reaction to the sort of theology he judged encouraged in Oxford by metaphysical idealism on the one hand, and by the attitude to the traditional conciliar orthodoxy encouraged by the *Quellen-forschung* of the synoptic Gospels, characteristic of Sanday's seminar, on the other.[2]

The events that go to make up the history of Jesus belong to the

[1] London, 1907

[2] Yet when Sanday read *The One Christ* he said that he was proud of his 'old pupil'; see *Life of Frank Weston*, Bishop of Zanzibar, 1937.

same time order as the conspiracy of Seianus against Tiberius Caesar which was contemporary with some of them. Indeed there are those who argue that Pilate was particularly vulnerable to the suggestion that if he let go one who might be thought to have spoken against Caesar, he could hardly be regarded as Tiberius' friend. (It is alleged of Pilate that he had been involved at least on the fringe of that conspiracy and therefore would wish to avoid even the faintest *soupçon* of disloyalty towards the all-powerful despot on Capri.) The life of Jesus, the last years of Tiberius, the principate of Caligula, the whole complex reality of the Roman world belong to that created order fashioned through the Logos, continually sustained by his power and owing its unity to his creative activity. Further it is not the world of human history alone that finds its ground in the eternal Word, but the natural world in which that history is set, which is itself moreover part of a universe of which in recent decades we have achieved, through empirical cosmology, a greater understanding than any previously possible to human kind. There was no single theological point more continually emphasized by Professor Charles Raven than the total impropriety of treating the natural world and, by implication, the universe, as if they were no more than the stage set for the drama of redemption. He greatly welcomed an article which the late Cardinal Jean Daniélou contributed to *Études* in February 1962 in which he claimed that Teilhard's most important contribution to theology was the administration of a *coup de grâce* to any and every tendency to treat the Christian God as a *deus ex machina*. The Word incarnate in Christ is continually at work. But how then are we to understand the relationship of the apparently datable concentration of his action in the ministry of Jesus, under the circumstances of that period in the history of the society into which he was born and in which he was schooled, to that pervasive continuing activity?

The charge is often brought against most forms of kenotic Christology that they fail in the end to make any sense of the relation of the 'depotentiated' Logos incarnate in Jesus to that same Logos eternally and changelessly abiding itself within the unity of the godhead.[1] The duality of the eternal *tropos huparxeōs* and the temporally manifested Logos which seemingly on such a view must be affirmed is dismissed as totally incredible, if not nonsensical.

So inevitably to those who would profess and call themselves orthodox, there was a certain attraction in turning away from the abysses of ontological speculation to the apparent simplicities of a theology that would insist that its fundamental categories were economic, in the sense of being embedded in the structure of the

[1] Cf. J. M. Creed, *The Divinity of Jesus Christ*, ed. by D. M. MacKinnon (Fontana), London, 1964.

economy of God's dealings with us. The very conception of God as Father, Son, and Holy Spirit must be construed as a conception of God in his relation to his creatures in creation, redemption, and sanctification.

Yet as we well know, such a view has failed in fact to sustain itself for more than a very short period. The reasons for this failure are several. I should like immediately to focus on one of them, and paradoxical though it may seem, I should like to suggest that I find this very powerfully expressed in Bultmann's great commentary on the fourth Gospel.[1] (I realize that this must appear paradoxical, in view, for instance, of the form of Cullmann's acute criticism of Bultmann's depreciation of the sacramental teaching of that Gospel.) In his commentary, affected as it is by his study of Kierkegaard, Bultmann powerfully brings out the extent to which radically Christocentric though John's Gospel is, that Christocentrism is parasitic upon a continued reference to the Father who sent the Son, that gives the book an ultimately theocentric emphasis. It is not Jesus who himself imposes significance on what he is and does; rather he continually advertises the fact that his significance lies in this, that it is wholly bestowed upon him *ab extra*. In Bultmann's own theological thought the central emphasis is always epistemological. 'Jesus reveals that He is the revealer.' His import is found in that God is uniquely disclosed through him, in his own preaching and then in the preaching which has him as its subject. Yet if Jesus is to reveal that 'He is the revealer', thus disclosing that his significance is not in himself, and that where he is concerned, the most important fact is this, that he is the identifiable historical individual through whom God has addressed the world, we may claim that this is only possible through the realization in his historical individuality of a total receptivity.

And here I quote another student of the fourth Gospel, of a very different temper from Bultmann, namely Dr W. R. Inge. In his oddly entitled study *Faith and its Psychology*,[2] he speaks of an 'infinite self-abnegation' as characteristic of the Johannine Christology. His idiom is ontological. Clearly he takes very seriously John's suggestion that what is realized in the Incarnate Word's earthly ministry is properly characterized as the achievement of such a total self-abnegation. Indeed he encourages his readers to ask themselves how far that which is incarnate in Jesus may not be characterized as infinite receptivity, infinite response. Few would deny that for John, the Word is pre-existent, even if in that sentence we are in fact saying

[1] London, 1971. The reader will realize that my debt is to Bultmann's theological exegesis and not to the *Quellen-forschung* which his commentary also contains.

[2] London, 1909.

(this is Cullmann's view) that what pre-exists is that to which *we* refer by the 'definite description', the Word.[1] That which is represented as coming into the world in Jesus, as transcribed in the conditions of his ministry into forms of speaking his Father's words and 'doing the will of Him that sent me', is what he eternally is.

It was an Italian prior who recently spoke of obedience as 'the most insidious' (the Italian word is *subdola*) of all the temptations. This characterization of obedience is certainly one of the most illuminating contributions to fundamental Christian ethics I have heard in years. But it is not only for Christian ethics that it is important; it is also deeply significant for dogmatic theology, both for soteriology and for the doctrine of God. The direction of the argument in the preceding paragraphs may have seemed to suggest that in Jesus we find a total obedience to the will of God. And of course the New Testament gives a certain encouragement in that direction, e.g. (a *locus classicus*), 'obedient unto death', Philippians 2:1 ff. Yet Paul says first that he made himself of no reputation (*doxa*). He implies a complete indifference to human judgment which is expressive not of a strenuous heroism, but of a total self-abandonment to the Father. Thus in the *third* Gospel the young Jesus chides his parents, who seek him after Passover, with the words that he must be in his Father's house, about his Father's business, and the dying man, the temptation to prove himself to himself and to the world at large finally resisted by refusal to descend from the Cross, utters as his last word: 'Father into thy hands I commend my spirit.' It is only after that last word that the centurion in charge of the execution squad confesses him an innocent man (*dikaios*). Yet it is his refusal to attempt descent from the Cross that enables him to receive the 'penitent thief's' confession of faith.[2] So, as Barth so clearly saw, Jesus is 'the man for others' in so far as he is 'the man for God'. Because his very costly, total indifference to human judgment is grounded in a loving self-abandon to his Father, it makes possible for him an analogous accessibility to the outcast and derelict.

[1] For Cullmann the designation 'Word of God' refers to Jesus in his relation to us.

[2] It is very important that in his account of Jesus' temptations, Luke finds the climactic temptation not in the offer of the Kingdoms of this world and their glory, but in the suggestion Jesus tests his status *via-à-vis* his Father by a descent from the pinnacle of the Temple. The devil then leaves him *achri kairou* to return in the hour of the power of darkness, to enter into Judas, to sift Peter as wheat, and above all to renew his challenge to Jesus to prove himself. Luke's narrative of the Passion is one of a final overwhelming temptation, and that temptation reaches its climax in the challenge to descend from the Cross, the axis of Luke's treatment of the crucifixion. Such a descent, if successfully executed, would confirm Jesus's status in his own right and achieve for him a 'bloodless victory'.

A man's conduct may sometimes be excused on the ground that he was obeying orders. Whether that conduct is good or bad in itself and/or by reason of its consequences is what determines whether or not we should approve it. No one would question the heroism of the German soldiers at Stalingrad in 1942; I trust that no one either would question the moral superiority of the action of the Munich students who that same terrible autumn, courted death by open protest against the monstrous evil the soldiers were sustaining by their brave obedience, or of Franz Jägerstätter in his solitary witness to death as an Austrian C.O. the next August.

If we find the starting-point of a Christology in the relation of Christ to the Father, realized for our salvation in flesh and blood, we have to recognize that what is thus realized is in itself an ultimate gentleness of receiving and of giving back, even of parting asunder and of accepted estrangement. My language here is anthropomorphic, and perilously nearly tritheistic. Yet the doctrine of the Trinity, of the essential as distinct from the economic Trinity, represents in part at least a grave attempt to preserve the doctrine of Christ's passion and work from lapsing into a saga of human achievement, or worse still, into that of a demigod, akin to Heracles. It is to engage in the task of so reconstructing the doctrine of the Ultimate that the form of Jesus' ministry, his life, his death, and his being brought again from death to boundless life,[1] is found in God as He is in Himself. At the heart of that ministry we find realized a final, a haunting receptivity. Yet that receptivity never rots away into a passive acceptance. It is not only that, for instance, the temple is cleansed; it is rather that tragic failure in the circumstances of Jesus' mission is characterized for what it is, 'Oh Jerusalem, Jerusalem'. 'Daughters of Jerusalem, weep not for me, but for yourselves.' The situation is not mastered, nor is it accepted; it is lived through and met by agony. We cannot say too often that Jesus failed in very much, even as Antigone in Sophocles' tragedy failed in her confrontation with Creon, bringing out the very worst in that self-conscious ruler. Of that failure Jesus bore the burden, but not in the mood of a ferocious, exultant self-denial; rather as expressive of an identification in love at once with those with whom He was involved, and with the One in relationship to whom is constituted eternally what He is. 'And the spirit drove him into the wilderness.' The theme of the Holy Spirit's role in the mission of the Incarnate needs much further treatment, if this picture is to be, I will not say, complete but tolerably adequate.

So I must turn briefly to the central enigma of the relation of the times of Jesus to the eternity of God. For it is in a proper under-

[1] i.e. life no longer moving to the frontier of death.

standing of this relation that it may be we shall find the key to the problem of the relation of the Word through which the world comes to be and the Word Incarnate in Jesus.

What is realized in the mission of Jesus and perfected in the Father's raising Him from the dead is the very unity of God, the consistency of God with himself in relation to his creation. We have to do with a prolonged human action that is grounded in God, that in fact provides the very rationale of creation itself. Yet it is unique because in it the very being of God is put at risk, and by the way in which it thus is put at risk, we learn, as nowhere else, what it is we *say* of God when we acclaim him all-powerful, all-knowing, etc. It is a weakness of the western Trinitarian tradition so to conceive and so to stress the unity of God that the whole theology of the divine attributes tends to be treated independently of the treatise on the divine tri-unity, and the unity of God itself regarded as conceivable independently of the tri-unity through which it is realized:

> 'The hands are stretched in weakness,
> not in power.'

So Archbishop William Dalrymple Maclagan in a Good Friday hymn,[1] a good deal better than most. But he is wrong. It is the power of God that we must learn to define by reference to those outstretched hands. For we are not passing through the hour of a temporary *eclipse* of the divine sovereignty where we are concerned. We are witnessing its supreme assertion in the setting of a deeply estranged world, an assertion that discloses its very substance, its arcane ground. Our images of the divine are always perilously suffused with anthropomorphic suggestions of a consummate mastery of the world. One catches an example in the prayer that speaks of God as 'high and mighty King of Kings and Lord of Lords', a magnified Henrican-style despot 'without body, parts or passions'. But the divine crown is one of thorns: 'Has he diadem as monarch etc.' One could say that the writer of that hymn[2] (hardly heard today) was (possibly unknown to himself) nearer the heart of the matter than the composer of the prayer!

It is only through the reinforcement of our Christology by a profoundly probing doctrine of the essential Trinity that the former is preserved from the sort of distortion which immediately in one way or another, overtakes any attempt to develop an autonomous and all-inclusive doctrine of Christ's person and work, as if both person

[1] A. & M. Hymn 115, *Lord when thy Kingdom comes.*

[2] *Art thou weary, art thou languid?* It is the translation of a Greek original by Dr J. M. Neale: but in the form of Hymns A. & M. 254, a very paradigm of Victorian hymnody!

and work alike could stand on their own feet. It is again only through such a doctrine that the full significance of Christ's revelation may be glimpsed from afar, and the sort of trivialization of the divine that finds expression in succeeding styles of idolatry avoided. If in such effort we often find ourselves reduced to silence by inability to eliminate apparent contradiction from the concepts we invoke, at least we may hope that this silence reflects disturbed movement towards, rather than comforting escape from, the unutterable love.

It is a commonplace of the histories of the doctrine of the Trinity to contrast the Western emphasis on unity expressed e.g. in the Augustinian invocation of psychological analogies in treatment of persons and processions, with the Greek (Cappadocian) pre-occupation with the three *hypostaseis*. Yet we do well to remember that it is fully in accordance with orthodox tradition to insist both that: *Omnia opera Dei ad extra sunt opera totius indivisae Trinitatis* and that: *Missiones sequuntur Processiones.*

Thus the grounds of the roles *quoad nos* of Son and Spirit are found in their processional relations within the Godhead. And (if I understand Aquinas' treatise *de Trinitate* aright) these relations are to be *identified* with the individual persons. At the outset of his two volume study of the history of Trinitarian doctrine de Régnon[1] illuminatingly suggests that the 'egoism' (in the sense of 'I'ness) of the three persons is exhausted in the relation in which that person eternally stands to his fellows. So the 'I'ness of the Son is the relation of Sonship in which he stands to the Father; what he is, is his eternal generation from and response to the Father. So with the Holy Spirit (though here the controversy of the *Filioque* must be treated), his being resides in his being 'co-spired' by Father and Son, posited in and through their mutual relationship; for him to exist as Holy spirit is *co-spirari.*

To work this out in full use would have to be made of the treatment in modern ontology (beginning with such works as Russell's *Principles of Mathematics* and Moore's famous essay on *Internal and External Relations*) of different sorts of relations, e.g., *transitive, intransitive, symmetrical, asymmetrical, ancestral,* etc. It is notorious that in Aquinas' treatise *de Trinitate* the frontiers between substance, and relation are blurred. The relations with which the persons of the Trinity are identified are characterized as quasi-substantial. But the notion of substance which the early Church theologians invoked, e.g. in treatment of the identity of deity when predicated of Father and Son, was partly useful to them in treatment of totally novel problems because the *aporia,* which remained after Aristotle's sustained and subtle 'exploration of its veins and sinews' (the phrase is

[1] *Études sur l'histoire du Dogme de la Trinité, vol. 1.* See Appendix C at the end of this essay for a transcription of the passage referred to.

that of the late Dom David Knowles, OSB), suggested a fluidity or 'openness of texture' in the notion that made it unexpectedly useful in articulation of unprecedented problems.[1] But what is true of the notion of substance will be found to apply analogously to that of relation.

Yet already I can imagine impatience with this apparent attempt to substitute for the Gospel of God a 'bloodless ballet of impalpable' abstractions. It is as if the *saltus de Christo ad Deum trinum* is a leap not into the abyss but into a world in which dexterity in handling fundamental notions in philosophical logic, and the adjacent territory of ontology (in Geach's sense) takes over from reverence and from humanity. Where what is imposed on us is a new dimension of the perennial work of faith seeking understanding.

Yet it is an inescapable aspect of theological existence as we know it, continually to encounter this paradox, viz. that is, if we refuse the philistine and spiritually distorting amputation of our theological reach that must be our lot if we accept Cullmann's restriction as finally authoritative. (We must remember that Karl Barth, for all his Christocentrism, or indeed Christomonism, will have nothing of it.) And here inevitably I refer again to my remark that God's consistency with himself, his very unity, is at risk in the ministry and expecially the Passion of Jesus.

My debt here to the work of Hans Urs von Balthasar is very great. As I remarked in an article I contributed to the *Clergy Review* in 1969, there are few (if any) living theologians from whom I have learnt and continue to learn more. In particular his essay, *Mysterium Paschale*[2] in the composite *Mysterium Salutis* III 2 (ed. Feiner and Löhrer) has been constantly on my mind.[3] This very dense monograph dares to treat the unity of the Triune God, the very consistency of God with Himself, as something needing affirmation in

[1] On this may I refer to my two essays—Aristotle's *Conception of Substance* in *New Essays in Plato and Aristotle*, London, 1965, and *Substance in Christology* in *Cambridge Essays in Christology*, Cambridge, 1972? I might also mention a hitherto unpublished paper on *The Concept of Being* in Aristotle's *Metaphysics*, given to the Southern Association for the Study of Ancient Philosophy at Cambridge on September 19th/69, when the Association devoted the greater part of its annual meeting to Aristotle's *Metaphysics*. See also J. M. Le Blond: *Logique et Méthode chez Aristote*, Paris, and various essays in the *Festschrift* for Monsignor A. Mansion: *Autour d'Aristote*, Louvain, 1962. For a different view, see the important study of Aristotle by Professor G. E. M. Anscombe in the volume: *Three Philosophers* by Professors Anscombe and Geach, Blackwell, 1962.

[2] An expanded version of this article has appeared as an introduction to the translation of von Bàlthasar's *Engagement with God* by Dr J. Halliburton, London, 1975. The interested student is referred to the excellent study of von Balthasar by Mr John Riches in *Theology* for 1972.

[3] Which I had not read in 1969 when I wrote the article mentioned above in its original form.

relation to the creation. It is as if that unity were not an eternal self-sufficiency, a transcendent and formally complete wholeness, but something which because its eternal realization is in and through the perpetual mutuality of the processions of the Three comprising it, may find itself at risk by the predicament of its creation, and by the cost exacted for that creation's fulfilment by reason of that predicament. It is as if the theology of the Triune God, understood as a completion of the theology of Christ's *kenōsis* and the complex simplicity of his redeeming mission, provided the context within which traditional debates concerning the alleged divine passibility, or impassibility are transformed. God is transcendent in the sense that the world's dependence upon it is totally asymmetrical. Yet in Himself He is such that the very dependence of the world upon Him is expressive of his eternal relatedness. The creator's humility before his creature is the centrepoint of the mystery of the divine humility, which is the very ground of the divine omnipotence. That power in its absolute sovereignty must not be conceived abstractly but in terms of the total and unfettered *perichoresis* of the persons. Indeed the humility of God may be identified with the Son as response to the Father *in vinculo Spiritus*.

If Raven was right in insisting that we must not treat the natural universe as the stage-set for the drama of redemption, so surely also was Oliver Quick when in private conversation with myself in the autumn of 1941, he said that he regarded as the very touchstone of orthodoxy the frankly mythological clause in the Creed—*descendit de coelis*. Quick was no pre-Copernican! Yet he insisted that this dramatic, mythological idiom was irreducible, the point at which the perennial search on the part of Christianity for a metaphysic in which to rest came to an end. The effort had continually to be made if only to bring out more effectively the irreducible surd of the movement of God to men.

Yet what is the doctrine of the Trinity if not the effort so to reconstruct the doctrine of God that this 'descent' may be seen as supremely, indeed paradigmatically, declaratory of what He is in himself? That God is ultimate humility, a selflessness that in the life of the Incarnate shows itself in a total indifference to the survival of 'institutional Christianity' if only the Father's truth may be affirmed redemptively for those 'lost sheep' to whom he came (cf. again the refusal to descend from the Cross)—these are strange, paradoxical truths: yet they may be arguably more easily perceived by a Church that must seek to redefine its *moyen d'être*, and in consequence made receptive of its *raison d'être* as the embodiment of Christ's sheerly precarious existence, in the new freedom of the post-Constantinian age. Because the built-in institutional carapace of the Christian reality (as we have known it) is being destroyed, we are coming to see that the concepts of the divine sovereignty, and the kingship of Christ must be schematized anew. Only this reschematization calls not for a facile self-dispensation from the burden of metaphysical thought, but rather for a deeper, because less artificially protected, engagement with its relation to the representation of Christ's reality.

It is paradoxical that at a time when there is great interest in the characteristically Christian doctrine of God, it is by no means uncommon for this interest to be accompanied by a certain impatience with the doctrine of the Trinity. Yet it remains true that the history of this doctrine represents the most sustained effort made to reconstruct the conception of the Absolute under the central conviction that the mission of Jesus (and here we include his resurrection and the coming upon his disciples of the Holy Spirit) is, in an altogether unique sense, the actuality of the divine self-impartation to the world. It is a commonplace to point out that how far remote the ontological categories, by which the Chalcedonian definition sought by the concept of hypostatic union to affirm the irreducible uniqueness of the union of ultimately incommensurables is from the simplicities of Galilee; in the doctrine of the Trinity, whether one attends to the tradition classically articulated by the Cappadocians or to the Latin concentration on the divine unity, we find ourselves involved in the use of the same notions—of substance, of property, of relation etc. But even a writer, as traditional as de Régnon, is firmly emphatic that whatever is said *de Deo Trino* is said *analogice*, and in analogy the way of *negation* is always sovereign over that of *eminence*. To claim otherwise is to plunge into the sort of anthropomorphism that involves either an almost overt tritheism or an ultimately monadic conception of the divine mind mitigated only by the sly introduction into the characterization of its activity, of the concepts of different intellectual dispositions which though very properly distinguished in analysis of human awareness, can hardly be extrapolated to the level of the divine without the most rigorous qualification.

What remains, however, unquestionably true, and this is a central thesis of this paper, is that the doctrine of the Trinity has to a very considerable extent been developed out of properly considered relation to the unresolved issues pertaining to the relation of time to God. Here the quotation from Hopkins' *Notebooks* at the outset of the paper was deliberately included to advertise the cruciality of this question. The conception of kenōsis is emphatically (in my judgment) the conception which alone enables us to approach the *arcana* of the divine condescension. It is a conception which is traditional in that it regards the pre-existence of the Word or Son as essential to a valid Christology. It is of course a part of the doctrine of the Trinity to suggest (it can do no more) concerning the manner of that pre-existence, to indicate the eternal relationship that is constitutive of it in so far as it is the pre-existence of a distinguishable person whose distinguishable uniqueness can easily be lost sight of in the torrential energy of the Deity, in the mutual interpenetration of its constitutent persons: energy that is at one and the same time expressive of a total spontaneity and absolute mutual response. Yet within the context of this totally uninhibited, but triadic aseity, we have to reckon with the actuality of limit, of *peras* or boundary. It is through this actuality that, for instance, the *idiotēs* of the Son as eternal receptivity is constituted, a receptivity that in the manner of the Incarnate life is expressed in his dependence, realized in the form of his human submission in respect of the hour of his agony and his glorification, and also in the role of the Spirit Who within his history is presented as effective in the order of his coming and going, but Whom he is also enabled to bestow upon his disciples in the setting of his glorification.[1]

If we suppose that in the theology of the Trinity an *analogia personarum* can be complemented by an analogy of *limits* (in the pregnant sense of the Greek *peras*), it may go some way towards grounding within the eternal, the essentially human element of temporality, the sense of inescapable limitation. For this element of temporality (clearly dependent, as it is, upon awareness of temporal direction as a cosmological ultimate) belongs to the substance of Jesus' comings and goings. What it was for him to be human was to be subject to the sort of fragmentation of effort, curtailment of design, interruption of purpose, distraction of resolve that belongs to temporal experience. To leave one place for another is to leave work undone; to give attention to one suppliant is to ignore another; to expend energy today is to leave less for tomorrow. We have to ask ourselves how far this very conformity to the complex discipline of temporality, this acceptance of the often tragic consequences that spring from its obstinate, ineluctable truncation of human effort, belongs to the very substance of Jesus' defeat. Jesus' acceptance of this part of his burden can arguably be interpreted as a painfully realized transcription into the conditions of our existence, of the receptivity, the defined, even if frontierless, receptivity that constitutes his person. It is indeed as that which makes such transcription possible that we must first see the divine relation to the temporal. It is a relation that we will misunderstand except we see the God so related as triune.

[1] One recalls how very clearly in John 20 the revelation of the risen Lord and the bestowal of Holy Spirit are integrated: indeed deep analysis of that chapter suggests that for the fourth Evangelist, the separate events of Easter, Ascension Day and Pentecost are presented as in fact falling within twenty-four hours, aspects of the single Paschal mystery.

APPENDIX A

Cullman & Bultmann

In fairness to Dr Cullmann, it should be remembered that in his last major work—*Heil als Geschichte*, Tübingen, 1966, he offered a penetrating and sustained criticism of the radical subjectivism that may be judged the central blemish of the theological interpretation of the New Testament by Rudolf Bultmann, and some of his followers, but still more by Professor John Knox. Granted that with the wide influence of the work of such theologians as Wolfhart Pannenberg and Jürgen Moltmann (and the latter's early deep indebtedness to the independent Marxism of Ernst Bloch has understandably proved effective as a liberation from an excessive servitude to the metaphysical studies of Martin Heidegger whether in his *Sein und Zeit*, or in his often very interesting later work), the attraction of the sort of radical subjectivism, which surely reaches its *reductio ad absurdum*, in the excursions into general theology by the much admired New York *Neutestamentler*, John Knox, has declined, it still remains true that Cullmann's contribution in *Heil als Geschichte* to the central theological issue of the last two decades is very valuable. He is indeed very self-consciously a theologian who seeks to eschew any involvement in metaphysical discussion, and in the hostages which in this connexion he is prepared to give to fortune, Bultmann has the edge on him. Yet in his argument against Bultmann, one catches quite clearly the vibration within theology proper, of the unresolved metaphysical controversy between idealism or constructivism and realism. (On this issue see especially Michael Dummett: *Frege: Philosophy of Language*, London, 1973, and his Henriette Herz Lecture before the British Academy in the same year: *The Justification of Deduction*, Oxford, 1973.) In conclusion it might be remarked that a comment on Moltmann's very profound essay *Der gekreuzigte Gott* from a theologian sensitive to the significance for specifically theological issues of the idealist-realist debate might be of considerable value.

APPENDIX B

Küng on Divine Impassibility

It is a weakness of Hans Küng's *Menschwerdung Gottes*, Herder, 1970, that after his very lengthy survey of Hegel's treatment of Christological themes, in a long and impressive chapter devoted to criticism, in the light of lessons extracted from his previous study of the notion of divine impassibility he largely averts from the Trinitarian issues to which inevitably his concentration on Hegel's characteristic theological emphases had directed his attention. The chapter that follows the treatment of impassibility is devoted to an informed, but strangely flaccid and pedestrian, survey of the 'old' and 'new' quests for the historical Jesus. It is a useful summary, and a part-indication of its acknowledged and unacknowledged hostility to the traditional treatises *de Verbo Incarnato*. But it lacks any clear conclusion and is intellectually unsatisfying. Only in the last appendix of his very long work, inspired partly by von Balthasar's *Mysterium Paschale* to treat of Kenosis, does Küng show how he might have converted to most valuable use his brilliantly impressionistic, and admittedly often vulnerable, presentation of Hegel's *oeuvre* in his grounding theologically his rejection of the traditional concept of impassibility in the doctrine of the Trinity, thus indeed showing the way in which the deep insights it enshrines, excellently caught in the late Dr J. K. Mozley's classical monograph on the theme, but also admitted by a theologian as different in temper as the late Dr Reinhold Niebuhr in his Gifford Lectures, might be reconciled with a proper sensitivity to the concrete actuality of the Incarnate.

APPENDIX C

From *Études de Théologie positive sur La Sainte Trinité* by Th. de Régnon, S. J., Vol. 1, Paris, 1892, p. 67.

1 II Section 7

Mais gardons-nous de pousser trop loin cette assimilation, de peur qu'elle n'égare notre pensée. Après avoir constaté les ressemblances, voyons les dissemblances. Saint Damascène nous signale la principale: 'Les hypostases créées, dit-il, sont isolées et non les unes dans les autres . . . En la sainte Trinité, tout le contraire . . . les hypostases sont les unes dans les autres, *ἐν ἀλλήλαις γαρ αἱ ὑποστάσεις εἰσιν*.'[1] Sans entrer encore dans l'étude de cette métaphysique, éclairons-nous à sa lumière.

La personne humaine est inclinée à tout rapporter à soi, et à se rapporter à soi-même. Je ne décide pas si c'est là une nécessité constitutive ou une défectuosité vicieuse. Mais il reste que bien des vices résultent de cette tendance: orgueil, ambition, jalousie, avarice; toutes passions se résumant en un seul mot: *égoïsme*. Par état, le moi est possesseur, je l'accorde; mais, par abus, il devient accapareur; facilement il repousse et exclut le non-moi. Encore un coup, la personne humaine tend à rapporter à soi et sa propre nature et tout le reste.

Hé bien! de la personne divine concevez tout le contraire. Les théologiens en donnent une définition qui semble un paradoxe. Chaque personne divine, disent-ils, est une *relation subsistante*. Expression étrange, puisque, d'après les idées communes, rien n'est moins substance qu'une relation. Mais cette définition a pour but de nous enseigner que, de même que dans une relation chaque terme se rapporte à son corrélatif, de même chaque personne divine, bien que subsistant dans l'identité de la substance infinie, se rapporte tout entière à une autre personne.

Qui dit: 'père', dit: 'père d'un fils'.—Qui dit: 'fils', dit: 'fils d'un père'. Être père, c'est avoir un fils; être fils, c'est avoir un père. Je sais que parmi les hommes la paternité est quelque chose de surajouté, car l'homme est constitué personne humaine, avant qu'il ne soit père. Mais en Dieu toute la personnalité du Père consiste dans la paternité. Tout entier il est père, et par conséquent sa personne tout entière se rapporte à son Fils. A son tour, le Fils n'est pas autre chose que fils au point de vue personnel, et par conséquent sa personne tout entière se rapporte à son Père.

Oh! que sont bien choisis ces noms de Père et de Fils! Ou plutôt que Dieu a été bon et sage, en créant la paternité humaine pour nous permettre de concevoir quelque chose de la Paternité divine! Voyez comme un bon père se penche vers son fils pour se déverser en lui, et comme un bon fils se tourne vers son père pour se rapporter à lui. La gloire du père est son fils, l'honneur du fils est son père.

O mon âme! abandonne-toi à ces nobles pensées. Oublie les égoïsmes humains pour contempler les égoïsmes divins. Conçois, si tu le peux, un père qui ne soit que père, un fils qui ne soit que fils. Tout l'égoïsme de ce père consiste à donner à sons fils toute la substance de ses richesses: *Pater diligit Filium et omnia dedit in*

[1] S. Damascène, *Foi orthod.*, liv. I, ch. VIII.–M. col. 828 et 829.

manu ejus.[1] Tout l'égoïsme du fils est de se rapporter à son père, soi-même et tout le reste, afin que soi-même et tout le reste accomplisse la volonté du père; *non quaero voluntatem meam, sed voluntatem ejus qui misit me*. Encore une fois, le propre d'un tel père est de tout donner à son fils; le propre d'un tel fils est de tout rendre à son père; *et mea omnia tua sunt et tua mea sunt*.

Telle est la manière dont nous devons concevoir une personne divine. Que cette lumière du coeur nous éclaire et nous échauffe, dans la discussion où nous allons reprendre la question d'une façon plus philosophique.

[1] Jean, III, 35.
[2] Jean, V, 30.
[3] Jean, XVII, 10.

8 Creation and Covenant

by ALLAN D. GALLOWAY

Creation and Covenant

The doctrine of creation presents a major systematic difficulty. This consists in its logical and hermeneutical interdependence with every other doctrine of the creed. There is, of course, some measure of logical interdependence between all the doctrines of the faith—otherwise systematic theology could not be the coherent and rational science which it is. But the doctrine of creation is an extreme case. It cannot stand alone. Unless we state or imply something about the nature and attributes of the God who creates, the statement 'God created the world' is vacuous. Consider the following conversation:

A: 'X' created the world.
B: Who or what is 'X'?
A: He is entirely beyond the reach of all our powers of observation. Therefore we can know nothing directly about him. However, we can form some idea of his nature by inference from the kind of world he has created.
B: What is the significance and importance of such inferred knowledge of 'X'?
A: If we know something of the nature and purpose of the being who created the world, we can learn from that, something about our own nature and destiny.
B: It seems to me that 'X' is an unnecessary complication in your argument. Since we can know nothing of 'X' by direct observation, he or it adds nothing to the information. In so far as such inferences are possible we can reach the same conclusions about the nature and destiny of man and his world from direct observation without reference to 'X'. Entities should not be multiplied beyond necessity.

The above conversation is, of course, an over-simplification. There are a great many subtle gambits which 'A' can still employ. But ultimately the outcome is the same. The above conversation is a fair caricature or cartoon of the fate of the doctrine of creation during the past century from Hegel through Feuerbach, Marx and Nietzsche.

The world can declare itself only as world. It cannot declare itself as God's action. Only God's own action can declare itself as such. God's action becomes articulate and declares itself in the history and tradition of Israel, in the culmination of that history in Jesus Christ, and in its continuation in the life of the Church. I do not make this statement in a spirit of dogmatic arrogance or perverse particularism. At this stage I state it merely as a fact of our religio-cultural history. This is how the Judaeo-Christian doctrine of creation came to us.

It is only in the context of a tradition in which it is claimed that God discloses himself to be more than and other than the world that the doctrine of creation becomes an informative statement, making its own distinctive truth claim. It is only thus that it can affirm anything more than can be affirmed directly about the nature and destiny of man and his world without any reference to God.

The heavens do not in fact declare God's glory (not, at any rate, until they have been made articulate and made to sing a new song). The heavens and earth declare their own glory. In this respect there is a measure of logical self-consistency in the kind of cosmogonic mythologies which originate outside the biblical tradition. In Egyptian mythologies Re/Osiris *is* the glory of the sun in its passage across the heavens by day and through the land of the dead by night. Taimat, Ea, Enki and all the host of the Babylonian pantheon *are* the elements and processes of nature in their own divine splendour. The Canaanite El, Ba'al, Anat, etc. *are* identified with the fertility cycle in nature. They are the world, the cosmos or nature declaring its own glory.

The biblical traditions about creation declare something different. It is well known, of course, that the biblical creation stories use conceptual and symbolic material from these cosmogonies. But this mythological material is set in a new context which altogether transforms its significance. This context is the self-revelation of the God of Israel.

But although the Judaeo-Christian doctrine of creation must therefore be regarded as a revealed doctrine this does not mean that its disclosure is something that takes place apart from and outside the created world. The doctrine of the creation of heaven and earth by the God of Israel, the Father of Jesus Christ, is not a secret, divine communication to inspired initiates. It belongs to public history. It takes place *in* the world. But it is not the self-expression of the world.

It was not speculation about the nature and origin of the world which gave rise to the Judaeo-Christian doctrine of creation. It was generated out of concrete, historical events. Indeed it was fairly late in the history of Israel that an *explicit* formulation of the doctrine of creation was developed. The initial events which ultimately generated the knowledge of God the Lord and Creator in the life of Israel were such that:

(a) They engendered an experience of radical insecurity for a people with no place, no identity, no future or destiny of their own. This alienating experience already implied an estrangement from the in-dwelling cosmogonic gods and their progeny. (Abraham left his household gods behind.)

(b) The events which engendered this experience of alienation and insecurity also engendered a faith in a God who could match and over-match this radical insecurity in the absolute consistency and irresistible efficacy of his support. This support was forthcoming in his concrete action in history. Such unshakable consistency and irresistible efficacy are conceivable only on the basis of absolute transcendence and sovereignty. At first this was expressed simply in affirming Yahweh's unqualified ascendancy over the cosmogonic and nature divinities in the provenance of Israel. Eventually it was expressed in an explicit doctrine of creation.

In all this there is little sign of speculation about the origin of the universe. The biblical traditions about creation do not arise as an answer to that question. They are not the answer to any prior question. The biblical doctrine of creation is rather the proclamation that there is only one god who is truly God. He is the God of Israel. When that proclamation is received in faith the speculative question about the origin of creatures does not arise. It is answered before it is asked. If God is truly God in the sense in which Israel believed in him, there is nothing else that can stand against or even beside him to limit his power or to share his glory.

Thus the doctrine of *creatio ex nihilo* is implicated in the faith of Israel from the beginning. The idea of *creatio ex nihilo* did not begin to receive explicit formulation until the inter-testamental period (2 Macc. 7:28). It was later threatened by the assimilation of the Christian doctrine to Greek cosmogonic philosophies. The *tohu wabhohu* of Genesis 1 was assimilated to the Platonic notion of unformed matter. But this was a deviation resulting from an incautious mixing of two quite different conceptualities.

The adoption of Greek conceptuality in the Hellenistic church to express and define the doctrine of creation and God's relation to the world was as necessary and inevitable as was the original use in the biblical sources of words and symbols drawn from Ancient Near Eastern mythologies. Otherwise Christianity would have remained an isolated sect of Judaism culturally irrelevant and historically moribund. But just as the mythological material had to be transformed by assimilation to its new context, so also the conceptuality of Greek philosophy. Indeed the two cases are quite similar in that the Greek philosophy of Being arose largely out of a demythologizing and sophistication of earlier cosmogonic myths. A dialectical relation between Being and non-Being (or unformed matter) could not adequately express the freedom of the biblical God. Despite initial vacillation, early Christian theology was quick to effect the necessary transformation in the doctrine of *creatio ex nihilo*. It is already taken for granted by both Irenaeus and Tertullian.

The 'nothing' which is implicated in the biblical tradition (I use the word 'implicated' rather than 'implied', for the doctrine of *creatio ex nihilo* was not so much deduced as discovered to be an unspoken content which was there all along) is not a non-Being dialectically related to the Being of God. It is not conceived in any kind of positive, ontological terms. It is conceived rather in terms of absence of power and meaning (cf. Aquinas' *non ex aliquid*). It is non-potency. It is the absence of power to effect anything. It is non-sense. In modern parlance, 'It doesn't mean a thing'. There is nothing which enters into relation with God—not even a negative relation—except by God's will and power.

It is this that determines the Hebrew metaphysics (if metaphysics is the right word) of spirit and flesh (so different from the Greek mind/matter distinction). Every aspect of creation—whether mental or physical—in respect of its relation to the positive will of God is spirit. In this respect it is efficacious and significant. Considered in itself—apart from its relation to God, the only source of efficacious power—it amounts to nothing. It can effect nothing. It means nothing. It is mere flesh (*basar*). This applies to heart and mind as well as body.

The whole creation is spirit in respect of its relation to God the creator and preserver. It is flesh in respect of its total inefficacy and insignificance apart from God. As flesh it bears the stamp of *ex nihilo*.

Covenant and Creation

The whole theology of the Old Testament cannot be written round the concept of covenant. Indeed surprisingly little of it is explicitly federal. But the idea is so fundamental to those aspects of Israelite theology which inform the doctrine of creation that I propose to concentrate upon it. I shall use the idea of covenant in a fairly broad sense.

Covenant is the freely given faithfulness of God upon which our faith rests. It obliges us to faithfulness not as a contract between two parties, but because it deserves no other response. Creation takes place in the free, unforced, unshakable will of God. It therefore has the character of God's initial covenant. He creates what is other than himself in order to have that kind of relation with it. Admittedly the word 'covenant' is not used in the creation narratives. But it is implied and is made explicit in the Noachic covenant with all creation.

What is the relation of this covenant with all creation to the special covenant with Israel?

The scandal of God's apparent favouritism towards the Jews has troubled many people from St Paul onwards.

One must remember first of all that the covenant with Abraham is one which takes place within the context of the universal covenant with all creation. It is not an additional covenant. It is a re-affirmation of the universal covenant as it relates to a specific person in a specific place and time. It is re-affirmed in such a way that what has been true all along of the relation between creator and creature, but has become hidden through a distorted perception of the world, is again uncovered in its meaning for this particular man and people. In this respect the covenant with Abraham is special only in the sense that it becomes the paradigm case which is the key to the 'grammar' of creation.

Consider what was promised to Abraham. He was promised a place which would be *his* place, a significant role in the fruitfulness of the created time process, and the confronting presence of his God to give and determine the meaning of his life. This is not a special privilege. It is the paradigm of what God gives to every creature he creates—a footing in space-time with and in the face of his own confronting and sustaining presence.

This last element in the universal covenant of creation is of crucial importance. Merely to have an existence which could be exhaustively described in terms of our measurable space-time relations would be to exist without sense or meaning. It would be mere happening. The doctrine of creation is not merely about the being of the world but also about its meaning. It involves not only the bare act of creation but also the address of the Creator to his creature—his coming to us in his Word. It is his *Ad*vent that turns mere *ev*ent into *ad*venture—i.e., into absorbingly significant life.

Creation and the New Covenant

But this confronting presence of God in and to the creature (which is central to the doctrine of creation because it is the whole point and purpose of creation, i.e., God's love of and delight in the creature) is not a pervasive property of creation as, for example, light is a constant in the space-time process. It is closer to us than mere ubiquity just as friendship or love is closer than mere proximity. It is advent rather than presence. It is an awesome, gracious coming which can never be taken for granted (any more than human friendship or love can). It is definite, local and particular. It took place in the history of Israel. It has its centre in Jesus Christ going about among the people of Galilee. Therefore Jesus Christ, crucified and risen, is the one who gives body and content to the doctrine of creation. He is the manifestation and the reality of what God's action in creation is all about.

Therefore when we affirm 'I believe in God the Father almighty, maker of heaven and earth' we are affirming that it is precisely the God who is revealed as the Father of our Lord Jesus Christ, and none other, who is the Creator. (Otherwise we go back to the uninformative or only trivially informative talk about a necessary and self-existent 'X'.) All things were made through or by the Word who became incarnate. In him all things consist. His resurrection anticipates the end of all creation.

The witness of creation to the Creator

I said at the beginning of this essay that the heavens do not declare God's glory. They declare their own. The world can declare itself only as world. This had to be said first. But when the world is perceived within the context of this covenant faith, then the heavens do disclose his glory and the hills sing out his praise. The stars and the galaxies witness to the mystery of his power and his majesty. 'When, however, through God's Word the "inward eye" of man is really enlightened, then he is also able to see the divine revelation in Creation, as it really is; then he is able to understand the *analogia entis* aright, and to praise God the Creator in the works of his creation.'[1]

In this respect the doctrine of Creation bears some analogy to these major scientific theories which are more than mere hypotheses in that in some measure they determine the way one looks at the evidence. To some extent they determine what is to count as a fact. They are thus to some extent self-confirming.

But this does not mean that either scientific theories or the doctrine of creation are arbitrary or subjective. It is not just a case of 'seeing as' where the evidence will bear either interpretation indifferently (cf. Wittgenstein's duck/rabbit, etc.). Major scientific theories are adopted in the process of adequating the mind to reality. They are adopted because they make sense of what would not otherwise make sense. Similarly the doctrine of creation.

[1] Brunner, *Dogmatics*, II, p. 23.

The prime fact with which we have to deal is that we have received this tradition which commends itself as God's Word. (There is neither space nor time to become embroiled with rival theories of revelation here.) This Word has the power to disrupt and disconcert our normal egocentric and concupiscent relation to the world.

We learn from that tradition that God created the world by his Word. What it means for 'Word' to be performative in this absolute sense cannot be imagined. (That would be to try to understand God's Word from the point of view of his speaking it rather than our hearing it.) But from the standpoint of our hearing it does mean that creation is an *intelligible* order.

This not only means that it is amenable to scientific, mathematical, logical treatment (though that is important, for it is the basis of science and the fundamentally irenic relation between science and theology). It means also that the created order is comprehensible in a wider sense. The Word of God is a personal word. It has the character of *personal* rationality. It provides a significant, comprehensible context for human life and action. It has a structure and a meaning which is correlative with the indwelling word which is the light that 'lighteneth every man that cometh into the world'. It is the basis of that quality of personal rationality which we know as *sanity*. Man can live out his sane, personal rationality only in an environment which has a meaning that offers him the opportunity for significant orientation in action and integrity of response. The doctrine of creation, entertained in lively faith, opens up the meaning and reality of the world to us in just this way. It tends to restore a sane and rational perception of and response to the world. It stands over against the twin *malaises* of our fallen human rationality—schizophrenic fragmentation and loss of meaning on the one hand and paranoid withdrawal from reality into private fantasies on the other.

But if this talk of perceiving of the world as a created order having a comprehensible rationality in which human rationality can thrive is to be more than empty words, it must be shown to have real cash value in Christian experience. The best way to approach this is through the inter-personal aspect of our wordly relations. It is well known and central to distinctively Christian encounter with the world that acknowledgment in faith of the truth of God's word and action in Christ involves a new perception of our neighbour. To see the neighbour in Christ is to see the meaning of his creatureliness in his brotherhood with Christ. It is Christ's eyes that look at us out of the eyes of the stranger. In ministering to his need, we minister to Christ. In encountering the neighbour thus, we perceive his reality as God's creature. We have begun to understand the 'grammar' of creation.

But it has recently been borne in upon us (through belated awareness of the ecological crisis which has always been with us) that the neighbourly relation cannot be confined and delimited to the realm of the inter-personal—though that is its centre. The neighbourly relation involves all our relations with the whole eco-system of which we are a part. Therefore the new perception of the reality of our neighbour as neighbour in Christ involves also a new perception of the whole world. It is then that the truth of the world as God's beloved creature begins to open itself to us. We begin to perceive the meaning of the doctrine of creation.

In the light of this one should not speak of the orders of creation—which, in any case, is a notoriously unbiblical concept. It suggests a system of static, institutional orders established by divine legislation. One should speak rather of the order of creation, in the singular. It is a single, comprehensible order. It is comprehensible in terms of the kind of rationality which constitutes the structural integrity and sanity of persons. An important aspect of the doctrine of *creatio ex nihilo* is that it not only affirms the absolute sovereignty and transcendence of God but also, in denying any kind of pre-existent substance or potentiality outside of God, it affirms the ontological priority of personal over impersonal Being.[1]

But the meaning of the doctrine of creation cannot be appreciated simply as a matter of 'pure' theological theory. Just as the perception of neighbour as neighbour in Christ cannot be separated from neighbourly action; so the perception of the world as created by God and made articulate through the Word who became incarnate in Jesus Christ is not independent of the way we use the world. A concupiscent misuse of the world dulls the ear to its voice.

The Creation of Heaven

God created not only the earth but heaven. It is likely that the *shamayim* referred to in the account given of creation in the Priestly Code in Genesis I refers primarily to the skies. But in a pre-Ptolemaic universe there could be an identity of the physical heaven and 'heaven' conceived as God's habitat or the place of his nearer or more intimate dwelling.

What, if anything, are we to make of the creation of heaven today? It seems to me to be of the greatest importance that the world has a heavenly counterpart which is its fellow-creature. Clearly this can no longer be thought of as a location. But we still use spatial metaphors to speak of it. Heaven is 'beyond' the world, 'beyond' space-time.

Much has been made recently of man's openness beyond his world.

[1] John Zizioulas, 'Human Capacity and Incapacity' SJT, 1975, pp. 401–44.

He is open beyond his given world in hope, freedom, aspiration, imagination as well as in his relation to such absolutes as truth, goodness, beauty. But the 'beyond' of man's world is also the source of his worst anxieties, fears and terrors. It is the whole realm of unfulfilled possibility out of which anything can come. It is the black hole of despair. It is the pit of hell. Our sanatoria are full of people who live on its brink and see only its black depth.

To be a whole and wholesome personal being, man needs to encounter meaning not only in his world, but also in the 'beyond' of his world. The doctrine that God created heaven as well as earth, whatever more it may mean, means at least this: that the 'beyond' of man's world is not an empty and meaningless ground of anxiety. It is full of the holy and blessed powers of God. It beckons us as a ground for hope and expectation. We may have demythologized angels long ago. But we must not discard what the idea of the heavenly creation represented.

Because the notion of the 'beyond' of man's world is so intimately bound up with the thought of the yet unrealized future some attempts have been made to identify transcendence and futurity—or to explain transcendence in terms of futurity. Thus there is talk—especially in Pannenberg and, in a different sense, in Moltmann—of the futurity of God. There is the suggestion that God creates out of the future rather than as *arche* or first principle at the beginning of time. He creates out of his own eschatological end-time where the beginning and the end, *alpha* and *omega*, meet and God is all in all. Like many others I have been greatly stimulated and excited by this complex of ideas. They bring together creation and eschatology, ethics and grace, politics and the kingdom of God, history and revelation in a new and fruitful relation.

But the idea of eschatological futurity can never become a substitute for that of a heavenly realm created 'in the beginning'. We have over-reacted so strongly against a dualistic understanding of the relation between heaven and earth that in our theologies we have almost lost the vision of heaven altogether. The 'beyond' of man's space-time world is not merely his future. It is also his past which slips away from him beyond recall. The created heaven is as much of the past as of the future. It is where our treasure lies.

The 'beyond' of man's world is not only the 'beyond' of outer space-time. It is also the 'beyond' of inner space-time. St Paul could speak of being caught up into heaven in his prayer and meditation. Nowadays, especially in the Protestant tradition, we have so neglected to teach and interpret the doctrine of the spiritual creation that when many set out to explore the inner space of their lives they do so in the hope of finding nothing better than an entirely empty Nirvana.

Here and now heaven is as much part of our created environment as earth. Man is the creature in whom heaven and earth meet.

The Dominion of Man and the Ecological Crisis

Until recently it was fashionable to upbraid Christianity—especially in its Calvinistic expression—for its denigration of humanity in the doctrines of Fall and depravity. In the present awareness of the ecological crisis it has become fashionable to blame the Christian exaltation of man above all other creatures—especially in the Calvinist tradition—for the rapaciousness of Western culture in using and abusing the earth's resources. This emphasis on the sovereignty of man over creation is based upon and derived from the model of God's sovereignty.

It used to be the boast of Christian theologians that the Hebraic emphasis on God's absolute and transcendent sovereignty over creation dedivinized and disenchanted the natural order in a way which made the objectivity of science and the controlling attitude of technology possible. There is probably some truth in this, though the claim has often been exaggerated. But this claim too has now been turned against us. This de-divinizing of nature, it is alleged, has engendered the controlling, technological, utilitarian attitude to nature which is the spiritual root of the present ecological malaise. There is some truth in this too, though the point is often made without appropriate qualification or substantiation.

John Macquarrie has recently addressed himself to this problem.[1] He contrasts two models of God's relation to creation—the monarchical and the organic. He argues in defence of the organic model. Certainly, the organic model avoids some of the worst abuses to which the monarchic model is open. But it does open the way to a renewed flirtation with the cosmogonic myths and the assimilation to God of some of the aspects of nature divinities. John Macquarrie is not unduly worried by this. He quotes Richard Rubenstein's remark: 'The priests of ancient Israel wisely never suffered Yahweh entirely to win the war with Baal, Astarte and Anath'.

I can agree with the intention of these remarks, though I reject their conclusion. Certainly we need to make more edifying use of the doctrine of creation to enable man to realize his holy communion with all nature within the covenant of God. We need to bring *eros* more frankly and fully into the content of *agape*. But this is not to be achieved by adding a dash of piquant paganism to our theology.

Our choice is not limited to the disjunction between monarchic and organic models. In an earlier part of this essay I referred to the Judaeo-Christian doctrine of creation as asserting the ontological

[1] 'Creation and Environment', *Thinking About God*, pp. 142 ff.

primacy of the personal. This suggests that our model should be personal and societal rather than either monarchic (at least in the narrow sense in which it was condemned by Tertullian) or organic. The model is the personal and societal nature of God himself in his three-fold being.

Hegel came as near to seeing and applying the richness of this model to the whole created space-time process as any man in the modern West. But he so confused and mixed the nature of the Creator with the nature of the created that he lost the primacy of the personal in the societal model and slipped back into the organic. This left the way open for Feuerbach and Marx.

It seems to me to be broadly true that the spirit of modern capitalism has its roots in a too narrowly monarchic view of creation. The spirit of dialectical materialism has its roots in an incautiously organic view of creation. Neither will do. A new perception of the covenanted character of the whole created order yields a new vision of society beyond these alternatives and a new mode of participation in the whole eco-system.

9 Creation and Redemption

by JÜRGEN MOLTMANN

I. *Two Problems*

(1) It is a well-known fact that since the beginning of modern times the relationship between belief in creation and natural science has become problematic. Natural science has broken free from the religious culture of the Middle Ages and established the foundations of modern secular culture. Theology has become apologetic and offered no more than token resistance to the triumphal progress of natural science: this has taken the form, in the case of *deism*, of reducing belief in creation to a concern for the contingent origin of the universe;[1] it has also taken the form, in the case of *existentialism*, of reducing such belief to a concern for the personal and contingent character of all human existence;[2] or it has taken the further form of so separating *Church Dogmatics* from natural science that the one has neither disturbed nor had anything to say to the other.[3] In its intention to co-exist with natural science, theology has itself deepened the division which it wished to overcome. If we, today, are striving to achieve some form of reconciliation between belief in creation and natural science, then this presupposes that both the traditional theological concept of creation, as well as the concept of nature found in classical natural science, must be revised. However, if man and nature are to have any chance of surviving—especially in view of the ecological crisis and the progressive destruction of nature brought about by both Christianity and natural science—then we must also revise both the understanding of man present in the traditional doctrine of creation: 'Have dominion over the earth' (Gen. 1:28), as well as the understanding of man present in Cartesian natural science: 'Master and possessor of nature'.

(2) Since the development of christian dogmatics within the context of Greek thought, theological method has always begun with an

[1] See A. Koyré, *From the Closed World to the Infinite Universe*, New York, 1959.

[2] F. Gogarten and R. Bultmann have advocated this solution. By way of criticism, see C. J. Dippel/J. M. de Jeng, *Geloof en Naturwetenshap*, 1965.

[3] See K. Barth, *Church Dogmatics*, III, 1, Edinburgh, 1958, Preface. It is evident from his anthropology, presented in volume 3 of the CD, that Barth did not maintain this peaceful separation of theology from natural science.

account of the creation of the world and only after that come to a concept of the redemption of the world. As a consequence of this way of thinking redemption has always been related to creation and understood from the perspective of creation. With the creation of the world everything was already fundamentally established. In the beginning was God, the Creator, and his creation was both very good and perfect. At the end it will once again be as it was in the beginning: *ta eschata hos ta prota.* Redemption is, therefore, to be understood as the restoration of the original, good creation: *restitutio in integrum.* If redemption is thus understood from the perspective of and in relation to the creation, then one is left with a *'protological' understanding of eschatology.* The history between creation and redemption becomes no more than the history of the fall of man. It can produce nothing new apart from the increasing deterioration and obsolescence of the creation itself. Redemption becomes, first and foremost, the restoration of the creation. The revision of the doctrine of creation, which is necessary today both (a) on exegetical grounds and (b) in the light of our experience of and dealings with nature, depends upon our conversion to an *'eschatological' understanding of creation.* This means that eschatology is no longer to be understood in the light of creation but rather that creation is to be understood in the light of eschatology.[1]

II. *Is creation a closed or an open system?*

The word creation (Schöpfung) signifies by its suffix both the completed act of creation and its product. Accordingly in talking theologically about creation we think involuntarily of the original condition of the world and of the beginning of all things: we conceive of this condition as being closed, completed and perfect. Belief in creation reiterates the judgment of the Creator upon his creation: 'Behold, it was very good'. Unfortunately, however, man cannot accept the judgment of the Creator for experience tells him: 'Behold, it is unfortunately not very good'. This difference between the judgment of faith and experience has had the following consequence. The creation which was very good has been placed before history and, as an idea of religious memory, has been represented in terms of myths and cosmic origins. Dogmatic theology has called Adam's state in paradise the *status integritatis.* As the man created 'very

[1] I am in full agreement with W. Pannenberg in trying to develop an eschatological doctrine of creation. See *Erwägungen zu einer Theologie der Natur*, Güterloh, 1970; *Theology and the Kingdom of God*, Philadelphia, 1969. I believe, however, that his presentation of the being of God as 'the power of the future' is one-sided because it ignores the power of the 'suffering of God'. See my book: *The Crucified God*, London, 1974.

good', Adam possessed *justitia et sanctitas originalis*. The first human beings were expelled from this perfect state on account of their sin. Redemption, however, leads men back to this sound condition. What, then, is history? It is, first of all, *paradise lost* and, as such, the way into the far country. What is redemption? It is the way back which finally results in *paradise regained*. Sin perverts the good creation. Grace restores it again. Out of the history of sin and grace re-emerges the good creation as it originally was. This outline corresponds, from the point of view of the history of religions, to that described by *Mircea Eliade*.[1] Did not *Thomas Aquinas*, moreover, have the same thing in mind when he said: 'Finis rerum respondet principio, Deus enim principium et finis rerum. Ergo et exitus rerum a principio respondet reductioni rerum in finem'? In any case time had for Thomas a symmetrical and circular structure: 'In exitu creaturarum a primo principio attenditur quaedam circulatio vel regiratio, eo quod omnia revertuntur sicut in finem in id, a quo sicut principio prodierunt. Et ideo oportet ut per eadem quibus est exitus in principio, et reditus in finem attendatur.'[2] Indeed does not *Rudolf Bultmann*, despite his 'demythologization programme', have the same thing in mind when he says: 'no other light has appeared with Jesus apart from that which already shines in creation. Man ought already to understand himself, in view of the revelation in creation and law, as God's creature and he does not have to understand himself any differently in the light of the revelation of redemption?' In any case time has also for Bultmann a symmetrical and circular structure: 'what meaning does the justice of God or the forgiveness of sin have? . . . It consists of the fact that the original relation to creation is restored.'[3]

According to the evidence provided by both terminology and the traditional interpretation, the original creation is non-historical. History only begins with the fall of man and it ends with the restoration of creation in redemption. Creation itself lies outside of time and history. The picture of creation which emerges from this is one of a closed, perfect and self-sufficient system.

This conception of creation, however, cannot be maintained in the light of modern exegesis of the Old and New Testaments. From the biblical point of view it is belief in the historical events of salvation which determines belief in creation: moreover, in so far as redemption determines belief in the historical events of salvation,

[1] M. Eliade, *The Myth of the Eternal Return*, Baltimore, 1957; W. F. Otto, *Die Gestalt und das Sein*, München, 1955; E. Hornung, *Die Geschichte als Fest*, Darmstadt, 1966.

[2] Thomas Aquinas, *S.Th.* I, 90, 3ad–2 and I.Sent.d.14 q 2 a 2. See M. Seckler, *Das Heil in der Geschichte*. Geschichtstheologisches Denken bei Thomas von Aquin, München, 1964.

[3] R. Bultmann, *Glauben und Verstehen*, III, Tübingen, 1960, 29, 26.

it also determines eschatology, the experience of history and belief in creation. We can list the following systematically important results of Old Testament exegesis:

(1) Israelite belief in creation arose out of her experience of God within history—Exodus, Covenant and Settlement—and it is moulded by this experience. Israel had a 'soteriological understanding of the work of creation'.[1]

(2) Creation in the beginning, both for the Yahwist and the Priestly writer, does not signify an original redeemed condition but rather that history which is prior to the history of salvation itself. Thus the creation along with its orders, is understood as a product of Yahweh's grace and it is narrated in the form of *toledoth*. 'The prospect of history is introduced,[2] through creation at the beginning. The history of God's relationship to the world begins with creation itself and not just the fall of man. Creation is executed with a view to the future, so that we are able to say: "Creation is an eschatological concept in the theology of the Old Testament".'[3]

(3) The expression 'in the beginning God created' places time within the context of creation. If time, however, originates with *creation in the beginning*, the creation must be subject to change from the very beginning, for time is only experienced through change. Yet if creation is both subject to change and temporal in character from the very beginning, then it cannot be a 'closed system' but must rather be an 'open system'. Moreover time that originates with the creation itself does not have a symmetrical structure in terms of which future and past, goal and origin relate to one another like the two halves of a circle. Rather it must have an asymmetrical structure. It is open towards a future which is not merely a return to the beginning understood as *restitutio in integrum*. Various scholars have noted that the consummation of creation 'at the end' is already brought into focus by the phrase 'creation at the beginning', because the idea of *acharith* also belongs to that of *reshith*.[4] In any case if

[1] G. von Rad, *Theology of the Old Testament*, I, Edinburgh, 1962, pp. 140 ff.; W. Schmidt, *Die Schöpfungsgeschichte*, Neukirchen, 1967.

[2] G. von Rad, *op. cit.*, p. 143. [The Hebrew word *toledoth* is used in Genesis 2.4, at the conclusion of the Priestly account of creation. RSV translates it by 'the generations', while NEB uses 'the story (of the making)'. Elsewhere *toledoth* has the meaning 'genealogy' or 'family history' (cf. Gen. 5:1, 6:9, 10:1 etc.), being a derivative of the verb *yalad*= 'he begot'. According to von Rad (*Genesis, ad loc.*), Gen. 5:1 was the beginning of an 'old *toledoth* book' (i.e. a series of genealogies), which formed the nucleus of the Priestly Work. In front of this the account of creation was placed, a link being formed by the (now wider) use of the word *toledoth* in Gen. 2:4. (Ed.)]

[3] L. Köhler, *Theologie des Alten Testamentes*, 1966^4, 72.

[4] H. D. Preuss, *Jahweglaube und Zukuntshoffnung*, Stuttgart, 1968, pp. 97 f. [*Acharith* is a Hebrew word for 'end' (as in the phrase 'in the end of the days',

that does not follow directly from the concept 'at the beginning', then according to the Priestly writer creation at the beginning is related to the 'rest of God' and according to the Yahwist this is related to the universal fulfilment of the blessing of Abraham. Objectives defined in this way may be designated eschatological. 'To the beginning there corresponds an end, to the creation a consummation, to the "very good" here a "quite glorious" there.'[1]

Thus it follows that theology must speak of creation not only at the beginning but also in history, at the end and in relation to the totality of divine creative activity. 'Creation' as the epitome of God's creative activity embraces creation at the beginning, creative activity in history and creation at the end. It embraces creative activity at the beginning, creative activity within history and the eschatological consummation. By limiting the concept of creation to 'at the beginning' the traditions have separated either 'creation from redemption', or 'nature from supernature' or 'the first from the second creation'. As a consequence of this the continuity and unity of the divine creative activity has been brought into question. Only through an understanding of the process of creation as coherent and eschatologically oriented can the concepts of both the unity of God and of the unity of meaning within his creative activity be maintained. If this is correct, then the place of man within creation is also altered: he is not just the creature made in the image of God, standing over against the non-human creation of God as its master; rather, he stands together with all other living things in the ongoing process of a creation which is still open and incomplete. For creation is not a *factum* but a *fieri*. This also leads to a new interpretation of the situation of man in creation. 'Have dominion over the earth' cannot be the last word concerning this situation.

If theology wants to offer a comprehensive outline of the creative activity of God, then it must focus upon the creation as that reality which is still open and in the process of being created. Expressed in terms of traditional concepts we understand by this the unity of the *regnum naturae*, the *regnum gratiae* and the *regnum gloriae*, all together viewed in an eschatological perspective. Creation at the beginning points forward to the history of salvation and both point beyond themselves to the kingdom of glory. It is the kingdom of glory, and not just the covenant of grace, which is the 'inner ground' of creation at the beginning, for the kingdom of glory is that which motivates the history of the covenant of God with man. Nevertheless

which is found in eschatological contexts, though not exclusively so). *Reshith* is the Hebrew word for 'beginning' (as in Genesis 1:1). (Ed.)]

[1] L. Köhler, *op. cit.*, p. 74.

in the uniformly oriented process of creation towards glory, we can distinguish, in accordance with various conditions, between:

(a) creation at the beginning
(b) creative activity in history
(c) creation at the end.

III. *Creation at the beginning*

Creation at the beginning is, according to the texts, clearly creation independent of any presuppositions. The expression *creatio ex nihilo* (in Platonic terminology *ouk on* not *me on*) ought to convey both the freedom of the Creator and the contingent character of everything that exists; this contingent character refers not just to the origin but to the ongoing fundamental nature of everything that is. The question 'why is there anything and rather than nothing?' cannot be answered by referring either to some prior necessity or to pure chance. *Creatio ex nihilo* expresses negatively the positive basis for the creation, namely the good pleasure of God. The Creator, out of the 'inner necessity of his love' (Barth), creates something that is congenial and well pleasing to himself. The creation, for all its contingency, is thus meaningful. This basis makes it, as opposed to *Chance and Necessity* (J. Monod) both gratifying and worthy of love.[1]

Creation at the beginning is simultaneously the creation of time; therefore it must be understood as *creatio mutabilis*. It is not perfect, but perfectible, in that it is open both to the history of damnation and salvation as well as to destruction and consummation. If we understand creation, in its individual parts as well as in its totality, as an *open system*, then the conditions for both its history and its consummation are established simultaneous with its beginning.[2] Creation at the beginning establishes the conditions for the possibilities emergent in the history of creation. It defines the experimental area for both constructive and destructive possibilities. It is

[1] Concerning necessity, chance and pleasure in the theory of play, see J Moltmann, *Theology and Joy*, London, 1973.

[2] The openness of a system means: (1) that the system has various possibilities for change, (2) that its future behaviour is not wholly determined by the present, (3) that it is open to communication with other systems, (4) that the final condition of the system is different from that at the beginning. Seen from the point of view of natural science, the 'closed system' is no more than a hypothesis for making quantifiable assertions. There is no such thing as a 'closed system'; at any rate no assertions can be made about closed systems because they are not amenable to observation. Assertions can only be made about open systems; with these an exchange of information is possible. A closed system may be defined as one that is not assimilated to its environment.

open to time and to its own alteration within time. We can see in it not the unvarying nature of history but, rather, the beginning of the history of nature. Creation at the beginning is not a balanced or fulfilled reality.

As the creation narratives themselves indicate, creation at the beginning is out of chaos: it is also the establishment of order within chaos. In the language of biblical mythology 'darkness' and 'the waters', the forces of chaos, rise up against creation until they are rejected and overcome by God. *Creatio ex nihilo* is thus also *creatio in nihilo* and consequently a creation that is threatened and yet only partially protected against such threat. In the apocalyptic visions of creation at the end the forces of chaos which rise up again are found wanting (Rev. 21:1; 22:5). Creation in the kingdom of glory shall no longer be either threatened or vulnerable. If God is 'all in all' in creation (I Cor. 15:28), then his glory shall visibly penetrate everything and conquer not only destruction and death but also the very possibility of both. The Augustinian doctrine of freewill makes the same point: the *posse non peccare* at the beginning shall be overcome by the *non posse peccare* at the end; the *posse non mori* at the beginning shall be overcome by the *non posse mori* at the end. Thus it follows, by way of conclusion, that man was created with open possibilities. He is destined, certainly, for justice and not for sin, for glory and not for death. He can, however, fail to achieve this appointed destiny. Such failure cannot be described, in ontological terms, as 'the impossible possibility' (Barth) but is better described, in ethical terms, as a possibility which has not been realized.

IV. *Creative activity in history*

If we attribute to Israel a soteriological understanding of creation at the beginning, then we must also acknowledge that Israel had an understanding of salvation in history which was itself related to creation. The word *bara'* is employed by the Prophets more frequently with reference to the divine creative activity in new, unexpected and unmerited salvation in history than with reference to creation at the beginning. The Prophets, like the Psalms, saw the historical exodus and the creation of the world, the creation of the world and the final, universal exodus all within one perspective. Moreover, belief in creation also gives support to belief in salvation, in that, for the latter, salvation arises out of God's new creative activity. So creation at the beginning can be praised as an act of salvation and redemption can be awaited as a new creation.

The *bara'* events in history are the free acts of God and, as such, contingent. However, like creation at the beginning, they are not without their presuppositions. They are presented as the new creation emerging out of the old, as salvation arising out of misery and as life being given to dead bones. The divine creative activity at the beginning through the Word is conceived of as being effortless: but the divine creative activity in redemption is understood in terms of the effort and work of God (Is. 43:24; 55). The creative and redemptive activity on behalf of those people outside the orbit of salvation arises out of the suffering of the love of God for his people. Because Israel understood herself as being an example for all people and for the whole creation, we can consider her experience of history as being exemplary for our understanding of history in general. The hidden activity of God in history is here made manifest in an exemplary fashion.

To what does the divine creative activity in history relate? Theological language relates salvation to sin and redemption to slavery. What, however, are we to understand by sin and slavery? If we have described creation at the beginning as a system open to time and to possibility, then we can now understand *sin and slavery* as the self-imposed isolation of open systems from their own time and possibilities.[1] 'Sin is isolation' (Ch. Péguy). If man closes himself off from his own possibilities, then he settles the question concerning his own reality and attempts both to establish his present situation and to maintain it against all possible change. He, thus, becomes *homo incurvatus in se*. If a human society establishes itself as a closed system, one that wants to be self-sufficient, then something similar happens: such a society will project its present reality into the future and merely perpetuate itself. The future is lost to it as the arena of possible change. As a consequence, it sacrifices its freedom. Such a society becomes *societas incurvata in se*. Natural history shows that if other creatures isolate themselves from the future, immunize themselves against change and break off communication with their fellow creatures, then this leads to self-destruction and to death. Although isolation among men and in human societies is quite peculiar in that both man and his societies have specific vocations, analogous phenomena among other creatures may also be pointed out. While the word 'sin' can only indicate human failure, the concept of fatal self-isolation can lead to a wider understanding of the 'slavery of the whole creation to futility', of which Paul speaks in Rom. 8:19 ff.

If God acts creatively in history to effect the salvation of these people who stand outside the orbit of salvation, then he liberates them from slavery which they have either brought upon themselves or had imposed on them by others. If he acts creatively in grace towards the sinner, then he liberates him from his self alienation. We can, therefore, describe salvation in history as the divine opening

[1] See W. Pannenberg, *Theology and the Kingdom of God*, p. 27.

of 'closed systems'. The man who has alienated himself is liberated and opened to his own future. A closed society is brought to life so that it can adopt an attitude towards the future which includes the possibility of its own metamorphosis. Non-human life systems enter into communication again with one another. In that closed systems can only be opened through renewed communication with other systems (unless, that is, they are to be destroyed), this opening to God takes place through God's suffering in isolation. Though God himself suffers on account of the fact that man is alienated from him, he still maintains his communication with man, despite being rejected, and creates the possibility that alienanted man can open himself to God and change.[1] So man's *openness to God* is brought about by grace and grace arises out of the suffering of God who is faithful to alienated man. In analogous fashion we can conceive of the opening up of closed human societies in the direction of one's *neighbour* and of the *world*. Closed systems resist both suffering and change. They become inflexible and bring death upon themselves. The opening up of closed systems and the overcoming of their separation and isolation can only take place through the acceptance of suffering. However creatures only achieve this in that they exhibit a higher level of vulnerability and changeability, i.e. freedom. They are not only living: they are able to bring life to others.

If we look at the statements about creation in the New Testament we arrive at some surprising conclusions. Looked at from the perspective of the beautiful 'lilies of the field', creation does not appear to be a new theme. However this impression only arises if we enquire concerning statements about creation at the beginning. The New Testament witness concerning creation is rooted in the resurrection kerygma and in pneumatology. There God's creative activity is understood eschatologically as the summons to life (*kalein*), as resurrection (*egeirein*), as the power to grant life (*zoopoieiv*), and these all relate to creation at the end of time.[2]

With the resurrection of Christ from the dead creation at the end of time begins for Paul. He describes it as a process which has begun with the resurrection of Jesus, which is effective in a wider context through the revelation of the Spirit and which is brought to completion through life being given to mortal bodies and through the resurrection of the dead (Rom. 8:11). Paul always relates the 'perfect tense' of the resurrection of Christ to the 'future tense' of our resurrection. Whenever he speaks, in various places, of a chronological order for this process (I Cor. 15:20 ff.) he does not mean that these are separated elements. Paul makes the unitary character of

[1] See J. Moltmann, *The Crucified God*, pp. 267 ff.
[2] H. Schwantes, *Schöpfung der Endzeit*, Stuttgart, 1962.

the process of the new creation intelligible by means of the concept of *aparche*.[1]

If the granting of life and resurrection are described in terms of divine creative activity, then they ought to relate to creation at the beginning (Rom. 4:17; 2 Cor. 4:6). The historical activity and work of the Creator is complete only in so far as it presupposes the surrender, suffering and death of Christ in our place and on our behalf. Because God in Christ has suffered our alienation, i.e., our death, he opens for us through the resurrection of Christ the fullness of his eternal life. Eternal life is no longer a life which is only preserved from death but the life that has overcome death. Moreover this opening of eternal life through the death and resurrection of Christ must be understood as the consummation of the process of creation. According to Paul the crucified Christ is exalted as Lord and has become a 'life giving spirit'. Moreover revitalizing powers of the Spirit radiate from him to the community. In Paul's doctrine of the charisma the Spirit is the power of the new creation in that it is the power of the resurrection. The powers of the new creation are meant to enter into the Christian community and, through this, to come upon all 'flesh', preparing it for eternal life.

If we want to interpret salvation in Christ more theoretically, then we may look upon it as the definitive and, in its general trend, universal opening up of alienated man and this alienated world towards the fullness of the divine life. God's openness for the world is revealed in the suffering and death of Christ. The resurrection of Christ effects, through faith, the openness of man towards God. The 'revelation of the Spirit' through the charismatic gifts of the Christian community gives substance to this mutual relationship between God and man by breaking down the barriers which man erects against his fellow-man: Jews and Gentiles, Greeks and barbarians, masters and slaves, men and women (Gal. 3:28). The liberation achieved through the passion and glorification of Christ is made operative through the charismatic restoration of life to the world. Openness to God, to one's neighbour and to the world are attained as actual possibilities. The community is founded upon freedom. Faith can even be described as the 'open identity' of man.

V. *The Consummation of Creation*

Assertions about the future of both creation and history in the kingdom of glory can only be made under the guidance of historical experience and hope. Conceptions of the end of history have, within

[1] E. Käsemann, *Exegetische Versuche und Besinnungen*, II, Göttingen, 1964, pp. 125 ff. I want to express, by means of the 'concept of *Aparche*', the positive aspect of what Käsemann calls the 'eschatological proviso'.

history itself, only an anticipatory form. In both prophetic and apocalyptic visions we find two ways of proceeding: (a) by the negation of negative elements and (b) through the actualization of that which is anticipated. In this twofold way the visions continue to be both realistic and futuristic at the same time. The negation of negative elements—'there shall be neither sorrow, nor pain, nor crying, and death shall be no more' (Rev. 21:4)—only describes the dimension opened up for the positive reality to come. In like manner the vision of the 'classless society' describes the future by means of negating certain negative elements. However out of the mere negation of negative elements no definition of positive reality emerges. For that reason eschatology cannot be developed only as negative theology.[1] The negation of negative elements must have its basis in a hidden anticipation of positive reality, otherwise the negation would not be experienced and criticized as such. It is in the experience of divine promissory history, ever striving for fulfilment, that biblical eschatology anchors the negation of negative elements. These models of promise-fulfilment and of the negation of negative elements bring into unison the various eschatological visions.

The completion of the creative process in the kingdom of glory is conceived in the new creation as the *indwelling of God*. 'Behold the dwelling of God is with men and he will live with them and they shall be his people' (Rev. 21:3). Heaven is no longer named as the only place in which God dwells; heaven and earth are created anew so that God himself may dwell in them: *finitum capax infiniti*. The hidden, anticipatory indwelling of God in the Temple and among his people shall be universally fulfilled at the consummation of creation. Creation at the beginning does not speak about such an indwelling. It is, however, open to that possibility and directed towards it. I Cor. 15 unites this fulfilment of creation and of promissory history to the negation of negative elements: 'Every rule, every authority and every power will be destroyed. . . . The last enemy to be destroyed is death' (v. 24–6). The Son shall fulfil his liberating lordship when he delivers the kingdom over to the Father, 'that God may be everything to every one' (v. 28). Moreover, according to Paul, the creator does not stand over against his creation but enters into it in his glory so that he is present throughout it. This includes the annihila-

1 Against E. Brunner, *Das Ewige als Zukunft und Gegenwart*, München, 1965, Siebenstern-Taschenbuch 32, pp. 219 ff., especially 221. 'The negative is clear and definite, that "the form of this world is passing", that death and transitoriness shall be no more. Apart from that which concerns the new being of man and humanity, the positive remains, however, almost completely indefinite.' See also J. B. Metz, *Theologie der Welt*, Mainz 1968, p. 88: 'Christian eschatology is not an ideology of the future but, above all, a *theologia negativa* of the future.' Thus Metz sees, in love for those that are deprived, a positive connection between present and future.

tion of all destructive powers as well as the new creation of all things through the glory of God. Man is not only restored to the image of God, but 'glorified' (Rom. 2:23, 8:30), i.e. he shares in the life and glory of God. Together with him the whole creation is liberated from slavery to nothingness and participates in the glory of God which pervades all things. Man and the world are not divinized but they participate in the divine life. However both glorified man and the glorified creation are finite, though no longer mortal, and temporal, though no longer transitory. The patristic doctrine of *theosis* attempted to think this through in terms of the life of the risen and transfigured Christ. If we must understand finitude qualitatively and not quantitatively—as we must—then infinitude must be something other than endlessness. If we experience time in terms of change rather than of transitoriness then a change from 'glory to glory' is conceivable. This being so, all these conceptions are not so unusual.

We have now described creation at the beginning as an open system and understood the historical activity of God as that of opening up in time systems that are closed. The question now arises: Is the completion of the process of creation to be understood as the final conclusion of the open and opened systems? Is the kingdom of glory the final conclusion to the universe? Then the new creation would be the end of time and in itself timeless. Man, understood as an open system, would then be only an unfinished system and the open systems of nature would be no more than systems that were not-yet-closed. History would then be the condition of a universe in its not yet wholly predetermined form. The consummation would then be the end of human freedom and the end of new possibilities for God. Time would be destroyed by eternity and possibility by reality. However, the consummation cannot be thought of in this way in theology. If the process of creation is to be consummated through the indwelling of God, then the unlimited possibilities open to God will indwell the new creation and glorified man will be free to participate in the unlimited freedom of God. The indwelling of unlimited possibilities open to God will signify, moreover, the openness *par excellence* of all life-systems and, for that reason, their eternal capacity for life not their rigidity. Thus time and history, future and possibility may be admitted into the kingdom of glory and, moreover, both to an unimpeded extent and in a way that is no longer ambivalent. Instead of a timeless eternity we should talk rather about 'eternal time'; instead of the 'end of history' we should talk rather about the end of pre-history and the beginning of the 'eternal history' of God, man and nature. We must, above all else, think of change without passing away, time without the past and life without death. However this is difficult within the context of life and death, of coming-to-be and passing away, because all our concepts are conditioned by such experiences.

Nevertheless both the systematic construction of nature and human experience in history point in this direction. Material structures already exhibit a capacity for indeterminate behaviour. When we pass from atomic structures to more complex systems, we discover a greater openness to time and a growing number of possibilities. With the evolution of complex systems indeterminate behaviour increases in that new possibilities also increase. The human person and human societies are the most complex systems which we know. They exhibit the highest level of indeterminate behaviour as well as the broadest degree of openness to time and the future. Because any actualization of a possibility by open systems itself creates a new openness for possibilities and does not merely actualize a given possibility and, thereby, transfer the future into the past, we cannot conceive of the kingdom of glory (consummating the process of creation with the indwelling of God) as a system that is finally brought to its conclusion and, as such, closed but, on the contrary, as the openness of all finite life systems for the infinity of God. This means, to be sure, that we cannot think of the being of God as the highest actuality of all realized possibilities but, rather, as the transcendent source for all possibilities.

VI. *The capacity for survival through the living together* (Symbiosis) *of Man and Nature*

The misunderstanding of creation as an original, complete and in itself perfect reality has led tradition to understand the true and essential destiny of man in terms of Gen. 1:28; 'Be fruitful and multiply, and fill the earth and subdue it'. This understanding of man has been taken from the Priestly writer but not, in accordance with the history of traditions, within the context of earlier texts, like that of the Yahwist—who interprets this 'lordship' as 'cultivation and preservation'—or even later Old and New Testament texts: on the contrary, all the later texts have been related to this one 'text of creation'. As a consequence of this there emerges a one-sided emphasis upon the special place of man in the universe. Man is the one who exercises lordship: all other creatures are subject to his authority. His lordship over the world was understood as proof of the fact that he was made in the image of God. Then, in modern times, the subject-object distinction divided reality into the *res cogitans* and the *res extensa*. According to Descartes man ought to become, through natural sciences, 'master and possessor of nature' and, in this way, fulfil his destiny within creation. Because he understood redemption from the fall as the restoration of the original creation, Francis Bacon declared the aim of a scientific understanding of nature to be 'the restitution and reinvesting (in great part) of man to the sovereignty and power . . . which he had in his first state of creation'. The reinstatement of man to lordship over the world through natural science and technology is supposed to restore man again to the image of God upon earth. In Bacon and Descartes we can recognize the fatal reversal of biblical thought which has led, through the success of modern technology, to the world-wide ecological crisis. According to the bible man's dominion over the world is established by the fact that he is made in the image of God. According to Bacon and Descartes man's dominion over the world establishes his divinity.[1]

Since Bacon and Descartes outlined the relationship between man and the world as that of a subject to an object—a model which was generally speaking, quite clear—the triumphal progress of classical natural science and of modern technology has continued. This model, however, is one that leads to domination and exploitation. Quantum physics certainly did not overcome this model but merely revitalized it: 'the old division of the world into an objective process within space and time, on the one hand, and the soul, within which this process was reflected, on the other hand, as well as the Cartesian distinction between *res cogitans* and *res extensa*, are no longer suitable as a starting point for understanding natural science. From the point of view of this science the network of relationships between man and nature stands above all else, providing the context in terms of which we, as physical entities, are dependent upon nature and which makes us, as human beings, an object for our own thought and action. Natural science no longer stands before nature as an observer but understands itself as involved in this exchange between man and nature.'[2] However, the model of domination and subjection does not give precise expression to this concept of exchange. With the model of communication and co-operation, on the other hand, nature is no longer an object subject to man but a collection of open life systems with its own identity. The Cartesian phase of presenting nature as an object is, in principle, exhausted and it no longer produces any new scientific insights. Knowledge of the complex open systems present in the world around us calls for a model based upon the theory of communication. Two aspects of reality with admittedly varying degrees of identity, enter into a reciprocal relationship. Whenever we encounter, in natural systems, indeterminate behaviour,

[1] See G. Liedke, *Von der Ausbeutung zur Kooperation*. Theologisch-Philosophische Überlegungen zum Problem des Umweltschutzes, in: *Humanökologie und Umweltschutz*, ed. E. von Weizsäcker, Stuttgart, 1972, pp. 36–65.

[2] W. Heisenberg, *Das Naturbild der heutigen Physick*, München, 1956, p. 45; similarly C. F. von Weizsäcker, *Die Einheit der Natur*, München, 1971, pp. 279 ff.

we can speak of a certain identity or 'freedom of choice'. The more natural science progresses in the knowledge of complex systems, so much the more will it produce not only technically useful results but also potential consequences of such a kind that we will not be justified—in relation to our 'environment'—in doing all that we are capable of doing. Investigations into the ecology of survival have demonstrated, on the sub-human plane, that where competing organisms adapt to one another (*symbiosis*) they have a much better chance of survival than those which continue to conflict with one another in the 'struggle for existence'. The subject-object relation between man and nature and the model of domination and exploitation do not provide a viable basis for the survival of both human and non-human systems: rather they lead to the mutilation of nature and to the ecological death of both man and nature.

Now all the factors which alter our natural environment have their roots in economic and social processes within human society and these are themselves rooted in man's self-expression; this being so, the task of Christian theology would appear to be that of cultivating a re-evaluation of contemporary values. Man will not rediscover the image of God upon earth through the domination of nature or by the exploitation, in demonic fashion, of natural systems for his own ends. For Christian faith, Christ is 'the true man' and the 'image of God' upon earth. 'All power is given to me in heaven and on earth' (Mt. 28:18). Moreover he came 'not to be served but to serve'. The service he rendered was that of liberating us for communion with God and openness towards one another. In the light of Christ's ministry, Gen. 1:28 ought to be completely re-interpreted: no longer 'have dominion over the earth' but 'liberate the earth through partnership with it'. According to Rom. 8 the enslaved creation is waiting for the 'revelation of the freedom of the children of God' through which it, also, is to be liberated. Karl Marx called this the 'true resurrection of nature' and fervently hoped for both the 'naturalization of man' and the 'humanization of nature'.[1]

As a consequence, the character of human society ought to be re-oriented in the direction of social concern (Solidarität) rather than the will to power, a contented life rather than a struggle for existence, justice rather than the pursuit of happiness. The most important element in the wider development of civilization is not the growth of economic power but *social justice*. Social justice, however, cannot be attained without justice for the natural environment nor can justice for nature be attained without social justice. For exploitation controls

[1] K. Marx, *Früschriften*, ed. S. Landshut, Stuttgart, 1953, p. 237. In *Capital*, however, he is less assured concerning the attainability of an essential unity between man and nature. See A. Schmidt, *Der Begriff der Natur in der Lehre von Marx*, Wien, 1971.

both human labour as well as the 'mineral wealth' of nature. If, today, the 'limits of growth' are becoming obvious and we are entering into a situation in which the basic resources for living are becoming scarce, then self denial becomes unavoidable. Social concern (Solidarität) and partnership are those values which make inescapable suffering and necessary self denial tolerable.

Justice is the form of authentic and life-enhancing interdependence between men and between society and its environment. It arises out of the capacity of different life-systems to live together and it is the basis for common survival. Its presupposition is the recognition of the independence and identity of other life systems. 'Independence, in the sense of liberation from oppression of others, is a requirement of justice. But independence in the sense of isolation from the human community is neither possible nor just. We—human persons—need each other within communities. We—human communities—need each other within the community of mankind. We—mankind—need nature with the community of creation. We—the creation—need God, our Creator and Recreator. Mankind faces the urgent task of devising social mechanisms and political structures that encouraged genuine interdependence, in order to replace mechanisms and structures that sustain domination and subservience.'[1]

This outline of an eschatological doctrine of creation, aided by the theory of open systems and their communication, should contribute to the solution of those problems which must be dealt with if man and nature are to have any probable chance of surviving.

[1] The Bucharest-Conference of the World Council of Churches on Science and Technology for Human Development, June 1974, Anticipation No. 18, August 1974, ed. by Church and Society, Geneva.

10 Creation and Participation

by N. D. O'DONOGHUE

I. *Creature and Creator*

In any theory of creation one is faced with the question of the relation of the Creator to the creature in *the activity of creation.* Is the creature without the least share in this activity, being entirely passive? Or is there some sense in which the creature shares in the creative activity?

Let us explore the first of these alternatives. It means that the creator communicates being without communicating the activity of its being as creator. This implies a radical distinction between the being of the creator (which is communicated) and the creativity of the creator which is not communicated, which is seen as incommunicable. It also applies a distinction in God between the divine being and the divine activity, which in turn implies a degree of potentiality or capacity. For activity, if it is distinct from essence or substance, must yet be related to it. The essence is not always and fully active (this would be to deny the distinction) so it must be *capable* of activity, have this capacity at all times which at a certain time emerges in activity. So, we are faced with all the implications of a finite God.

Are we, then, forced to assert that the first alternative is out? Not just yet. Our dismissal of it rests on the assumption that creation involves the giving of being and that this means that the creature participates in the being of God as Being Itself. It may be argued *either* that being is not given, or that the being that is given is entirely different from the being that gives, so different that there can be no question of the creature's sharing or participating in the being of the creator.

The first alternative brings up the opposition of being and nothingness. If creation means anything more than and distinct from making, if it really differs in kind from making, then it involves the emergence of being somehow held in contrast with nothingness. In other words there is no *thinking* about creation unless one has this opposition at hand or in the background. Even with this opposition at hand the concept is by no means an easy one; without it the concept slides back into that of making. It would seem then that if we are to talk intelligibly about creation we must assume that the creature which is its *terminus ad quem* somehow 'receives' being or is established as being. A certain kind of analytical philosophy will object to the use of the term 'being' as meaningless, and it is in a sense meaningless for it cannot be given meaning. But it is, nevertheless, involved in all meaning: it gives meaning and is indeed the core of meaning, for meaning can only be grounded in being or else it has no ground at all. There is no call for apology then in this kind of grounding of creation in being, nor is there any need for the theologian to claim privilege, as Brunner tries to do against Fichte. What is necessary, however, is that an ontology of creation should face the consequences of its own basic affirmation, and it is this kind of exercise that is in question here.

Let us, then, look at the second way of evading the consequence that creation means participation in the very activity of creation. Allowing that creation means that the creature is made to be, to share in being, it can be argued that this being of the creature is totally other as being from the being of the creator. *Ens creans* and *ens creatum* are both *ens*, both being, both reality, but the word 'being' is used quite equivocably in its application to the two. Now the difficulty about this position is that it forces us to say either that God is not being or that man is not being, being that is to say in opposition to nothingness. In other words if one is opposing being to nothingness, then all being has at least this in common, that it stands in opposition to nothingness. So, if creator and creature are utterly distinct, this common factor is ruled out. We are forced to say that one or other is *not* being in the sense of being-in-opposition-to nothingness, and this means that one or other is identical with nothingness. Let the opposition to nothingness go and being falls away into nothingness. Either God or the creature is identified with nothingness. Both alternatives are absurd, though either one or the other may well be implied in certain statements of the kind which sees God as totally other.

We are forced then to give a definite 'no' to the first of the alternative questions raised at the beginning: is the creature without the least share in the activity of creation? And this forces us to face the other alternative and to ask *in what sense* the creature participates in the creative activity of the creator.

II. *Participation*

At this point it is necessary to examine the concept of participation. It is a central concept in the philosophy of St Thomas Aquinas: this has been clear since the work of Geiger (1942) and Fabro (1950) though the time has gone when participation was seen as the key to

Aquinas' philosophy.[1] It is bound up with the notion of grades of being, inasmuch as the lower is seen as participating in the higher order so that, for instance, the fact that animals participate in human qualities is rather an indication of hierarchy than of indistinction.[2] Obviously it belongs to the Platonic and neo-Platonist line of influence which had its effect not only on Aquinas but on all medieval philosophy and theology, an effect all the greater because of the respect accorded to Proclus's *Liber de Causis* as an Aristotelian writing, and to the writings of Pseudo-Dionysius as quasi-scriptural. This principle of the continuity of the grades of being was, however, but a special instance of participation, which in fact ramified into all the main themes of medieval, and especially Thomist, metaphysics. The notion in its generality is expressed as follows by St Thomas himself:

> 'To participate is, as it were, to take part of something. And so, when something receives in some particular way, that which belongs to another in a general way, he is said to participate in that thing. For instance, man is said to participate in animality because he has not the quality of animality in all its generality. . . . So, too, Socrates participates in humanity, a subject participates in accidents, matter shares form.'[3]

We are very near to the world of Plato here, the conception of a general idea finding various concrete embodiments. It would be

[1] The standard treatment of participation as a key-concept in medieval philosophy is *La Participation dans la philosophie de S. Thomas d'Aquin* by L. B. Geiger, O.P., Paris, 1942. Participation is also a major theme in Joseph de Finance's remarkable book *Être et Agir*, Paris, 1945. The most easily available treatment of the topic in English is to be found in the *New Catholic Encyclopedia*. The article is written by C. Fabro whose work *La notione metaphysica di partecipatione* is also a standard work on the subject (3rd ed.), Turin, 1964. Both Geiger and Fabro, the latter especially, tend to keep within the limits of Thomist orthodoxy, and so rather play down the more extreme implications of the concept.

[2] This principle of continuity has both ontological and epistemological aspects, and it dominated the thinking of the Middle Ages as much as evolution dominates our thinking today. The two views seem at first sight irreconcilable, yet they are identical in so far as they both affirm the inter-relatedness of things. According to Teilhard de Chardin 'the broadest, deepest and most unassailable meaning of the idea of evolution' is that 'everything in the world appears or exists as a function of the whole', *The Future of Man*, p. 222. This kind of participation (by which the whole is in each part) is implied in the very notion of a cosmos.

[3] In 2 *de Caelo*. 18g; *In Boeth. de hebdom.* 2.24. *Participare est quasi partem capere*: this etymological definition comes up again and again. Strangely, Fabro's article in the *New Catholic Encyclopedia* translates the phrase *quasi partem capere* as 'to take a *quasi* part'. In fact the *quasi* obviously qualifies *capere* rather than *partem*, being directly adverbial. St Thomas wants to use *partem* quite literally, and this is important in the whole conception of participation.

interesting to try to estimate the relative reality of *participans* and *participatum* in this doctrine, but this is not immediately relevant. What is in question is not really St Thomas' doctrine on anything, but whether the concepts he uses are still useful to us in trying to work out a concept of creation. Here it is enough to notice that participation asserts a real sharing of what A, the giver, has or is with B, the recipient.

Creation is a giving of being, so that the creature participates in the being of the creator. Geiger distinguishes between participation by similitude and participation by composition, i.e. by sharing in a common characteristic. It is in the second or strong sense of the concept that we are concerned with it here. Thomists speak of sharing in *esse*, which is seen as the perfection of perfections, *actus actuum*, and this sharing is seen as the basis of all analogical predication. All proportionality rests on a basic ontological proportion. It is this proportion that we must try to analyse further. St Thomas does not in fact take the analysis very far in the direction of our present purpose, so it must be noted that what we are engaged in is not a restatement of a Thomist doctrine but rather an explanation that takes its rise from a Thomist insight.

If the supreme being shares its being this would seem to involve some kind of division; at least this is the usual meaning of sharing, the usual meaning of a phrase such as *partem capere*. To take a part implies that there are parts to take. It would also seem to imply that when a part is taken, what is left is the less by the part taken. Yet here there is question of an indivisible and undiminishable source. But what if it is this itself that is shared, the very indivisibility and immutability? And it would seem that that by which a thing *IS* cannot be seen as either divisible or mutable, for these characteristics can only belong to that by which a thing is a particular kind of thing or is this individual thing. *Esse*, the being of beings, existence, can only be divided by union with essence; in itself, of itself it is indivisible and immutable. So the sharing of *esse* is the sharing of indivisible unity. But this would seem to be self-contradictory. What is one and indivisible cannot be shared. The one cannot give itself, for so it will cease to be one.

But what if the one is of its very nature a giving and a sharing? What if existence is itself a force of giving? What if the Supreme Being is essentially creative?

III. *Coincidentia Oppositorum*

If God is essentially and infinitely giving then this indivisible unity and absolute reciprocity involves a duality of giver and receiver. If God is essentially infinite giving then it would seem that there is an infinity of givings and receivings. In other words we are faced with a combination of absolute unity and absolute multiplicity. So also this givingness while supremely independent will depend on receptivities in order to be fully and actively giving. We are here in the world of the dialectic of the *coincidentia oppositorum*, explored in the fifteenth century by Nicholas of Cusa and taken up again in our own time by process theology.

The logic of the theology of *coincidentia oppositorum* is that all opposition implies a context which unites the opposites. The more radical the opposition the more extensive the context. To call the opposition dialectical is to say that it is not static but dynamic, that there is continual interplay between the poles of the opposition and that this in turn affirms the context and is affirmed by it. The logic of process theology is that the absolute and the relative share a common context, interact and affirm their context, and are affirmed by it. It is also part of this logic that our thought cannot define or systematize this context, we can know it only as direction and horizon. This is the logic of infinity thinking, and we must look at it more closely.

IV. *The Logic of Infinity*

According to Nicholas of Cusa the man who would truly investigate the nature of God must plunge into darkness. Long before Hegel, the fifteenth century theologian tried to develop a theology based on the dialectic of affirmation and negation. He rejects the Aristotelian system—logic based on the principle of Non-Contradiction. Discursive reasoning has its place even in theology but it does not really penetrate into the most secret doctrine of God to which none of the philosophers has access so long as the principle common to all philosophy is recognized as valid, the principle that things that contradict one another do not coincide. This is not to deny the Principle of Non-Contradiction but to limit its scope, or rather to allow full scope to its inner dialectic of limited being. Within the world of limited being affirmation is always exclusive: in affirming that A is B I am excluding from A whatever is not B. Both A and B are limited, and their belonging can only be within the mode of limitation. A and B belong together within a totality, within which to belong is to be limited by all else that belongs.

But the limited implies the unlimited, the finite implies the infinite, so there is a sense in which totality thinking is less primary than infinity thinking, in which the logic based on the Principle of Non-Contradiction is itself secondary and derivative. So it is that in spite of the great achievements of a science based in totality logic and a philosophy which keeps in step with this, every new impetus in philosophy tends to question this mode and try somehow to escape from it. Aquinas' *via eminentiae*, Descartes' return to the thinking subject, Kant's categorical imperative, Hegel's dialectic of being and nothingness, Bergson's intuition, Heidegger's ontological difference, Polanyi's tacit dimension: all are efforts to break out of the circle of system and totality, though, ironically, each breakthrough has become itself systematized and sometimes doctrinaire. Always, for each successive generation of thinkers, there has been felt the need to break out of the thought-circle of the previous generation, not so much a desire for novelty as a desire for space and freedom.

This impetus has expressed itself very intensely and explicitly in a recent book *Totalité et Infini* by Emmanuel Levinas, a Jewish thinker who owes much to Martin Buber and whose philosophy deploys itself within the horizons of the *I-Thou* attitude, though he speaks rather of the *Other* than of the *Thou* or *You*, and he criticizes Buber for having enclosed the *I-Thou* relationship in system and totality.[1] For Levinas the Other forces the I out of its framework of ready-made categories and attitudes. It is only in so far as I reduce the Other to an *Alter Ego* that it finds a place within my world, my total scheme, my world for-me and about-me. To meet the Other in his Otherness, in real Face-to-Face, I must break out of my totality and open outwards to the unknown and uncharted world of the Infinite. The Face of the Other cannot be defined, cannot be categorized, cannot be made to reflect my demands and expectations, if I am to allow the Other the freedom to be himself. So it is that the common experience of the Face of the Other leads me into the world of the Infinite and away from the world of the totality. It is because men fail to make this ex-stasis that they fight and kill each other. For Levinas all war arises from totality thinking which leads to totalitarian behaviour. Levinas does not attempt to work out a logic of infinity thinking to replace, or rather to complete, the Aristotelian and other systems of totality logic, and it is doubtful whether he would regard such an effort as legitimate. Does not logic of its very nature imply totality, system, a closed world? So Newman thought also, but he spoke of formal logic and wanted to substitute for it what he called variously material or natural logic. Logic is based ultimately on the distinction between good and bad ways of thinking, and this distinction is surely just as valid in the case of the thinking that transcends the self towards the other as in the thinking that remains within the circle of the self-world. All logic affirms coherence as a negative criterion of truth, that is to say, affirms that what is incoherent is not true (at least part of it must be false) and this criterion is just as valid in an infinite as in a finite context.

[1] *Totalité et Infini. Essai sur Exteriorité*, La Haye, 1961. There is an English translation in the Duquesne Philosophical Series (Duquesne University Press, Pittsburgh), *Totality and Infinity* (Tr. by A. Lingis).

This is not the place to attempt to work out this open logic, but it may be suggested that at its basis is the principle that all infinities coincide in the one infinity. This is an analytic principle, being really nothing more than a description of infinity. It follows from this that whatever conception contains the infinite within it is compatible with every other conception that contains the infinite within it, provided that the conceptions are used in their infinite aspect. So unity and multiplicity coincide provided there is a question of the highest unity and the highest multiplicity. So, too, freedom and necessity, with the same proviso that there is a question of a freedom and a necessity that includes the conception of infinity.[1]

Of course most of our conceptions are generalizations resting immediately on perception, and all perception is limited. Book, picture, pen, table and the rest, are, like Plato's bed, capable of being referred to a perfect and immutable idea but the idea is as limited in its contours as the objects it covers. This is the stuff of the world of ordinary discourse and within this world the Principle of Non-Contradiction holds absolute sway. Some minds are incapable of operating or simply refuse to operate outside of this world, and they are forever calling back to sanity and sense those who find their intellectual kinship in the infinite. 'Keep with the perceived facts or in sight of them' say the empiricists of every age. This protest would be unanswerable if we *only* perceived; it immediately destroys itself once we begin to *think* about our perceptions, once we begin to look at our limits. For one can only look at a limit if one can also look beyond a limit; one can only think of a limit if one can use the background of the unlimited. So it is that even within the world of ordinary discourse the nature of thought reveals the world of the infinite. It is not surprising, then, that we are moving within the atmosphere of this world as soon as we begin to think about the relation of man to the source of his being.

[1] Maurice Blondel attempted to work out an open logic, not primarily in terms of infinity but in terms of action. He speaks of an 'internal norm more supple and precise and at the same time more demanding than an extrinsic logic which so often injures reality by its generality', *L'Être et les Êtres*, Paris, 1935, p. 485. This logic of action reaches upwards to include the divine action. 'Do created beings add anything to Being? The answer is "no" if one looks at the question from the point of view of absolute reality, of omnipotence and of the perfect divine sufficiency. But the answer is "yes" if, while maintaining the full truth of what one may call the ontological attributes, one considers the perspectives of an infinite and unconditional charity, not indeed in as much as it is uncreated, full and perfect, but in as much as it is a manifestation of that paradoxical generosity of which it has been said that it seemed folly and scandal to wise men and believers' (*ibid.*, p. 466). Here we have already the 'dipolar' conception of God of which process theologians speak today.

V. *The Divine Sharing*

To return to the question posed above: what if existence is itself a giving? What if the Supreme Being is Supreme Giving? Being, Existence signifies independence, subsistence *per se*. Giving signifies a relationship to the Other and therefore a kind of dependence on the Other. So, too, participation conceived as sharing implies a relationship with the being who shares, and if the Supreme Being is Supreme (Active) Participation, it follows that the Supreme Being must have beings other than Himself with whom He can share.[1] There is no limit to this relativity any more than there is any limit to the being which shares itself. We are here in the realm of the infinite wherein the logic of non-contradiction does not apply: the completely absolute is completely relative, where there is the question of a relativity that itself implies infinity. This implication is clearly present inasmuch as the sharing which generates the relativity is infinite.

The presupposition here is that the concept of sharing is itself open to the infinite even though we come to this concept from finite experiences. The particular instances of finite sharing which we experience are each unique and individual, but we fix on a similar aspect and ignore the differences, e.g., between sharing bread and sharing information, between sharing this piece of bread and this other. All these instances of sharing are in fact finite, but their finitude does not enter into the concept itself which is therefore an open concept, open to the infinite. And since the concept of the infinite is already implied in the concept of the finite, we can pass from the conception of finite sharing to that of infinite sharing without any distortion. But the Principle of Non-Contradiction does not go along with us; it dissolves in the atmosphere of the infinite.

It may be asked, however, with regard to sharing (as with regard to giving) whether the note of relativity may be bound up with its finite applications. Does not the very nature of the infinite exclude otherness? What is infinite fills all the 'space' there is, leaving no 'place' for others. But, again, the question arises: what if the infinite being is of itself infinite sharing, infinite giving? Does infinite being exclude all generosity, all ek-stasis, all going beyond itself? Or does it imply rather the fulness of this generosity, ek-stasis, self-giving? If we accept the basic principle of an open logic stated above, we can accept this coincidence of self-sufficiency and ek-stasis, absolute and relative.[2]

[1] See preceding note.

[2] It would seem that Geiger was conscious of the fact that the notion of participation when linked with creation leads on to these paradoxes and 'coincidences' of opposites, but he is too cautious to allow himself more than a look in this direction. He writes: 'Participation because of its very subtlety

One can accept, too, as a background to this coincidence, the coincidence of freedom and necessity, and, thereby, help to heal that thought-chasm which divided Christianity and Islam in the Middle Ages, and still makes mutual understanding difficult. That which is by its very nature free to create or not to create, to share or not to share, to give or not to give, is yet by its nature infinite sharing and infinite giving, necessarily sharing and giving. But this infinite freedom reaches out beyond the horizon of our definite affirmations and negations. Who can say what it means for an infinitely giving being to be free in its giving: if it gives of its very nature how can it be free not to give, yet if giving is not entirely free how can it be called giving? So too with sharing, which is but the fulness of giving. At the finite level this kind of dilemma or double-bind is self-destructive. At the level of the infinite these opposites support each other, for each of them loses itself in the infinite and thus attains its own fulness and truth. To be utterly free is to be Freedom Itself, free by a kind of inner necessity; to be fully and finally necessitated is to have the necessity of Being Itself, to coincide with the Ultimate Act of Existence, which is supremely and independently itself. We cannot see all the way towards this coincidence of opposites in the Infinite, but we can catch a glimpse of the way of it, and we have with us from the beginning the concept of infinity as we have the concept of finitude which implies it. Here it is well to recall Anselm's distinction between having a concept of 'unthinkability' and thinking the unthinkable—the latter is impossible, the former is self-evidently possible. So, too, we can think of the infinite without thinking the infinite; we can cogitate infinity without claiming to explore the nature of the infinite.

It does not, then, seem impossible that Being Itself, *Actus Purus*, the Ultimate, the Deity should be of its nature giving, self-giving, sharing, participation. And this brings us back to the question posed at the head of this paper: Is there some sense in which the creature shares in the creative activity?

VI. *Creation as a Philosophical Concept*

If the giver is essentially giving then the giver can give itself only by creating givers. If the sharer is essentially sharing then it is this sharing that is shared. If the creator is essentially creative then it is this creativity that constitutes the creature.

Or, to put it another way: a doctrine of creation asserts the

---

(subtilité) could well dazzle the mind that entertains it. Since it is less unworthy of the divine reality it is nearer to it' (*op. cit.*, p. 388). He finds that the idea of the artisan-creator is more crude but less dangerous to orthodoxy.

creativity of being, asserts that there is a centre to this creativity, refuses to allow creativity to sink into routine or monotony.

It is commonly said that creation is a theological or Christian-theological thesis, that the concept holds no proper place in philosophy, that a philosophy will find a place for it only in so far as it is a Christian philosophy, or only in so far as it forsakes its own rational standpoint and allows itself the luxury of a leap of faith. I have already referred to Brunner's attempt to claim a kind of privilege for the notion of creation against Fichte's dismissal of it. Brunner writes as follows: 'In point of fact to "posit" a creation is, as Fichte says, philosophical nonsense, but the Christian faith does not "posit" the idea of Creation, but accepts it as posited by God.'[1] This kind of distinction, dear to a certain kind of neo-orthodoxy, simply begs the whole question, but I am not concerned with this here, rather with the assertion of both Brunner and Fichte that the notion of creation has no place in philosophy. In fact the notion of creation provides philosophy with the only alternative to the great circle of eternal recurrence. If there is supposed to be anything *new* anywhere in the world, as for instance a new thought in the mind of a philosopher, then we are already on the road to accepting creation as a central focus of meaning in the universe. We have been prevented from seeing this only because we assume that creativity can only be applied equivocably to creation and creature, to God and man. Yet not only is divine creativity incomprehensible apart from creaturely creativity but creaturely creativity is illusory apart from divine creativity. I have already explored somewhat the way in which creation implies a sharing in the very activity of creation. Here I want to look at the way in which creaturely creativity implies a creator.

VII. *The Metaphysics of Agency*

In maintaining that human (and in general creaturely) creativity is impossible apart from divine creativity I am, with the process theologians, linking the two creativities. This is to deny that the terms 'creation', 'creativity' etc. are used equivocably of creator and creature, but it is not necessarily to plump for univocity as process theology seems to do. There is a third option, that is usually termed analogy, according to which man's creativity is truly and formally creation, as is God's, but with all due proportions guarded. What is assumed here, as in all cases of analogy of the traditional Thomistic type, is that some concepts, creation/creativity among them, have an inbuilt variable which allows formal application of the concept to

[1] 'The Christian Doctrine of Creation and Redemption' (Dogmatics: Vol. II), Tr. by Wyon, Philadelphia, 1949, p. 12.

both finite and infinite reality. (The variable may operate in between, but this is its principal applicability.)

With this proviso, I am assuming, then, that human and divine creativity are covered by the one concept. Now human creativity is finite and relative. It initiates new being, but not quite. It needs material to work on. It labours and gropes. For the artist there is inspiration, but, as Shelley says, inspiration is a fading coal. All this we take for granted in our experience of human creativity, yet if we examine it, it can only appear as a limitation of creativity, a limitation that creativity *as creativity* does not imply or entail, and can only suffer, becoming diluted or diminished.

Finite agency is never pure. It involves a certain receptivity in its very exercise. Not simply *for* its exercise but *in* its exercise. This is one of the basic insights of Thomistic Aristotelianism, an insight already implicit in Aristotle and some of his predecessors, explicated by the medievals, basic in the metaphysics of St Thomas. It is bound up with the principle that the limits of a being are partly constitutive of that being. Finite being is composite, resulting from a principle of being (act) itself unlimited and a principle of limitation (potency) which limits its principle of being. Neither of these is a thing or the physical part of a thing. They are distinguishable and really distinct principles which emerge from a metaphysical analysis of finite being.

From the standpoint of this ontology, to exist is to act, pure existence is pure act, and imperfect existence is imperfect act. This imperfection reveals itself in the admixture of potentiality in finite activity. The finite essence does not exist of itself, it is not a coincidence of existence and essence. It *receives* existence, rather it is a receptivity of existence. So, too, the finite agent is of its nature, as finite, not act but the capacity to act. Its activity rests on another activity by which it receives that complement of being which changes the capacity to act into activity. There is only one agent that is pure activity, and all activity rests on this agency. This is the inner logic of the *Prima Via* of St Thomas, and it rests on the basic insight that reality *as such* is unlimited, an insight that establishes itself as soon as we reflect on what philosophy is about. For no matter whether we accept this metaphysics or reject it out of hand as nonsense, our *concern* is with the truly real, the absolutely real, reality in itself. Once we bring this light steadily to bear on human action we see that it must rest on a purer kind of action, or else all agency becomes illusory.

From this standpoint process theology is right in linking human (and creaturely) creativity with divine creation. Where it errs (again from this point of view) is in working with an imperfectly analysed concept of agency and therefore of creativity. For creativity is no more than a special purity of agency, action that is truly initiatory, and agency is pure itself only in that which is agency of itself, eternally, infinitely. Of course Whitehead grasped the nettle of the paradox of change by making change itself, process itself an ultimate. But to make process ultimate is to destroy process. It is to refuse to allow process to proceed to anything beyond process. If this great novelty of proceeding beyond itself is denied to process how can it be seen as creative within itself? Surely, as sheer creativity, the process beyond process is far more basic and genuine than process within process. The latter is, in fact, a limitation of process, a limitation within process. And what is the principle of this limitation? Surely not reality *as* process.

From any standpoint we should I think be grateful to process theology for its forthright assimilation of creaturely and creator activity. But the creature can only participate in creation if there is a final ground of this activity: otherwise all agency, all creativity falls away into nothingness. A true sharing in creation is possible only if this is first of all true creation.

VIII. *The Source*

Human creativity, human agency looks to divine activity, divine creativity as its exemplar and primary analogue. Only in this pure and ultimate activity does finite activity make sense in terms of reality. If there is such a thing as human creativity there must be an ultimate creativity. The concept of creation is essential to any complete metaphysic of human agency and human creativity.

But creativity at whatever level is affirmation of the Other, a giving of being, a sharing. *Actio fit in passo:* the activity of the agent is *in* the other, *is* the other as brought into being. But the other is in turn a centre of action and creativity. The picture, the song, the poem has its own life and its own activity, and so with all the works of man. The gift is the giving that is given. What is shared is itself a sharing. So, too, to heal, truly, humanly, to heal, is to give the power to heal, to free a stream that flows on and on. To love is to give the power to love. To teach is to give the power to teach. In this sense process is everywhere, and man the maker is a free flowing that goes on and on, to infinity.

But there is a source. There must be a source. For if all agency is the giving of agency, so, conversely all agency is the receiving of agency. Here there is no process to infinity. For the source must also be the ground here and now. The creator is present here and now in all creative agency. This insight of an indwelling infinite in the finite is the theme of Teilhard's *Le Milieu Divin* as it is the focus of St Thomas' *Prima Via.* It is an insight shared implicitly by every true artist as he wrestles with the infinite: once he settles for anything less he has sold his birthright: he may gain the world's acclaim but he has lost his place in the flow of creative power and presence.

But at the source itself what is happening? Total giving, total sharing, here especially. Since God is total agency, complete self-giving, utter generosity of sharing, we can assert that here if nowhere else nothing is held back, nothing is given by measure. Yet it is here especially that the gift has to be limited if there is a passing from the infinite to the finite. How can the infinite which is infinite giving give less than itself, give less than the infinite? Yet how can the infinite be given? Must we suppose a second infinite, an infinity of infinites?

This is the dilemma or the kind of dilemma to which all metaphysical questioning leads. Time and again it has led philosophers to question this questioning. It led Kant to his famous *ne plus ultra*: thus far and no further can human speculation go: the source must be postulated but the source is beyond the range of metaphysical questioning. But, of course, what happens is that the speculative reason hands over the reins to the critical reason, so that the source is still placed firmly within the domain of system and totality.

I have been arguing, in the wake of Nicholas of Cusa and Emmanuel Levinas, that the kind of thinking that apprehends the source has its own logic. The light by which one journeys towards the source, that primary apprehension of the being of being which is called the Principle of Non-Contradiction, becomes at the source not extinguished but absorbed into the light of the source itself. The very logic which guides us onward demands this, demands at the source a transcending of the method by which the source is reached: otherwise the method will push us further on, to find the source of the source.

Sharing then, participation (in the active sense) is, at the source, at once the sharing of infinite sharing, and the giving of an infinite capacity for receiving: *infinites meet in the finite*. The creature is no less infinite than the creator, in the infinity of its radical dependence, its radical nothingness: on this ground rests the infinity of its receptivity: *homo capax Dei*. The mystic makes his own of this negative immensity of openness to the infinite that shares its own being, and in this lived appropriation, experiences the logic of infinity, experiences that finitude reaching to the infinite which is the centre of all creativity as it is the centre of all prayer. Here existential apprehension takes over from metaphysical analysis. Infinity-thinking takes over from totality-thinking.

In his deepest religious experiences man realizes in himself the coincidence of finitude and infinity: the infinity of his finitude, how immeasurable is his radical nothingness (*of himself*; that is to say, in truth), his kinship with the eternal and unlimited (wherein alone he finds rest), his lover's right to equal the Beloved in loving, to equal an infinite Beloved. Such in man is the sharing in God's gift of Himself, the very pulse of creaturely being daring to create a new heaven and a new earth. The infinite has shared its own infinite sharing.

This is all in the order of lived experiences and we can find plenty of statements in the great Christian mystics to justify all that has been said, even if we do not use the Palamite tradition where the divinization of man is a central theme.

But what can we make of it philosophically and theologically? In other words, how do we fit this notion of creation as participation (in the creative being) into any theory of reality or of Christian reality without breaking through the theory, without injury to the system. There seems to me only one way of doing this: by going beyond the system while affirming it, by introducing into the system a thesis of self-transcendence, by affirming a totality which includes a view of the infinite. This does not at all mean that we cry 'mystery' and cease to explore any further. No, it means discovering a new logic which leaves intact the logic of system and finitude.

One basic principle of such an open logic I have tried tentatively to enunciate: that opposites which have an infinite aspect or 'note' coincide in the infinite reality, for example, freedom and necessity, unity and multiplicity. Another such principle arises from what has just been said. It is that the infinite is not limited to the infinite, but is also open to the finite. As long as we remain within the logic of system and finitude we treat the infinite as if it were finite, placing it in a situation which it cannot transcend. Hegel saw this when he said that the infinite is a finite notion. But, as Anselm saw, it is a unique notion, and it takes man's thinking into a new sphere. If the infinite is not limited by its own infinity the way is open to participation in creation. The infinite creates the finite, yet remains infinite in its relations with the finite. Moreover the finite participates in the infinite from whence it comes. Indeed its creaturehood is this very participation. To be a creature is then to be both finite and a sharer in the infinite. In the case of man it means intelligence and love that is *capax infiniti.* It means a share in that infinite sharing which Christianity has called the (infinite) love of God in the (finite) heart of man.

11 Theological Aspects of Creative Science[1]

by STANLEY L. JAKI

Historical Background

When Whitehead put on the seventeenth century that happy label, the century of genius, no explanation was needed about the kind of genius he had in mind. Kepler, Galileo, Descartes, Harvey, Boyle, Huygens, Leibniz, and Newton showed their genius as men of science. They created science, or rather they raised science to a stage where it seemed to be possessed of an undying vigour. This truly creative achievement had several characteristics of which the most conspicuous was the close alliance of natural science with natural theology. Kepler spoke of Copernican scientists as priests officiating around the altar of the Creator.[2] Newton in turn made no secret of his pleasure that Bentley had found the *Principia* to be a storehouse of pointers toward the Maker and Creator of all. Between Kepler and Newton the virtuosi made it a tone of thought that scientific work was, in Boyle's words, a vehicle to the 'seraphick love' of God.

A hundred years later the atmosphere between science and theology was noticeably different. Far from echoing sounds of jubilation, the air was quiet, though not entirely so. Small sparks of electricity broke the silence with their crackling sound. One such spark was Voltaire's complaint about the piety of Euler, the greatest scientist of the day, a piety which Voltaire ascribed to Euler's senility. About the same time, in the early 1760's, Lambert, the self-made genius, became the butt of snide remarks as he regularly took part in communion services in the Reformed Church of Berlin. It was a city where the academicians were overawed by Voltaire, to say nothing of those many who stood in uninformed awe of the academicians. The same age saw d'Alembert become the victim of unsavoury libels by Diderot, who found it intolerable that the greatest French 'geometer' did not follow him on the primrose path to rank atheism. Diderot did not live to see

[1] This paper is based on a lecture given at Princeton University on Feb. 20, 1975, in commemoration of the centenary of Albert Schweitzer's birth.

[2] See his letter of March 26, 1598, to Herwart von Hohenburg, in *Johannes Kepler Gesammelte Werke*, vol. XIII, *Briefe 1590–99*, edited by W. von Dyck and M. Caspar, Munich, 1938, p. 193.

the day when Laplace, the foremost student of d'Alembert, stood up to the First Consul, who deplored the absence of any reference to God in Laplace's account of the solar system. The witness of the dispute was none other than Herschel, who quietly commented in his diary of his visit of 1802 in Paris: 'Much may be said on the subject; by joining the arguments of both we shall be led to "nature and nature's God".'[1] But Herschel kept his belief in God largely to himself. Half a century later his son, himself an illustrious astronomer, had to defend his father's name against innuendoes of atheism.

Those innuendoes were part of an open warfare which was declared, shortly after the middle of the nineteenth century, on religion in the name of science. The names of great scientists were conspicuously absent among those in the forefront of that virulent attack. Moleschott, Voigt, Büchner, Engels, Huxley, Spencer, Littré, White, Draper are not names of scientific discoverers, but of propagandists of an interpretation of science which rested on the conviction that science and religion were in irreconcilable conflict. The means of spreading this conviction consisted in setting off the 'latest' in science against antiquated accounts of theology. The victims of this strategy were many and some very illustrious. After reading some 'popular' accounts of science, Einstein reached the firm conclusion at the tender age of twelve that biblical revelation had no rational foundation.[2] Whatever he wrote and said in later life about religion remained within the confines of that youthful self-instruction.

On a cursory look nothing much positive emerges when a survey is made of the relatively little written about religion by the most prominent figures of twentieth-century science.[3] Planck, with his belief in a personal God, still belonged to an older school, which, however, shied away from historical revelation. Bohr's views on religion were those of Harald Höffding, the Danish forerunner of William James. They amounted to the recognition of some purely natural aspirations in man complementing sheer rationality. In Schrödinger's Buddhism there was no room for a transcendental,

[1] *The Herschel Chronicle: The Life Story of William Herschel and his Sister Caroline Herschel*, edited by Constance A. Lubbock, New York, 1933, p. 310.

[2] This is, of course, the broader implication of what Einstein states in his 'Autobiographical Note': 'Through the reading of popular scientific books I soon reached the conviction that much in the stories of the Bible could not be true.' See *Albert Einstein: Philosopher-Scientist*, edited by P. A. Schilpp, Evanston, 1949, p. 5.

[3] While science is certainly much broader than physics, to speak of science as if it were but physics has some methodological justification. Conceptually, physics is, in a sense, the foundation of all other natural sciences; indeed, most cultivators of the various life-sciences aim at reducing their subject matter to that of physics. The various aspects of that reductionist trend were treated extensively in my *The Relevance of Physics*, Chicago, 1966.

personal God, let alone for His stepping into history through a specific revelation. The *Physics and Beyond* of Heisenberg contains no metaphysics worthy of that name. Its concluding note, the enthralment of a Beethoven trio, is certainly beyond physics, but not at all beyond *physis* or nature. Pascal's fervent commitment to the God of Abraham, Isaac and Jacob, revealing Himself in Jesus, had no appeal for Heisenberg.[1]

Others, like De Broglie and Dirac, kept a studied silence about religion, in accordance with the widely shared view that science alone is public knowledge, or a knowledge with objective validity, whereas religion is merely a private knowledge, that is, a respectable personal opinion at best.[2] The twentieth century is not, of course, lacking in prominent scientists with faith in a personal God and even with genuine commitment to historical, revealed Christianity. Today, like at any other time, the statistical distribution of scientists along the gamut ranging from rank disbelief to strong belief matches the distribution of other educated men along the same scale. It was even claimed by C. P. Snow that among the younger ones there were more with a penchant for religion than without.[3]

Still, the largely prevailing attitude among scientists of our times is that religion is not to be mentioned publicly and certainly not in connection with science. Open attacks on religion and God are not applauded as loudly as they were a century ago. It is largely recognized in at least the civilized parts of the globe that rude attacks are counter-productive. At any rate, religion and God seem to have been successfully eliminated from the public arena of intellectual discourse. Such is a striking contrast not only with the witness on behalf of God and Christian religion by Oersted, Ampère, Faraday, Fraunhofer, Helmholtz, Joule, Maxwell, Fizeau, Clausius and Kelvin, a blue-ribbon list of nineteenth-century physics, but also with the list stretching from Kepler to Newton. The rise of science to a unique level of creativity during the century of genius is an indisputable fact and so is the sound of jubilation which accompanied the advance of those geniuses from nature to nature's God. The twentieth century is certainly a match to the seventeenth as far as scientific genius is concerned. But the erstwhile jubilation is now largely echoed by a lame silence or by inept words about God and religion. Is it then still legitimate to speak about the theological aspects of creative science?

[1] W. Heisenberg, *Physics and Beyond: Encounters and Conversations*, translated from the German by A. J. Pomerans, New York, 1971, p. 215.

[2] For a recent expression of this conviction, see J. M. Ziman, *Public Knowledge: An Essay concerning the Social Dimension of Science*, Cambridge, 1968, pp. 39 and 144.

[3] C. P. Snow, *The Two Cultures and a Second Look*, Cambridge, 1964, p. 10.

Creative Science

Unfortunately, the word creative has lost much of its meaning in its present-day overuse. There was a time when only God was the proper subject of the verb create. In the Old Testament the word *bara'* was reserved to an action which only God could perform and wherever Christianity made its imprint on a culture, it became part of the cultural consciousness that God alone could create. Those aware of the workings of inner logic will not be surprised by the very different use of the verb create in non-Christian cultures. Our post-Christian culture is no exception. Today it is a mark of scholarship to claim that it is not God who created man or anything, but it is man who creates his gods. Whatever the merit of such scholarship, it is certainly a sign of our cultural poverty that, in many of our schools, courses in creative writing are offered on levels where spelling and grammar still could be taught with great profit.

This abuse of the word creative, and many other examples could be mentioned, is not merely the doing of those who are usually called the humanists. The abuse is just as much present in scientific literature. A good example is *The Creation of the Universe*, one of the 'musts' in the 1950's. From its second printing on it carried the warning of its author, George Gamow, that he meant creation only in the sense 'of the latest creation of Parisian fashion'.[1] Gamow was right. It was in that sense that he used the word. It was, of course, his privilege to use 'creation' in the sense in which the world of fashion uses it. It is another matter whether truly creative scientists have ever claimed the privilege of looking at the world as if it were a mere fashion.

About the time when Gamow's book had its heyday, the rage in cosmology was the steady-state theory. It is based on the postulate that hydrogen atoms are constantly created everywhere in cosmic spaces to maintain the density of matter the same while the galaxies are receding from one another. Like Gamow, the proponents of the steady-state theory, Bondi, Gold, and Hoyle, had to explain themselves before long on the meaning of creation. As Bondi made it clear in his *Cosmology*, the creation of hydrogen atoms was a formation of matter out of nothing.[2] Such is truly a creation which, when severed from any reference to the Creator, merely begs the question. Compared with it the teaching of creative writing to practical illiterates may seem a minor self-deception.

Gamow, Bondi, Gold and Hoyle certainly deserve to be called good scientists. Hoyle, in particular, will certainly be remembered by historians of stellar physics. Future cosmologists and especially

[1] See note for the second printing, New York, 1952, p. [vii].

[2] H. Bondi, *Cosmology* (2nd ed.), Cambridge, p. 144.

historians of cosmology will remember Hoyle, as well as Bondi and Gold, as curiosum, in much the same way in which historians of gravitation today recall George Louis Le Sage. He was the author of a very attractive but wholly wrong explanation of gravitation by impact. With his mechanical theory of gravitation Le Sage merely gave around 1780 another application of the mechanistic creed according to which all physical influences derive from physical contact. By claiming that the universe has since eternity been the same and will always remain the same, on a large scale at least, the steady-state theorists only give a new twist to an age-old dogma, the eternity of the world, which in the hands of Aristotle put physics and cosmology into a straitjacket for two thousand years.

As to Gamow, he has certainly made some memorable contributions. Among them are his explanation of the emission of alpha particles from radioactive elements and his prediction that the start of the expansion of galaxies should produce a background radiation. With his theory of alpha tunnelling Gamow did not create quantum theory; he merely worked within its context. He did not discover a large new continent, he was merely the first to survey one of its hidden valleys. Exactly the same holds true of his prediction of the cosmic background radiation. By predicting it Gamow did not discover general relativity and its cosmology. He merely unfolded one of its many implications.

The creators of quantum theory and of general relativity were Planck and Einstein. They were the great discoverers; the many other great names following in their footsteps were the pioneering surveyors. Of such great discoverers, there are very few in science. They seem to have come in groups as science progressed. Planck and Einstein form one such group. Leucippus and Socrates would form the earliest of such groups. The next group is that of Copernicus, Kepler, Galileo and Newton. With some reservations one can add another group, Faraday, Helmholtz and Maxwell. A total of less than a dozen names. If any reduction is to be made in that list, neither Planck nor Einstein would be among those to be omitted. While the unity of forces was a much-talked-about topic some time before Faraday, to say nothing of Helmholtz and Maxwell, nobody before Planck spoke of quanta of radiation and nobody dreamed of the equivalence of accelerated inertial systems before Einstein. Again, Copernicus was not supported by any previous trend toward heliocentrism and nobody before Newton spoke of gravitation in the sense he did.

So much in defence of limiting the number of eminently creative scientists to less than a dozen, and to a mere two in this century of science explosion. Such a stringent definition of scientific creativity is certainly not in opposition to the fact that all recent efforts to probe into the psychology of creative thought[1] only strengthened its mysterious character. At any rate, such a stringent definition of 'creative' and 'creative science' will not lend itself to marketing children's toys under the same label. The rarity of great creative thought is not its only aspect that can be handled with some ease. Another can be studied with profit in the literature on the problem of scientific discovery. This ample literature[2] makes clear at least two features of scientific creativity. One is its considerable independence of social parameters. Sociology may explain many things; unfortunately in the hands of some of its cultivators it explains everything. But the sociology of science does not explain even such minor details as, say, the conflict of Gassendi and Descartes. Both came from the same seventeenth-century French bourgeoisie, both were Roman Catholics, and yet they became the spokesmen of radically different philosophical and physical theories. Sociology does not explain why the stiff Prussian, the vaguely Christian and socially conservative Planck, became the most perceptive supporter of Einstein, an agnostic Jew, a political radical, and very informal in his behaviour. Of course, those who derive both quantum theory and general relativity from the gentle decadence of the turn of the century[3] will find it difficult to explain why the lives and personalities of both Planck and Einstein were free of symptoms of what is commonly called decadence.

In addition to being remarkably free of social parameters, scientific creativity is also elusive to psychological probings. The best that had been found about scientific creativity through psychological investigations is to be credited to Gestalt psychology. But when Gestalt psychologists, or philosophers and historians of science working with its tools,[4] state that the sudden insight marking the moment of scientific discovery is an indivisible whole, they merely state the fact. Gestalt psychology is a statement, a recognition but not an explanation of the process of intellectual perception in general and of creative perception in particular. Gestalt psychology is not so much an explanation as a reaction, a most valuable one against psychologies

[1] See especially C. W. Taylor and F. Barron (eds.), *Scientific Creativity: Its Recognition and Development*, New York, and A. Koestler, *The Act of Creation*, New York, 1964.

[2] For an emphasis on the historical aspect, see R. Taton, *Reason and Chance in Scientific Discovery*, translated by A. J. Pomerans, New York, 1962. The conceptual aspect is stressed in W. I. B. Beveridge, *The Art of Scientific Investigation* (rev. ed.), New York, 1957; in N. R. Hanson, *Patterns of Discovery*, Cambridge, 1958; and in R. J. Blackwell, *Discovery in the Physical Sciences*, 1969.

[3] Thus, for instance, L. S. Feuer, *Einstein and the Generations of Science*, New York, 1973. Feuer is also the author of *The Scientific Intellectual: The Psychological and Sociological Origins of Modern Science*, New York, 1963.

[4] The works of this kind that created the greatest following are *Personal Knowledge*, M. Polanyi, London, 1958, and *The Structure of Scientific Revolutions*, T. S. Kuhn (2nd ed.), Chicago, 1970.

based on Hume's empiricism and Mach's sensationism. With Hume and Mach, the bits of sensory impressions could never really come together into that wholeness which Gestalt psychology rightly takes as the hallmark of cognition. While not an explanation, Gestalt psychology is a wholesome antidote to empiricism and sensationism in which science and scientists are created by sensory data, instead of scientists creating science with the eyes of their minds fixed on the data.

There is a third branch in present-day literature on the history and philosophy of science which sheds a useful light on the question of creative science. This literature is concerned with the scientific revolutions.[1] As in the case of the word creation, the word revolution, too, can be used in a sense which is almost a parody of its original use in the scientific context. In our times the word revolution is inseparable from the impression which compares well with the one given by fermenting grapejuice. In the process the whole surface becomes covered with unseemly foam and the air above it is filled with a heavy odour. Yet such a description of revolutions is a bit Manichean. Human nature, even those of revolutionaries, is never wholly evil. It can be terribly misguided at times, but even then it is driven by a vision about a perfect state of things. The more ferocious a revolution is, the more forceful is that vision of the ideal. All revolutions, however bloody, were preceded by the Utopian vision of social mystics. Unfortunately, before a place becomes actually called 'Place de la Concorde', the guillotine has to flood it with innocent blood.

Scientific revolutions also involve, if not head chopping, at least some head hunting. Luther called Copernicus a fool, Galileo was muzzled by two Popes. Around the turn of this century Boltzmann was driven to suicide in part at least because of Mach's bitter campaign against atomism. Mach's efforts to discredit Einstein were more veiled but no less resolute. Planck, another target of Mach, drily noted that before a new theory is accepted its opponents must die out.[2] By a new theory Planck meant not some novelty but a novel vision of a perfect order of things that lies behind scientific revolutions. Copernicus called his immortal book *On the Revolutions of Celestial Orbs*, precisely because those revolutions mirrored a perfect order, the order of planets revolving in concentric orbits around the

[1] This literature is largely the outgrowth of the studies on Galileo by A. Koyré whom R. S. Westfall aptly called the 'dean of historians of the scientific revolution'. See R. S. Westfall, 'Newton and the Fudge Factor', *Science* 179, 1973, p. 751.

[2] M. Planck, *The Philosophy of Physics*, translated by W. A. Johnston, New York, 1936, p. 97. In the same context (p. 96) Planck refers to Mach as one of those who vindicated to themselves an authority 'simply above argument'.

sun. The vision was partly philosophical, partly theological. It was steeped in a faith in the Creator's eternal wisdom and decree. The same is true of Kepler, Galileo and Newton. This is a fact of the historical record, and it was a very important fact for those who like Copernicus and the others created at that time the scientific revolution. Unfortunately, no justice is done to this in much of the current literature dealing with scientific revolutions.

A happier fact about that literature is the general agreement that scientific revolutions are few and far between. The very small number of scientific revolutions may sound a truism hardly worth any excitement. But in this age when consensus among scholars is so hard to find, this particular agreement should be the cause of some rejoicing. It is agreed that there have been two scientific revolutions so far. One was initiated by Copernicus and completed by Newton, the other is ascribed to Planck and Einstein. If the Greek background of science is considered, then a third may be added, the Socratic revolution. It was first outlined in the *Phaedo* and on this Plato and Aristotle were to elaborate. Socrates advocated a world view in terms of the biological organism. The Copernican revolution changed the organism to mechanism. In the twentieth century science looks at the world as a mathematical pattern.[1]

Equally important is the fact that the shift from one world view to the other was a very conscious process. Moreover, eighteenth- and nineteenth-century physicists were fully aware of the fact that they were not creators or discoverers on a par with Newton, but merely surveyors of a new continent discovered by him. No less an authority than Lagrange said precisely this around 1800 as he remarked on the good fortune of Newton to have made the discovery which could be made only once.[2] Lagrange also showed in detail that all subsequent advances in theoretical mechanics were only the unfolding of principles laid down by Newton. At the end of the century, Mach emphasized the same in the successive editions of his *Science of Mechanics*.[3] The awareness of twentieth-century scientists of their debt to Planck and Einstein is too clear to need any illustration.

The very small number of scientific revolutions and the very small

[1] See the first three chapters in my *The Relevance of Physics*, quoted in note 3, page 150.

[2] As reported by M. Delambre in his 'Notice sur la vie et les ouvrages de M. le comte J. L. Lagrange' in *Oeuvres de Lagrange*, Paris, 1867–92, vol. I, p. xx.

[3] The English translation itself went through six editions of which the last corresponded to the ninth German edition. Mach supported his view with a reference to Gauss who noted that no essentially new principle can be established in mechanics. *The Science of Mechanics: A Critical and Historical Account of its Development* by Ernst Mach. Translated by Thomas J. McCormack (6th ed.), La Salle, Ill., 1960, p. 441.

number of scientists to be credited with initiating those revolutions is worth stating partly because it constitutes a point of agreement among quarrelling scholars. Compared with those few giants in physical science there are an immense number of scientists of different stature, some very great, though not giants, many more of common stature, and an enormous number of plain dwarfs, when compared with giants. The seven dwarfs, it should be recalled, were crucial for the success of the only Snow White. Although dressed alike, they were individuals. The same is true of ordinary scientists in spite of their uniformly white lab coat. Individuality means diversity and there is indeed a great diversity among scientists even when it comes to their scientific philosophy. That many of them subscribe to a kind of operationist philosophy of science should seem to be of no surprise. Almost all scientists remain all their lives within their specializations and these become increasingly more narrow. Scientists by and large are not so much interested in spotting problems as finding solutions to very obvious and very specific problems, most of the time very practical, technical problems. In other words, since they must produce solutions which work in concrete and immediate contexts they want tools, including conceptual tools, which provide immediate solutions. Hence the kind of work they do makes them subscribe to operationism. The same kind of work makes them form specialized associations, it keeps them within the confines of their own specialized trade, it makes them develop a special jargon, which is particularly suited to the kind of scientific operations which they perform. The kind of operations in question is best compared with the work of a surveyor. He may perhaps ask a question or two about the geological history of the land to make sure that his instruments will be placed on a stable spot. He will not, however, be interested in relating the stretch of land he surveys to the features of the whole continent, let alone to the whole surface of the earth, and much less to the position and distribution of stars and galaxies.

Quite different is the work of the great creative scientists. They, too, have their specialities. Faraday's field was electrochemistry. By training and trade Helmholtz was more a physiologist than a physicist. Much of Planck's work was in thermodynamics. Happily for Einstein, Planck soon saved him from the distractions of a physics teacher by bringing him to the Berlin Academy where Einstein had the sole duty to think in the broadest possible terms about physics and the physical world. Thinking in such terms about physics and the physical world implies a deep concern for the problems of epistemology and for the rationality of the universe. It should be some source of satisfaction that there is a fairly general agreement on this point among philosophers of science. This is true at least in the sense that today it is rather unsafe to make a Copernicus, a Galileo, a Newton, and an

Einstein appear as positivists devoted to the 'economic' correlation of sensory data.

Theological Aspects

Contrary to the operationist and positivist clichés about the great creators of exact science, their main concern was a vision of the whole cosmos, a vision steeped in the belief that the whole world was a unity kept together by rational laws. An equally important feature of that vision was that those rational laws could not be simply derived in a Platonic, or a priori fashion from the preferences of the mind. Plato and his circles were certainly admired by Copernicus, but he was not merely a Platonist. He was a Christian Platonist and this made a world of a difference. As a Christian, Copernicus firmly believed that the world was not a self-explaining entity. His Christian faith told him that the ultimate explanation of the world could only be found in the wisdom and will of the Creator. From the wisdom of the Creator it followed that the world had to be fully rational. The will of the Creator implied that the specific pattern of rationality embodied in the world was a choice which man, himself a creature, could not dictate to the Creator. Consequently, man's Platonic, a priori speculations had to be shown to agree in all minute details with the data of experience. Those data were of man's gathering but not of his making. While this was very clear to Copernicus, the Christian Platonist, it was almost completely missed by Plato, or by any other purely pagan Platonist.

All these points can easily be found in substance at least in the Preface and First Book of Copernicus' great work. They stand out very clearly in the writings of Kepler, Galileo and Newton. Although very clear they are all too often ignored or slurred over in the present-day literature on the sixteenth- and seventeenth-century scientific revolution. It is, therefore, not enough to say that Copernicus was 'un bon catholique'[1] and leave it at that. Kepler might have been a sleepwalker, but certainly not when it came to his belief in the Creator. The effort to turn Galileo into a herald of agnosticism[2] entails a systematic oversight of many of his statements. That Newton's faith in God needs Freud for an interpreter,[3] or that the same faith is akin to Newton's preoccupation with alchemy are claims that do violence to very plain texts.

[1] A. Koyré, *La révolution astronomique*, Paris, 1961, p. 19. However, two pages later Koyré describes Copernicus as a humanist 'dans le meilleur sens du terme', a sense which Koyré does not explain.

[2] L. Geymonat, *Galileo Galilei: A Biography and Inquiry into his Philosophy of Science*, translated by Stillman Drake, New York, 1965.

[3] Frank E. Manuel, *A Portrait of Isaac Newton*, Cambridge, 1968.

All these and similar efforts seem to be based on the assumption that Christian faith in the Creator has little if any rationality to it. Such an assumption is not so much a reflection on the rationality of that faith as a reflection on the state of mind of those who try to create credibility for it. Psychologically, this state of mind is easily understandable. Few things would seem more difficult than for an agnostic to grasp what it really means to hold and to hold firmly that the whole realm of existence, including one's own very existence, borders on the realm of nothing and if there is existence as we know it, it is only so because of the exclusive power of the One who alone can create. This psychological difficulty is not something to be quarrelled with or to be criticized lightly. Such a quarrel and criticism would be sheer arrogance to which no licence can be had in one's faith in the Creator.

Things are somewhat different when it comes to scholarship. Here Christians and agnostics are much in the same boat. The risk run by a Christian historian of Buddhism is similar to the risk run by an agnostic who writes the history of Christian philosophy or portrays the mental physiognomy of a great scientist who is also a firm believer. When for instance Pierre Duhem's devout faith is written off as religious extremism,[1] one cannot help suspecting that a serious narrowing of horizons is at play. Although a very fine physicist, a very incisive philosopher of science, and possibly the most creative historian of science so far, Duhem is a minor figure compared with Copernicus and Galileo. Thus a Duhem can be turned into a practical non-entity. Obviously, the same policy cannot be risked in connection with Copernicus, Kepler, Galileo and Newton. The only thing that can be done about them by an agnostic historian who is not watching his agnosticism is to minimize the significance of their Christian faith in the Creator for their scientific thinking and to emphasize out of proportion apparently contrary aspects of their mental physiognomy. Such a tactic is feasible as long as one handles their actual statements in a very selective manner. When the statements of Copernicus and others are taken in their fullness they constitute an impressive evidence of the theological aspects of creative science.

About the scientific creativity of Faraday, Helmholtz and Maxwell two remarks should suffice. One is that their creativity was in a sense a variation on a theme articulated by Newton, namely, that all forces in nature must ultimately be reducible to mechanical laws. The work on the unity of forces as done by Faraday, Helmholtz and Maxwell was considered a triumph of mechanism, a triumph more spectacular than original in the creative sense. The other remark concerns the broader perspectives in which Faraday, Helmholtz and Maxwell did their work. For them, and the proof is their having been practising

[1] D. G. Miller, 'Pierre Duhem', *Physics Today*, 19, 1966, p. 53.

Christians, the world was susceptible of a creative investigation because the world was the handiwork of a rational Creator.

The evidence in the case of Planck and Einstein should seem all the more telling because it is immune to a standard objection. The objection is that if one is a believer, especially if one is a practising Christian, one is walking around with blindfolds on one's eyes and one's reflections will instinctively be formulated within a firmly set conceptual framework. Neither Planck nor Einstein can be suspect in that respect. On all evidence Planck was at most a nominal Christian. Such an assumption is strengthened by Planck's negative remarks on the question of the supernatural and on historical, organized Christianity, or the Church in short. In other words, whatever philosophy of science Planck had, he did not owe it to positive Christianity.

This seems also to be borne out from the fact that as a student Planck grew up in an academic atmosphere which was strongly neo-Kantian in its philosophy departments, and strongly anti-philosophical in its science departments. In the latter half of the nineteenth century, scientists in Germany were still aware of the intensive campaign of Schelling, Hegel and their successors on behalf of a 'true' physics. About the champions of that 'true' physics Gauss once wrote to an astronomer friend: 'Don't they make your hair stand on end with their statements?'[1] Later Helmholtz summed up the German academic conflict with the words: 'The philosophers said that the scientists were stupid and the scientists charged that the philosophers were crazy.'[2] Scientists could therefore have only contempt for philosophy and especially for metaphysics, and the only kind which was spoken about was idealistic metaphysics. It was with an eye on that metaphysics that Maxwell spoke of the 'den of metaphysicians strewn around with dead bones'.[3]

Planck certainly did not wish to take up residence in that smelly den. The most natural thing for him to do would have been to adopt an empiricist philosophy which was rapidly gaining in scientific circles largely because of the writings of Ernst Mach. But Mach found his staunchest opponent in Planck. The conflict between them came to a head on the question whether physics was about external reality or whether it was merely about one's sensations. About that external reality Planck held that it was fully ordered and that such an order existed independently of the thinking mind. Furthermore, Planck

[1] *Carl Friedrich Gauss Werke*, Göttingen, 1870–1933, vol. XII, p. 62.

[2] 'On the Relation of Natural Science to General Science' (1862), in *Popular Lectures on Scientific Subjects*, translated by E. Atkinson, New York, 1873, pp. 7–8.

[3] 'Address to the Mathematical and Physical Section of the British Association' (1870), in *The Scientific Papers of James Clerk Maxwell*, edited by W. D. Niven, Cambridge, 1890, vol. II, p. 216.

perceived that holding these propositions was a metaphysical stance in the sense that it demanded far more on the part of the intellect than a registration and economical organization of scientific data. The additional demand consisted in going beyond physics, or engaging in meta-physics. He never endorsed metaphysics as such, but his whole philosophical conviction was deeply steeped in it.

It was clearly an endorsement of metaphysics when Planck argued that it was legitimate and necessary in physics to assume a deeper layer of physical reality to explain spectral lines, black-body radiation, and the like. The layer below was the realm of atoms. Planck also perceived that when a physicist endorses a layer of physical reality lying beneath what is actually experienced, he is engaged in an act of faith. Planck's repeated statements about the role in science of this spirit of belief are too well known to be quoted here. Somewhat less known are the details of his conflict with Mach. Mach, the radical empiricist, could have no use for metaphysics and for metaphysical belief. Accepting such a belief and going along with the trend Planck represented seemed to him to be tantamount to joining a church.[1] His remark was uncannily expressive and perceptive. Mach was a good enough philosopher to see what could be the long-range implication of endorsing certain philosophical tenets about the physical world.

Mach was no part of the debate that was to rage about Planck's creative act in science, the quantization of energy. Long before that debate broke into the open in the late 1920's, Planck fully realized that the quantization of energy might suggest a basic disorder in nature. Such a possibility pained him a great deal. As late as 1910, a full ten years after he solved the black-body radiation by postulating discrete or quantized energy emission from atomic oscillators, Planck was still trying to find fault with his derivation of quanta. What seemed to be at stake immediately was the question of mechanical causality in nature. Planck insisted that the fall of mechanical causality cannot mean the absence of ontological rationality in nature. He asserted that rationality with the kind of commitment which is usually ascribed to strong faith. It was with such faith that he opposed the Copenhagen interpretation of science, nature and knowledge. By the time he died in 1947 he had practically only one ally, Einstein. Not a poor ally, if witnesses are weighed and not merely numbered.

It cannot be emphasized enough that Einstein's reluctance to accept the Copenhagen interpretation went far beyond matters of technicality. For him the question at issue was not merely whether (or not) in quantum mechanics a theory of hidden variables could be constructed. He tried it and failed and so did others. For all that he

[1] See P. Carus, 'Professor Mach and his Work', *Monist*, 21, 1911, p. 33.

stuck to his philosophical and scientific belief that the cosmos was the embodiment of full rationality, especially in its deepest layer. While his opponents could press him with their famous thought experiments, he kept reminding them of some deeper philosophical issues about the kind of physical reality which is assumed by science. His best known opponent was Bohr, a thinker sensitive enough to see the weight of Einstein's disagreement. Once, while working on the history of his epistemological debate with Einstein, Bohr was found gazing out the window muttering: 'Einstein . . . Einstein.'[1]

The story should not distract from an issue which is ultimately philosophical. But the issue at stake here is the historical record. For a historian of science Einstein's philosophical position is a fact, hardly a negligible fact in view of his towering stature as a creative scientist. If a historian decides to evaluate Einstein's philosophical position, he should at least realize that in that case the historian is no longer a historian but a philosopher. He would certainly be mistaken if he tried to do the work of a philosopher with the tools of a historian. A historian still remains within his bounds if he wants to know how Einstein came to take up a position in epistemology which widely separated him from empiricism, sensationism, positivism, and related trends. After all he started out as an empiricist, an admirer of Hume. Then as a young physicist he thought that he was working according to the prescriptions of Mach. But Mach soon began to suspect that Einstein's reasoning implied views diametrically opposite to his. The matter became crystal clear to Mach after Einstein's work on General Relativity became public. Mach's last writing, the preface to the second edition of his history of optics, was a broadside against Einstein, the philosopher-scientist.

The broadside had one good effect. It shook the scales from Einstein's eyes. He began to see the true physiognomy of the philosophy implied in his creativity in physics. The theory he created, General Relativity, implied that the notion of the world, the universe as a whole, was a valid notion. This put him apart from idealists and empiricists by the same stroke. For Kant and for his followers the notion of the world as a whole was an illegitimate product of the urges of the intellect. Empiricists from Hume on left no stone unturned to discredit the very same notion. They might have done so out of disinterested scholarship, but other motivations might have been at play as well. John Stuart Mill, a prominent empiricist and a candid autobiographer, supports this suspicion. In his autobiography he tells why he wrote his chief work, *The System of Logic*, in which he upheld the possibility that the universe might consist of rational

[1] As reported by an eye witness, A Pais, in S. Rozental (ed.), *Niels Bohr*, Amsterdam, 1967, p. 225.

and irrational parts.[1] In the notion of a fully rational universe Mill saw the vindication of metaphysics, and according to the *Autobiography* he deemed it to be of paramount importance to expel metaphysics from what he called its stronghold, namely, its appeal to mathematics and physical science.[2] Only then could society live free of aberration in morals, politics and religion.

Whether Mill was right or wrong in speaking of metaphysics as being equivalent to idealism and in attributing to such metaphysics serious ties with science, is beside the point. Mill's empiricism could not be reconciled with non-idealist metaphysics, nor with the theism it supported. For that theism the heavens could declare the glory of God only as long as they were ordered throughout. It was hardly an accident that Mill, who advocated the possibility of irrational sectors in the universe, ended up recognizing two gods, both partial, one good and one evil.[3] Undoubtedly, nothing could so badly discredit the glory of one God than cutting the universe into parts of which some were rational and some irrational. While this procedure is compatible with certain philosophies, it is wholly alien to the philosophical framework of creative science as found in the thinking of all great creators of science.

This philosophical framework has been endorsed by Einstein ever more explicitly as he continued reflecting on what he had done in science. The evidence constitutes an extraordinary travelogue of a uniquely creative scientific mind.[4] The record of that travelogue shows Einstein's awareness of two points emphasized in this paper. One is the difference between ordinary and creative science. As Einstein wrote on January 1, 1951, to Maurice Solovine, a long-standing friend: 'I have never found a better expression than the expression "religious" for this trust in the rational nature of reality and of its peculiar accessibility to the human mind. Where this trust is lacking science degenerates into an uninspired procedure. Let the devil care if the priests make capital out of this. There is no remedy for that.'[5]

[1] *The System of Logic, Ratiocinative and Inductive*, Book III, chapter xxi § 1. The chapter in question is 'Of the Evidence of the Law of Universal Causation'.

[2] *Autobiography of John Stuart Mill* with a Preface by John Jacob Coss, New York, 1924, p. 158. This edition is the first to contain the integral text of the manuscript.

[3] See especially Part II, 'Attributes' in *Theism*, which in turn is a part of Mill's *Nature, the Utility of Religion, Theism, Being Three Essays on Religion* published a year after his death.

[4] G. Holton, 'Mach, Einstein, and the Search for Reality', *Daedalus*, Spring 1968, pp. 636–73. Holton's article begins with a characterization of Einstein's mental development as a 'pilgrimage from a philosophy of science, in which sensationism and empiricism were at the center, to one in which the basis was a rational realism'. The following quotations are not in Holton's article.

[5] Albert Einstein, *Lettres à Maurice Solovine*, reproduits en facsimilé et traduites en français, Paris, 1956, pp. 102–3.

The other point, the theological relevance of creative science, can easily be spotted in another letter of Einstein by anyone familiar with the handling of the traditional proofs of the existence of God in modern philosophy since the time of Hume and Kant. As Einstein wrote on March 30, 1952, again to Solovine: 'You find it surprising that I think of the comprehensibility of the world (in so far as we are entitled to speak of such world) as a miracle or an eternal mystery. But surely, a priori, one should expect the world to be chaotic, not to be grasped by thought in any way. One might (indeed one *should*) expect that the world evidence itself as lawful only so far as we grasp it in an orderly fashion. This would be a sort of order like the alphabetical order of words of a language. On the other hand, the kind of order created, for example, by Newton's gravitational theory is of a very different character. Even if the axioms of the theory are posited by man, the success of such a procedure supposes in the objective world a high degree of order which we are in no way entitled to expect *a priori*. Therein lies the "miracle" which becomes more and more evident as our knowledge develops.' To this Einstein added the even more revealing passage: 'And here is the weak point of positivists and of professional atheists, who feel happy because they think that they have not only pre-empted the world of the divine, but also of the miraculous. Curiously, we have to be resigned to recognizing the "miracle" without having any legitimate way of getting any further. I have to add the last point explicitly, lest you think that, weakened by age, I have fallen into the hands of priests.'[1] Einstein was then seventy-three.

As everybody knows, Einstein did not fall into the hands of priests but in that eagerness of his to assure Solovine on that score there seems to be more than his well-known bent for fun. In fact his remark is as serious as a cartridge that can explode at the slightest touch. Those who would be the first to touch off that explosion would not be from the ranks of priests or theologians. Rather, it seems to be a safe expectation that had Comte, Mach and Carnap had the opportunity to read these words of Einstein, they would have exploded. They would rise as a man and ask with a touch of indignation in their voice: 'Has it not been proved in Hume's *Dialogue*, in Kant's *Critique*, and in Mill's *System of Logic* that the notion of the universe is not a valid notion? And has it not been proved that anyone who accepts the notion of the universe as fully ordered, has no escape from admitting God as well, and the soul thrown in for good measure?' As a man they would tell Einstein: 'It is indeed strange that you fail to see that once you have gone as far as the universe in the way you did, you have no right to say that there is no legitimate way to go any farther.'

1 *Ibid.*, pp. 114–15.

Although Einstein did not fall into the hands of priests, his creativity in science put him in a philosophical position about which he recognized that it was uncomfortably close to those old, often abused, and almost invariably dismissed proofs of the existence of God. Such is one of the theological aspects of creative science. Another of those aspects can be spotted in the repeated stillbirths of science in ancient cultures. Those stillbirths constitute a monumental pattern in cultural history which should loom even more so in an age of science like ours. Yet in this age of morbid preoccupation with 'cultural patterns' this monumental pattern received but slight attention even by historians of science. The reason for this curious neglect is not difficult to identify. It derives from the unwillingness of our age to accept religion except as a cultural pattern. This relativistic approach to religion may serve the disbelief of our age, but it also acts as a blindfold. While the same approach can free a scholar from the perspective of perennial truth in his comparative studies of religion, it will prevent him from facing up to the interaction between science and religion in their historical completeness and true creativity. Obviously, since there is only one viable science, no scholar with indifference, let alone with covert hostility towards Christianity, will consider at length the failure of science in ancient cultures all of which were steeped in paganism. In contrast with these stillbirths of science, its only viable birth took place within a distinctly Christian cultural matrix, hardly cheerful news for the kind of scholar described above.

This difference between repeated stillbirths and one viable birth is a difference between two distinctly theological world views. One is invariably anchored in the idea of eternal recurrence, the other is the fruit of belief in a once-and-for-all creation.[1] For the historian of ideas, or of science in particular, there is another fruitful field to document the theological aspects of creative science. The field is the history of the classic proofs of the existence of God viewed in relation to the development of science.[2] That history shows that all attacks on those proofs when unfolded in their full implication became attacks on the epistemology and world view which proved themselves to be essential ingredients in truly creative science. The correlation is certainly a historical fact. Its detailed account is therefore a proper task for the historian of science not unmindful of the ever present philosophical presuppositions in the methodology of creative science. That methodology also lends itself to a speculative approach which

[1] This contrast forms the basis of my *Science and Creation: From Eternal Cycles to an Oscillating Universe*, Edinburgh, 1974. See also my article, 'God and Creation: A Biblical-Scientific Reflection', *Theology Today*, 30, 1973, pp. 111–20.

[2] This is the subject of my Gifford Lectures given at the University of Edinburgh in 1975 and 1976 under the title, *The Road of Science and the Ways to God.*

can indeed show that science at its creative best can be a genuine help for the theologian if he is to achieve in this age of science a proper handling of divine truths which are always revealed through human words. It is no small satisfaction for this historian of science that the pioneering work in this respect is being done by the very same theologian to whom these essays are dedicated.[1]

[1] See especially his 'The Integration of Form in Natural and in Theological Science', in *Science, Medicine and Man*, London, 1973, vol. I, pp. 143–72.

12 Authority, Community and Church

by THOMAS A. LANGFORD

Authority is a chimera; or at least it seems so to contemporary persons. Since the seventeenth century, the notion of authority has taken on grotesque connotations; often identified with oppression, tyranny, insensitivity, narrow-mindedness, and illegitimate power, the very idea has become overlaid with negative and limiting implications, especially as it is associated with political and ecclesiastical modes of operation.[1]

Contemporary sensibility seems to have derogated two dimensions of experience which are closely related to the idea of authority: the past and the future. Historically, at least in the western world, the present century has witnessed a decline in the functional influence of tradition. The past is past. Historical events are anachronistic and the recalling of history is often taken to be an escape from the responsibilities or enjoyment of the present. Moreover, there is increasing scepticism about the future. While people continue to live doggedly, sometimes thrusting themselves and their ambitions ahead of the specious present, they no longer credit liberal optimism or messianic expectations. For many contemporary persons, the past is gone and the future is uncertain. Both etiological and eschatological categories seem increasingly inoperative and the authorities which once perpetuated what had gone before or projected what should come to be have been replaced by entrenchment in the immediate context—a context in which persons feel more comfortable, even if more restricted, and one which they can, to some extent, control.

As represented in institutions or ideas which attempt to retain the past or to gain the future, authority is thought to be static, unproductive of social change, or insensitive to human need. Freedom has been set in antithesis to such authority and autonomy has been counterposed to these seemingly heteronomous pressures. To over-

[1] Hannah Arendt has declared that 'authority has vanished from the modern world'. *Between Past and Future*, New York, 1961, p. 91. Although she is working with a definition of authority which is overly restricted—namely, that authority refers to a hierarchial ordering of society in which persons in subordinate positions should necessarily accept the direction of those who by tradition have the right to rule—she is correct in pointing to the demise in contemporary culture of any consensus about ordering or generally sanctioning values.

throw falsely limiting authorities may, of course, be a sign of cultural vitality. Hence, the rejection of ecclesiastical intolerances and political privileges has opened new possibilities for spiritual and social fulfilment. But to recognize limiting or negative modalities of authority is not enough, for it can, at times, lead to confusion of forms of false authoritarianism with legitimate expressions of authority.

What has happened is that authority—which historically has been associated with the impingement of the past or the attraction of the future—is denied. Because of its associations with an inherited sanction for life or a demand for the future, authority has been declared an enemy of persons finding their rightful place as free and responsible citizens in the present.[1] But such an interpretation of authority is too narrow; and an inadequate understanding of authority has issued in a failure to recognize a fundamental constituent of personal and societal organization.

A predictable consequence has followed: while there is a sense in which the previously instrumental authorities have been eclipsed, there is a concomitant awareness that social cohesion is eroded and that viable community is difficult, if not impossible, to establish. The result is an ambivalent attitude towards authority. The sense of emancipation which contemporary people eulogize is countered, if not rendered insignificant, by anguished solitariness and isolation. Thus, while people congratulate themselves for overthrowing impeding authorities, they search with anguish for new forms of community.[2]

[1] John Oman has claimed that, from the standpoint of cultural development, the Enlightenment caused greater dislocation of values than did the Protestant Reformation, for while the Reformation brought about important changes within the inherited religious context, the Enlightenment called every authority into question, including the authority of God, in the name of autonomous rationality. See *Grace and Personality*, Cambridge (2nd ed.), 1919, p. 3. This observation must be enlarged by an inclusion of the development of science and technology during this same period. The issue may be focused in terms of persons' growing sense of their inviolate personal freedom as this was set in opposition to inherited political and ecclesiastical institutions and the regnancy of an attitude of the possibility of self-making.

[2] Part of the contemporary malaise is the awareness that the Enlightenment ideal has failed. Persons neither have the autonomy they pretend nor use what freedom they possess for personal and social well-being. The cultural anguish of the present has been occasioned by doubt about Enlightenment principles and the beneficence of technology.

Some political philosophers, however, have denounced the continued search for authority as a desire for an illicit certainty. Hence, Charles Frankel, in *The Democratic Prospect*, New York, 1962, and *The Case for Modern Man*, Boston, 1956, from a liberal perspective argues that the quest for authority represents a refusal to accept the human responsibility for planning and directing historical existence. But Frankel has misunderstood the nature of authority and the extent of the cultural vertigo.

It is the case that even though people tend to announce their liberation from authority, authority remains and continues to function in formative ways in both personal and communal development, although the functioning is often covert. Covert authority is still authority, and it has unusual potential for perniciousness precisely because it is not consciously recognized.[1] In part, such a lack of recognition is due to a tendency to identify authoritative sanctions with external social powers. But to move to more internal sanctions —which is a major bequest of the Enlightenment—is not to escape the influence of authority. The persistent presence of authority, often in covert form, indicates the necessity of understanding the character of authority more adequately and explicating its meaning more fully. Moreover, if authority is to be rightly appreciated and once again gain its proper place in personal and social reality it must be freshly understood.

Toward a Definition

The failure to interpret authority in an adequate fashion is a major cause of current misunderstanding of the notion; hence I want to suggest a definition for this discussion—a definition which may be characterized as functional and relational. Authority, as I understand the term, represents the commanding sanction or sanctions for a way of life; it is the expression of power which structures communal and personal life. This is to say, in a rather simple way, that life is organized around basic sanctions, external or internal, and such integration is necessary for human life at both personal and social levels. The identity crisis of contemporaries—individually and corporately—results from a failure to recognize or locate viable sanctions and gives rise to a search for such ordering authorities.

Authority functions as a complex, many faceted dynamic. It is not a simple, noncomposite element of an experience or set of experiences. The authoritative sanctions of life are found in constellations of experience. Such dominion is exceedingly involved in character and functions through both direct and indirect motilities. As constellations of factors, authoritative directives vary with each community, tradition, or historical grouping, and they function variously for

[1] See Eric Fromm's discussion of anonymous authority in *Escape From Freedom*, New York, 1941, pp. 166–8. Fromm, however, persists in interpreting authority as authoritarianism and, consequently, sees it primarily as a negative factor. This understanding has been almost universal in psychological circles and was given a major early impetus by the work of T. W. Adorno, D. Frenkel-Brunswik, D. J. Levinson and R. N. Sanford, *The Authoritarian Personality*, New York, 1950. The argument of this book is that authoritarianism characterizes a basically weak and dependent person who confronts the world with a spurious strength. In all of these cases, it is assumed that for a person to become free he or she must overthrow the authoritarian influences (usually derived from the super-ego or self-uncertainty) which negatively affect personal development.

different persons within a particular historical setting. Thus, authority is a concept which points to actual processes by which human life is structured in concrete historical situations;[1] the word 'authority' denotes specific and dynamic intersection of givenness and reception, of command and obedience, of rule and compliance, of structure and conformity.

The primary function of authority is the organization of life in communal and personal patterns. However loosely or closely a particular ethos of a bonding group may be defined, the group has its degree of cohesion as a result of commonly shared values, symbols, convictions, conventions, language, beliefs and rituals. However loosely or closely the personal self-definition is achieved, it has its cohesion as the result of ordering values as these are nurtured by tradition, present social participation, eschatological expectation and personal ascription. In both of these cases, authority is found in its sanctioning activity; that is, authority is known as it functions to shape life. Authority is its own criterion, the power of sanctions is discovered as they operate in the process of moulding corporate and personal existence. The integrating sanctions of community order constitute the authoritative process of a particular social organization and for persons who are participants in that systemic arrangement. Moreover, the qualities which are cohesive for corporate life constitute the informing tradition for subsequent generations. As a consequence, the primary performance of community is the conveyance of sanctions. Authority creates order in life and is transmitted through vital communities, so that there is processional utilization of the past even as there is affirmation in the present and a creation of a future.

Acknowledgment of primal sources of communal life may be tacit as well as consciously intentional.[2] Such acts or dispositions of

[1] One of the most important and influential discussions of authority is to be found in Max Weber, *The Theory of Social and Economic Organization*, trans. A. M. Henderson and Talcott Parsons, ed. Talcott Parsons, New York, 1947. In this study Weber distinguishes rational-legal, traditional, and charismatic types of authority. Because the categories are so comprehensive and are applied so insightfully, it has been difficult for political scientists to devise new conceptual models to challenge Weber's description.

[2] Roger L. Shinn, for instance, in 'The Locus of Authority: Participatory Democracy in the Age of the Expert', *The Erosion of Authority*, ed. Clyde L. Manschreck, Nashville, 1971, pp. 92–122, fails to recognize the multiple dimensions of authority and especially the tacit and emotive levels. In essence, by concentrating upon theological authority he misses the more basic authority of faith commitment. Hence, he distinguishes two types of authority, operational and rational—which is a separation of Weber's rational-legal type—into rational-noetic and legal-operational types. The effort to refine Weber's types is significant, but Shinn has simply reduced the understanding of authority. What is required is an awareness of the complexity of the character of authority and an exploration of its function in concrete Christian communities.

acceptance involve indwelling, trust, utilization and extension of the self into the contextual framework. As a result, authority deals with more than the rational dimension of human experience. To emphasize constellations of sanctions in this manner is to claim that authority is a matter of affective drives and concrete activity as well as cognitive processes. Such interpenetration of thought and action implies that the commanding orders of life are acknowledged in activities, both private and public, as well as in conscious, reflective rationality. The dynamics of sovereignty are expressed in or through the total complexity of communal life, personal assessment, and commitment, tacit and reflective reason, activity and intellectual evaluation. All of these media of authoritative sanction are interfaced and intrinsically related to form a holistic frame for life.

To clarify further the concept, authority must be distinguished from sheer power. Authority represents the exertion of compelling sovereignty which is acknowledged as value. Although authority is always based upon power, it is not to be identified simply with power. A primary way of distinguishing authority from brute—and therefore tyrannical—power is to emphasize the quality of the responsive acknowledgment of those upon whom authority is exercised. The notion of authority is intrinsically bound up with axiological dimensions; authority conveys value and elicits a response of acknowledgment of value. Hence, to speak of legitimate authority is to speak of legitimated power, that is, power which is accepted—at explicit and/ or implicit levels—in its sanctioning potency and value.[1]

At this juncture we are involved in a potentially circular argument. Authority establishes itself; it sets its own criteria. To acknowledge authority is to concur with its claim. Is not such acknowledgment a simple yielding to an imposing power? Does the distinction between authority and power hold? It does hold if it is recognized that in any given historical situation there are multiple authority claims and multiple power incursions. Decisions about authority are made within this arena of counter-claims, so that there is always a necessary discrimination among options. Nevertheless, it is also true that decision for an authority is initiated and directed by that authority itself. No neat line may be drawn between the influence of the authority and the responsive decision, but the integrity of both the imposing authority and of the responding person or group must be maintained. The dynamics of interrelation cannot be sharply

[1] Although the distinction between power and authority has been emphasized by some recent and contemporary political scientists, the distinction is very old. A difference was indicated by Augustus who stated that his 'authority (auctoritas) was greater than that of any of his colleagues although his power (potestas) was no wider than theirs' (*Res Gestae Divi Augusti*, chapter 34). This reference is made in R. M. MacIver, *The Web of Government*, New York, 1947, p. 475, fn. 82.

or precisely indicated, but in so far as they are dynamics of relationship (and this is the theological and philosophical presupposition of this paper) then the interaction must be insisted upon.

Authority and Faith

Perhaps this dynamic of interrelationship can best be illustrated in religious faith where the function of authority may be more narrowly delineated. For faith as an actuality grows out of participation in the life of a concrete community; it involves an indwelling of a particular ritual, language, thought, and action of that community; and it requires an acknowledgment and adoption of the values which created and are regnant in that community. Faith is the legitimating act in the authority complex. Hence, while the roots of religious faith are to be located outside of the self in a community and in that community's primal origin and sanction, faith as response is an integral part of the dynamic of authority. That which one accepts as authoritative is that which functions to initiate, shape, and project his or her dominant life-style.

Authority and faith are intrinsically bound together. Authority is the initiator of faith and is expressed in faith. Or to put this in the reverse way, faith completes the character of authority as response to the claim of sovereignty. Authority sets a claim upon life, faith is the responsive act of legitimation which concedes to, acknowledges, and affirms the claiming impingement. Faith gives the authenticity of concurrence to a sovereign claim. In the total dynamic of authority there are polar tensions, namely the dimensions of claim and acknowledgment, of givenness and reception, and one must speak of authority as including both the power of the initial claim and the answering response.

Every historical religion has its own unique originating, traditional, contextual and eschatological sources of power-authority. In Christian faith, the history of Israel as it culminated in Jesus Christ, the present life of the Christian community as parochial and ecumenical, and enduring eschatological hopes define the frame of God's impinging sovereignty. None the less, from this total complex it is possible and necessary to indicate that the primary authority of God is found in Jesus Christ. In Jesus Christ is found the authoritative origin, presence, and expectation of Christian faith.

Christian faith has its origination in the initiative taken by God in the historical event of Jesus Christ and in responsive commitment to Jesus as Lord. To confess Jesus as Lord is to acknowledge his sovereignty in the life of the community and in personal existence. Although both givenness and reception are concomitantly present, there is an order of priority: Jesus encounters persons with a claim of lordship, persons respond with a faithful commitment as disciples. To be a disciple is to be disciplined by this claim and, as a consequence, by the intention to live under its aegis.

Christian faith has its present reality in the continuous encounter of God as Holy Spirit with human life. This encounter comes as the Spirit bears witness to the Christ and functions to elicit continuous response to Jesus as Lord. It is to this continuously active, creative encounter that every moment of Christian existence is referred. Christian faith also lives with keen expectation of God's consummating providence. And this also is rooted in and derives its meaning from the historical presence of Jesus Christ. That which was begun in Jesus Christ will be carried to completion; the lordship of Jesus is the expression of the rule of God who shall—in his time and in his way—bring his Kingdom. Faith lives upon the creative, preservative, and promissory activity of God in Christ, and it takes into its own character these dimensions as it responds to and participates in the life of God.

Authority, as it refers to God in his relation to persons, always operates within the tension of the incapacity/capacity of persons for this relationship. The majesty and freedom of God in Christ is the primal source of all Christian organization of personal and communal life. The primacy and finality of God must be affirmed and insisted upon; at the same time, the existential reality of faith is located in persons' concrete humanness, and this must also be affirmed and insisted upon. Faith, while it is human faith, is also God-given faith, it is faith willed by God. It is faith, however, which is also an expression of the integrity of human existence and which is willed by persons within, in response to, and in concurrence with the will of God. Here it is necessary to acknowledge both poles, to recognize the order of priority, and to assess—even in the limited ways possible—the interactions which are a part of the dynamics of faith.

Authority and Historical Change

To refer to an order of priority and to indicate that the lordship of Jesus is the primal authority for Christian faith leads to the necessity of distinguishing levels of authority. The dynamic of authority works through multiple modalities and is known only in the interaction of the various claims which are made upon each individual and historical community. But there is an organization of life, whether in terms of ego-structure or of community order, only because there are primary expressions of authority which integrate life and set into complementary arrangement other claims. Such integration is never complete or totally comprehensive, but what order there is results from the constellation which is effected by authority or primary claim and response.

In Christian faith, such levels of authority are found to exist within the context of Christian origination, tradition and present community; and they are also found in terms of the relation of Christian commitment to the cultural and social environment in which it exists. Hence, the authority of God as this is expressed through the lordship of Jesus is the primary value and possesses the most comprehensive scope in Christian faith. The lordship of Jesus, however, is itself confirmed by the Holy Spirit as this lordship is mediated by the scriptures and tradition of the church. In addition, the confession of Jesus as Lord is set within a cultural context which includes philosophical, psychological, and sociological presuppositions and formation. One of the continuing tensions in determining the nature of Christian commitment is the need to distinguish the role which each of these impinging factors plays and the valency which they possess.

In every confession or acknowledgment of Jesus as Lord there is a nucleus and a cultural embodiment. One must look for the nucleus in the embodiment and one must look at the embodiment in terms of the nucleus. In short, the confession of Jesus as Lord is an historically conditioned event. Primary confession of Jesus as Lord may be compared to the most distinctive movement in a dance or the theme upon which a symphony is built. In each of these illustrations the effort is to point to a primal reality which gathers other aspects of reality around itself. It has an intrinsic value of its own and yet the full richness of its implications is only recognized as the theme gives itself for development, rephrasing, approaches from new directions and for setting within a fresh context. It also represents a decision from among strong and tempting counter claims and competing values.

As cultural matrices change, the confession of Jesus as Lord is made from within new environments. The lordship of Jesus is primary; but this lordship is always present as a concrete manifestation in an historically conditioned situation. Hence, the confession of Jesus as Lord is, for instance, related to its cultural enfoldments (such as a confessional community living within a particular cultural ethos) as the theme of a symphony is to its elaboration in the total composition. There could be no symphonic construction without a theme, and the theme takes on its richness of character only in its development and in terms of its elaboration and variations.

The heterogeneity of human experience allows for, and indeed, demands, a recognition of the variety of ways in which the lordship of Jesus may be affirmed. Although the confession of Jesus as Lord is a personal act of commitment it is dependent upon transmission through an historical community and is set within a particular cultural matrix. The possibility of such a confession is dependent upon the presentation and the representation—through proclamation, sacrament, fellowship and service—of Jesus as Lord by a continuing historical community. But since every community also changes in time and experiences mutations of sensibility, its presentation of the lordship of Jesus also undergoes change and, consequently, response to the lordship of Jesus evidences wide variety.

The church is presently faced with the problem of recognizing the ordering of authority claims, of acknowledging principal authority and acknowledging its establishment among counter-claimants and in relation to its derivative expressions. Hence, the crisis in community which characterizes present Christian life is fundamentally rooted in the adjudication of claims of authority, and principally between primary and subordinate modalities of authority. The integrating sanction, the basic theme, of community order, which constitutes the authoritative centre of a particular social organization, must be rediscovered and reaffirmed.

The church, in spite of the presently dominant ahistorical sensibility, is bound to its past; and it cannot continue to live without a vital appreciation of that past. Consequently, whether or not other institutions in contemporary culture live on memory, the church must continually rediscover the significance of the Bible and tradition. Reference to scripture and tradition re-emphasizes an inexpungeable part of the Christian consciousness and an inviolate element in the constellation of authoritative sanctions for the present community; and this joint reference points to the complex interinvolvement of the scriptures and the life of the church. The Bible is the primary and normative embodiment of response to the lordship of Jesus as Lord, it is the generative historical factor in Christian community and individuals in such community, and it is the continuing focus of concrete authorization of Christian tradition. As such, the Bible functions as a central element in the authoritative dynamic of present Christian experience. Theology does not possess the logical power or the persuasive potency to generate or preserve the authoritative role of scripture, rather scripture as an originator and sustainer of tradition becomes authoritative as it is used by the Holy Spirit to create and preserve actual Christian community.

The authority of the Bible is not to be confused with a direct identity of its content with the Word of God, with the inspiration of the scriptures, with the issue of what unifies the Bible, or with the discernment of that which is distinctive in the Bible. Each of these matters has an importance which deserves separate consideration, but the authority of the Bible is to be found as it authoritatively asserts itself through the work of the Holy Spirit, that is, as it constitutes an essential, concrete factor in the constitution of historical Christian community and personal life within that community.

The Old and New Testaments were formed in and as a part of the life of the church; through time the scripture has shaped and been interpreted by the developing life of the church; and the vitality of scripture and tradition projects the future possibility of hope for and in the church. It is necessary to recognize the shaping of scripture by the church, but in terms of the levels of authority—and to assert a Protestant perspective—it is necessary to recognize the primacy of scripture over tradition even as one recognizes the complex interactions.

The interaction of scripture and tradition is continuously evident; for the tradition of the Christian church—with all of its diversity and multiplicity—is formed by the inter-relatedness of scripture and the concrete life of the church. Here interactive assessment, judgment, and new promulgation are all to be found in ongoing creativity of new community which is founded upon previous community and its sources. Throughout the interactions of the Bible and tradition with the creation and preservation of community and permeating all of its sanctioning influence there is the interaction of God as Holy Spirit speaking with creative power and authorizing life under the lordship of Jesus Christ.

The church is rooted in this document and in the history which scripture has formed. But more, scripture and tradition represent not only a past which retains present potency, but also they represent an historical transmission of continuously new, creative activity of God. Consequently, scripture and tradition have ongoing effectiveness and point to eschatological expectations. The anticipations of the church as well as its memory constitute its frame of reference. The hope which the church possesses is a hope rooted in and determined by Jesus Christ; it is hope predicated upon the present creative witness of the Holy Spirit; it is hope anticipating the providential faithfulness of God. The authority of God which is expressed in eschatological terms points to the historical mission and responsibility of the church. To live towards the future is to strive for those qualities which begin to make life human under God. Here the rule of God as expressed as his kingdom is extended into engagement with the social order which acknowledges other regnant values. Eschatological hope has also, in the Christian tradition, carried transcendent import; and this too must be affirmed in the face of secular incredulity. In so far as God's sovereignty is viewed providentially, the Christian lives toward a parousia in which the authority of God is finally asserted.

Community and Church

The issue with which we began was the mistrust of and a tendency to reject the notion of authority in contemporary culture. Such a rejection invites a study of the concept, the reason for its dismissal, and an assessment of the possibility of developing an interpretation which properly retains the importance of the concept—especially in Christian existence at both the personal and communal levels.

Christian faith, as this exists historically, has been the focus of our investigation, and this concrete embodiment led us to emphasize the centrality of Jesus as Lord and the need to discuss levels of authority; this, in turn, led to an evaluation of the role of scripture, tradition and eschatological hope in the establishment and continuation of Christian existence. By emphasizing the important role of these dimensions we have come to an interpretation of authority which possesses both memory and anticipation, and have affirmed the primacy of community for Christian authority and for Christian life. We shall, in this last section, turn to the issue of community as a concrete and significant arena of the dynamic of authority in present experience.

The loss of a sense of authority in contemporary life has resulted in a loss of the experience of genuine community. The two are necessarily interrelated, for communal life is established only when there is a centring authority, and the lack of community is witness to the erosion of singular potency and dispersion into multiple centres which contend with each other.[1] The loss of community seems endemic to contemporary western life, and present sensibility is keenly aware of the difficulty of sharing life in meaningful ways. Since the Enlightenment (and perhaps as a stream of the Protestant Reformation) there has been an increase in atomic individualism and a transition from social cohesion to a dominance of the private,

[1] The emphasis on communal life I take to be of prime importance. Edward Shils, for instance, has written;

> 'Society has a centre. . . . This central zone impinges in various way on those who live within the ecological domain in which the society exists . . .
>
> The centre, or the central zone, is a phenomenon of the realm of values and beliefs. It is the centre of the order of symbols, of values and beliefs, which govern the society. It is the centre because it is the ultimate and irreducible; and it is felt to be such by many who cannot give explicit articulation to its reductibility. . . .
>
> The centre is also a phenomenon of the realm of action. It is a structure of activities, of roles and persons, within the network of institutions. It is in these roles that the values and beliefs which are central are embodied and propounded.'

'Centre and Periphery', in *The Logic of Personal Knowledge: Essays Presented to Michael Polanyi*, London, 1961, p. 117.

isolated domain. Persons have become free for and responsible to themselves alone.[1]

Tokens of contemporary cultural life, such as drama, novels, poetry and painting explore with devastating thoroughness this condition of human existence; the general appeal of individualistic psychiatric therapy and the intensification of nuclear family life illustrate centripetal forces in this movement; and the frustrating search for political order within nations and among nations emphasizes the difficulty of finding enough consensus for public order. There seems to be a general sense of the value and need of community, and indeed a poignant desire for community is too common to need extended explication; but the search has turned upon itself and has tended towards tight in-group ideology or even solipsistic inclinations.

All of this is an intensely practical matter. For instance, with the shifting centres of authority—a condition which might be described as social entropy—there has been, as a reaction, a concomitant rise of identification with narrowly defined ideological positions. Ideologies promise strong sanctions and order, for they are usually narrowly conceived, rigorously logical, and thoroughly demanding. They are also simplistic, but this perhaps only adds to their appeal. Ideologies also focus upon an in-group; and while doubting or denying the possibility of commonly shared values in a larger community—here reflecting the general cultural *aporia*—the votaries of a specific ideology tend to become fanatical about their own values and turn tyranically upon those who differ with them.

For many individuals, the vision of life is even more restricted to their own person or to their most immediate context. There is a tendency to solitude in the sense of loneliness rather than in the sense of purposeful withdrawal in order to be renewed, and there is a simultaneous sense of frustration in finding meaning in such narrow

[1] Leander E. Keck has insightfully written in an unpublished paper, 'The Problem of Biblical Authority', pp. 3–4.

'. . . authority is not rightly understood when it is regarded as the antonym of freedom, in which case one would choose between them. But authority need not constrict freedom. Actually, authority can confer freedom as readily as it can cancel it. This is precisely the case when authority is regarded not as an external coercion but as that which establishes inner authorization. . . .'

'. . . the real antithesis of authority is the absence of accountability for one's freedom. This is why it is virtually impossible to avoid authority altogether, for even if one were to insist that he is accountable only to himself, he would merely proclaim that he is his own authority. Actually, human life, being social, consists of accountabilities (and hence of authorities), often in unresolved conflict with one another because they have not been ordered or because a particular ordering proves to be unstable. The question is not, shall I acknowledge an authority to whom I am accountable? but, how is my accountability pattern to be ordered?, how shall I deal with the several authorities which already hold me accountable? . . .'

circumference. Community which is the principal desideratum of many persons is known more in its absence than in its presence. Here is a fundamental challenge to the church and to the possibility for Christian community.

But the crisis in community also faces the contemporary church. The crisis is rooted in the failure to perceive and allow the adjudication of the claims of authority, and this principally between primary and subordinate modalities of authority. It is important, at this juncture, to note that the current tendency to speak of a loss of authority is a misidentification of the problem. What is happening is a repositioning of the counter-claimants for authoritative sanctioning. For the church this means a continuous adjudication of the interactions of the competing authoritative sanctions.

Yet it is not possible to speak of authority in the church in a simple manner, for both the dynamics of authority and the multiple facets of church existence in a particular culture are highly complex. In the dynamics of concrete, historically specific authorities we are faced with the interlacing and interfacing of multiple sources and influences, so in the formation of life within Christian community, there are relative groupings of strength *vis-à-vis* the primary authority of the lordship of Jesus. Hence, any concrete Christian community inherits and absorbs from its culture sets of values which are relatively uncriticized, but which must be critically assessed if primal value is to be understood and responded to in its authoritative sanctioning.

From a theological perspective, the creation of Christian community must be understood in terms of its primary authority. But here one must speak carefully, for the nuances are important. Since primary commitment is always embodied in organized life which lives in the matrix of an inclusive culture, and since organized life includes elements of this culture as indigenous ingredients in its formation, we cannot speak of a 'pure' Christian community which must relate to a 'wholly other' social order. Rather, tensions exist within every community—including every particular Christian community, for within the inner life of community the struggle between value claims is felt, as are the tensions among communities which differently embody these contending values or which are integrated around different values.

When these dimensions are not kept in lively tension, the church becomes an isolated, inwardly directed community with an unreal sense of its organic union with culture, or the church loses its distinctive identity as the Body of Christ by capitulation to dominant cultural values. What this means in practice is that in regard to any self-identity, such as concrete decision or any projection of life-style, the church must come to an understanding of, and a critical evaluation of, the authoritative groupings and relative strengths of the various authoritative inputs as these relate to the primary authority of the lordship of Jesus.

To speak of primary authority or to use analogies of theme and elaboration sounds much like the effort of liberal theology to distinguish the kernel and the husk of Christian faith. The issue which liberal theology fastened upon is fundamentally significant, but it must be cast in a new perspective. Hence, to speak of levels of authority is not done in order to discard limited, parochial, or less important authorities. And it is not to ask: what is the minimum which faith requires? Rather, to raise the issue of levels of authority is to recognize the dynamic input of numerous sanctions, all of which have importance, and precisely because they are important their relative weight must be ascertained. The levels of authority for Christian communal existence are self-establishing but they must be responded to in a way which acknowledges their legitimate weight and which allows them to establish themselves and the centre from which faith, and thought, and action flow. The church needs to bear the injunction to let the Lord be Lord, and it must respond with a willingness to let the lordship of Jesus become the ordering principle of personal and corporate life.

It is for this reason that it is important to understand the hierarchy of authority in Christian faith and life. The primal sanction is Jesus who is Lord, and in witness to him there is the Bible, then tradition, then concrete cultural context. The theme organizes its developments and extensions, and each development reflects back upon the theme. Each aspect must be recognized in terms of its relative valency in the formation of any particular community. But now a final point must be made: since the life of Christian community is centred in the lordship of Jesus, worship and service are the most important responses which can be given and which continuously function to represent the vital life of the church. Concrete community is transmitted by concrete signs which focus the church upon its true centre; here Christian worship and service are indispensable for Christian community. Once the centre is recognized in its legitimate power in the formation of community, the multiple modes by which it is transmitted, interpreted, and projected must also be recognized, appreciated, judged, and utilized.

It is here that theology has one of its significant roles in the life of the church. For theology must be subject to, and then serve to interpret, the primal centre, and also to assess the manner in which cultural factors influence the functioning of authority in Christian life. The fact of the impinging cultural influences is neither surprising nor regrettable; this is simply an attestation to the historical conditioning of community. But it does emphasize the necessity of principally honouring the authority which has formed Christian community and which structures life as worship and service.

13 Precepts and Counsels

by J. HOUSTON

This paper tries to make systematic sense from a Christian point of view of the body of injunctions which are found in the New Testament; it sets off on the assumption that the New Testament's ethical teaching does make a consistent whole at least in the respect with which I am concerned with it now, and that that consistent whole is a commendable whole.

I wish to consider a distinction which has been made by Christians between two sorts of injunctions: (1) those, obedience to which is necessary for salvation and, (2) those which set forth the (higher) requirements of perfection by obedience to which a man may arrive quickly and better at eternal life. The former are precepts, the latter counsels—counsels of perfection. To illustrate and, perhaps, to justify the distinction appeal has been made to the story of the rich young man as found in Matt. 19:16–22. A distinction seems to be drawn here between what he has to do to gain eternal life ('to enter life') namely keep certain precepts, and what more he has to do to be perfect (obey a counsel of perfection):

> And behold one came up to him, saying, 'Teacher, what good deed must I do, to have eternal life?' And he said to him, 'Why do you ask me about what is good? One there is who is good. If you would enter life, keep the commandments.' He said to him 'Which?' and Jesus said, 'You shall not kill, You shall not commit adultery, You shall not steal, You shall not bear false witness, Honour your father and mother, and, You shall love your neighbour as yourself.' The young man said to him 'All these I have observed; what do I still lack?' Jesus said to him, 'If you would be perfect, go, sell what you possess and give to the poor, and you will have treasure in heaven; and come, follow me.' When the young man heard this he went away sorrowful; for he had great possessions.

This distinction between what he has to do to gain eternal life and what more he has to do to be perfect is not drawn in the parallel-seeming Gospel accounts.

It has also been said, as a further development, that these different kinds of injunction lay claims on different sets of people. Thus precepts are said to be binding on everyone, while counsels lay a claim only upon some, namely those who pursue or occupy (if these are the words) the *perfectum officium* as opposed to the *medium officium*. The Latin phrases are those of St Ambrose who explicitly appeals to the Matthew 19 passage. Those who seek perfection will, for example, give their goods to the poor and will remain unmarried for the Kingdom's sake. Nevertheless in accordance with St Paul's remarks in 1 Cor. 7:25 ff., specifically on marriage, those who do not take up the way of perfection and who do marry are not thereby sinning. And in general the ordinary Christian in the *medium officium* is not to be held *blameworthy* because he doesn't give away his goods to the poor, nor turn the other cheek to an attacker, nor carry out the other counsels, many of which are to be found in the Sermon on the Mount. In due course twelve counsels in particular came to be distinguished including loving enemies, giving alms not merely from our excess goods, and not swearing without necessity! Of course those who entered religious orders afford the most obvious examples of people who followed the way of perfection. Whether it is correct to describe the way of perfection as voluntary on the part of those who enter upon it I am not wholly clear. Were they regarded as choosing this higher way for themselves, so that phrases like 'optional extra' apply to the higher way? It seems to be the case that those who embarked on it did not at any rate believe themselves, within their Christian obedience, free to follow or not to follow the higher life, as they might decide for themselves. Rather they saw themselves as required or called to take the course they took even though no one else would blame them for doing otherwise.

The ordinary run of Christians who do not think themselves subject to the counsels of perfection, on the double *officium* thesis, are not obliged to attend to the counsels any further, except to admire and be humbled by the way of life which the counsels enjoin.

There appears to be a number of things to be said (if we are to love God and neighbour as we are called to do) in favour of there being a distinction between precepts which are binding on all and counsels.

(1) Some Scriptural warrant can be claimed for these views; some of this warrant I have indicated.

(2) If we regarded both sorts of rules as laying down duties for everyone, requirements which everyone is obliged to meet, human nature will perhaps find the burden of the specially demanding injunctions more than it can bear. These rules will be broken so often that first they will come to be ignored, and then the whole body of rules brought into some disrepute. An analogy from positive law may be helpful. Strict rationing of scarce essentials commonly lays upon people a burden too heavy to be borne. The upshot is not only

the widespread disregard of the rationing laws themselves, but a lessening of respect for all law. Hence it may well be that to require that everyone lôve his enemy and give away his coat on request, will result not only in disregard of these precepts but in a general moral cynicism which will lead to less love of God and of neighbour. I would not argue that situation ethics is a species of moral cynicism, only that (as a further tangential point) disregard of the distinction between precepts and counsels has possibly contributed something to the view that no moral rules whatever are binding on us.

(3) Whereas some simply specifiable rules can be laid down to exclude behaviour which is at least almost always undesirable (like stealing) and to enjoin behaviour which is at least almost always desirable (like promise-keeping), there are kinds of desirable and highly praiseworthy behaviour which will be desirable only for some people while other kinds of saintly behaviour will be appropriate for others. If everyone were alike enjoined to give all his goods to the poor in the spirit in which we are all told not to kill, the result would be a redistribution which it is hard to picture rightly but which isn't obviously one which love would seek. Would the poor themselves exchange goods among themselves? Would the erstwhile rich man who gives away all his wealth become the poor man to whom others should then give in turn? Taken as the sort of rule binding on all we might have the following crazy situation: initially there are ten rich men who give away all they have to the many poor. They then become the poor men in the community. So everyone else, in order to obey the command to give away all to the poor, has to give all he now has so that the ten rich men now have their original wealth back plus the accumulated wealth of all the many who were initally poor and are now totally without possessions. So it might go on. Less artificially, if everyone did as Kagawa did, going to live in the worst slums to help the people there, the result would not be obviously desirable. A distinction between precepts which do bear on everyone and counsels which can each only be a call to some people, seems to deal rather well with this sort of point.

(4) Following some secular moralists a fourth point might be made: the minimum standard of morality whose observance by the general citizenry is at least a generally recognized necessary condition for the maintenance of society is Strawson's *Social Morality*; whatever goes beyond it will for Strawson and those who follow him constitute an *Individual Ideal*. This distinction might be thought to correspond to that between precepts and counsels, and to provide an additional rationale for the latter distinction. However, as against Strawson's distinction, may it not be the case that to maintain society, it is necessary for at least some to rise beyond the mere basic obligations whose observance by all is only one necessary condition

(and not alone a sufficient condition) for society's maintenance? How can one be confident or even tentative about what is a minimal sufficient condition for the maintenance of a society?

Nevertheless, as a consequence of what I have so far argued, it seems plain that a root and branch rejection of any distinction between precepts and counsels is unreasonable. However, I wonder whether they should be distinguished as laying down necessary conditions for salvation, and going beyond the minimum necessary; whether the distinction isn't simply between rules which are binding on all and injunctions which are not each binding on everyone; and whether the distinctions between those people who can properly disregard all the counsels of perfection and those who are bound by the counsels, or between the *perfectum officium* and *medium officium*, are as readily defensible.

Consider Scripture: All are surely told to love the Lord and to love their neighbours with all their heart and soul and mind and strength? All Christians are told to take up their cross and follow Christ. In Philippians, Christ's self-emptying is held up as an example to all, and in I Peter, to all ill-treated slaves, and not merely to those who feel themselves challenged by the ideal he embodies. Also it looks as if the injunction that God's people are to be perfect as he is perfect is binding on all. If Christians are to be salt and light, must they not aim at more than the minimum standard of morality whose observance by the general citizenry is at least a generally recognized necessary condition for the maintenance of society? Further, the Bible insists that we all come far short of what God requires of us and that only by his forgiveness can we be accepted by him. Now if we are only required to keep the precepts it seems hard to see why there may not be some, like the rich young ruler claimed to be, who have kept them perfectly, or pretty nearly. And as for the rest of us who do fail from time to time, it seems reasonable to suggest that we might ourselves make good our lapses by some especially worthy action which goes beyond the requirements of the precepts. But since this seems at odds with the Biblical insistence I mentioned I would hold with St Anselm that perfection is what is required of us, with the result that we can only be accepted by God through his forgiveness; we have no spare capacity, as it were, for good work going beyond what is required, wherewith to atone for our own lapses. If perfection is all the time demanded of us, this is why we must be forgiven our sins.

One Protestant suggestion has been to insist that loving God to the utmost and being perfect, to which we are all called, is to be done simply by obeying the precepts. And the so-called counsels of perfection are variously addressed to those particular, weaker people who can only obey precepts by following counsels. Thus some can only avoid stealing and covetousness by giving away all goods to the poor. Others can only be chaste by celibacy. On this account counsels are for the weak, to enable them to obey the precepts in spite of their particular weakness; and a particular counsel is addressed to these individuals whose weakness calls for this help. If there is value in this suggestion, it seems unlikely to be the whole truth. Loving enemies and giving away goods and taking up crosses can surely have great value in the lives of people who do not require to adopt these courses of action out of any weakness on their part? I am thinking of people who are saintly, in the familiar Catholic sense, if not the New Testament sense, whose saintliness goes beyond precept-keeping, and whose lives have a value higher than those of mere precept-keepers. To suggest that St Francis did well to give away his wealth and position only because of his weakness is a bit like saying that Walker the athlete does well to train particularly hard because only so will he manage to totter round the track at all. Many people are obviously better than they would have been because they've taken counsels seriously, people who had no need to embrace these counsels out of weakness in order to keep the precepts. Many have surely been inspired by the counsels and thereby drawn beyond mere precept righteousness.

What are we to say then? The Gospel seems to call from all Christians for more than is required by the precepts, i.e. more than what can be asked of everyone alike. On the other hand, there are great difficulties (noted already) in saying that the counsels are binding on all Christians in the same way as the precepts. But we do not wish 'ordinary' Christians to think the counsels have no advice for them.

My suggestions would aim to take the counsels without distorting their obvious meaning and to require everyone to consider them seriously, without saying that they are all binding on everyone as the precepts are.

As a first try, perhaps the distinction should run somewhat as follows: Precepts lay down necessary conditions for love of God and neighbour, conditions which must be met if any person is to live what is overall a life of Christian love. Thus everyone who wishes to adopt a policy of love for God and for neighbour must obey the precepts. But Christian obedience which goes beyond the behaviour covered by the precepts will not be the same (i.e. lead to the same sort of action) for everyone. So no universal rule will cover everyone in this area. Possibly a weak disjunction of many rules may cover everyone. By a weak disjunction of Rules 1, 2 and 3 I mean (of course) Rule 1 or Rule 2 or Rule 3, or any combination of these rules. If the body of counsels is regarded as a weak disjunction of several rules, no particular one of them can be pointed out as necessarily binding on each Christian. But some one or other of this set of rules will be binding on each Christian. And what is not binding at one time may come to be his duty or calling at another. And every Christian must constantly consider all the counsels of perfection and obey those which challenge and inspire him, because for him they will be the best way to love God and neighbour as he is called to do. In this way the counsels cannot be disregarded by the ordinary Christian as having no claim on him. He has, as it were, a meta-duty to review this body of counsels again and again, to contemplate the lines of action there enjoined, and consider honestly by which of them he will most fully love God and neighbour. He then has a duty to follow out those lines of action.

But it may properly be objected that much of, for example, the Sermon on the Mount does not consist of precise rules for behaviour, such that we would almost always know what is and what is not a breach of them. Thus the suggestion just sketched is too rigid and formal in its conception of the body of counsels. The Sermon is obviously non-literal, proverbial, suggestive rather than precise and legalistically literal. Hence counsels should be regarded as inspiring, prompting, suggesting, lines of action and even types of life-style, rather than as rules. This might introduce a further distinction amongst counsels, no doubt rather a difference of degree than of kind. It does seem justified by the character of much of the moral teaching in the Gospels. If we took going the second mile as literal law we might end up going to infinity. And it would obviously be contrary to the teaching of the Sermon on the Mount if, while turning the other cheek, we kicked our attacker on the shins—though it would not infringe the letter of the Sermon. In addition, the scope for imaginative, discerning, loving action is not to be exhausted by even a set of many rules. Perhaps, therefore, we should regard the counsels as one body of teaching by which all Christians should allow themselves to be prompted, by opening themselves again and again to its suggestions. Perhaps attending to the counsels is but one important way of being influenced by the inspiration and example and ideal of Christ himself in his love of God and man. The criteria to be employed, in deciding what faithfulness to such an ideal requires, will be impossible to formulate at all fully. Will it do to suggest that while keeping the precepts is a necessary condition for loving, taking the counsels seriously and sensitively in the way described is also a necessary condition for loving, even if it is one about whose fulfilment (even by ourselves) it is not easy to be confident. But in so far as the moral man is an artist who uses his raw materials imaginatively, though not indeed arbitrarily, we should expect love to be in some respects beyond precise legal definition. Of course, neither strictly obeying the precepts nor taking the counsels seriously is a *sufficient* condition for loving, if Paul in 1 Corinthians 13 is to be believed.

14 Morality and Prayer

by ENDA McDONAGH

I. *Introduction*

In the theological as distinct from the practical co-operation between the Churches which has become such a feature of our times, insufficient attention may have been paid to the character of the Churches which most impresses the ordinary believer and unbeliever, that they are worshipping or praying communities which uphold certain moral standards. Of course there has been extraordinary development in prayer shared between the Churches and quite valuable growth in inter-Church moral activity, particularly on social issues. But has there been adequate theological reflection on the relationship between prayer and morality as distinguishing characteristics, particularly in the light of the rather 'radical' developments in both of these which have taken place in recent years? The liturgical changes in the Roman Catholic Church in the wake of Vatican II[1] would have been almost inconceivable fifteen years ago. And they are now being followed, for some overshadowed, by the renewal in personal and community prayer, described as 'charismatic' or 'pentecostal'.[2] The changes in moral understanding are no less far-reaching and have long since crossed Church boundaries. For two Churches such as the Church of Scotland and the Roman Catholic Church in Ireland, where traditionally church-attendance, personal prayer and a fairly rigid moral code have enjoyed great strength, the changes are, despite certain enriching and liberating effects, also the source of

[1] The basis of these developments is contained in the first document issued by Vatican II *Constitutio de Sacra Liturgia*, Constitution on the Sacred Liturgy, cf. Abbott/Gallagher (Eds), *The Documents of Vatican II*, London, 1966, pp. 137–77.

[2] A useful account of the early developments of the movement in the Catholic Church is contained in Edward D. O'Connor, CSC, *The Pentecostal Movement in the Catholic Church*, Ave Maria Press, 1971. Since then a flood of literature has appeared: the most prestigious, because of his office, the book of Cardinal L. J. Suenens, *A New Pentecost?*, London, 1975. A thoughtful symposium on the Prayer and Renewal, Movement in the Catholic Church appears in *La Vie Spirituelle*, juillet-aout, 1975, No. 609 T 129. For the older movement outside the Roman Catholic Church, cf. W. J. Hollenweger, *The Pentecostals*, London, 1972.

some confusion and pain[1] and place the traditional bonds between prayer and morality in urgent need of theological reconsideration.

Such reconsideration was inevitable. The age-old association between religion and morality,[2] which subsumed the relationship between prayer and morality, has had its own peculiar swings even within the Judaeo-Christian tradition. While presumed to be mutually illuminating and supporting, in fact one frequently enjoyed periods of dominance at the expense of the other. Those who honoured with their lips but not with their hearts (Is. 29:13) belonged to a long line of Hebrews and Christians for whom a certain distortion of religion suppressed or distorted morality. But moralism also had its turn in obscuring or reducing the central saving truth and power of the Covenant of God and ultimately of Jesus Christ. The creative tension which ought to exist between the two and was proclaimed and lived by Jesus has frequently turned into a destructive exploitation of the one or the other. It would be too much to expect that Christians and their Churches today were not exposed to these perennial temptations and did not sometimes yield to them. The *semper reformanda* of the Reformed tradition, which the Roman Catholic Church has proclaimed once again as hers also will provide the stimulus here as elsewhere for the theological task which is a necessary part of the reform and which has become all the more urgent in the face of radical change.

Such a theological attempt in its bearing on the day-to-day living of Church members (in prayer and moral activity) could have the useful side-effect of overcoming the divisions between Christian theologians and Christian preachers/practitioners which have appeared and sometimes in ugly form. The ultimate goal of the theologian's task is to attempt out of his study of the Word and the Christian tradition to assist ordinary Christians and Christian communities to understand and respond in prayer and life to the divine call offered to them in Jesus Christ. In grappling with the prayer-morality relationship in the new situations he will be more directly than usually attempting to provide that assistance and finding himself more closely engaged in his reflections with daily Christian living.

It is hardly necessary to point out as a final introductory note that this is a theological and not a sociological exercise. No attempt will (can?) be made to correlate Church attendance, personal and other

[1] In liturgical affairs a certain resistance to the developments has been associated with groups upholding the Latin and Tridentine form of the Mass. The charismatic prayer movement has also its critics and opponents, but as it has not official status it does not cause the same difficulties.

[2] Again there is a vast literature but quite a helpful recent collection of essays is to be found in Gene Outka and John P. Reeder Jr, *Religion and Morality*, New York, 1973. Some of my own thoughts on this wider issue are developed in my recent book *Gift and Call*, Dublin 1975, particularly chs 1, 4 and 12.

prayer, statistically considered, with moral achievement, also statistically considered. Yet attention must be paid to experience, the obvious experience of changes in prayer and morality which require no statistical back-up and the personal experience, individual and shared, of new forms or needs in prayer and morality. It is with this kind of experience as stimulus that these theological reflections began.

II. *More Recent Understanding of Prayer, Morality and their Relationship in the Roman Catholic Tradition*

Scholarly qualifications can be fatal long before they reach their first century, let alone their first millenium. Yet it is necessary in reassessing the relationship between prayer and morality to define fairly exactly one's starting point. I speak of the 'more recent understanding' and in 'the Roman Catholic tradition'. It is with the Roman Catholic tradition that I am most familiar and to it my professional competence is really confined. However, I hope that what I have to say will find traces of convergence as well as divergence across the denominational divide. 'More recent understanding' is deliberately chosen to refer to the period prior to Vatican II and, as far as the relationship is concerned, exemplified particularly in the Manuals of Moral Theology[1] which enjoyed such influence in the training of Roman Catholic clergy and their subsequent preaching. It does not mean 'traditional' which is much broader in scope and rightly should take us back to New Testament times. A prevalent (controversial) weakness is to identify one particular phase of tradition with all of tradition, the particular phase which happens to suit us.

However, before tackling the Manual treatment of the association it is necessary to recall the popular understandings of prayer and morality which were dominant at least among Roman Catholics in that period and to a large extent still are.[2] Prayer was simply understood as speaking to God or communication with God (and this included listening to Him). It did not, of course, confine itself to petition but included praise and adoration, thanksgiving and regret or sorrow leading to repentance and reconciliation. For Roman Catholics, the public and central act of prayer was the Mass although it was an event (the word was not used and certainly not in any technical and theological sense) as were the other sacraments. There were other public prayers, paraliturgical as one might now call them,

[1] Typical manuals in common usage at that time were Nolden-Schmitt, *Summa Theologiae Moralis*, I–III, Barcelona, 1951, or M. Zalba, *Theologiae Moralis Compendium*, I–II, Madrid, 1958.

[2] The various catechisms such as the Maynooth Catechism dealt with the matter in these terms and a fairly comprehensive account of the theology on which they were based is to be found in the article by A. Fonck, 'Prière', *Dictionnaire de Théologie Catholique*, XIII/I, Paris, 1936, pp. 169–244.

such as Benediction of the Blessed Sacrament, novenas and devotions of numerous kinds. And there were private prayers for the individual, the family or a particular group on a special occasion. For completeness one would have to advert to a variety of practices of private personal prayer, oral and silent, meditative, contemplative and mystical. But some elements of the more advanced forms were considered to reside in the more primitive types.[1] There was in addition the wider understanding of prayer as all that one does: *laborare est orare*. This was given concrete expression in the practice of the 'morning offering' whereby one 'consecrated' to God all one's activities for that day. It could also be expressed in terms of one's intentions to offer this or every work to God or by describing one's work as always done for the love or glory of God in sound Pauline terms (I Cor. 10:31).

The morality[2] contemporary with the prayer-phase catalogued earlier was for the most part expressed in terms of a legal code of does and don'ts, commands and prohibitions. God's will was the moral law and it was either directly revealed in the Judaeo-Christian tradition (e.g. Ten Commandments) or accessible by reflection on human nature, the natural moral law (or both). The expression of these primarily in legal form and their intertwining (e.g. the content of the Ten Commandments was for the most part also Natural Law Morality) were further compounded by the admixture of a voluminous code of Canon or Church Law, so that the prohibition of eating meat on Friday (a purely Church Law) could be taken as morally equivalent to the prohibition of adultery—as both could be thought equally to involve serious sin and merit eternal damnation. The resilience of priests and people, more importantly perhaps of the Spirit of Christ, rose above many of these confusions and limitations but by no means all.

This rather obvious and simple outline of pre-Vatican II approaches to prayer and morality seemed a necessary introduction to considering how the relationship between them was understood.

Presuming an awareness of the tension and temptation between the prayer and morality poles discussed earlier and presuming that the tension was not always creative or the temptation always resisted, one still wants to know how the manual theologians and the people envisaged the relationship and so could hope to cope with it.

[1] This point is made by Fonck *art. cit.* I find it difficult to accept very sharply distinguished and contrasting typologies in the classic study of Friedrich Heiler, *Prayer*, London, 1932, particularly the total contrast between what he calls mystical and prophetic prayer. I would largely agree with criticisms of him by M. Nedoncelle, *The Nature and Use of Prayer*, London, 1964, pp. 106–11.

[2] For a description of the manual tradition and criticism of it cf. E. McDonagh, 'Moral Theology: The Need for Renewal' in *Moral Theology Renewed* (Ed. E. McDonagh), Dublin, 1965, pp. 13–30.

Prayer[1] as a duty of the virtue of religion was regarded as of moral obligation in various ways. This involved as usual a combination of divine (revealed and natural) and human ecclesiastical law. So Catholics were obliged by law to attend Mass on Sunday. They were also obliged to pray frequently throughout their lives (this was sometimes interpreted as daily or in terms of morning and evening prayers). And they were obliged to pray in particular situations for light to know their moral duty and strength to do it and to resist the temptation to evil.

One might not unfairly characterize the relationship as predominantly extrinsic in concept. There was a moral obligation to pray and this was couched in rather legal and so extrinsic terms—coming at the individual as it were from the outside, whether from God or the Church. In relation to other moral obligations prayer was of assistance in seeking light from God to understand the obligation correctly and strength or grace from him to fulfil it as correctly understood. Undoubtedly the light and strength became internal to the person as granted by God, but the concept and image of the connection between them and the prayer for them was, I should say, also predominantly extrinsic. One asked God for help and the help came or it did not, but any inner connection between the asking and the help was not given much attention, at either theological or popular level.

The prayer for forgiveness and the gifts of repentance and forgiveness for moral failure suggested a more intimate connection but it was not expanded upon in other areas. The 'morning offering' and 'good intentions' consecrating all of one's activities to God was also extrinsic in concept as referring to God activities somehow foreign to him and so to communication with him, i.e. prayer.

There were appeals to experiences of inner illumination and strengthening by God which did issue for example in special vocations, but these were not considered in the typical moral treatment but as exceptions to be dealt with in theology of vocation for example, with criteria for distinguishing true from false or, in more advanced cases still, under the rubric of mystical theology. Moral theology and popular moral thinking was not concerned with such exceptional phenomena. The predominant links were extrinsic in moral obligations to pray or in the use of prayer to obtain light and strength to fulfil one's moral obligations, although in the prayer to obtain forgiveness the connection was understood in a more intrinsic way, but the potential for intrinsic connection in the 'morning offering' was scarcely adverted to.

[1] For this section cf. Noldin-Schmitt, *op. cit.*, II, pp. 132–47; M. Zalba, *op. cit.*, I, pp. 531–62.

III. *Prayer and Morality in the post-Vatican II Era*

The developments in understanding of prayer, particularly liturgical prayer, and of morality which we attribute to this era had emerged in various ways to prepare for Vatican II itself. But they became predominant and official modes of teaching and practice after the Council.

The earlier simple and unscientific catalogue of types of prayer has been profoundly changed in its contents in the last decade. The community character of the Mass or Eucharist (a term in increasing use) has been newly emphasized for example by the use of the vernacular, the priest facing the people, the participation of laity in reading, bringing up gifts, bidding prayers, the kiss of peace. These reforms have also been extended to the other sacraments. However, the other forms of public prayer in novenas and other devotions have undoubtedly declined, although they may be seen as increasingly replaced by prayer groups and developments such as the Charismatic Renewal Movement, although without as yet the same clerical leadership or backing.

The most recent theological attempt to overcome the limitations of the Manual approach to moral theology and its popular presentation began before World War II in Europe and reached its peak in the 'fifties and sixties'.[1] A theology of Christian life, based on the human being called to share in Christ's sonship of the Father and brotherhood of all mankind, and derived more directly from the New Testament, began gradually to displace the legal system of the manuals although the undoubted achievement of these works provided a valuable challenge and corrective to some of the woollier forms of 'love-ethic' which began to emerge.

This development of moral theology as a theology of the Christian life based on a Christian anthropology (ontology) is still far from complete.[2] Yet at the same time a quite different, if complementary rather than contradictory, approach is emerging, to which I shall have to return later.

The most striking consequence of these developments for our problem, the connection between prayer and morality, is the mani-

[1] Two of the great pioneers in this work were: Fritz Tillmann, in *Handbuch der Katholischen Sittenlehre* I–VI, particularly his own volume Bd. III, *Die Idee der Nachfolge Christi*, first published in 1933 and in 4th ed., Dusseldorf, 1953; Bernhard Häring, *Das Gesetz Christi*, Eng. trans. *The Law of Christ* I–III, Cork, 1961–7. For some account to the background to these developments cf. McDonagh *art. cit.* in *Moral Theology Renewed.*

[2] An attempt to provide such an 'ontological' anthropology is found in E. McDonagh, 'The Law of Christ and the Natural Law' published in G. Dunstan (Ed.), *Duty and Discernment*, London, 1975.

festation of inner and intrinsic connection between the liturgical activity of the Christian and his moral activity.[1] The liturgical activity explicitly proclaims his incorporation into Christ's response to the Father in self-surrender as Son, his resultant adoptive sonship of the Father and brotherhood of all men. And this is effected through the gift of the Spirit whereby we are buried with Christ to rise with him to a new life (Rom 6) in which we are empowered to cry Abba, Father (Rom 8). The prayer which Jesus himself taught us to say begins Our Father (Lk 11). The moral living which he summarized as love of God and love of neighbour (Mk 12:28–30 *par*) finds its basis in this share in the gift and call to divine sonship of the Father and of the universal brotherhood of mankind which this entails. Each particular moral act and the moral life as a whole is to be a realization of that sonship and brotherhood which we explicitly recognize, manifest and celebrate in liturgical and private prayer. The Christian life, like the Christian liturgy, has a basically trinitarian structure, directed towards the Father through sharing in the sonship of Jesus Christ by the sending of the Spirit. Our prayers for light and strength in moral situations are articulations of our need that the spirit of sonship within us would find expression in our moral understanding and in our moral response.

A good deal more might be said about the more precise content of such a Christian way of life and how one is to discover it, if one does not accept any simple theory of divine inspiration in every moral situation. However, that is a task for another time and place.

More relevant here is the theological basis which such a trinitarian approach to moral theology could provide the prayer-renewal that is at present such a feature of the Roman Catholic and other Churches. It must be admitted that the moral theologians themselves in their work did not anticipate such a powerful development or have the fully developed theological understanding adequate to the task. Despite a recognition of his essential place in the scheme of things, the Spirit remained the poor relation of the Trinity in the renewal of moral theology as well as in the renewal of the liturgy. The appeal to the Spirit in the new prayer movements has put the theologians on their metal and one of the great practical advocates of shared prayer was one of the great pioneers in the renewal of moral theology, Bernhard Häring. Other theologians writing in these islands too, such as Simon Tugwell[2] and Peter Hocken,[3] have attempted to do fuller justice to the role of the Spirit, while keeping Him within the

[1] I have developed this point elsewhere in the essay, 'Liturgy and Christian Living', in B. Devlin (Ed.), *The Christian in the World*, Dublin, 1968.

[2] S. Tugwell, *Did you receive the Spirit?*, London, 1972.

[3] P. Hocken, *You, He Made Alive*, London, 1972. Cf. M. Thornton, *Prayer, A New Encounter*, London, 1972.

Trinity. The temptation to treat Him in isolation is not one all prayer enthusiasts can resist.

Yet formidable work remains to be done in theological reflection on this prayer movement itself and its relation to daily living and morality. It would be impossible to deny the sense of liberation, which ought to be a feature of authentic prayer, which the movement has given to many people, as well as a sense of personal and communal integration at least as far as the group is concerned. (In this context the phenomenon of healing requires careful if positive evaluation.[1]) The dangers of excessive emotion undoubtedly exist, although the sheer lack of any emotional dimension in so much of even the reformed liturgy is not particularly praiseworthy either, given that the emotions are a God-given and integral part of man. More worrying from the ecclesial point of view are the dangers of elitism and sectarianism, although how far they exist is very difficult to judge. And for the moral theologian, with his sensitivities to the complexities of moral situations and to the mysteriousness of God's providential relationship with the world, there may appear to be for the less discerning a too easy temptation to appeal without question to what 'the Spirit told me'. Indeed there may be a deeper danger that the world in itself would be ignored in such an exclusively religious atmosphere.[2]

In my view these renewals in liturgy, shared prayer and moral theology remain basically positive, and include solid achievements which will undoubtedly persist. It is perhaps too soon to offer any final theological analysis of or balanced judgment on the Charismatic Renewal Movement, yet it might attend to some of the limitations which have emerged in the liturgical and moral theological renewal. And these limitations may lead in turn to posing the question of association in reverse form, that between morality and prayer, rather than prayer and morality.

IV. *From Morality to Prayer: A Reconsideration of the Bond*

The more obvious difficulty which renewal in prayer, liturgical, shared and private, faces is what is rather loosely known as the

[1] The best 'insider' account of this is probably Francis MacNutt, *Healing*, Ave Maria Press, 1975.

[2] These reservations are based on limited personal experience of the movement itself and so should not be exaggerated. Yet the history of not entirely dissimilar movements in the past would suggest that they may not be without some basis. P. Baelz, *Prayer and Providence*, London, 1968, would, together with some of the more classical treatments such as St Thomas Aquinas *Summa Contra Gentes*, Bk. III, provide useful balance on this matter. R. A. Knox, *Enthusiasm*, Oxford, 1950, still provides a very valuable historical counter-balance to other temptations of such a movement.

phenomenon of secularization. Without wishing to enter the tangled debate on this thorny issue, I think that it can be safely said that the cultural context in which our minds are shaped and so our prayer(s) learned and expressed has far fewer explicitly religious elements in it than it had even some decades ago and even in countries with such obvious public and private religious expression as Scotland and Ireland. For many people this secular cultural context has made God, the transcendent and religious dimension of life, unnecessary or irrelevant or at any rate much more remote and obscure. It has made the traditional prayer concepts, formulae and structures, however renewed, strangers to one's daily thinking and living. A lack of inner connection which threatens a lack of inner conviction can sometimes be discerned even among those with a firm desire to maintain and develop their prayer life.

This would in fact explain a certain sense of disappointment with the liturgical renewal in the Roman Catholic Church which some experience. Undoubtedly the expectations of many were raised too suddenly and too high, while the implementation by others has been partial and grudging.

More profoundly perhaps the expectations were simply mistaken at times. There was a suggestion that a community-based liturgy with fuller participation by the laity would quickly inspire and sustain the reform of society as a whole, breaking down in twentieth century America or wherever the barriers of race or sex or nation. When this did not happen except in particular groups and for individuals, the liturgy lost its significance for many earlier enthusiasts. The value of the liturgy in wider social renewal should not be ignored, but it is not a substitute for social moral action and the connection between prayer and moral action needs to be soundly based.

At popular and more reflective level the problem of the relationship between morality and prayer, a facet, as I have said, of the relationship between morality and religion, has to face the reality that, while there has been a traditionally very close association between morality and religion/prayer, morality itself is older and wider than the Judaeo-Christian tradition and that today it is taken for granted as essential to human living by people who reject or neglect religion and prayer. Confirmed and perhaps accelerated by the secularization process, however that is to be more precisely understood, morality in its popular impact as well as the subject of rigorous reflection, is increasingly regarded as an autonomous human phenomenon.[1] Where the autonomy is absolute and no relationship to any transhuman or transcosmic reality is accepted, one is faced with one of the many brands of humanist morality. Accepting morality in its immediate

[1] This is the point of departure of my recent book *Gift and Call*. What follows is, in the analysis of morality, largely based on that work.

and reflective state as autonomous does not however commit one to such absoluteness, which is basically derived from a philosophy of life that is not necessarily implicit in the analysis of morality itself but attempts to answer questions raised by, but going beyond, what that analysis provides. Such questions are not answerable in terms of moral analysis alone although they open the way to a discussion of philosophies of life, including Christianity, as providing (or not) some satisfying answers for enquirers.

Among the many possible approaches to moral analysis, I prefer for the task in hand to concentrate on the moral experience as it occurs in the concrete situation. This experience is, at its purest, of unconditional obligation to do or avoid something however unpleasant or disadvantageous it may be to me. And the final source of this obligation is another person or group of persons. In its most developed form the morality is an aspect of interpersonal relations (individual or group) which expresses an unconditional obligation or call, at least to recognize and respect the person(s) as person(s) and to make a particular response of food or shelter or education or comfort, according to the particular situation. The unconditionality which affects recognition, respect and response as three not always distinguishable phases of the same reaction, is founded in the character of the personal source as constituting a world of its own, a creative centre of knowing and loving, deciding and acting, which I as subject may not seek simply to use/abuse, to violate, to possess, to diminish or to eliminate. He is in that sense ultimately other than I am.

Because I am equally person and other, the call to recognition and respect is mutual, although the particular concrete response, e.g. providing food, may affect the first one (the subject) more immediately than the second (source of the call). In the reciprocal interchange, recognition or distinguishing the other in his otherness, develops identification of the self; respect for the other involves accepting and respecting the self; responding to the other involves seeking potentialities in the self or self-development.

The other person is however not simply source of call and so of burden, but comes to one as a creative, new and unique world, a gift or present in the literal sense of being driven or presented to one and in the further sense of being (at least potentially) enriching for one. But this has to be qualified by our equally undoubted experience of the other as threat, potential or actual, at an individual or group level, and provoking us to fear and self-protection. This ambiguity affects all our moral interchanges, although the direction of the overall moral call would seem to be to enabling the gift to triumph over the threat.

This moral or ethical analysis could be taken much further as have the meta-ethical[1] questions which it raises about the meaning of this human otherness with the unconditional obligations and inviolability which it involves; about the value or ability to go on attempting to enable the gifts to triumph over the threat in a world which has experienced Auschwitz and Hiroshima and a thousand lesser horrors; about the fulfilment available for subject or source even in the most favourable circumstances; and about the possible undermining of the whole moral enterprise by the absurdity of death. It is here, it seems to me, that Christianity corresponds and responds to the ethical analysis and meta-ethical questions: with its covenant structure relating God to man and man to man in a basically gift-call compounded by threat (sin) situation, with its understanding of human otherness as originating in the image of God the Father, the absolute other, and completed through its sharing in the divine sonship of Jesus Christ, and as finally assured of the triumph of gift over the most horrible threat, of meaning over absurdity in the suffering, death and resurrection of Jesus.

This mutual coherence, illumination and intrinsic connection which the Christian can observe is not offered here as a proof from moral analysis for the existence of God or the truth of Christianity. The humanist of whatever ilk would try to answer the meta-ethical questions, supposing he accepted the ethical analysis, from his own world-view. The scope of my argument is to provide Christian believers with a way of accepting the autonomy of the moral experience, but then seeking to understand its deeper connection with their faith in Jesus Christ—their awareness and acceptance of the God of Jesus Christ which have been given to them in the gift of the Spirit at Baptism.

Morality and faith are of course only a step away from morality and prayer. And it is by considering morality in terms of this analysis of human relationships and understanding what our moral responses as between people involve, first at the genuinely moral and human level, that I believe our awareness of God, our prayer-life can be enriched and expanded.

The recognition and respect of the other as other, which are essential phases of genuine moral response, are often simply implicit and taken for granted. Yet precisely for the task in hand they deserve more attention. Sensitivity to the unique world of the other in its actuality and potential, that is to the mystery of the other, with the respect and even awe which this induces in one's best moments, are in themselves enriching for me and my relationship, implying enhanced self-awareness and self-acceptance; moral awareness and the awe it inspires enrich the humanity of the world generally and can provide in a changing and more secular culture a new context for

[1] *ibid.*, particularly chs 4, 10.

religious awareness and awe.[1] Prayer may be formal and empty, lack inner connection and conviction because of the poverty of our human relationships and their moral implications. Unless more attention is paid to recognition and respect for the penultimate other, the recognition and respect for the ultimate may lack any real roots. The true basis for an intrinsic relationship between morality and prayer is to be found here.

In the Christian perspective the human otherness which demands this unconditional recognition and respect derives from, if it remains (inadequately) distinct from, the final other we call God.[2] Image and sonship are the Judaeo-Christian ways of understanding how the ultimate mystery is accessible to us in human form. So the moral response to the human other can and should by its own inherent dynamism expand into a response to the ultimate other; it can and should expand into prayer.

A fresh insight into this is provided by the Hebrew understanding of God as holy,[3] in a word which meant absolutely other, or, as it was later (more obscurely) termed, transcendent. This holiness, with the awe it inspires, he shared with people. The renewal of holiness as awareness of and sensitivity to otherness will have to be alive for people with people if it is to be alive for people with God. Renewal in prayer is not just dependent on or related in some extrinsic fashion to a good moral life and relationships, it can be seen as an expansion of these relationships.

The reciprocity of such relationships and the dialectic of other-recognition/respect and self-identification/acceptance shed a certain light on a problem rendered acute at least at the popular level in our own time,[4] the contrast between the God-up-there or out-there or beyond and the God-within, between the transcendent and the immanent God. In recognition and respect for the human other one can and should be opened up to the God-beyond, while in the dialectic effect of further identification and acceptance of the self (also a

[1] Although I was helped by them at the time, I do not find very satisfactory as theological analyses the previous attempts to deal with this challenge of prayer in a secular culture, by J. Daniélou, *Prayer as a Political Problem*, London, 1967, and D. Rhymes, *Prayer in the Secular City*, London, 1967.

[2] The interesting work of M. Nedoncelle already cited does move from an analysis of *prayer* between men to prayer between men and God. But this is an entirely different approach from the one used here although it could have some useful connecting points.

[3] This is obviously related to Rudolf Otto's *The Idea of the Holy*, London, 1968. For more recent useful comments cf. John P. Reeder Jr, 'The Relation of the Moral and the Numinous in Otto's Notion of the Holy' in Outka and Reeder (eds), *op. cit.*

[4] Whatever its ultimate theological limitations John Robinson's, *Honest to God*, London, 1963, and the ensuing debate did clearly find echoes of recognition among many Christians.

human other) one can and should be opened up to the God-within, the immanent God. It is this God-within, the immanent God, which is also accessible to us in our community identification. By taking account of the historical character of human relations and moral responses as they build up and move into the future, one is summoned to an awareness of the God-ahead, the eschatological God. And all this is dependent for its historical offer to each one and for its understanding on the original divine creation and incarnation. The absolute other, whose creating and saving deeds in the history of Israel and Jesus Christ gave human relations their divine significance, is also accessible in these relations as the God of the past as well as the present and the future, of man's origin and development as well as his present sustaining and transforming power and his future destiny.

In this necessarily compressed treatment of one aspect of moral analysis and its impact on understanding prayer, the perennial temptations to distortion and suppression are the more blatant. Clearly, sensitivity to human others may not in fact be expanded into awareness of the absolute and divine other. And for non-believers this seems undeniably true. (I do not wish to get engaged here with the quite different problem of how far this sensitivity may have an inevitable 'implicit' or 'anonymous' relationship with the God of Jesus Christ,[1] because even if one granted this, prayer in the strict and explicit sense does not arise for such people). For Christians also the temptation could be to reduce their Christianity and their prayer-life to 'good neighbourliness' on family, local, national or world-scale. The penultimate would have obscured the ultimate, perhaps to the point of becoming the ultimate itself and so created an idolatrous humanism.

Such temptation can only be avoided by insisting on the true meaning of the penultimate as derived from, dependent on and directed towards the ultimate. And for this, of course, direct and explicit attention to the ultimate in liturgical and personal prayer, shared or individual, is essential. Although again one has to be aware of being misunderstood, the close relationship between true and full other-recognition (including relationship to the absolute transcendent other) and true and full self-identification (including relationship to the absolute immanent other) would mean that the 'idolizing' of the penultimate would prevent the true and full self-identification, which in more traditional terms might be called 'damnation'.

The other temptation, to which the earlier presentation in both pre- and post-Vatican II phases might seem more open, could easily

[1] This problem was given considerable recent attention in Roman Catholic theology in the discussion of 'anonymous Christianity' associated in particular with Kark Rahner.

arise here too; the distortion or suppression of the penultimate for the sake of the ultimate, the distortion or suppression of morality for the sake of religion or prayer, where the human other is seen as finally derived from the ultimate other, the temptation to use him as a means to the ultimate other could become very real. Yet unless the human other is taken fully seriously as a world in herself/himself and for her/his own sake, his true reality is lost and the God we seek at his expense is not the God of Jesus Christ, of creation and salvation. And as one, in the move towards God, suppresses the other, so one suppresses the self and there is no basis for a proper relationship between God and the self either. Like all other human and cosmic realities, the call to renewal of prayer and of awareness of God by a renewal of human relationships and of morality, has its threat as well as its gift elements and can never be entirely unambiguous.

It is worth recalling at this stage the gift and threat aspects of human relationships and their moral dimensions. Concentrating on the gift for the moment, I feel that one of the primary moral activities is simply that of thanksgiving for the presence of the others, a celebration of their presence as gift. With the source and guarantee of this human otherness in mind, it is fairly easy to establish an inner connection between this primary moral call and activity and the thanksgiving for and celebration of the gift of the ultimate other. Where the Eucharist forms the explicit centre of such thanksgiving and celebration, it is easily connected in mind if not in practice with thanksgiving and celebration parties for immediately human reasons. And proper understanding and genuine celebration of both can and should be mutually enriching. The mission which began with a (wedding) party concluded with a last (Eucharistic) supper. The inner connection is based on the genuine humanity of the man who was God but was practically exemplified in the life of one who came eating and drinking, only to be accused of being a drunkard and a glutton (Lk 7:34).

The gift is always qualified and sometimes obscured and apparently overwhelmed by the threat. At both individual and group level, from battered babies and wives, to football hooliganism, to Northern Ireland or to the Middle East, one can hardly escape noticing the prevalence and reality of the threat. The cry and the prayer are for peace and reconciliation, for the triumph of the gift over the threat. To many people these cries and prayers seem hollow and evidently fruitless. Perhaps once again the penultimate has been ignored for the sake of the ultimate, the moral situation misunderstood or ignored or inadequately responded to, while refuge is taken in prayer. At least a moral awareness of threat as obscuring gift and of the call to enable the gift to triumph over the threat would shift the prayer from the lips to the heart (Is. 29:13). Efforts at reconciliation begin by taking the others fully seriously with their own unique world, their limitations, fears and hatreds, as well as their actual and potential achievements. Such moral response may be rebuffed or inadequate or meet with what is for the present at least, an intractable situation. Yet it has to go on, for the call is insistent and persistent, that we should seek to enable the gift to triumph over the threat. And the battering husband or mother, the hooded gunman or hostile soldier, the football hooligan or threatening rapist, are also gifts whose enriching potential one cannot see (perhaps they cannot see) and yet one must seek to discover and encourage to emerge.

'Love your enemies' (Mt 5:44) is how Jesus summarized the appropriate moral response to threat, the effort to transform it into gift. In pursuing this line, great risks may be involved and at the high point of moral response, one may have to lay down one's life even for one's enemies. The significance of this only becomes clear in the life and death of Jesus, but in the persistent attempts to reach the other as gift rather than threat, one is reaching for his mystery as image of God and Son of the Father. So, one is reaching for that divine mystery. The explicit prayer which one then voices for peace and reconciliation is the translation into words of what the search for God involves, as one seeks the true gift of humanity in one's enemy. Reconciliation is no cheap grace as Jesus showed, and it is frequently bought only at the price of human suffering as one or both individuals or groups persist in their efforts to overcome the threat element by the gift element, and so liberate true humanity and encounter its final mystery.

Such struggles today are conducted on the grand scale between exploiting or warring groups.[1] The efforts at reconciliation will be efforts to restore true recognition of and respect for the other group as gift rather than threat and then to find the appropriate solution which will embody that recognition and respect. The final argument against violence is that by eliminating one side to the dispute, it refuses ultimate recognition and respect and prevents mutual gift from replacing mutual threat. The immediate excuse for violence is that the powerful and entrenched (the basically threatening) refuse to recognize and respect the exploited and oppressed (the basically threatened) and provide structures adequate to enabling that recognition and respect to grow into mutual enrichment and the removal of threat and exploitation. The commitment to overcome exploitation and oppression imbued with a sense of justice for all and ready to undertake the same training programme, the same risks, as the men of violence (institutional or physical) will enrich our sense of human others and provide flesh and blood (incarnation) for the words of

[1] As I have noted before (*op. cit.*) there is still no fully satisfactory moral analysis of the relationships between groups.

appeal for peace to God or to others, which flow so readily from the mouths of the comfortable. And in the faith which fuels the loving commitment, the committed discern and experience the mystery of God even as Jesus did, above all in the oppressed and the marginal people, while remaining aware of it in the oppressor, his needs and even his particular impoverishment. Engagement in the pursuit of social justice at local, national and international level is about recognizing, respecting and responding to the inviolable otherness of all human beings; at the level of Christian understanding it is also an encounter with the absolute other in whose image and sonship all men share.[1]

It is, I believe, possible to consider other areas of moral activity, such as sexuality or verbal communication, and to discover the same kind of inner connection between the appropriate moral response to the other and the response to the ultimate other or God. From a different angle it is equally possible to take most of the traditional categories of prayer, adoration, thanksgiving, petition, contrition, in their vocal and silent forms or even more developed and mystical forms, and see how they have their parallels at the level of moral interchange between people and could be greatly enlivened and enriched by starting from the understanding of moral response and expanding into prayer. Along the same lines, the theological virtues which might well be called the 'prayer' virtues in their traditional meaning of having God as their immediate object (unlike the moral virtues which related directly to men) could be more richly understood by considering their human parallels, faith and hope in men as well as love of them, not simply as parallels, but as human realities relating human others but open to expansion to the ultimate other and to the transformation which that involves. However, if the point has not been sufficiently made by now that through moral experience and a deeper understanding of it one is opened up to prayer-experience and a fuller commitment to it, further elaboration will scarcely help.

Conclusion

Theologians are sometimes known to yield in arrogance to the temptations of exclusivity or totalitarianism in their analysis and solution of difficulties. It is not a temptation which I experience particularly strongly here. I am too well aware of the strength of the prayer-life and moral-life of the people in that era which I criticized as (inevitably) having a somewhat extrinsic understanding of the relation between prayer and morality, at least at the theological level.

[1] Cf. McDonagh, 'Human Violence: A Question of Ethics or Salvation', ch. 10, *op. cit.*, for a fuller discussion of this question.

Again, I am very well aware of the achievements of liturgical reform in my own Church and of the potential for good which the new prayer movement is already displaying, despite my reservations born of the inability of some very good people to connect inwardly with the predominantly religious thought and words used here. Threat elements are inseparable from gift elements in these movements, and could lead to liturgical and prayer communities estranged from, if not indifferent to the world in its 'secularized' state. My object has been simply to complement these developments by endeavouring to show that a reconsideration of moral relationships and responses can provide the dynamism for a prayer-development which avoids some of the limitations or threat-elements of the others discussed, while inevitably involving its own. And it is an approach which could increase communication between the 'study-bound' theologian and the Christian on the street, while it would seem also to have the advantage of cutting across denominational boundaries.

15 Theology and Method

by JOHN McINTYRE

1. One of Professor Torrance's most absorbing interests in recent years has been the nature of theological method. What he has said on this subject has set in motion many discussions about the relation of theological method to the methods of other sciences; the internal relation of theological method to the content of that discipline and whether either should precede the other and if so, which; the logic which is to be employed in deploying theological subject-matter—to mention but a few of the topics which have risen particularly in the wake of his *Theological Science*.[1] It is not proposed to offer here a critique of the views held by Professor Torrance on these subjects, but rather to set out an account of the nature of theological method prompted by a reading of his views. Since this account deals with some topics which he was not called upon to examine, it can not in any way be regarded as an alternative account, nor is it to be regarded as derivative of his views for which he must be somehow held responsible. It is rather by way of being a contribution to a subject which is dear to his heart.

1.1. Investigation into the nature of theological method requires that first of all we answer the question: What is theology? That requirement is a fair one in that the definition of a discipline in itself prescribes the kind of answer we are able to give to questions of method, quite apart from the other contention that the nature of the discipline may actually determine the method. There are in the main two answers to be given to the question: What is theology? the one extensive, the other intensive.

1.2. We may begin with what looks remarkably like the roll-call of any Faculty of Divinity, naming the subjects which are studied by those who are interested in theology: Old Testament and New Testament, both with study of the relevant languages, church history, Christian ethics, pastoralia, liturgiology, philosophy of religion and apologetics, as well as sociology of religion and comparative religion. The list is not meant to be exhaustive but its purpose is plain: it answers the question about what theology is by enumerating the subjects that you find under that heading in a library, or in a faculty

[1] London, 1969.

which teaches the subject. The following comments may be made upon the list:

1.2.1. What must surely strike us first of all is the tremendous heterogeneity of the subjects named. We seem to have in our discipline, literature, history, ethics, metaphysics, logic, and psychology; their presence within the discipline giving them all a religious characterization; and while it could be argued that as theological disciplines they are autonomous and may be practised without reference to any external norms or methods, nevertheless the fact that we can identify the disciplines named does suggest that the matter should be taken farther and even formalized.

1.2.2. We would then go on to say that the theological disciplines have a penumbra of closely related disciplines, whose methods are patently similar to, even if they do not actually impose criteria upon, those of the theological disciplines. So close do those disciplines stand to the contents of theology that it will be necessary at some time to indicate the exact nature of their relation to theology. The disciplines which I have in mind are: logic, philosophy, archaeology, epistemology, metaphysics, ethics, history, sociology, psychology, psychiatry, linguistics, and several language-systems.

1.2.3. If, instead of speaking of disciplines, we change to speaking of fields, two quite major problems connected with theological method come into focus. On the one hand we have the question of whether all the theological disciplines constitute one unitary field distinct even from the penumbral disciplines which may be thought to constitute adjacent fields. Despite their *prima facie* dissimilarity, it could be argued they are internally related to one another in a very special way in which no one of them is related to any apparently similar penumbral field. On the other hand there is the complementary question of whether the theological disciplines each share a field with one of the penumbral disciplines most akin to it. In a sentence, is the philosophy of the Christian religion more akin to philosophy than it is to church history? Those who would answer this last question in the negative and maintain generally that the theological disciplines form a unitary field and have a common factor which they do not share with the penumbral disciplines, would base their case on an intensive answer to the question: what is theology? and to their answer we now turn.

1.3. The simplest form of answer to the question which I know was given by Professor Torrance's old mentor and my own, the late Principal John Baillie, many years ago, when he said that 'theology is the *logos* of *theos*'. Dr Baillie was shrewd enough to realize the delphic quality of his answer, pointing out that it may mean either the reasoned and reasonable statement of the nature of God, or the reasoned and reasonable statement of what men and women thought and think about God. When we remember Dr Baillie's insistence in one of his earliest books[1] upon the fact that theology is a science and that the kind of enquiry which it prosecutes is scientific, then we will be struck by the similarity between his view and that stated by Professor Torrance forty years later: 'theological science has for its primary object the one God who is the source of all being and the ground of all truth'.[2] Unless we are going to say that every theological discipline can in fact be seen to be in the same way a scientific enquiry into God—and I do not think that either Professor Torrance or Dr Baillie wishes to do so—then we have to show how this intensive statement about the nature of theology is related to our earlier enumeration of the different disciplines normally called theological.

Extemporizing upon a theme of Anders Jeffner's[3] concerning the nature of religious statements, I should like to propose the following as going some way to meet the problem of relating the individual theological disciplines to the intensive concept of theological science with God as its single primary subject:

CTD is a Christian theological discipline = df. CTD is a discipline which is connected immediately or mediately (i) with some aspect or aspects of the central facts of the Christian faith, particularly with the life, death and resurrection of Jesus Christ as the fulfilment of the purposes of God for mankind and the whole creation; and (ii) with the response of men and women to these central facts, to the anticipation of them or to their sequel. Such a discipline is seen to be so connected by those who practise it and is so felt by them to be a condition of their practice of it, that if the connection were invalidated or severed, they would cease to regard it as a Christian theological discipline. The following points are being made in this definition:

1.3.1. First of all, it is being affirmed that the theological disciplines exhibit unity of centre rather than unity of system. They derive their character from the relation in which they stand to the central facts of the Christian faith, and not primarily at any rate from the relationships which they set up with one another. At a later stage these lateral relationships develop; but they are only possible because of a primary radial relationship which the disciplines hold to the centre.

1.3.2. Secondly, and instantly we have to add that their connection with the centre varies considerably in immediacy. In some cases, the link is direct, for example, in the study of the literature of the New

[1] *The Interpretation of Religion*, Edinburgh, 1929. See particularly Chapters 1 and 2.

[2] *op. cit.*, p. 282.

[3] *The Study of Religious Language*, London, 1972, pp. 8 ff.

Testament, or the doctrine of creation, or the obedience of faith. In other cases, by contrast, the connection is more accurately described as mediate. Some parts of the Old Testament have no connection either with prophetic anticipations of the Messiah, or with the mighty acts in which God demonstrates his will to redeem Israel, or with the covenant which he has made with them. The study of such parts of the Old Testament is rightly regarded as part of the theological discipline because they can be related indirectly or mediately to one or other of these great themes which link directly to the centre of the faith. Some parts of church history which deal, for example, with the economic circumstances which existed in Scotland in the century before the Reformation are of great significance in the account of the way in which the Reformation rooted itself and expressed itself in the Scottish scene, but their relation to the central facts of the Christian faith can only be said to be mediate. The point does not require to be laboured in examples from other disciplines.

1.3.3. I do think, next, that it is important to draw attention to the special role which must be assigned to Jesus Christ in the definition of any discipline which calls itself Christian, while at the same time recognizing that his place in the faith can only be properly understood when he is related to the whole purposes of God, the Triune God. In other words, theological disciplines are not exclusively christocentric. On the contrary, the centre as I have been calling it, to which these disciplines are variously related is in fact very complex indeed, nor can its boundaries be demarcated with any complete precision; it is the responsibility of some of the Christian theological disciplines to concern themselves with demarcation problems.

1.3.4. The definition, moreover, takes note of the fact that an increasing number of theological disciplines have very much to do with the range of human response to the central material of the Christian faith and facts. These disciplines are necessarily included in our line-up because of the recognition that the human response is itself a theological fact, without which the centre of the faith would be incomplete.

1.3.5. The practitioners of these disciplines must themselves see that their connection, either immediate or mediate, with the central facts is a genuine one, and regard it as their reason for pursuing their studies. If at any time in the further course of these studies it was eventually shown that their connection with the central facts of the Christian faith was neither immediate nor mediate, then these disciplines would have to surrender their title Christian. For instance, if the marxist thesis about the origins and course of the Reformation in Germany were proved to be correct; if the whole theological content of the interpretation of Luther's stand and that of all his supporters and his opponents could be drained away in the alleged interests of historical truth; and if that presentation carried such conviction to the practitioners of the discipline which had been known as church history that they abandoned all their previous views about the relations of the events in Germany in the early part of the sixteenth century to the Christian Gospel of forgiveness; then these practitioners would no longer claim to be engaged in a Christian theological discipline, at least in dealing with that segment of history.

1.3.6. What has emerged from this discussion is that though the several theological disciplines cohere in a unity of centre, they are not to be thought of as so many embodiments of some universal concept called theological science. They will all be pursued with devotion to their centre, and they will be practised with all the rigour, control and reasoned organization imposed upon them by the truth and integrity of that centre. But we have no reason to think that they are uniform in structure; nor have we at this stage grounds for concluding that the methods which are to be associated with them are identical and uniform, beyond their common devotion to their centre. In fact it is logically possible that the methods are as diverse as the disciplines, and that this diversity may be found even within one discipline. That fact does not depress me nor confuse me. I think of a discipline such as medicine which may be defined as the science concerned with the cure, alleviation, and prevention of disease, and with the restoration and preservation of health of the human person. Yet this apparently single science has within it many disciplines and by implication many methods; but these, it seems to me, are held together in unity through their radial relation to the unitary human person, in health and in disease, and through that radial relation they acquire and develop many further lateral relationships with one another.

2. Having committed ourselves to a definition of theological discipline, there is perhaps a continuing responsibility to give like treatment to the other half of our subject, method. In a rough approximation we could say that method is the way you present your material in treating your subject, the kinds of figures, images, and language you regard as appropriate to it, the arguments you employ to defend your statements, and the whole variety of interpretations that you bring to its understanding. Let me therefore formalise this rough approximation with a view to drawing out its full complexity. The formal statement will then be examined section by section. M is the method of a theological discipline = df. M is the series of procedures, originating within the 'given' of the discipline, which are to be followed (i) in establishing the central facts and concepts of the discipline; and (ii) in interpreting, describing, expounding, explaining and defending the subject-matter of the discipline contained within

the 'given' and the claims arising out of it. These procedures enunciate criteria of truth and validity that operate in the discipline, define the kind of evidence that is quoteable as warrant for its claims, schematize the arguments that are to be employed in its explication or substantiation, as well as the language, models, figures, imagery and analogies which function across its whole range.

2.1. It should be said at once that a definition of this sort is a classical case of wisdom after the event. In fact there would be justification for the view that methodological reflections such as are the theme of this study are third order activities. The actual practice of the Christian faith in worship and obedience and in total commitment to God through Christ is and remains the first order activity. The second order comes with the systematisation, and reflection upon that basic material, such as is found in the many disciplines mentioned at 1.2. The consideration of how these second order disciplines operate is our present task. While its third order status should be a constant warning to us that we are at two removes from the reality of the faith and so in danger of being out of touch, that fact is not in itself inhibiting or frustrating; we may at any time move to the second or even first orders for fresh checking and renewed insight. The *ex post facto* quality of the methodological enquiry certainly does not entail its irrelevance to the second order where the disciplines are practised. To become self-consciously aware of what we are doing, of the criteria we are employing and of the arguments we are permitted to adopt, is a very sure way to a much more efficient practice of the discipline.

2.2. When the definition is taken with what was previously said about the heterogeneous disciplines that constitute Christian theology, the comment has to be made that we must not expect to find every detail of this method instanced in each one of them. Some are more concerned with exposition than with defence, with systematization than with inference, so that across the different disciplines the emphasis will vary, nor will we be surprised if there is variation in the detail of the way the procedures operate. What is unlikely to happen is that any of the major features of this method will be totally absent from any one of those disciplines.

2.3. It will be fairly obvious that no serious attempt has been made in this definition to allow any pride of place or paradigmatic priority to the method of the natural sciences. It is remarkable that even a theologian of the stature of Bernard Lonergan[1] should feel obliged to make his deferential nod in that direction, 'We shall appeal to the successful sciences to form a preliminary notion of method'. Even though in the next sentence he appears to escape the full implications of that statement by saying that 'we shall go behind the procedures of

[1] *Method in Theology*, London, 1972, p. 4.

the natural sciences to something both more general and more fundamental, namely, the procedures of the human mind', the damage has been done. His own method is to universalize on the basis of the particular method of natural sciences, and to proceed through the transcendental method as he calls it to more special methods appropriate to particular fields. The only justification he offers for this allocation of paradigmatic and prior status to the natural sciences is their 'success', a curious nineteenth century view of their achievements. I see no reason whatsoever for saying that the natural sciences have been in any way more 'successful' than, say, history or linguistics or philosophy. Professor Torrance in his study of *Theological Science* seems almost to be taking the same line as Lonergan, saying that 'there is an important sense in which physics has played an exemplary role, and may still be allowed to stand as a model of pure science' (p. 107). Yet if you look closely at his presentation of the nature of scientific activity, you will find that his starting point is not an analysis of the method of physics which he subsequently universalizes but his theorem about general science, namely, that 'in all science reason behaves in terms of the nature of the object' (p. 111). Special sciences, physics included, are particularizations of that general procedure, modifications dictated by the distinctive nature of the object in each case.

2.4. Clearly in the definition we have made ample allowance for the way in which the procedures to be followed in the theological disciplines must be appropriate to the disciplines concerned, and for the sort of consequence which will inevitably follow upon the importation into one of these disciplines of a method alien to it. Professor Torrance has described this position in his own way by saying that 'a scientific theology . . . will have nothing to do with a method that is not governed by the material content of its knowledge . . . it must be controlled knowledge that operates with proper criteria and appropriate methods of verification'[1]. He would argue further that the appropriateness of the method to be followed in any science and *a fortiori* in theological science is determined by 'the unique nature of its own particular object'.[2] This assertion echoes so many similar statements of his throughout his writings such as that the nature of the object prescribes the mode of rationality proper to its investigation that it may repay a little further examination.

2.5.1. When it is said that the object determines the method in any study, it might seem that at least two invalid assumptions are being made. The first is that the object with which any study is concerned is apprehended in some veridical way at the very outset of the study. Without some such clear initial apprehension, it would be difficult

[1] *op. cit.*, p. 116.
[2] *id.*, p. 112.

to see how, on this present reading of their relationship, the object could possibly determine the method to be followed in investigating that object. This assumption would seem to be false for the reason that it is doubtful if any discipline—apart from a completely aprioristic one such as pure mathematics or logico-mathematics, which begins from axioms and postulates clearly stated at the beginning of the deductions—ever originates in a clear knowledge of its object. In fact, there is a very real sense in which knowledge of the object of the science comes only at a very late stage in its development. In the case of biology, for example, it is only in very recent times that scientists have begun to speak with any assurance about the nature of life. Even the physicists who are in this respect further ahead than most of their colleagues would be as reluctant as any of them to claim anything approaching certainty about the nature of the object that they investigate. When we move over into the theological disciplines then the situation might initially appear to be somewhat better. The claim might here be made that the object of theological disciplines is self-revealing, and that without knowledge of God from the start these disciplines would never have begun. While one can not but admire the piety of such a view, he would have to question its realism. The fact of God's self-revelation is not in question; what is not so incontestable is agreement about what the content of the revelation is, a single unique *revelatum*, agreement about which might form the starting-point for the prescription of the method to be followed in theological investigation. One of the complicating components in that starting-point Professor Torrance has indicated: 'the fact of our knowing God enters into the content of that knowledge, so that there is an interplay between human subject and divine object'.[1] When we pass from the strictest theology concerned with the doctrine of God into such areas as church history or missiology, it is even more difficult to identify one single object for the discipline.

The second invalid assumption that appears to be being made in the assertion that the object of a discipline determines the method is that prescription or determination is the right way to describe how object and method are related to one another. If it is the case as has been argued that the object of a discipline may well not emerge with clarity till a late state in the process, then the relation of object to method is much more subtle than that of determination of the latter by the former. The object yields itself to the increasing sophistications of the method, which in their turn are validated by their ability to enable the investigator to penetrate to the fullest nature of the object. The last say must be with the object, but only the last say.

2.5.2. How, then, can we best state what we are now seeking to establish—the relation of method to object? Perhaps we shall fare

[1] *id.*, p. 97.

better if we speak not so much about the object with which any discipline deals, for that is a simplification of its subject-matter, as about the field of discipline. The object will be found or it will occur within the field, but it will not be isolated necessarily within any one part of it. In fact the task of the method to begin with may turn out to be that of locating the object in the field, which in these initial stages, if not also later, will be equivalent to what we shall soon be going to examine under the name of the 'given'. The term which I would prefer to use to describe method and field is correlation, which would allow for adjustment on both sides; and since in any relation of correlation there has to be ultimately a dominant term even when there is a functional relation between the two terms, it will be the field, which in the end of the day will have to be regarded as dominant. It should be pointed out at once of course that by stating the relationship in such a fashion, I have not solved any major problems. The task remains to give content to that rather formal description by showing how the method actually operates on and in the field.[1]

3. Taking up from now onwards the detail of our definition of method at item 2 above, and following the suggestion that the field of a discipline certainly in the initial stages of its practice is what has been already named the 'given', we must now analyse this concept more carefully. As I have indicated elsewhere,[2] the concept of the given is extremely ambiguous; and it behoves anyone using the term to declare his interest and intention.

3.1. It may help what we have to say about the given of the theological disciplines if I recapitulate and partly modify that analysis.[3] There are at least six senses in which the concept of the given is understood in modern philosophical usage.

3.1.1. First we have the given as the directly intuitable, what is so presented to the observer that simple examination of its content reveals its nature. The percipient is thought of as in no way contributing to what is in front of him, or if not a sense-percept, to what is presented to his mind or emotions. In this sense the given is to be contrasted with interpretations which the observer might later impose upon it. It is regarded as being beyond all reasonable doubt. Consequently it tends to become a kind of court of appeal, a norm of truth to settle an argument.

3.1.2. Secondly, a more advanced epistemology might refine upon sense one of the given, and, pointing out that any perceptual situation is an amalgam of two components, sensation resulting from external stimulus, and categorical conceptualization, assert that the given is

[1] *vide infra*, pp. 216 ff.
[2] *The Shape of Christology*, London, 1966, pp. 13 ff.
[3] *ibid.*

to be equated with those components in the perceptual situation which come from outside the perceiving subject. As distinct from the former sense, this view would hold that the given is never sensed in its purity, in isolation from the conceptual categorization. It is one element in a complex situation, and can be abstracted only in analysis.

3.1.3. Thirdly, while a technical notion of the given runs all through Heidegger's *Sein und Zeit*,[1] there are other features of his thought which lead to an interesting view of the given. 'The way things have been interpreted by the "they" has already restricted the possible options of choice to what lies within the range of the familiar, the attainable, the respectable—that which is fitting and proper. This levelling of Dasein's possibilities to what is proximally at its everyday disposal also results in a dimming down of the possible as such. The average everydayness of concern becomes blind to its possibilities and tranquillizes itself with that which is merely "actual".'[2] The given can be the circumscribed situation in which I find myself due to pressures of the past, of other persons or of my own blindness to the possibilities of my position. Heidegger condemns this view which I take of my position as 'inauthentic existence', but for many people it is the only existence they know. Transposed into our discussion, this existentialist insight presents the given as the system of parameters within which our thinking or action on a certain matter has to operate.

3.1.4. Fourthly, we must include for the record the sense of the given which we all probably first encountered, the given of Euclidean geometry. Given triangle ABC such that angle ABC is equal to angle ACB; prove that . . . In this sense the given is the point of logical departure in a proof of some kind. I have been careful not to say that it constitutes the premise of the subsequent argument. As we all know who have come through the process of Euclidean indoctrination, the subsequent argument depends upon a whole range of pertinent propositions and postulates which have to be kept in mind as we set down the so-called proof. The given both presupposes the previously established propositions and the stated axioms and postulates and prescribes the point of departure for further logical argumentation and exposition. Just because the Euclidean given—if I may so describe it—is part of an aprioristic system, it has been responsible for a widespread impression that what is subsequently derived from the given is somehow implicit in the given. That view is not necessarily true even of the Euclidean given: but that understanding of it has spread into other fields where this view of the character

[1] See particularly pp. 36, 115, 129 (references to German text).

[2] Quoted by John Macquarrie in *Studies in Christian Existentialism*, London, 1966, p. 67, from *Sein und Zeit*, pp. 194 f.

of the given is also accepted. We shall have to return to this notion; for the moment we merely note its origin.

3.1.5. The given received a rather different assessment from Professor Kemp Smith from those which we have examined. For him it was the problematical rather than the crystal clear first statement in a deductive argument, or the veridically intuitable. It was some situation which confronted us with some kind of problem requiring a solution, for it would not be immediately explicable in terms of our existing knowledge. The situation constituting the given might be only an unusual reading on an instrument, the apparent movement of the station while the train in which we were travelling appeared by contrast to be stationary, or just the odd, out-of-character behaviour of our friend, or a whole vast new range of scientific data. Kemp Smith used to make a great deal of the fact that the given as the problematical was the key to all intellectual advance, and that it demanded great perceptiveness to realize just when you were in its presence.

3.1.6. It is not a long step from Kemp Smith's account of the given to one which regards the given as the subject-matter of a discipline. When we find occurring together a sufficient number of apparently related problematical situations, and that in attempting to solve one set we are beginning to discern solutions to others, while all the time the field is growing and becoming more comprehensive; then we have on our hands the subject-matter of a discipline. In an interesting way that definition gathers up quite a few of the emphases that were made by the others. For example, this subject-matter is imposed upon us and is not the result of our own devising. It constitutes the starting-point of our enquiries, even though we do not think of it as the first line of a logical deduction. It provides the contextual framework within which our researches will be conducted.

3.2. Let us now discuss the character of the given in the theological disciplines in the light of these general reflections upon its varied nature.

3.2.1. In speaking of the given, I find myself in ever increasing sympathy with the claim contained in the existentialist position that we must begin where we are. The given is what is given to us. It does not consist of some set of logical propositions from which all else follows—and here I part company with at least part of the Euclidean notion of the given. It is what confronts us where we are, and even when we try to disentangle, say, church history from Christian origins, the very process of disentangling requires us to begin where we are. If we do so, we shall find ourselves in the position which Kemp Smith so much welcomed, for then we have before us the problematical which is so creative of further reflection, definition and insight. We shall also be reluctant to identify the given with any single *one* of those entities with which theologians in the past have been so anxious to identify the given to the exclusion of all the others. By contrast I should be willing to include most of these entities with which the given has been variously identified. Let me therefore itemize the constituents of the given as I see them, indicating wherever relevant why it seems to me to be wrong to isolate any one.

3.2.2. A strong claim is made, particularly in the Protestant line, to give absolute prime and sole place to the Bible in defining the given of Christian theology. Clearly the claim has much attraction. We come out of a period when so-called 'biblical theology' was regarded as normative of all theology. Even yet, wherever our sympathies lie in the matter of the authority of the Bible, we all invariably turn to the Bible when searching for light upon a major doctrine of the faith, or when challenged about the Christian character of some statement that we have made. If I am pressed for an answer to the question how I came to know originally about the relation of the Father to the Son in the Holy Trinity, I can not but reply that it was because the Bible told me so. On that point and quite a number of others fundamental to the Christian faith, I would have to say that that answer is true not only for myself but for the whole church at least from the time when the scriptures began to be accepted in the worship and scholarship of the church. But I have instantly to add that when the Bible told me so, I heard what it had to say, not in a vacuum or some kind of splendid isolation, but in the context of a tradition and accepted interpretation and theological commentary. These, too, have entered into the given and constituting part of it require to be acknowledged.

3.2.3. Of those other components of the given perhaps the primary is the creeds and confessions adopted by the Protestant churches or the formally recognized tradition of the Roman Church. It may be that their strictly logical status in relation to the Bible is that they are interpretations of it; it may be, alternatively, that they represent the further working of the very revelation which gave us the Bible, and provide knowledge of God and his works that goes beyond the Bible. To such matters we shall have to return. In the meantime we simply note that for us they form part of the given. But that is not all: in addition to what might be called the official agencies of interpretation others have been operating—biblical and theological commentaries as well as Sunday school lessons and sermons and talks. These all operating together serve to demonstrate how internally complex a body of material the given is.

3.2.4. One term to which exclusive claim to be regarded as the totality of the given is sometimes assigned is revelation, and clearly it must be allocated a place even if not an exclusive one. A place is to be given it in two ways. First, it has come in recent times to be the dominant characterization of the events of the Incarnation for many of our contemporaries. Even though it is in itself a description of what happened when the word was made flesh and depends for its meaning upon all the other things which the church has had traditionally to say about Jesus Christ, nevertheless it has come to colour much of our substantive understanding of the given and can not therefore be neglected. Secondly, some parts of the given do themselves actually present this character of revelation to us here-and-now. Through them we are ourselves confronted with the realities or the Reality with which and with whom they were concerned. What must not be affirmed is that this quality pervades the entirety of the given. There are areas which do not shine with this light; some which are very opaque and which may long remain so.

3.2.5. In order to fix the different concepts on some kind of map, I should like to give a placing of the given in relation to what has been called at item 2 the subject-matter, and also in relation to the discipline in item 1.3. As I read the situation the subject-matter is initially located within the given, but with the development of the discipline it will expand beyond it. For example, we read in the Bible that God acted in this way and that, said this and that, but as the discipline of dogmatics grows, the doctrine, say, of the attributes of God develops and we find ourselves saying things about God that are not contained in so many words in the given. It has to be noted however that the development of a discipline must not be such that it loses contact with the given, which remains even to the end a form of check upon what is said in the developing subject-matter. Concerning discipline and the given, we may observe that the given is, as it were, the founding charter of the discipline, which is by that charter commissioned to present its content with clarity and conviction, expound it and defend it, and generally to perfect the procedures which most competently achieve that end. The discipline does all of these things by means of its method; and so we must now turn to the next stage of our discussion, which is an examination of the way the method handles the given and the nature of the procedures which it follows.

4. When we turn to the series of procedures which the method follows in dealing with the subject-matter located in the given of the discipline, we can not fail to observe that there is one single procedure which appears to be omni-prevalent both throughout the different procedures mentioned in our original definition of method and throughout the different theological disciplines themselves, namely, interpretation. That, however, is not the whole of the truth, for interpretation is to be found also in the given which forms the starting-point of the discipline. The complex problems which arise over the precise nature of interpretation, and we shall soon be

indicating what they are, would be very much simplified if we could be assured of starting from a given which was uninterpreted, a bare datum, as it were. Such a datum would constitute a norm for the variety of interpretations which might subsequently be imposed upon it. It might even be accepted by all the supporters of the different interpretations. The sad and difficult truth is that the given itself is permeated with interpretation, and much of the subsequent variety of interpretation derives from that initial variety.

4.1. The prevalence of interpretation upon the theological scene has prompted me to present what I would call the spectrum of interpretation. It begins with the events that happened in biblical times and runs through to the most developed of the theological disciplines, thus: events; biblical narrative (in Hebrew or Greek or in the languages of their sources); translation; paraphrase; exegesis; exposition/sermon; creeds and confessions; biblical theology; dogmatic theology; philosophical theology; ethics. The items on the spectrum are fairly self-explanatory. Events are the happenings which form the story of the Bible. They occurred before witnesses who saw them not simply as occurrences of an ordinary sort, but as having a much deeper significance; and if they had themselves failed to perceive that significance themselves, there was a prophet or a priest nearby to offer the fully religious interpretation. The events with this interpretation are what we have in the biblical narrative, recorded in the appropriate language; and since we know that in some cases, the narrative which we have depends on some earlier account, we have to include that source in its original form. Proceeding along the spectrum we come to translations, which as we realize perhaps more than any previous generation because of the enormous number of modern translations which are available to us involve an enormous amount of interpretation. Sometimes the original is untranslateable, or can not be translated without some loss of meaning, a classical example being the first verse of the Gospel according to St John where the Greek reads 'the Word was with the God and the Word was God'. According to Hoskyns[1] 'it is impossible to reproduce in English this contrast. The Coptic version alone has been able to reproduce the meaning of the original Greek'. Paraphrase is free translation which does not seek to abide too closely by the *ipsissima verba* of the original, and does so in the interests of a presumed better understanding of the original. In exegesis the possibilities of interpretation appear to be infinite. Sometimes the exegete will quote non-biblical uses of terms used by the biblical writer, or their use by other biblical writers, sometimes the philosophical, or sociological or cultural overtones of the terms, sometimes their theological

[1] Sir Edwyn Hoskyns and F. N. Davey, *The Fourth Gospel*, London, 1940, Vol. 1, p. 136.

contribution to the understanding of the message of the writer—to mention but a random few of the devices that he may employ to interpret the words of the text. In exposition/sermon, we move into the area of still freer handling of the biblical material, but even here, especially when we are thinking of expository preaching, the presentation claims to derive from the original text, and to be an application of the text. Creeds, confessions, biblical theology and dogmatic theology carry the formalization of the biblical material to the final stages of systematization and definition; and by a curious paradox which reverses the whole process, provide the structures, the hermeneutic as it is so popularly called, for the re-interpretation of the more original elements on the spectrum. If we may quote yet another classical example, this time from Athanasius,[1] he employs the theological doctrine of the consubstantiality of the Son to the Father in order to propound what he regards as the proper exegesis of St John, 10.3, 'I and the Father are one'. The spectrum could be extended to include the other disciplines normally included under the generic term of theology; and in these cases there would be involved in the original given—in addition to the material provided by the rest of the spectrum—historical records, liturgical practices, social behaviour, religious experiences and so on. . . . The principle would be the same—an original given which came before the practitioner of the discipline would be subjected to still further interpretation. This spectrum is so wide, and one might feel so all-embracing, that it will be impossible to find any formula to cover such a range. We shall, therefore, be on our guard against any premature universalization of elements present at limited points on the spectrum. Let us then tease out some of the senses which the notion of interpretation seems to have.

4.2. To begin with we see that it is equivalent to translation, a term which may be given a literal and a metaphorical sense, both of which are valid. On the one hand, when a word is translated from one language into another, it is very often very difficult to get an exact equivalent. It is difficult enough when we use modern languages, but when we move into the classical and biblical languages, major sources of misunderstanding appear. Obvious examples are the New Testament words *Logos* and *agape*. Words, it could almost be said, do not have exact translations in other languages, for they all belong to an ethos, a culture, a society, a literary tradition or a spoken folklore. They have their place within these and they derive their significance and their value from them. On the other hand, this literal sense of what interpretation means at one end of the spectrum is a clue to the metaphorical meaning that it may have at the other end.

[1] *Four Discourses Against the Arians*, Oxford, 1842, Discourse IV, Subject IV, pp. 523 f.

Here interpretation involves the transposition of given biblical material or credal affirmation from its original *mise-en-scène* into some more modern setting. At 1 Corinthians 15:10. St Paul wrote: 'By the grace of God I am what I am . . . I laboured more abundantly than they all: yet not I, but the grace of God which was in me'. Donald Baillie[1] has transposed that Pauline statement into a setting which included such notions as the paradox of grace and the prevenient activity of God. Peter Hamilton[2] transposes the whole situation which St Paul has described into a Hartshorne-type of process theology which in his judgment does greater justice than Baillie's account to the reality of human freedom, not allowing it to be 'swamped by God's influence'. Many theologians in modern times have attempted a similar transposition for the doctrine of the Trinity and the doctrine of Creation. The logical formal structure of what is happening is as follows: x, it is assumed, has the same relation to a, b, c to n, and plays the same role within the system S as x, bears to a_1, b_1, c_1, to n_1, and plays within the system S_1. The merit of the transposition lies in the way in which it attempts to replace what may be a frame of reference not easily accepted by some modern reader with one which he will more readily understand. The difficulties which it has to face lie in the possibilities that a_1 may not be equivalent to a in the first place, or S and S_1 may be so dissimilar to one another that it is impossible for them to impart identity of meaning to any two elements within them. It could be argued that maladjustment within a psychological system can not be accepted as equivalent to sin within a conservative theological system. There are many, however, who would say that Christian thinkers have to take the risk of failing to establish such equivalences if they hope to present an intelligible message today.

4.3. Because of the extremely important part which interpretation has played particularly in the history of creeds and doctrine, as the link between the given, which may be the Bible or revelation or some such original datum, and the creeds or doctrines, the logical status of this relationship has understandably come in for serious examination.

4.3.1. One way of describing the relationship is to say that the interpretation is implicit in the given and that it is the making explicit of the full interior nature of the given. Thus it has been held that the statement that the Son is *homoousios* with the Father is implicit in the biblical statement that 'I and the Father are one'. The theological statement is the unfolding of a truth that lies hidden in the Johannine statement. This idea that the interpretation is somehow implicit in the given springs I believe from a fear of the consequences that will

[1] *God was in Christ*, London, 1948, pp. 116 f.

[2] *The Living God and the Modern World*, London, 1967, pp. 91 f.

follow if we conceded that the interpretation adds something new to the given. The fear is twofold, first that thereby we might be implying some inadequacy in the original datum of scripture or revelation which prevented it from being sufficient not only for man's knowledge of God, but for his salvation by God. As the Westminster Confession puts it[1]: 'The whole counsel of God concerning all things necessary for his glory, man's salvation, faith, and life, is either expressly set down in Scripture, or by good and necessary consequence may be deduced from Scripture: unto which nothing is at any time to be added, whether by new revelations of the Spirit, or traditions of men'. The Bible does not require anything to be added to it by way of interpretation, to provide what is necessary for man's salvation. The second element in the fear of the consequences of the interpretation adding anything to the original datum is that we might seem thereby to be denying that the Bible in its simplicity is immediately accessible to all, and particularly to children and the child-like, and suggesting that there is a higher way to glory for the sophisticated. If it is acknowledged that an interpretation makes no claim to provide a means to salvation not already in scripture, and that it does not pretend to some higher personal knowledge of God even though to some fuller knowledge about him; then I do think that the way is clear to asserting that the interpretation does say new things about the subject denoted by the given. When Athanasius says that 'the Son is consubstantial with the Father' he is saying more than St John said in the verse, 'I and the Father are one'. There is a semantic gap; I am not yet saying that it is a logical gap, for that remains to be examined. That gap, and sometimes it appears more like a gulf, is an essential feature of the relation of an interpretation and its original.

4.3.2. A not dissimilar view of the relation of interpretation to original is that the interpretation says the same thing as the original but says it in a different way. A formal construction of this view would be that the original denoted a certain situation to which we are directed on reading it or hearing it. Having turned our attention to that situation we are then in a position to forget the original signpost, and describe the situation in alternative terms which then constitute the interpretation. I have two faults to find with this view. First, it relies too heavily upon an ostensive understanding of the nature of definition or meaning. A word, a sentence is not an expendible item in the process of communication; it imparts something of its character to the situation it describes or denotes. Secondly and consequently, the interpretation has to take account of its original and not simply walk away from it forgetful of its character. If originally we have spoken of Jesus as Logos, and in a different setting proceed to describe him in strictly messianic terms, we are

[1] At Chapter I, VI.

not entitled to think that the latter is simply an interpretation of the former. That is not to say that both sets of terms are descriptions of the one person. It *is* to say that they are different ways of talking about the same person, and that we have a quite major problem on our hands of combining these two ways of speaking about him. Even in the case quoted above from Athanasius, we can not hold that Athanasius is saying the same thing about the Son as St John, but saying it in a different way. They are not saying the same thing, even though the one is interpreting the words of the other.

4.3.3. An earlier quotation from the Westminster Confession[1] that 'the whole counsel of God . . . is either expressly set down in Scripture or by good and necessary consequence may be deduced from Scripture' gives us a clue to another possible way of looking at the relation of original to interpretation, namely, that of logical entailment. It has often been felt particularly in theological circles that the only way in which the validity of an interpretation of a credal or doctrinal statement could be assured was to claim that it was logically entailed by some scriptural original. The doctrine of *creatio ex nihilo*, albeit an essential part of the Christian doctrine of creation, is not logically inferrible from the story of creation as we have it in the opening chapters in Genesis, or yet from the Hebrew word *br'*. Even Athanasius seems to rely more upon the weight of the 'catholic faith' to browbeat Arius than powers to deduce the *homoousios* from the text, 'I and the Father are one'. Were it not so, the heretics who are of all men the most logical and frequently exceptionally well-versed in the scriptures could not have long survived. It is because of the absence of the logical nexus that they stake a claim for their rival interpretations, and why so often the orthodox are reduced to falling back upon authority. There must be recognized to exist between original and interpretation a logical gap, a discontinuity, which will always make the transition from the one to the other an occasion of risk.

4.3.4. Discussion of interpretation in recent years has derived from a now famous statement of Wittgenstein's[2]: '. . . we can see the illustration (in this case a cubic figure) now as one thing now as another—So we interpret it, and *see* it as we *interpret* it.' It is however his duck-rabbit which has achieved the greater fame, and the process of 'seeing-as' has been the key to the interpretation of interpretation in our time. In the sequel Wittgenstein makes a variety of comments—such as that the two heads, the one seen like a rabbit and the other seen like a duck, are not in the slightest way similar, and yet are congruent; or that when it is a puzzle-picture my visual impression of it changes, acquires a new 'organisation'; or that the

[1] *supra* at 4.3.1.
[2] *Philosophical Investigations*, London, 1958, xi, p. 193[e].

difference between the two visual experiences lies in our *thinking* of what we see—which have greatly influenced later reflection upon religious epistemology. Wisdom takes up some of these themes both with his parable of the garden[1] and with his suggestion that we experience things in patterns or arrangements of connections which we point to in order to enable others to see them as we do. John Hick in turn prefers 'experience-as' to 'see-as'.[2] Religious faith is the interpretative process which constructs significance within the world, and which recognizes that there are viable relational patterns in the given which has to be admitted to be ambiguous. Hick emphasizes the correlation between the religious interpretation and the actions which it elicits, and affirms the importance of the freedom of the individual to make a voluntary act of interpreting the world in a religious way. Ian G. Barbour makes the further conversion from 'experience-as' to 'interpret-as',[3] though he is anxious not to make too much of the difference. This fascinating account of the nature of interpretation deserves much fuller treatment than is possible in the present context, but we must try to relate it to the spectrum of interpretation. It is at once obvious that it is applicable more to the interpretation of events, phenomena, entities and persons—the members of the left-hand end of the spectrum—than to the others which are of a propositional character. The scribes and pharisees experienced Jesus as a blasphemer and the friend of publicans and sinners; Peter experienced him as the Christ, the Son of the living God. The centurion out at Calvary experienced Jesus Christ as an innocent man; the rest of the soldiers experienced him as a common criminal. So as Wisdom, Hick and Barbour have claimed, the theory can be applied to the contemporary problems in religious epistemology, and, we may add, to those in ecclesiastical history, a discipline deeply concerned with questions of interpretation. To that extent the theory could be thought to cover the right-hand end of the spectrum. But I do not see its relevance to that range of interpretation that deals with propositions, or its merits over the view we have advanced above[4] which amounts to an extension of the notion of translation.

I should perhaps add that I have certain misgivings about it as a totally satisfactory explanation even of the range of interpretation to which we have allocated it. For example, in the original Wittgenstein illustration the duck aspect and the rabbit aspect, in spite of their dissimilarities, are co-ordinate with one another; they are both empirical realities; whereas in the religious transposition, the new

[1] In paper, 'Gods', *Proc. Arist. Soc.*, Vol. 45, 1944–5, p. 187.

[2] Ed. G. N. A. Vesey, *Talk of God*, London, 1969: contribution by John Hick, 'Religious Faith as Experiencing-as'.

[3] *Myths, Models and Paradigms*, London, 1974, p. 53.

[4] *Vide supra:* 4.2.

pattern or organization involves what Anders Jeffner calls 'a new entity or ontological category'.[1] It is the very fact of this difference which requires explanation when we are dealing with questions of religious epistemology, so that an illustration from a situation which does not contain the difficulty may not be altogether helpful. Also, at p. 195[e] of *Philosophical Investigations,* Wittgenstein considers the case of someone who on being shown a duck-rabbit and asked what it is, may actually reply, 'A duck-rabbit', because that is what he perceives and he is reporting. This kind of conflation is impossible in the cases of a religious and an atheistic aspect of, say, the life of Christ. The fact that the duck-rabbit can be perceived does prompt the question whether the options were correctly stated by Wittgenstein in the first place. They are three in number not two: duck, rabbit and duck-rabbit. Had they been so stated they might not have proved so useful to the understanding of the religious epistemological problem. Further, I find it a little difficult to equate 'seeing-as' or 'experiencing-as' with interpretation. Take the simple case with which Wittgenstein begins,[2] the cube, and the comment he makes upon it, 'So we interpret it, and *see* it as we *interpret* it'. He here indicates two elements in the situation, the first, what he later in the page calls 'a particular experience', and secondly, the interpretation of the figure which involves some placing of it in a category, in this case, that of a box. The interpretation and the seeing-as are therefore distinguishable, the interpretation being part of the process of seeing-as and not equivalent to it. For that reason, I can not accept Dr Barbour's view that we have to substitute 'interpreting-as' for seeing-as, or experiencing-as, which would produce a tautological situation. That problem takes me to the final one which I wish to mention in this connection. It is a fact that it is not absolutely clear what the *as* means in all the participial phrases which we have met in this discussion. Shades and echoes of Vaihinger's *als ob* haunt the pages, and it would not distort Wittgenstein's text to read it as 'I see the figure as if it were a rabbit'. This reading brings out the notional character of the perception, and shows how low the ontological commitment is. When these elements are extrapolated into the religious epistemological situation, problems ensue. The believer does not simply see the world as if it were the creation of God; for him it *is* the creation of God. There may have been a time when he looked on the world as a kind of rabbit-duck, seeing it now as the fortuitous concatenation of atoms in motion, now as the creation of a provident God. But when he has become a believer, he has passed that point, and the world is for him the product of God's creative power. An *as* would be as out of place in the way he looks at the world as it would be in the

[1] *op. cit.*, p. 118.
[2] *Philosophical Investigations,* London, 1958, ix, p. 193[e].

statement and the situation it refers to, 'I see this woman as my wife'. It is for me significant that John Hick departs from his original use of the *as* when he describes the state of the believer who is well advanced in the faith,[1] 'and conscious . . . of the divine will as a reality in the background of his life, a reality which may at any time emerge to confront him in absolute and inescapable demand'. It is not now a case of the believer seeing some situation as the divine will confronting him; he perceives the divine will as reality. That I am sure is the right placing of *as* for faith but it does not derive from Wittgenstein's duck-rabbit.

4.4. Earlier in this essay,[2] I mentioned that perhaps the most characteristic activity of interpretation is the transposition of a biblical text or concept, a credal affirmation of the church, or a doctrine of the faith, from its original *mise-en-scène* into a totally different cultural, philosophical or sociological context. Interpretation is the way in which that transposition takes place, and the media which it predominantly employs are models, paradigms, analogies and symbols. The choice of model, if I may regard that as the generic term for them all, is of paramount importance for the success of the interpretation. It must be sympathetic to the material to be interpreted; it must be readily assimilable by those to whom it is directed; it must be capable of deployment as the description proceeds; and it must be ready and able to rally to the defence if the original comes under attack. The history of theology is full of models which have met these tests, and it is not altogether empty of those which have equally grossly failed. And interpretation may turn out to be worse than the model it employs; it can not ever turn out to be better.[3]

5. In what we have said about interpretation and the use of models in theological method we have now explored fairly extensively the process of description in theology. I wish now to examine what happens when argument is employed in theology, and should like to say to begin with that the reference is not exclusively to what is known as apologetic literature, the theology which is concerned with the defence of the faith against the objections that are brought against it from whatever source—philosophy, science, psychology or sociology. The reference is also to more dogmatic theology as well, for much of it contains within itself arguments against critics, the theologian himself being often in sympathy with the problems raised

[1] *Faith and Knowledge*, 2nd ed., London, 1967, pp. 116 f.

[2] *viz.*, at 4.2, p. 218 *supra*.

[3] The topics associated with 'Myths, Models and Paradigms' have been so recently and so expertly marshalled and assessed by Professor Ian G. Barbour in his book of that name (see fn. 23 *supra*) that I have decided not to go over similar ground. Cf. also Ian T. Ramsey, *Models and Mystery*, London, 1964; also his *Models for Divine Activity*, London, 1973.

by the critics. An interesting modern example of this view is the way in which Emil Brunner handles the doctrine of the Virgin Birth in his *The Mediator*.[1] Brunner comes out quite openly with the admission that there is practically no historical evidence from Jesus' parents on the subject. He rejects the theological arguments which have been advanced in its support to make up for the absence of historical evidence. He has little time for explanation of the Virgin Birth which argues from the biological possibility of parthenogenesis. Most of the traditional difficulties he seems to accept. Nevertheless he uses each of them as a means whereby he may positively and dogmatically propound his account of the Incarnation. But Brunner is by no means an isolated example. That, I believe, is how theology has been written in this or any other century. Let us look, then, at the arguments that theologians use.

5.1. We shall not expect, and we shall not be disappointed if we do not find, that they use syllogistic arguments of the traditional formal logic as their standard form of argument. I am encouraged in this direction by a remark of Stephen Toulmin: 'The ability to follow simple predictive arguments, whose warrants are backed by sufficiently wide and relevant experience, may just have to be recognized as another simple rational skill, which most men possess but which is lacking in some mental defectives; and for other fields other basic skills. Could this be said for arguments in all fields whatever? Is the ability to follow and see the force of simple moral arguments (say) also such a skill? Or simple aesthetic arguments? Or simple theological arguments?'[2] On the basis of this statement Toulmin goes on to distinguish analytic arguments, which conform to the formal pattern of the syllogism and to be valid must fall within the 'barbara celarent . . .' modes, from substantial arguments which in spite of the fact that by the standards of strict analyticity (viz., conclusiveness, demonstrativeness, necessity, certainty, and validity) they appear to involve invalidity in the movement to their conclusion must nevertheless not be charged with inconclusiveness. If the analytic criteria are not allowed to determine the final judgment about the validity of substantial arguments, then the question of relevance becomes all-important. 'All this means is that we must judge each field of substantial arguments by its own relevant standards.'[3] It remains for us to outline what appear to be the relevant standards which have been traditionally employed in the theological disciplines, backed as they are by 'sufficiently wide and relevant experience'.

5.2. Before proceeding to the actual enumeration of these standards or criteria, I should like to revert briefly to a matter which

[1] London, 1937, pp. 322 ff.
[2] *The Uses of Argument*, Cambridge, 1958, pp. 134 f.
[3] *Id.*, p. 234.

arose when we were discussing[1] the distributive definition of theology, the question of how much the theological disciplines share with one another in virtue of having a common centre, and how much they share with what I earlier called the penumbral disciplines which adjoin most of the strictly theological disciplines. It is the question: when does an extra-theological over-ride an intra-theological norm, and when not? May I make two replies to this question?

5.2.1. The first answer is to admit that I can not answer it, largely I fear because it is unanswerable. Certainly no one seems to have succeeded in answering it. On the whole theologians may appear to come down on the side of the intra-theological norms. To take an example dealing with Jesus' resurrection Pannenberg says: 'The natural sciences can not, therefore, be the final court of appeal in the decision as to the possibility or impossibility of Jesus' resurrection. . . . For the historian this means that in forming a judgment about the past he must not from the outset permit only those possibilities which are in line with the normal and superficial course of events. . . . The permanently controversial character of Jesus' resurrection need not disturb the Christian, however.'[2] But that last statement must not be allowed to go unchallenged. There have been many Christians who have been very greatly disturbed by this very subject of the historicity of the resurrection events. Professor Torrance in relating the procedures of theological science and historical science[3] says: 'In turning back to the consideration of Jesus Christ, it must be said right away that we cannot but treat this historical event as we treat other historical events' of which we have documentary evidence itself based on evidence of eye-witnesses and oral tradition. It has all to be exposed to critical investigation, its evidential value tested, its testimony traced back to source. But since at the heart of this event there is a personal divine movement, we must not allow preconceived notions about what is and what is not historically possible to lead us to tamper with the evidence. What is not clear however is whether the divine heart of this historical event obliges us to accept *all* the historical data. That, I believe, is the problem to which we receive no clear answer anywhere, that is, apart from the fundamentalists.

5.2.2. Since what I am in effect saying is that the theologian appears sometimes to avail himself of extra-theological criteria and sometimes of intra-theological criteria, no great purpose is served by indicating which is which. In fact it might well prove misleading to do so. Very often an extra-theological criterion is used intra-disciplinarily.

[1] *Vide supra*, 1.2.1. to 1.2.3.

[2] Wolfhart Pannenberg, *The Apostles' Creed in the Light of Today's Questions*, London, 1972, pp. 111 ff.

[3] *op. cit.*, pp. 322 ff.

5.3. What we are not prepared for is the plethora of criteria which theologians employ in their arguments within their disciplines. The following list is not by any means exhaustive, and it is meant not to be repetitive even though it contains criteria that look rather like one another. They are fourteen in number:

5.3.1. Right at the beginning we have to nominate two of the oldest veterans in this territory, the first being *coherence*, which is a theory about both the nature and the criterion of truth. Any proposition which does not contradict the already established system of true propositions is itself true. 'The mark of falsehood is failure to cohere in the body of true propositions.'[1]

5.3.2. The second veteran is *correspondence*. 'A belief is true when it corresponds to an associated complex and false when it does not.'[2] This veteran has served in many wars, and has been used to re-inforce many of the other criteria, which denote the referent in the correspondence relationship mentioned in this present criterion. Correspondence may be required with scripture or tradition or one of the others.

5.3.3. The third we have just mentioned, namely, the *scriptures*. With the widespread popularity of the so-called biblical theology of the past thirty-five years or so, this criterion which was for a long time the preserve of the strictest conservatives in theology has come in for a completely new term of office, and is still running. A sub-criterion which ought to be recognized in this connection is the canon which even the most convinced biblicists operate when using scripture as the basis of theological assertion. Some parts of the Bible enshrine the truth of the Bible in a much more unequivocal way than do others, and they gradually become a criterion within the canon.

5.3.4. Reference to Scripture as a criterion of theological truth takes us by association to *tradition* by which I intend, in addition to the normal Roman Catholic concept, the early Christian notion of the *quod semper, quod ubique quod ab omnibus creditur* as well as the creeds and confessions which have formed themselves into a great catena to which all have access who are Christian interpreters.

5.3.5. While tradition may operate on its own from time to time as a single criterion, as does scripture, more frequently they operate *in tandem, scripture and tradition*. This joint criterion is normally attributed to the Roman Catholic Church, but is as characteristic of the Reformed Churches, which universally after they had put the Bible in the common tongue into the hands of the common people, almost immediately devised confessions by which they were to be rightly interpreted and understood.

5.3.6. We now come to a cluster of criteria which are rather similar to one another but which appear sufficiently frequently as separate

[1] Bertrand Russell, *The Problems of Philosophy*, London, 1970, p. 70.
[2] *Id.*, p. 74.

operatives in modern, particularly Protestant, theology that they deserve separate notice. The first of these is *Jesus Christ.* He is the supreme subject of our faith. His is the mind that we seek so that our minds may be conformed to his truth. It is sometimes said that all theological statements have an ostensive purpose of pointing to Jesus Christ, and that when we go in the direction of their pointing, we come to him and we then have the opportunity to check their authenticity against Christ himself.

5.3.7. Another related form of this previous criterion is the *Word of God* as the phrase is used in the theology of Karl Barth, particularly in the earlier volumes of the *Church Dogmatics.* The Word of God exists in three-fold form—revealed, written, preached. Our access must therefore be through the latter two, which are not in themselves the Word of God; they become the Word of God, the Word revealed to us, and it is that Word which is the criterion of theological truth.

5.3.8. Neo-orthodox theologians have made great play with the concept of *revelation* as the criterion of theological truth, a term to which it is very difficult to give an identifiable fix of meaning. In Brunner, for example, it appears often to be simply a proper name substituting for Jesus Christ, but at other times it seems to be almost equivalent to the Bible. In both of these cases it means something more than either of the original terms, yet how much more is not exactly clear.

5.3.9. An extension can be made to the previous criterion to read the *self-revelation of God.* The distinction between this form and the previous one is that whereas the previous form could be almost reduced to two other more usual criteria, this present form unfolds what it is that Christ reveals of God. In other words this form takes the notion of revelation seriously as the revelation of God by Christ, and treats that content of the revelation as more ultimate than the medium.

5.3.10. We now move into another ethos, and consider those theologies which give evidence of the influence of existentialism. Some are more extreme and these I would call hard-line existentialists; but others, the soft-line existentialists have been much more selective, and have chosen those elements in existentialism which in their judgment facilitate the communication of the traditional content of the faith for our time. They have been remarkably successful. For them, it could be said that the criterion of truth is convertibility into *existential significance.* It is the method which John Macquarrie adopts in the handling of biblical episodes and Christian doctrines. For example, he writes: 'The story of the ascension would be senseless if regarded as an account of a journey into the upper regions of the sky, but it makes sense if we regard it as expressing what has happened to Jesus in the experience of his disciples. The crucified One has become the exalted Lord of their existence.'[1]

5.3.11. Hard-line existentialists would list the *existentialia*, the categories appropriate to human existence, applicable that is to man's existence-in-the-world, as the true criterion which determines all truth be it theological or anthropological, there being no real difference. Man's pre-understanding determines truth and falsity.

5.3.12. The demythologizing controversy brought to the fore a somewhat popular but none the less very influential criterion, namely, *compatibility with contemporary culture.* The criterion operates in a negative and a positive form. Negatively, what is unacceptable to modern man is out: demon-possession, large numbers of nature miracles, a three-deck cosmology, divine transcendence, and the indwelling grace of God. Positively, the criterion encourages and blesses a theory or a principle which appears to get backing from some modern discipline.

5.3.13. The logico-philosophical controversies of the past forty years have produced a criterion which I would call *logical performance*, that is, the capacity of a theological statement, as it were, to make the right logical noises. Sometimes this criterion seemed to favour a type of religious positivism which regarded religious phenomena as subjects of experience very much in the style of sense-data, with their modes of perception and methods of verification. Sophisticated views emerged, such as that of D. D. Evans,[2] which located the meaning and validity of theological statements in their performative function.

5.3.14. I have mentioned the role of *existentialia* in existentialist theologies, but it would be wrong to ignore the equally important role which hermeneutical categories have played in other theologies. I think of the concept of 'covenant' in many theologies of the Old Testament, or *eschaton*, *Heilsgeschichte*, acts of God, *kairos* in many books on the so-called biblical theology; *Gabe* and *Aufgabe* in Emil Brunner, ultimate concern and Being in Paul Tillich, Teilhard's omega point, Buber's I and Thou. These concepts are not just expository devices; they gather around themselves such a constellation of fixed ideas and accepted notions that very soon they are acting effectively as criteria of theological thought. Theology in the past thirty years has seen a lot of this criterion, the criterion of the *dominant motif.* It is at this point that we have to make a cross-reference to what I called the penumbral disciplines, and say that various theologians have not hesitated to use the criteria of such disciplines within their own theological process of theological validation. When Oscar Cullmann said that 'All Christian theology

[1] *op. cit.*, London, 1966, p. 108.
[2] *The Logic of Self-Involvement*, London, 1963.

in its innermost essence is biblical history',[1] he was not concealing his preferences. Others in adopting the paradigms of natural science or psychology or sociology are committed to giving credence to criteria derived from these disciplines.

5.4. I have not attempted to assign any order of priority to these many criteria. Not only are they not all to be found in any one theologian; they will not individually or severally be employed uniformly by any one theologian within a sustained piece of writing. Nor do I expect theologians to be constantly explaining which criteria they are using; I would be just a little suspicious of them if they did. There is a sense in which if we are all the time bothered about the method we are following or the criteria that will keep us right when we are writing theology, we shall not be writing the best kind of theology. It will be contrived and self-conscious. As in art the technology, to be effective, has to be totally unobserved, if the final product is to be truly aesthetic; so in theology the artifice of the method will have to be concealed, if the reader is to grasp and be grasped by the Reality whom it is our duty and our joy to describe and interpret, to serve and love. The price of that concealment is that the method and the criteria may remain to the end somewhat ambiguous.

[1] *Christ and Time*, London, 1952, p. 23.

16 The Truth of Life: Observations on Truth as the Interruption of the Continuity of Life

by EBERHARD JÜNGEL

John's gospel, by means of an 'I-saying', calls Jesus Christ the truth. In this way it understands him to be the truth of human life. In what follows I shall discuss, from a theological point of view, the sense in which Jesus Christ can be called the truth and, as such, can be understood as the decisive authority for human life.

I

To talk of truth is to talk of man. Man alone of all creatures is concerned with truth in the specific activities of his intellectual life, that is, in the judgments he makes and which he expresses in the form of assertions. Of all creatures man alone asks whether something is true or is not true. Indeed the life of man, in the context of creation as a whole, is the place where something is apprehended, or as we ought rather to say, is known to be true. To know something to be true means to apprehend it and to reproduce it as it really is. The correspondence between the reproduction and what it reproduces is what we call truth: *adaequatio intellectus et rei.* Man alone is able to apprehend and to reproduce something as it really is, he alone is able to know something to be true. Only man is capable of truth. Therefore it is only man who can lie. Only man can be concerned with everything that is in such a way that in principle nothing is beyond the sphere of truth. If truth is indeed correspondence between knowledge and known facts, then while the question of truth can be asked with reference to *everything that is*, it is only *posed* within the context of human life; for, of all creatures, it is only in the mind of man that the correspondence between *intellectus* and *res*, knowledge and facts, can arise. To that extent, it is always the case that the question concerning truth is, at the same time, a question concerning human life, as a life that is capable of truth. The more detailed discussion of this subject is the task of epistemology or of related *philosophical* disciplines. *Theology* can contribute to this only indirectly.

However, theology has a direct contribution to make to the question of what is so specific about the nature of man that truth is located precisely within the continuity of his life. In this sense, theology inquires about human life when it inquires about the truth of life. That is, for theology, the question 'What is man?' is meaningful and can be answered only in connection with the question 'What is truth?' Both man and truth share one and the same origin. They are both branches on the same tree of life. To put it succinctly: man is, only because there is truth in the continuity of life. Not the other way round! Truth is not dependent upon man but man is dependent upon truth. In biblical terms this means that man is dependent upon the faithfulness of God. For what the Greeks understood by *truth* is called, in the Old Testament, *faithfulness*; and faithfulness belongs specifically to *Yahweh*—it is God's prerogative. So we speak of the faithfulness of God distinctively characterizing human life when we discuss the questions 'What is truth?' and 'What is man?' in relation to one another. In my discussion of these questions I shall proceed from what is commonly understood by truth.

According to the classical definition, truth is the correspondence between assertion and fact, between knowledge and object, this in the sense of *adaequatio intellectus ad rem*. In brief: truth is correspondence. Knowledge that corresponds with a given object presupposes that this object also corresponds with itself. It is only the object that corresponds with itself that can be known in such a way as to allow knowledge and judgment to correspond with it. Thus, as pertains to truth, there is presupposed in the object of knowledge a correspondence with itself (identity).

However, the situation is more complicated as regards the knower, that is, the human subject. If man is to be able to know at all he must, in a quite specific sense, interrupt this correspondence with himself. He must, as it were, step out of himself without thereby ceasing to be man. It is rather the other way round: to be human is precisely *not to be in immediate correspondence* with oneself. For that reason it has been said that man has an ec-centric existence (Plessner); it is as though man is always looking back over his shoulder at himself. But he can only look back over his own shoulder, if he is able to go beyond himself, that is, if he is able to step behind himself, as his own double so to speak. In a certain sense man in fact can do this; in a certain sense he is his own double. This is what is known as having a relation to oneself, being able to relate to one's own existence. However, this is only possible if the immediate correspondence with himself is interrupted. Only where this occurs, does man truly exist as man. Man is that creature whose being is not in immediate correspondence with itself but is capable of being interrupted at any moment by other things that exist, and in fact is always being so interrupted. Only in this manner can any fact be known; only thus can truth or the correspondence between the *intellectus humanus* and a particular *res* emerge: namely, in that the continuity of life is interrupted by something that intervenes. Human life occurs, then, when the continuity of earthly life and existence is interrupted, in that something intervenes and is apprehended (and thus comes to be known). Human life, therefore, *is* the interruption of the continuity of created life by the occurrence of truth.

II

It may be useful to elucidate the significance of this ontological definition by reference to the ontic characteristics of human existence. If human life is understood ontologically as the interruption of the continuity of creaturely life by the occurrence of truth, then what must take place in human life is that its continuity be interrupted for the sake of something other than itself which intervenes and is apprehended (that is, comes to be known) as something else.

The most acute and effective ontic interruption of the continuity of human life occurs, undoubtedly, through death. However, it is not our own death but rather the death of someone close to us that interrupts the continuity of our own life. (Our own death does not merely interrupt our life; it brings it to an end). This is confirmed by 'words of comfort' such as 'life goes on' in so far as they try to show that the interruption of the continuity of our own life through the death of someone close to us was 'only' an interruption. (The man who refuses to have anything at all to do with such 'comfort' fails to overcome this interruption, and will thus himself be destroyed by it). The interruption of the continuity of our own life through the death of one close to us is our participation in the event of this death and through this quite specific possibilities for our own existence are removed and vanish irrevocably. And death is always somehow involved when the continuity of human life is interrupted. However, if we only come to the apprehension and knowledge of something else through such an interruption, then all our knowing contains an experience of death. We can then understand why ancient myths considered the truth to be deadly, because truth is only attained where life is interrupted by death. The moment of death is, in the most profound sense, the moment of truth. For the human mind 'arrives at its truth only as it finds itself in being utterly torn asunder' (Hegel, *The Phenomenology of Mind*), so that death appears as the 'energy of thought'.

The interruption of our life through the occurrence of beauty can elucidate the fact that every interruption of the continuity of human life involves a relationship with death. For beauty also interrupts the continuity of life. It intervenes. The cry, the exclamation, the shout of ecstasy or even the (no less eloquent) stupified speechlessness, which is clearly nothing other than an interjection, a cry turned inwards: these are all unmistakable indications of such an interruption through encounter with beauty. Such a shout, such speechlessness in the presence of beauty are exclamations by means of which man—whether aloud or in silence—breaks out of himself and expresses the fact that something has intervened within his life. These are shouts of joy. As such, however, they are also the twin cries of lament through which an 'I' erupts *de profundis*, and cries out—into and over against the total continuity of being—when *death* interrupts the continuity of a man's life. The experience of beauty has therefore always been related to death, without thereby in the least diminishing its joyful character: 'For beauty is nothing other than the beginning of the terrible, which we just about still manage to endure; and we admire it so much because it calmly scorns destroying us. Every angel is terrible' (Rilke).

From such moments of intervention spring attentiveness and discovery. These are the consequences (not the presupposition!) of events and encounters which interrupt the continuity of human life. Where such interruption evokes attentiveness and discovery and permits their realization, there the interruption is being assimiliated, and, at that point, there emerges an *enhancing* of the continuity of life so that life takes on a new quality. This, then, is another integral aspect of the truth of human life: the possibilities open to man may be enhanced precisely through the assimilation of those occurrences which interrupt the continuity of life.

If, however, man wants to make his self-correspondence so secure that he can no longer be interrupted, the result is both the suppression of truth itself (as an occurrence which intervenes in and interrupts the continuity of life) and the restriction of the *occurrence* of truth to the sphere of the correctness of a particular correspondence—a correspondence which, indeed, improperly is not even seen as the negation of that very interruption which enables this correspondence to occur in the first place. This is precisely what modern man does. From the time of Descartes, at least, man has been intent on safeguarding his own self-certainty, on continually securing his ephemeral existence, which is already made secure in any particular moment by his 'I think', and thus on ensuring the continuity of his existence—even making use of God's help for this purpose. He wants to be left undisturbed in his self-correspondence. For Kant, this happens in the following way: *reason*, in the realm of theory (what can I know?), corresponds to itself, in the realm of practice (what ought I to do?), comes to a correspondence with itself and, in the end (what may I hope for?), is postulated as having definitely achieved this self-correspondence. For Nietzsche it is the *will* in respect to oneself which guarantees self-correspondence. For Marx it is *labour* liberated from alienation which brings humanity into correspondence with itself. As a matter of fact, however, his determination to achieve an uninterrupted *correspondence with himself* brings man into *opposition to nature*, which he threatens to denaturalize completely, in terms of a second, artificial and thus unnatural, creation through technology. However, this opposition to nature shatters the correspondence which (modern) man desires to achieve with himself, inasmuch as man would thereby destroy himself along with nature. If, therefore, he does not want his striving for self-correspondence to lead to self-annihilation, he must significantly *limit* his opposition to nature (that is, his exploitation of the creation). However, every limit placed upon his self-correspondence lays man open to the possibility of an interruption of the continuity of his life through something else (namely nature). The final elimination of such an interruption can only be purchased at the price of the final abrupt ending of the continuity of life itself. That is the dilemma of modern man. But it is also his opportunity.

III

If we now return from the ontic characteristics to the issue of the ontological definition of the continuity of human life, then it should be clear that what is distinctive about man is that he is a being who can be interrupted and thus enhanced. Theology recognizes in this ontological definition of the continuity of human life the expression of a creaturely relationship to God, which is creaturely but also, as distinct from the rest of creation, specifically human. For, of all creatures, man is that being to whom God wishes to draw near. Man is chosen and created as the covenant partner of God: as a creature he is set apart from God but as a partner he is drawn near to him. God does not want to remain set apart from this particular creation of his but to draw especially near to him: so near, in fact, that he, God, is closer than anyone to man. Thus it is not man who can be closest to himself. It is precisely in his desire to be closest to himself in his self-correspondence that man is interrupted by God. God wants to draw nearer to man than man is ever able to be to himself. It is just for this that man is created as man in such a way that he can be interrupted, and he is human precisely in that he allows himself to be interrupted. God is man's original interruption. He intervenes. For this reason God is, at the same time, the truth of life. He is this as the one who intervenes. And precisely for this reason men have believed the encounter with God to be deadly.

That it is *not* deadly is the Easter experience of a God who allowed the continuity of his own life to be interrupted through the death of Jesus Christ. For the cross of Jesus Christ is that event through which the living and eternally alive God accepted death for himself. That this death did not lead to the *abrupt ending* of the divine life, but only to its interruption, is the consequence of a life and death struggle. It is *love* which engages in this life and death struggle and love which conquers by enduring death for the sake of life. The cross of Jesus is that event in time through which God allowed the continuity of his own eternal life to be interrupted so as to prove himself *to be love.* It is as the unity of life and death for the sake of life that God *is* love. God *reveals* himself as love in that he allows his own eternal life to be interrupted by the death of Jesus and thereby confers divine life on the one who is crucified. The revelation of God as love is the way in which the God of Easter encounters us in the mode of the Holy Spirit; that Holy Spirit who—as the *vinculum pacis inter patrem et filium* and, at the same time, the *vinculum caritatis* between God and ourselves—overcomes our well-grounded expectation that the encounter with God is deadly. It would be deadly if it were the case that the life of God was uninterrupted eternity and his eternity uninterrupted life in which there were no place for death. The cross of Jesus Christ disallows this possibility. It represents the appropriation of human death by God and the granting of divine life to man: this is the joyful exchange, the reversal brought about by love.

In so far as the death of Jesus Christ is an event which interrupts God's own life it is *a fortiori* an event which interrupts the life of humanity and not just that of the disciples, relations and women companions 'left behind'. For what concerns God concerns all men, the whole of humanity, because God is the one who is of absolute concern for all men. God interrupts the continuity of our life as the one who allows our sin and death to interrupt his own life. The crucified and risen Christ *is* this twofold interruption which, in the mode of the Holy Spirit, is given concrete form as the *enhancement* of the continuity of the life that is interrupted. Theology knows man as that being who is defined by God's interrupting him in this way. That is, man is defined by the eternal Father who allows himself to be interrupted by the crucifixion of his Son and, in this way, interrupts the continuity of our life; and, at the same time, in the loving unity of the Spirit with his Son, he enhances his life and ours. Luther formulated this in his famous thesis that *man* (and not just the Christian) is defined by the *iustificatio sola fide*. He thus asserted the cross and resurrection of Jesus Christ to be the *truth* of human existence.

From this perspective it becomes intelligible why in John 14:6 Jesus Christ himself is called the truth.

17 Historical Relativism, the Appeal to Experience and Theological Reconstruction

by RICHARD W. A. McKINNEY

I

The problems facing contemporary critical theological reconstruction are formidable. The ongoing debate about theological method is, in itself, evidence of this fact. How is theology to proceed? What constitute the *data* for theology? What are the sources and norm or norms with which theology has to operate? These are familiar questions which are dealt with in the *prolegomena* to every systematic theology. Other issues, however, press in upon the systematic theologian and pose powerful and inescapable questions for him. Two such issues are: (i) the challenge of historical relativism and (ii) the difficulties associated with an appeal to experience. These issues are not new: they have been implicit to theological debate for a long time. They have, however, taken on a new power and significance since the time of the Enlightenment. This has been largely a function of the emergence of historical method and critical philosophy at that time. The former has developed our sense of the historical, the contingent, the unique and the particular; the latter has developed our scepticism as to the possibility of transcending the limits of human experience and making metaphysical claims on the basis of the same. Let us look more closely at the nature of the problems raised by these two issues.

(1) History, says Heinz Zahrnt, has become our fate.[1] It has become an inescapable element of our critical self-consciousness. We have come to understand the sense in which we not only live in history but our own lives are historical in character. We are all caught up in the flux and change of history and, moreover, this is something over which we have no control. It is not a matter of choice. We do not decide whether or not to be historical any more than we decide whether or not to be born. Being historical is part and parcel of being a human being, it is an integral element of our creaturehood.

This sense of history and of the historical, of the particularity and

[1] *The Historical Jesus*, London, 1963, p. 19.

contingency of all historical phenomena, has led to a considerable transformation in the self-understanding of man. All the old metaphysical certainties and securities have been swept away. Indeed the 'historicization' of man's self-consciousness made a considerable, and not always acknowledged, contribution to the collapse of the old metaphysical systems. Prior to that time, history itself had been subject to metaphysical interpretation: *Weltgeschichte* had been subordinated to *Heilsgeschichte*. History had been placed within a metaphysical framework of interpretation which gave to it a *ratio essendi*. But the emergence of historical method and the sense of the historical meant that all such interpretations were pulled down into the vortex of the historical and threatened by the spectre of relativism. Man lost, as a consequence, both his metaphysical innocence and confidence. He also discovered his own autonomy and historicity.

Now if all this was so, then how could history or historical phenomena be significant? Did history have a meaning? Could there ever be such a thing as historical explanation? Or could an appeal to historical phenomena ever explain anything else? Could there be any positive relation between truth and value, say, on the one hand and history on the other? Lessing was quite sure that no such relation could exist:

> 'accidental truths of history can never become the proof of the necessary truths of reason'.[1]

In this view he had the support of both Kant and Fichte. For Kant said:

> 'the historical can serve only for illustration, not for demonstration'.[2]

And Fichte maintained:

> 'only the metaphysical can save, never the historical'.[3]

But this was no more than a holding operation until the realization fully dawned that reason itself must be 'historicized', that reason could no more insulate itself from the relativizing acids of history than could any other human faculty or capacity.

Theology, then, had to grapple with the problem of history and the course of nineteenth-century theology exhibits the faltering way in which this was done. Schleiermacher showed considerable understanding of the problem both in his original schematization of theology in his *Brief Outline* as well as in his insistence upon the 'positive' character of all religion in both the *Speeches* and the *Christian Faith*. Yet the full implications of historical method did not

[1] *Lessing's Theological Writings*, ed. by Henry Chadwick, London, 1956, p. 53.
[2] *ibid.*, p. 32.
[3] *ibid.*, p. 32.

fully enter into his theology as the christological sections of the *Christian Faith* and his lectures on the *Life of Jesus* clearly show. Strauss' own devasting *Life of Jesus*, for all its inadequacies, opened up the nature of the problem as well as exposing the limitations of Schleiermacher's position. Baur struggled with these issues further but the Ritschlian school retreated into a Kantian redoubt and, effectively, turned its back on the emergent problems. For all their appeal to the historical, the Ritschlians did not take the challenge of history with relevant seriousness. They sought a historical basis and foundation for faith and, paradoxically, sowed the seeds of their own destruction in so doing. Tyrell's comment is often quoted: the Liberal Protestants looked down into the well of history and found reflected therein their own image. Actually this is very misleading for by the time of Ritschl's death in 1889 his disciples were finding not their own reflection but a stranger belonging to a different world, a Jesus they could scarcely recognize.

Indeed it was the *religionsgeschichtliche Schule*, and in particular Ernst Troeltsch, the 'systematic theologian' of this school, who first grappled seriously with the problem of historical relativism. Though he dedicated his life and immense intellectual talents to resolving the problems involved, he never actually succeeded in doing so. In his tentative reformulations, Troeltsch was compelled to fall back upon a form of philosophical idealism which seemed, *ex hypothesi*, to require more justification than he was able to offer. For him the historical and the relative were one and so they remained. The problems were not solved by Troeltsch, merely given their definitive modern expression.

(2) The appeal to experience in modern critical theology dates, likewise, from Schleiermacher. It was he who sought, in terms of his theological method, to establish his critical theological reconstruction on the basis of an appeal to religious experience. He also launched the quest for the essence of religion and of Christianity. For Schleiermacher, the essence of religion was to be found in religious experience which he characterized in various ways and understood as the *fides qua creditur* in terms of which alone we could understand the *fides quae creditur*. Christian doctrines or theological assertions thus became for him 'accounts of the Christian religious affections set forth in speech'.[1] The hermeneutical significance of this move was immense and highly influential. Albrecht Ritschl could say:

> 'the immediate object of theological cognition is the community's faith that it stands to God in a relation essentially conditioned by the forgiveness of sins'.[2]

[1] *The Christian Faith*, Edinburgh, 1928, p. 76.

[2] *The Christian Doctrine of Justification and Reconciliation*, New Jersey, 1966, p. 3.

And he went on to develop an account of theological statements as 'value-judgments' which arise out of the situation in which the individual is affected by and responds to the activity of God in Christ in his life. In analogous vein Wilhelm Herrmann could say:

'faith can find its basis only in the experience which produced it'.[1]

But the appeal to experience proved to be both elusive and unsatisfactory. On the one hand the character of the experience in question was insufficiently explored. What was it and did it require the weight of theistic interpretation which the nineteenth-century theologians, in their various ways, wished to place upon it? Moreover, Schleiermacher's paradigmatic handling of the issues, for all its brilliance, left much to be desired. In the early sections of the *Christian Faith* Schleiermacher appeared to be defending the 'objective referent' of religious experience, indeed to be saying that religious experience was only possible in relation to that object designated by the term 'God'.[2] However, in later sections of the same work, his highly unsatisfactory treatment of the attributes of God[3] as well as his distinction between 'the being of God in Himself' and 'the being of God in the world'[4] seemed to call into question the very possibility of knowing God. This, and other weaknesses, exposed Schleiermacher to Barth's devastating criticism in the early part of this century. The unfortunate tendency of *Kulturprotestantismus* of identifying the essence of Christianity with the spirit and ideals of the German nation provided an equally valid target for Barth,[5] though it would be quite unjust to blame Schleiermacher, for all his own nationalism, for the aberrations of the later Ritschlians. Barth, himself, always maintained a high respect for Schleiermacher.[6] Indeed one should, I believe, draw a distinction between the failure of Schleiermacher to draw out the full and proper potential of his own method and the possibility of developing a new critical theology in a manner analogous to that proposed by Schleiermacher. His proposals, in my view, need not *necessarily* have led to the weaknesses of his own theology, let alone the later catastrophes of *Kulturprotestantismus*.[7]

[1] *Systematic Theology*, London, 1927, p. 76.

[2] *op. cit.*, p. 16.

[3] *ibid.*, pp. 194 ff., *passim*.

[4] *ibid.*, esp. p. 748. How can Schleiermacher, on the basis of *his* theological method, justify such a distinction?

[5] 'The ethics of the *Ritschlian* school are the ethics of the bourgeoisie growing prosperous in the time of the consolidation of the Bismarckian empire', Barth, *The Word of God and the Word of Man*, London, 1928, p. 145.

[6] Cf., especially Barth's *Nachwort* to *Schleiermacher-Auswahl*, ed. by Heinz Bolli, München, 1968.

[7] Cf. the interesting article by Van Harvey in *Journal of Religion*, 1962, pp. 151–70, 'A Word in Defense of Schleiermacher's Method'.

(3) As far as the twentieth-century handling of the problems of historical relativism and the appeal to experience is concerned, Barth's contribution to the debate is of enormous influence and significance. One cannot understand our present dilemma without taking him into full consideration. In his monumental *Romans*,[1] one of the greatest theological works of this century, Barth launched an attack against all *Erlebnistheologie* and *Gottesbewusstseinstheologie*, against every attempt to make the experience or self-consciousness of man *qua homo religiosus* the proper object or subject-matter of theology. Theology, said Barth, was about God and not man. In the nineteenth century it had become religionistic, anthropocentric and humanistic.[2] He sought, indeed, to 'stand Schleiermacher on his head'[3] and to restore 'the great Calvinist distance between God and man'.[4] We must, he said, oppose any tendency which led to the 'secret identification of ourselves with God'.[5] To this end he espoused the radical disjunction between the finite and the infinite, the temporal and the eternal advocated by Kierkegaard. Other Kierkegaardian notions, such as the Moment, the Miracle, the Paradox and the Leap of Faith were also utilized.

In the *Romans*, moreover, Barth also took up the challenge of historical relativism. Though he did not study under Troeltsch or, indeed, make much reference to his work in his early writings, there is no doubt that the problems of historical relativism agitated Barth greatly at this time. Indeed, in many ways he 'out-relativized' the relativizers. For him, history was the realm of the temporal, the finite, the relative and the human. As a consequence:

> 'in history, as such, there is nothing as far as the eye can see which can provide a basis for faith'.[6]

As such, and in and of themselves, the world and human history are without meaning and value.[7] Thus:

> 'The judgment of history is that those devoted to its investigation are driven to a final deprivation: they become dumb before God'.[8]

In the light of all this the only move open to the theologian is an appeal to 'the non-historical (*Unhistorische*), the invisible and the incomprehensible'.[9] He has to appeal to that which transcends the

[1] *The Epistle to the Romans*, trans. by Hoskyns, London, 1933.
[2] *The Humanity of God*, London, 1961, p. 39.
[3] *ibid.*, p. 43.
[4] *Revolutionary Theology in the Making*, London, 1964, p. 104.
[5] *The Epistle to the Romans*, p. 45.
[6] Quoted by Zahrnt, *op. cit.*, p. 68.
[7] *Epistle to the Romans*, pp. 107–8.
[8] *ibid.*, p. 88.
[9] *ibid.*, p. 145.

relativity of history and it is with this that Christianity is concerned. In developing this response, Barth was influenced not only by Kierkegaard but by Overbeck who said:

> 'The only possible abode for Christianity lies . . . not in history, but in the history before history, the superhistory (*Urgeschichte*)'.[1]

The concept of *Urgeschichte* was most important for Barth. It gave content, if rather problematically so, to the distinction between the finite and the infinite, the temporal and the eternal. It also presaged the introduction of the famous model of the intersection of the horizontal plane by the vertical, the insistence that revelation, to be revelation, must come 'from above', from the other side, from the realm of the 'non-historical, the invisible and the incomprehensible'. The fundamental effect of this upon Barth's thinking, upon his later christocentrism and his understanding of the centrality of the incarnation, cannot be over-emphasized. Nor can its impact upon his contemporaries. Brunner, Gogarten, Tillich and Bultmann, among others, were all influenced by Barth at this time even if, by the mid 1920's, they were all to set off in different directions.[2]

However, the 'Barthian epoch' is now behind us. Barth's monumental contribution to modern theology no longer commands the assent it did, say, twenty years ago. Indeed there is no contemporary theological consensus. All of the big questions are back again on the agenda, in particular the issues of historical relativism and of the appeal to experience. These issues have just refused to go away or to lie down. Barth's attitude to historical method as well as his exegesis[3] have caused growing concern. Can historical method be subject to dogmatic method? This is, to say the least, an open question. How is dogmatic method to escape the snare of historical relativism which, *ex hypothesi*, is being confronted? Why accept the way out of the impasse provided by Kierkegaard and Overbeck? What grounds have we for making assertions about the 'non-historical, the invisible and the incomprehensible'? Renewed interest in the problems of historical method, in the work of Ernst Troeltsch and, indeed, in the problems posed by 'other religions' evidence a renewed consciousness of the problems of historical relativism. In similar fashion Barth's attitude to the role of experience in theology has not proved satisfactory. An appeal to revelation, to 'the reconciling and revealing activity of God in Jesus',[4] can never be insulated from the issue of experience, for that reconciling and revealing activity must impinge

[1] Barth, *Theology and the Church*, London, 1962, p. 62.

[2] The Barth–Thurneysen correspondence, *Revolutionary Theology in the Making*, gives some insight into the developing disagreements.

[3] A good example of this is the section of the 'Royal Man', CD 4/2, pp. 154 ff.

[4] CD 1/1, p. 11.

upon my self consciousness, must enter into the orbit of my experience, must become part of my history. Indeed, only as it does so can it be real for me: but, in doing so, it thus becomes vulnerable to all the questions that must be asked about any appeal to experience. Gordon Kaufmann, with explicit reference to Barth, has also rightly observed:

> 'The fact that man theologises is an anthropological fact which must and can be understood anthropologically'.[1]

In making these criticisms, we are not ignoring the importance of Barth's development of his 'Anselmic method', his later christocentrism or his insistence that faith depends upon the primacy and givenness of its object. We are only maintaining that the problems involved require a degree of sophisticated treatment which, scholarly consensus would say, neither Barth nor Schleiermacher has satisfactorily provided.

So the problems of historical relativism and of the appeal to experience still haunt us. Their ghosts have not been laid. In the next two sections I want to explore some of the ramifications of this for contemporary theology.

II

Historical method poses fundamental questions concerning the identity or essence of Christianity. Granted the historical character of the traditions and of their diverse development, what sense can we make of the same? Can, indeed, we even talk about development? Can the various christologies and theologies of both the New Testament itself and the patristic period as a whole be organized into a coherent scheme exhibiting development? Faced with the complex material, there seem to be two fundamental ploys open to us. (i) We might take what is, basically, the Catholic view: we might maintain that the traditions exhibit a process whereby the truth emerges into fuller clarification and finer definition. It is clear that in other spheres of knowledge our understanding does increase with time and reflection, so why should this not be the case with doctrinal traditions. The trouble with this analogy is that it remains an open question whether it can be applied to the New Testament and patristic traditions. Biblical and patristic scholarship have produced a wealth of information and understanding about these traditions. The conceptual and cultural shifts involved are of such an order that assumed progress and development is just *prima facie* implausible. Appeals to authority, such as that of the Councils of the *magisterium*, just beg

[1] *Relativism, Knowledge and Faith*, Chicago, 1960, pp. x–xi.

the issue.[1] (ii) On the other hand, we might take what is, basically, the Liberal Protestant view, as well as that of biblicistic Protestantism: we might maintain that we have to go behind the traditions to the original *data*, to the historical *Anknüpfungspunkt*. Adolf von Harnack, for example, took the view that the development of doctrine within the Hellenistic world led to its progressive falsification through illegitimate entanglement with metaphysical speculation and that we must, consequently, return to the original *data*. But this position will not do either. It is far from clear what constitutes the original *data*. Appeal to the Bible, as such, solves little for the problems of complexity and development are present within its covers, raising again the question as to the sense in which it can function, as it must, as a norm for Christian theology. Moreover, to repeat the point made earlier, it is surely significant that the Liberal Protestant position collapsed under attack from the *religionsgeschichtliche Schule* perspective. The original historical *data*, as the liberals themselves came to realize, did not solve the problem concerning the identity of Christianity or its development, but merely restated it. For these historical facts have to be interpreted for us, if they are to make any coherent and comprehensible impact upon our contemporary self-understanding. So the modern dilemma takes on the following shape. We cannot assume development towards a clearer understanding of the truth, nor can we do without the interpretative activity of tradition. Mere appeal to the original facts or to tradition will not do in and of itself, yet we cannot do without these original facts and the consequent tradition. How then are we to proceed?

It is around this dilemma that modern concern with the question concerning 'the essence of Christianity' and, indeed, with the whole 'hermeneutical debate' has centred and continues to centre. As both these questions, in their modern form, date explicitly from Schleiermacher it is clear that our problems are still those posed so fundamentally for theology by the emergence of historical method at the end of the eighteenth century.

The question concerning 'the essence of Christianity' is, however, a puzzling one. In the first instance it is a highly metaphysical question. Why introduce the notion of essence into the debate concerning the development of doctrine, especially if, with von Harnack, you are committed to a theological method which is supposedly anti-metaphysical? The question, of course, can be changed into one concerning the identity and continuity of Christianity but even that does not eliminate the problems. Let us formalize the issue by saying

[1] One is reminded of A. E. Taylor's remark that those who invoke the authority of the Bible and the Church must first show why these authorities should be accepted.

that the biblical and patristic material presents us with traditions *a, b, c, d . . . n*: *a* might, for sake of argument, be the Jesus tradition, *b* the Pauline tradition, *c* the Markan tradition, *g* Athanasius and *n* Chalcedon and so on. Now what connection does *n* have with *a*? Is there some inherent and essential connection between the two or is the connection merely coincidential, through the various stages *b–m*, leaving *a* and *n* essentially unrelated to each other? The first thing to be said is that these elements of the tradition are not logically isolated from each other. Nor do they stand in what may be called a radial relationship to some common factor. It is not as though all the elements *a–n* stood equidistant to a common denominator or subject matter, merely recording different, though similar, responses to this common factor. On the contrary the various elements interrelate and build up upon one another like layers of a cake. The history of christological development in the New Testament exhibits this phenomenon for us. I am not saying that every tradition literally builds upon all that has preceded it, only that the many traditions interrelate and interconnect in a highly complex way. Why, then, to press the question, assume that there is continuity and identity persisting throughout the various developments? Why search for the elusive 'essence'? It is clear that Paul and Athanasius are not, in any obvious sense of the words, saying the same thing. Even the invocation of the Wittgensteinian concept of 'family resemblance' does not help. The 'family resemblances' between what Paul is saying and what Athanasius maintains are, at best, general and oblique. The basic question we are here pressing is not answered in this way.

The 'hermeneutical problem' poses analogous difficulties. What presuppositions are to govern our understanding and interpretation of historical phenomena? Dilthey and others, following the lead given by Schleiermacher, have pursued this question with vigour. Twentieth-century theology, from Barth onwards, has wrestled with the issue but has been unable to come up with a lasting satisfactory answer. Perhaps no such answer exists though, again, to admit so would be to surrender to scepticism. The multivarious historical *data* compel us to search for a hermeneutical method which will, on the one hand, take with full seriousness the challenge of historical relativism while, at the same time, providing us with the possibility of finding a coherence and unity of some sort in our interpretation and appropriation of the *data*.

Thus the problems of history and historical method continue to haunt the critical theologian. It used to be said that philosophy was the handmaiden of theology. It has been claimed by some, in the wake of Kant and Hegel, that theology has been made the handmaiden of philosophy. In the light of the issues raised by modern historical method, it would surely be more accurate to say that *theologia et philosophia ancillae historiae*. History, as it were, is the reality that brackets all our theologizing and philosophizing. Both the theologian and the philosopher are historical beings, operating within all the limitations we have been analysing. There is no easy theological or philosophical escape from the dilemma. The response of both the theologian and the philosopher must be adequate to the nature of the challenge. It is interesting to note that even a philosopher as historically minded and conscious as Heidegger, whose philosophy explores in such a suggestive way the historical character of man's being, also makes assumptions as to the universal and uniform character or structure of that being. Since when, we are driven to ask. Since our progenitors came down from the trees or roamed the savannah plains? Since the dawn of civilization? Since . . . when?

III

Since, again, the time of Schleiermacher, a solution to the problems of historical relativism and hermeneutical method has been sought in experience. Experience gives us the 'key' to understanding, the means whereby we are enabled to interpret the traditions passed down to us. Bultmann's demythologizing proposals provide an excellent example of this. Having mapped out his own procedure, derived largely from the influence of the early Heidegger, Bultmann claims to know, not only the 'real purpose' of myth but also its 'real meaning'.[1] But this claim is widely contested, especially by Barth. Accusations of 'existentialist reductionism' are directed against Bultmann and the hermeneutical appeal to experience called in question. Leaving aside the dispute between Barth and Bultmann, it is clear that there are difficulties involved in *any* appeal to experience, difficulties of both a historical and a logical order. To some of these difficulties we now turn our attention.

(1) In a sense it must be admitted that an appeal to experience, as we saw in our initial critique of Barth, is unavoidable. To what else can we appeal? The question is thus not whether we are to appeal to experience but what experience we are to appeal to and what such experience will allow us to say, what weight of interpretation it will bear. The fact of the matter is that a concept like 'experience' and claims about the 'evidence' or 'significance' provided by experience are essentially contestable and systematically elusive. They are shrouded in ambiguity and open to constant dispute as the Bultmannian example shows. The trouble is that experience is a sort of pantechnicon word into which and out of which one can read whatever one wants to read. This being so, the appeal to experience looks logically, at first sight, like a jump out of the frying pan into

[1] *Kerygma and Myth*, 1, ed. by Bartsch, London, 1953, pp. 10, 38, 43.

the fire. The concept requires further analysis and elucidation.

(2) At the same time we must not become unduly sceptical about the appeal to experience. We have already emphasized not only the inescapability of such an appeal but the still promising character of Schleiermacher's methodological proposals if only these can be worked out in a more rigorous and consistent fashion. In addition, certain key distinctions must be kept in view, especially that between the *ordo cognoscendi* and the *ordo essendi*. The appeal to experience is an appeal to the *ordo cognoscendi*; as such it does not rule out the realm of being, the question of ontology, at all. It is only in and through and out of our experience that we are able to make the ontological claims that we do. Those who appeal to experience do not ignore or reject such ontological concern or interest. Every theologian, whatever his position, would claim to be dealing with objective and ultimate reality. That being so, the question is not whether we appeal to experience but what experience permits and compels us to say. The dispute about this is, therefore, not a dispute about appealing to experience but a dispute about the *data* provided by experience and how this *data* is to be understood and interpreted. However a whole cluster of difficulties congregate at this point.

(3) 'Experience' is never neutral. There are no bare facts, confronting us in their pristine nakedness and awaiting our 'interpretation' of their 'significance'. Experience is always somebody's experience and thus experience that is subject to, or has passed through the sieve of, a particular person's presuppositions, interpretative framework or culturally induced and historically relative attitudes. Likewise, and in a similar fashion, evidence is always somebody's evidence. Thus the appeal to experience must take into consideration *whose* experience is being appealed to. If it is the experience of someone else, then how are we to weigh or evaluate this experience? If it is our own experience, then the problems we have been trying to elucidate come to the surface again.

(4) Schubert Ogden, in the preface to his fine book *The Reality of God*, makes an important distinction between:

> '(1) the bases in our common human experience for talking about the reality of God at all; and (2) the conceptuality or system of fundamental concepts in which that reality is most adequately conceived and understood'.[1]

This distinction is a good one in that it highlights the difficulties involved and, indeed, the contentious character of the conceptualization of our experience. Just as important, however, is the insistence that our experience deals with the reality of God. Here the Barthian concern for the 'givenness' of God in revelation can be met. It is that

[2] London, 1968, p. x.

'givenness' which, in some mysterious way, gives us the bases for doing what theology does. But note, most importantly, that Ogden's distinction allows us to distinguish between this 'givenness' and the way in which this has been conceptualized in the various traditions. The 'givenness' in question is not reducible to any one particular conceptualization of it. Thus the way is, in principle, open to taking seriously the relative and culturally determined character of all conceptualization while, at the same time, maintaining the possibility that experience provides us with access to the reality thus variously conceptualized. The question, of course, remains as to whether or not experience does so operate. Indeed, how would we know that we were all dealing with the same reality, that our experiences were in some sense experiences of the same object? The logical difficulties here are considerable, but they are no different from those involved in other knowledge claims. This approach to the problem at least promises a possible solution.

(5) It might be argued that this tentative approach does less than justice to the question of truth in theology. To that I can but reply that this question is indeed a very difficult one. However, the approach outlined, for all its difficulties, at least gives some hope of evaluating truth claims. We do not arbitrarily commit ourselves to a particular conceptual system. We sift and test, seeking a more adequate way of expressing what, on the basis of experience, we must say. There are no guarantees or infallible procedures in this matter. To suggest that there were would be to deny our historicity and creaturehood. Nor will we ever be free from contradiction and dispute. Every critical theological method must take into consideration, for example, the various reductionist accounts of religious belief put forward in the post-Feuerbach and post-Freud context. Indeed the sifting and testing of our experience will entail taking these accounts into consideration. Only in the light of such radically honest and well-informed analysis of our experience will we be justified in making the truth claims that we end up making. As Schleiermacher says in his *Dialektik*, we must only believe in God if we have to, if we have no other choice, not because it pleases us to do so.[1]

(6) The complexity of such evaluation of our experience must, however, be re-emphasized. We do not have a number of beliefs which we can, somehow, validate or invalidate *seriatim*. Our beliefs interrelate and interconnect, providing what John Hick has called a 'total interpretation'. This point is important for our 'total framework' will condition how we evaluate particular elements of our experience. In this respect, however, the theist is not uniquely threatened. The Marxist, to take the most obvious example, equally operates with a 'total interpretation' which governs how he 'reads his

[1] 'Ihr könnt ihm nicht glauben willkürlich, sondern weil ihr müsst'.

experience'. In making this point, I do not want to suggest that such 'total interpretations' bear no relation to experience or that, even worse, they are of a non-cognitive character. I am only insisting that the relation between belief and experience is a complex one which is not reducible to a 1:1 correlation between specific beliefs and specific experiences. This means, of course, that the verification or falsification of such 'total interpretations' is a complex matter and both conversion and loss of faith, whether of a theistic or a marxist variety, occur within this complexity.

Thus the appeal to experience, like the problem of historical relativism, poses severe difficulties for the theologian, though, we are suggesting, these are not insuperable. We must not expect too much of our theologies or our theologians. Humility is demanded of us not just as a virtue in itself but also in the light of the immense problems with which we have to wrestle. We must always keep before us the difficulties outlined in this paper and, at the same time, eschew any Procrustean procedure which would assume that we, as *beati possidentes*, already know what experience must say. Everything we say must be, in principle, corrigible. We must never forget the fate of those poor fishermen who, having cast their 2″ mesh nets into the sea, drew the unfortunate conclusion that all the fish in the sea were more than 2″ long.

18 Life After Death: the Christian Doctrine of Heaven

by S. W. SYKES

Professor Torrance's fundamental contributions to the relation of the doctrines of the Incarnation and of creation indicate a whole series of consequences which may be drawn in relation to life after death.[1] We see this, for example, in the following:

> The Incarnation [is] to be understood as the chosen path of God's rationality in which He interacts with the world and establishes such a relation between creaturely being and Himself that He will not allow it to slip away from Him into futility or nothingness, but upholds and confirms it as that which He has made and come to redeem. Thus while the Incarnation does not mean that God is limited by space and time, it asserts the reality of space and time for God in the actuality of His relations with us, and at the same time binds us to space and time in our relations with Him. We can no more contract out of space and time than we can contract out of the creature-Creator relationship and God 'can' no more contract out of space and time than He 'can' go back on the Incarnation of His Son . . .[2]

Thus, although no careless assumptions can be made about the form of relation between the doctrines of creation and of the Incarnation on the one hand, and the Incarnation and eschatology on the other—in view of the fact that man's time is 'closed' on the one side and 'open' on the other—nevertheless the 'whence' and the 'whither' of man and the created order are mutually related and full of consequences for man's self-understanding.

The exploration of this relationship reveals one important parallel, whose methodological consequences must be drawn out. This parallel consists of the way in which, in the history of theology, the enterprise of natural theology, understood in separation from revealed theology,

[1] I wish gratefully to acknowledge help in the preparation of this paper from members of the Theological Society in Durham, who heard an early version of it, and from Dr Ann Loades, who provided me with valuable criticisms of its penultimate form.

[2] *Space, Time and Incarnation*, London, 1969, p. 67.

has played upon the content of the doctrines both of creation and of eschatology. In relation to creation, the 'old dualisms' of material existence and absolute space and time, or of nature and supernature (cf. p. 69), when developed independently in a natural theology, have exercised an undesirable tyranny over theological rationality. It is precisely the same dualisms which, in the form of propositions about the soul, have had a long history of influence in eschatology; and it is evident that we are still far from clear how that history is to be interpreted and the present position clarified. From the standpoint of the *method* of theology, however, what is proposed here is not an independent philosophical examination of the theme 'life after death', but an attempt to articulate 'the inner material logic of knowledge of God as it is mediated within the organized field of space-time' (p. 70) with special reference to the Christian doctrine of heaven. This formulation, therefore, distinguishes the treatment of the subject given here from two other approaches; the philosophical, as depicted above, a genre of literature in Western intellectual history devoted largely to the question of the immortality of the soul, taking its bearings from Plato and Aristotle, and reflecting the substantial critical contribution of the eighteenth century; and the mystical, stemming from various traditions, in which accounts are offered of the soul's communion with, and desire for, God.

In drawing attention to these other two approaches one could scarcely claim to be doing more than observing distinguishable sections, as it were, of a library catalogue. Neither the philosophical nor the mystical literature emerges from a religious vacuum. Both commonly draw upon themes from the religious traditions to hand, and even if they do so selectively, their 'independence' of them is only a relative matter. To refuse to follow these approaches and to attempt rather to tackle the problem of life after death by considering the Christian doctrine of heaven should not be interpreted as a sign of retreat into a theological ghetto. It is precisely by means of awareness of the existence and force of alternatives to such a Christian doctrine that a theologian receives the impetus to formulate out of the resources of the Christian tradition a doctrine which meets the present situation.

One further preliminary point must be clarified. I use the phrase 'life after death' because it remains, in my view, the clearest way of speaking of what I have in mind; which is, life, continuous in certain fundamental respects with the individual's present personal consciousness of living, temporally following on, and in that sense 'after', the cessation of life on earth. To speak of life after death is not to commit oneself to any theory of natural immortality. But I maintain that in order to provide minimum conditions of intelligibility for the doctrines of a resurrection to judgment and of the enjoyment of heaven, which it will be argued are integral to a coherent Christian theology, the term 'life' will inevitably carry temporal connotations which cannot be thought away in some a-temporal conceptuality.[1]

The present essay will advance along two parallel courses; first, by means of an enquiry into one recent attempt in theology to dispense with life after death, and secondly, by means of the presentation of an alternative way of viewing the coherence of a Christian doctrine of heaven with a total view of God's way with men. The intention is less to provide explicit arguments for believing in life after death, than to provide a contemporary statement of a tradition whose power to claim our allegiance may be allowed to speak for itself.

I

The contemporary context in which Christian belief in life after death is articulated is, inevitably, a complex one. The Christian himself, as he even superficially surveys the history of his own traditions, must be conscious of an embarrassing plethora of opinions. Hades, purgatory, the immortality of the soul, intercession for the dead, the second coming of Christ and the events preceding it, the resurrection of the body, the millennial kingdom, the last judgment, the fate of Satan, and the existence and form of heaven and hell provide a series of *quaestiones disputatae* of unpleasing memory, creating the formidable impression of the sheer unverifiability of eschatological doctrines. The inspection of the nineteenth century reveals two major problems on which considerable divergence still exists, the salvation of the unbaptized and the question of universalism. But even in the nineteenth century, and largely as the result of the influence of Kant and Hegel, it is evident that the character of the question about life after death has changed for Western intellectuals; now the very value and significance of the belief has become a problem. The doubts raised are philosophical, as to the doctrine's intelligibility, psychological, as to its coherence with contemporary theories of psychodynamics, and sociological, as to the social effect

[1] Karl Rahner objects to speaking of life after death in the sense characterized by Feuerbach, as if the soul were a kind of rider who, at death, merely changed horses and rode on. By contrast he proposes to speak of eternal life as 'something radically withdrawn from the former temporal dimension and the former spatially conceived time', 'Ideas for a Theology of Death', *Theological Investigations*, Vol. XIII, London, 1975, p. 175. But the meaning of this 'radical withdrawal' is far from clear. It is, according to Rahner, the self-realization of radical interiority (our personal freedom) losing itself in loving immediacy to God and thereby discovering its own fulness. But only if the notion of self is wholly withdrawn in such loss and discovery would time disappear as a dimension of life after death. Indeed the more emphatically Rahner insists on the primacy of human freedom realizing its true self in God, the more necessary it becomes to do proper justice to time.

of so believing. The extent to which any aspect of the objections may be consciously held varies, no doubt, from group to group within the Western world, but the modern theologian is unavoidably aware that he writes in the context of a common consciousness which rarely entertains belief in life after death as a matter of vital importance.

It is not too strong, in other words, to speak of this situation as a 'collapse' or at least of a 'transvaluation' of eschatological doctrine.[1] The situation is portrayed with startling clarity by a recent commentator upon contemporary historiography. Introducing the notion of 'horizon', Professor Gellner writes:

> The horizons of a society, or at any rate of many societies, consist of a cosmogony and eschatology, of an account of how things began and how they will end. As the horizon is dramatic, it is often easy to pick it out: the locals know how to talk about it, and ritual occasions abound which remind them to do so.[2]

Gellner proceeds at once to expound the view that our society has surrounded its traditional cosmogony and eschatology with a cloud of ambiguity 'according them "symbolic" status or what not, and it has been obliged to invent a special term, "fundamentalist", for those who actually claim to take them seriously'. Thus, in effect, our society's horizons, he believes, have collapsed into the present, and man is constantly faced with the 'logic of an absolute Creation situation' and no eschatology whatsoever. The facile dichotomy between a fundamentalist and a symbolic understanding of traditional cosmogony and eschatology need not detain us. What is of interest, however, is the transformation of cosmogonies and eschatologies. Their 'collapse into the present' implies, according to Gellner, that:

> contemporary history is not merely very dramatic, but, more significantly, it is crucial for the formulation, selection, validation of such alternatives as humanity may face (p. 17).

The crucial word is, of course, 'validation'. That certain courses of action were 'valid' would have been known in traditional societies by means of reference to the morality implicit in their cosmogonies and eschatologies. Here the possibility that man could fulfil the will of

[1] Thus, very properly, Karl Rahner, insists against this tendency that eschatology 'really bears on the *future*, that which is still to come, in a very ordinary, empirical sense of the word time' and rejects de-eschatologization, in 'The Hermeneutics of Eschatological Assertions', *Theological Investigations*, Vol. IV, London, 1966, p. 326.

[2] E. Gellner, 'Our current sense of history', in J. Dumoulin and D. Moisi (eds), *The Historian between the Ethnologist and the Futurologist*, Paris, 1973, pp. 3–4. Cf. Karl Rahner, 'Man possesses himself, disposes of himself, understands himself, in and by the anamnesis by which he retains his past and the prognosis by which he lays hold of what is to come', *op. cit.*, p. 331.

God would have been dramatically set forth, and his success and failure subjected to judgment. That for contemporary man 'the crucial events which are the charters of moralities . . . are not on the skyline, but, on the contrary, very close to home' (p. 17) is, according to Gellner, the direct consequence of ours being a naturalistic society, rather than one which thinks in terms of discontinuities.

This presentation of the phenomenon of 'collapse' or 'transvaluation' in relation to cosmogony and eschatology sets in perspective the observable tendency in some modern theology to deny, for example, that statements about creation have anything to do with the origins of things.[1] It also renders questionable the creation of easy 'correspondences' between what is referred to as 'contemporary anthropology' and theological eschatology. The risk here is a double one. On the one hand, the inherently controversial nature of work purporting to set out the anthropological presuppositions of modern man or of 'our society' is overlooked, and disagreements and contradictions ignored in the interests of selectivity and simplification. On the other hand, the radical gulf set by 'contemporary thinkers' between the naturalistic and any kind of theological perspective on man is minimized or concealed in the interests of a form of theology which proposes to have the best of both worlds.[2]

[1] J. Macquarrie, *Principles of Christian Theology*, London, 1966, esp. p. 199. The 'existential-ontological' interpretation of creation is applied similarly to the last things, p. 317. Macquarrie goes so far as to state: 'Let me say frankly, however, that if it were shown that the universe is indeed headed for an all-enveloping death, then this might seem to constitute a state of affairs so wasteful and negative that it might be held to falsify Christian faith and abolish Christian hope' (p. 318). In this sense Macquarrie's doctrine of creation is clearly more compatible with the theory of 'continuous creation', and the earlier strict demarcation between theology and science is eroded. Similarly in W. Pannenberg, *Jesus, God and Man*, London, 1968, pp. 225–31, both creation and last things are interpreted as affirming the 'nearness of God'. Those 'who direct their vision beyond their own accomplishments and possessions towards God's future have salvation already in this attitude' (pp. 227 f.). Both here, and in certain essays, Pannenberg shows awareness of the modern fallacy of robbing the eschatology of Jesus of its relation to time and converting his 'passion for God's future' into the presence of eternity in the momentary 'now', cf. 'The God of Hope', *Basic Questions in Theology*, Vol. 2, London, 1971, p. 237. Whether Pannenberg escapes the charge of having collapsed the content of the doctrines of creation and of the last things depends entirely on what is made of his interpretation of the doctrine of God as 'the power of the future' (*ibid.*, pp. 243 f.).

[2] These remarks apply to W. Pannenberg's essay, 'Eschatology and the Experience of Meaning', *Basic Questions in Theology*, Vol. 3, London, 1973, esp. pp. 196–202. Here Pannenberg attempts what he calls 'an anthropological interpretation of the traditional eschatological conceptions'. But his method confuses two distinct issues; (a) no 'interpretation' is involved if his intention is merely to state that the doctrine of future judgement has a profound meaning at every moment of man's life. This was already clearly part of the content of traditional eschatology. On the other hand, (b) it is quite another matter if a

Not falling into either of the above errors, however, is the theologically-formulated attack on the notion of life after death by Professor Moltmann in *The Crucified God*. This occurs in the section dealing with Jesus' resurrection from the dead which proposes to 'subject belief in the resurrection to the history of the crucified Christ as its true criticism' (p. 161). In simple terms Moltmann is seeking to mount a theological counter-attack on the long-standing tradition of theological optimism, which has presented the resurrection as the 'happy ending' to the temporary set-back on Golgotha. The passage, which must be examined in full, runs as follows:

> 'Resurrection of the dead' first of all excludes any idea of a revivification of the dead Jesus which might have reversed the process of his death. Easter faith can never mean that the dead Jesus returned to life, which leads to death. Were that the case, then he would have to be expected to die once more like Lazarus, who according to John 11 was raised by Christ, although his corpse was already stinking, and who then later died again. The symbol of 'resurrection from the dead' means a qualitatively new life which no longer knows death and therefore cannot be a continuation of this mortal life. 'Christ being raised from the dead will never die again', says Paul (Rom. 6:9). Resurrection means 'life from the dead' (Rom. 9:15), and is itself connected with the annihilation of the power of death. On the other hand, 'resurrection of the dead' excludes any idea of 'a life after death', of which many religions speak, whether in the idea of the immortality of the soul or in the idea of the transmigration of souls. Resurrection life is not a further life after death, whether in the soul or the spirit, in children or in reputation; it means the annihilation of death in the victory of the new, eternal life (I Cor. 15:55). The notion of 'life after death' can coexist peacefully with the experience that this life is a 'life towards death'. But the 'resurrection of the dead', understood as a present hope in the midst of the 'body of death', contradicts the harshest facts of life which point in the opposite direction, and cannot leave either death or the dead in peace, because it symbolizes the future of the dead. Thus the expression 'resurrection of the dead', which seemed to follow from the Easter visions, does not deny the fatality of death, whether this death is the death of Jesus on the cross or death in general, with the help

doctrine of God as 'the power of the future' is held to replace all previous notions of his transcendence. The fundamental question in the interpretation of Pannenberg's work is the precise sense in which the theological anthropology (which he affirms must serve as fundamental theology) is, in truth, a *theologically* formed anthropology, rather than an uneasy compromise between disciplines with radically different commitments, cf. 'Anthropology and the Question of God', *ibid.*, pp. 86–94.

of ideas of a life after death in some shape or form. Nor does it reduce the new element which the disciples perceived in Jesus to a dimension of the earthly Jesus, like the continuing influence of his cause or his spirit, or to a dimension of the faith of the disciples, like their longing for their own justification despite the disappointment of the cross or their desire for hope for their crucified past. It is therefore appropriate to the two experiences—the experience of his death on the cross and the experience of his appearances in the light of the coming glory of God (pp. 69–70).

Why does Moltmann apparently gratuitously go out of his way to exclude 'life after death'? Two reasons stand out. The first is that *a*-after-*b* talk is sequential in character, and basically inconsistent with the alternative 'double-conclusion' idea, which Moltmann is proposing as the outcome of Jesus' life.[1] The second reason is that, of course, life after death is spoken of in more than one religion, and Moltmann is strongly committed to the thesis that religion (catagorized with wisdom and power politics) is part of the 'world', to which the Christian is crucified (p. 24). A third reason takes the shape of an hypothesis, which it might be instructive to test by reference to Moltmann's book; that is, that by 'resurrection' Moltmann means, in plain language, that the crucifixion symbolizes a promise about the future of the world made by God, that 'the executioners will not finally triumph over their victims' (p. 178); or, alternatively, that there is an inherent order in things which will ensure that hate and vengeance will be broken down in a new humanity. That this hypothesis is worth investigating may be seen from the following statement in which Moltmann distinguishes his view, from, among others, Bultmann's that Jesus was raised into the kerygma or into faith. This is how Moltmann characterizes his own view:

> According to this analysis of the Easter appearances and visions, the original significance of the Easter faith is that the eye-witnesses perceived the earthly, crucified Jesus of the past in the glory of God's coming and drew conclusions from that in their experience of a call and mission. In that case it must be said that Jesus was raised into God's future and was seen and believed as the present representative of this future, of the free, new mankind and the new creation. In that case he was not raised into heaven and in that sense eternalized or divinized. Nor was he raised into the kerygma

[1] Cf. 'He [Paul] did not understand the resurrection of Christ as an event which simply followed his death, but as the eschatological event which characterized the earthly Jesus, crucified under Pontius Pilate, as the *Kyrios*' (p. 73). 'The question of Christ in the form "Who do you say that I am?" is posed by Jesus himself and by the two-fold conclusion of his life, from life into death and from death into new life' (pp. 105 f.). Cf. also p. 97 for the phrase, 'the double conclusion of the life of Jesus'.

> or into faith, for both kerygma and faith are understood eschatologically as the promise and hope of what is to come. Jesus 'rose into the final judgment of God' [U. Wilkens, *Auferstehung*, 1970, pp. 145 ff.] to which both kerygma and faith bear witness (p. 168).

We note that when Moltmann denies that Jesus was raised into heaven, he intends the denial to cover any personal form of 'divinization'. But when he negates Bultmann's theory that Jesus rose 'into the kerygma', he adds a qualification which indicates that he stands closer to Bultmann than to the tradition. This qualification consists in the fact that whereas Bultmann wishes to make the presence of the crucified Christ vivid to the believer existentially now, Moltmann is concerned to emphasize the *promisory* character of any faithful reflection on the crucifixion, the 'anticipatory vision' that 'salvation' or 'new life' can and will come about on earth. But it is nothing to do with 'reward' 'after death'.

> Therefore the resurrection hope of Christian faith is no longer ambivalent, threatened by an uncertain final judgement and its verdict; it is unequivocally a 'joyful hope'. It shows the cross of Christ as the unique and once-for-all anticipation of the great world judgement in the favour of those who otherwise could not survive at it. Thus resurrection is no longer the ontic presupposition of the accomplishment of the final judgement on the dead and the living, but it is already itself the new creation. So the Pauline resurrection kerygma contains within itself the proclamation of the new creation. In that case righteousness no longer means the rewarding of the righteous with eternal life and the punishing of the unrighteous with eternal condemnation, but the law of grace for unrighteous and self-righteous alike (p. 176).

The whole context of Moltmann's presentation of the resurrection is that of theodicy, and his criticism of the 'hope of immortality', with which he seems to identify talk of 'life after death', resides in 'the resigned attitude to life that goes along with it'.[1] The main question for him is thus not the physical, biological or historical possibility or conceivability of resurrection, but the righteousness of God. For Moltmann it is impossible to be alive with the resurrection life and to be resigned to the evil of the world. This is the point of the remark about the impossibility of peaceful co-existence between resurrection faith and the experience that life is a 'life toward death'. In plain language, he objects to the kind of fatalism which maintains that this life is a wretched existence, from which death is a blessed release into eternal life. Such fatalism, which has had dire conse-

[1] *Theology of Hope*, London, 1967, p. 208.

quences for the Christian attitude towards the evils of society, is the implicit object of his criticism.

This criticism is well made, and its point well taken. It is an example of a thoroughly traditional homiletic gambit, employed by more than one of the writers of the New Testament letters and preachers ever since, that those who believe *x* ought to be incapable of practising *y*, or alternatively, that those who practise *y* show that they do not really understand what *x*, which they say they believe, is all about. But the criticism is incompetent to accomplish what Moltmann intends. For it is impossible to establish a simple cause-effect correlation between belief and practice, so that it can be stated that those who practise *y* and say they believe *x* demonstrate that, because *y* is a wrong action, *x* must be a false belief. It is notorious that a single professed belief is compatible with a whole range of different attitudes and policies, reflecting a bewildering range of other factors entering the picture, among them psychological and social conditioning. Clearly not all Christians who have believed in life after death or the immortality of the soul have fatalistically resigned themselves to the 'miseries of this sinful world' or uncritically accepted the oppressive structures of their own societies. It would be difficult to demonstrate how such non-passivity arose. The inspiration might have derived from many elements in Christian faith, for example, from the example of Christ's concern for the sick and for the outcast, or from a doctrine of creation, or from a theory of natural law, or from a sense of brotherhood in Christ, or from the application of Old Testament prophetic criticism. There are numerous sources, other than resurrection faith, which might prompt opposition to the evils of the world. Similarly, on the other hand, there are numerous extraneous sources, in addition to a doctrine of the soul's immortality, which might be responsible for the fostering of a tendency to flight from the world, not least of which (it behoves a technologically developed society to remember) has been the sheer impossibility, in most of past history, of significantly altering the primary physical determinents of human existence. In short, Moltmann's criticism of belief in 'life after death' leaves ample room for the initial reply that such belief and an active opposition to the evils of man's existence, or a realistic attitude towards the 'deadliness' of death, are by no means alternatives to each other.

The second part of the reply to Moltmann pursues further his own chosen context for the discussion, the problem of the righteousness of God. Should it not be asked whether his own position is exposed to criticism precisely from the standpoint of theodicy? If it is the case, as my hypothesis suggests, that Moltmann's ambiguous references to resurrection may be translated into more readily intelligible speech about the constitution of this world, what account is he able to give of a world in which dying has not been, and is not, for very many people, in any way related to the 'new life' or 'new creation' of which he speaks. There are deaths which are the longed-for release from bodily pain or from insufferable mental tension, or which occur from sheer loss of will to live. There are, moreover, the uncomprehending deaths of children or the mentally deficient. The ancient pressures of theodicy which derives from a perceptive observation of the sheer undeserved hell suffered by some upon earth, cannot be set on one side by the disparaging observation that hope for life after death occurs in more than one religion. For a theology of the religions has to do not merely with the form, but also with the occasion, of religious beliefs. The facts are that living is an experience quite unequally enjoyed by human beings and that some discernibly suffer appalling deprivations, and that this is one powerful 'occasion' for the hope of life after death. It does not alter the situation for those who have no news of it, that some others may have evidence that life is not ultimately as they have experienced it, a lottery in which their luck has gone brutally astray. Of course, Moltmann knows all this, and correctly asks the theodicy question of those who are murdered and gassed, or who are hungry and oppressed:

> As Paul says in I Cor. 15, 'only with the resurrection of the dead, the murdered and the gassed, only with the healing of those in despair who bear lifelong wounds, only with the abolition of all rule and authority, only with the annihilation of death will the Son hand over the kingdom to the Father. Then God will turn his sorrow into eternal joy. This will be the sign of the completion of the trinitarian history of God and the end of world history, the overcoming of the history of man's sorrow and the fulfilment of his history of hope' (p. 278).

This passage, which could simply be read as a reaffirmation of Paul's doctrine of resurrection, is not without its ambiguities in the light of the denial of life after death. Moltmann cannot mean, unless he is in self-contradiction, that the individuals who were murdered or gassed in Auschwitz rise again to live in the kingdom of God. The phrases 'resurrection of the dead' and 'annihilation of death' refer rather to a total consummation of history, 'after' which there is only God—and, furthermore, God as totality without trinitarian 'history'. There is, in this theodicy, much about being given a ground for living in openness to the future of God; but no grounds for hoping for those who have died. In the nineteenth century it was observed in Britain that thoughtful men were becoming Roman Catholics on the grounds that the hope of purgatory provided a more consistent picture of God's righteousness towards the deprived than strict Evangelical orthodoxy.[1] The argument against the evangelicals was, precisely, on the basis of theodicy; that a God who had no discernible interest in the mass of mankind was a monster. It is still the mass of mankind, of all who have ever lived and died, who have had no news of the 'hope' which has transformed the Christian's existence and have not participated in his liberation. An understanding of the resurrection hope which does not recognize this as a serious dimension of theodicy, which is its context, is not yet in touch with human reality.

II

At this point the discussion may be best advanced by stepping back from close criticism to consider the context in which, as a dogmatic theologian with a view of resurrection hope different from that of Moltmann's, I view the discussion as taking place. On the one hand, some understanding has to be offered, even if only in the broadest outline, of the history in which one's protagonist stands; on the other hand, some indication has to be given of the alternative view taken by the critic. These two are closely connected. The significant moments in the history are invariably chosen with an eye to the substantive position being defended. Hence these two parts of the context of this discussion may be presented together.

From the point of view of the dogmatic theology being defended here there are two fundamental themes in Christian theology, whose ramifications permeate all Christian thought, aspiration and activity, and which require for their integrity the notion of life after death. These themes can be understood as doctrines, though they are not restricted in their application to intellectual considerations, and thus resemble rather Newman's 'principles' in their range of application.[2]

They are the concern with true life and the recognition of judgment. Both of these, it can be shown quite briefly, are integral to Christian discipleship, and both seem to demand the notion of life after death.

First, then, the concern with true life. Antecedent to all developed forms of theological anthropology, yet providing a distinctive alternative to all forms of naturalistic monism or fatalism, is the view that the life of man is only properly conceived in personal interaction with God's will for it. Even where there is explicitly no hope for the dead, life, long life and happiness is available for those who do God's will and feed on his word; and in the New Testament its nature and

[1] F. D. Maurice, *Theological Essays*, London, 1853, pp. 439 f.

[2] Cf. Principle 6: 'It is our Lord's intention in His Incarnation to make us what He is Himself; this is the principle of *grace*, which is not only holy but sanctifying', and principle 8: 'involved in this death of the natural man is necessarily a revelation of the *malignity of sin*, in corroboration of the forebodings of conscience'; *An Essay in the Development of Christian Doctrine*, Pt. II, Ch. 7, Image Books edn., New York, 1960, p. 311.

availability is defined in relation to the resurrection of Christ. This state of affairs becomes a reason for maintaining a doctrine of life after death inasmuch as the resurrection tradition corresponds to that self-transcending urge for a quality of life not fully appropriated—because of the fact of death—here and now (John 11:25–7, 'No man who is alive and has faith shall ever die'; Philippians 3:12–14, 'I have not yet reached perfection but I press on hoping to take hold of that for which Christ once took hold of me').

The second of the two reasons why Christian theology requires the notion of life after death lies in its concern with judgment. Again, antecedent to all developed eschatologies is the fact that life can only be lived in the light of a discriminatory perception of the human situation, the knowledge of good and evil. Judgment itself is thus a theme integral to the understanding of life; that men may do both good and evil and be held responsible for what they do is an inescapable corollary of the knowing and doing of the will of God, in which alone true life consists. From this flows the fundamentally moral character of Christian discipleship, and the fact that salvation is not merely deliverance from the power of death, but specifically deliverance from sin as a form of life. The concern with judgment provides a reason for maintaining life after death because it is clear that the span of a mortal life does not itself contain the resolution of that effort at discriminatory perception which is the fundamental motif of Christian discipleship. 'The sting of death is sin' in the sense that dying leaves for dead and living alike a hopelessly incomplete agenda. The resurrection to judgment provides the theological recognition that that agenda is, in God's time, completed.

It will be apparent to the critical reader that neither of these two reasons supply more than indications explaining the internal connection within Christian theology between its major theme of salvation and the hope of life after death. But, as reasons for preferring one interpretation rather than another of Christian affirmations about 'eternal life', they go a certain way towards establishing a case for a total view of God's dealings with mankind which includes, rather than excludes, speech about 'life after death'.

Thus heaven, the attaining of life in all its fulness, is, in the promise contained in the Christian's faith, the result of the perfect judgment which will be passed on his own life by God himself. This simply articulated hope is the emotional dynamic behind the diverse formulations of belief in life after death in Christian theology.

Life and judgment, and their correlatives, death and sin, are two themes permeating the whole of Christian theology. That *fulness* of life and that *true* judgment are both possible is given in the knowledge the Christian has of the human situation. According to this, man is not simply a lonely creature working out a *modus vivendi* for himself with his neighbours in a wholly obscure corner of the cosmos. He is part of a design, a scheme and an order of things, which he may rightly believe to exist and of which the author and originator is God. He speaks of God in personal language because he knows no other way of expressing the notion of free creative activity in this order of things. Furthermore, God, he believes, entered into our world himself. He was not, like an architect, personally immune from the stress of his own building. Of that of which he was the originator he is also the consummator. In particular, of the human lives of which he was the originator he is the consummator. He personally took the responsibility for the freedom of human life. He took responsibility by living through the freedom of an individual man, Jesus of Nazareth, to the point of that freedom's total defeat in death. This defeat makes clear the real situation of man, ultimately powerless to prevent the betrayal and destruction of love by fear, by cynicism, and by tragic weakness. The defeat makes clear also the real intention of God, and his disposition towards men.

The death of Jesus of Nazareth upon the cross is, none the less, the first of a series of victories, each of which are integral to each other. It is the victory of the obedience of love. It shows that God, in taking responsibility for the freedom of men, is prepared to take responsibility *utterly*, even unto death. It is thus a paradigm and consummation of human love, in whose experience there is nothing greater than personal self-giving.

The second victory is the resurrection, where the grip of mortality, binding and stamping with finality the powerlessness of man, is broken. Through the resurrection the now risen Lord is able to give to all humanity the rational hope that their personal lives have a capacity likewise to defeat the betrayal and destruction of love, and to be consummated outside the conditions of mortality.

The third victory is the exaltation of the risen Lord and the sending of the Spirit. In the exalted Lord man's freedom is given its ultimate point of consummation—namely communion with God; and in the gifts of the Spirit are bestowed the means whereby the relationship between God and man is here and now brought into existence. Man's powerlessness is transformed by power from on high, is the power of the exalted Lord.

The themes of life and judgment intertwine throughout this picture; life, in the realistic assessment of our present situation and in the promise held out that man is not ultimately imprisoned within the limits of his heredity and environment; and judgment, in the necessary discrimination between good and evil implied in the notion of 'fulness of life' and in the promise that it is good, not evil which, in the power of the victories of Christ, will ultimately triumph. In the history of Christian thought the balancing of the twin negativities of mortality and sin has been a recurrent problem, over which indeed Greek and Latin Christianity have diverged in emphasis. In the writings of the Greek fathers, up to and including the fourth century, the fundamental problem of man was his corruptibility, his transient hastening to death. In Latin theology, the situation is different. In the highly influential form given to the soteriological structure of theology by Augustine, who combined elements derived from Ambrose and from Cyprian, the emphasis is placed rather upon the inevitability and culpability of sin as the prime determinant of the human situation.[1] This structure is reproduced in certain of the developments of medieval theology even where Augustine's complex balance of themes is distorted. Thus in the later medieval doctrine of the sacraments (especially of penance), of justification and in the eschatological doctrine of purgatorial punishment, the development in each case presupposes the prominence given in theology to sin, its punishment and remission. Within the reformers' transformation of theology, both in respect of content and of method, the characteristically Western emphasis on sin and judgment is further maintained, especially by Luther.[2] Nor is it difficult to show the continuity in this respect between Luther and Kant. Despite the latter's radical alteration of hermeneutical stance, the problem-context in which the human situation is viewed is again that of the gravity and universality of human sin.

With Kant, however, the balance of the themes of mortality and sin has now emphatically shifted still further. In the Latin patristic and medieval context of soteriology, life *after* death was unambiguously affirmed as part of revealed knowledge, and the immortality of the soul was regarded as one of the certainties of natural theology. Thus although the present life was overclouded by the awareness of sin and judgment, there remained in the balance 'the blessed hope of everlasting life'. In the Kantian criticism of dogma, however, the status of life after death as theological knowledge is denied. The 'objective doctrine' that man's destiny is eternal blessedness or woe is classed as beyond the limits of reason's insight, even as a defense is offered, both in the *Critique of Practical Reason* and more strongly in the essay, 'Das Ende Aller Dinge' (1794), of the immortality of the soul as a postulate of pure practical reason. Such an immortality, however, is comprehensible only on the basis of the 'hypothesis of the spirituality of world beings', which denies the resurrection of the body.[3] What, in other words, occurs in Kant's treatment of the topic

[1] Cf. J. Pelikan, *The Christian Tradition*, Vol. I, Chicago, 1971, pp. 279–92.

[2] Cf. T. F. Torrance, 'The Eschatology of the Reformation', in W. Manson *et al.*, *Eschatology*, SJT Occasional Papers 2, Edinburgh, n.d., p. 40.

[3] *Religion within the Limits of Reason Alone*, Harper Torchbooks edn., New York, 1934, p. 119.

is that a tradition, already concentrated upon sin and judgment, has had its counterbalancing element explicitly 'spiritualized' and 'moralized'.

This procedure has far-reaching repercussions. The neglect of the ontological question posed by death in favour of the moral question of culpability and sin has posed severe questions for those Protestant theologians who believed they followed Kant most closely. The more completely the latter question dominated the discussion, the more difficult it has been found to answer the question with which the hope of life after death dealt, namely, whether man lives and ends his life, however it may have been intensified, transformed or improved, solely a creature of time. If the question is asked of the individual the doctrine of eternal life, when moralized, turns into a way of holding out the hope of reward for moral endeavour. But the problems with this are legion. What of those who repent before being able to set their lives on an appropriately moral course? What of those whose lives are wholly morally ambiguous? What of those whose personalities have been damaged by upbringing, or by the coincidences of nature and upbringing? What of the mentally deficient? What of those who suffer senile decay in their declining years or whose personality alters after an accident? It is in these cases that the consequence of the progressive shift away from ontological issues, from discussion of the intrinsic nature of man and his relation to God, becomes apparent.

The question concerning the temporal limits of human life may be asked, similarly, of the goal of society as a whole. Here we can observe, in a substantial section of post-Kantian Protestant thought, a progressive moralization of the doctrine of the kingdom of God. Contemporary discussion of the significance of Utopianism and interest in Christian-Marxist dialogue are both signs that the intramundane perfectibility of man has become a live theological issue. The kingdom of God shows a recurrent tendency to take on the features of Kant's ethical commonwealth, and the doctrine of a new heavens and a new earth those of an unrealistic and potentially inhuman utopia.

But in Moltmann's case, as he himself makes clear, it is with Hegel's contribution to the Kantian tradition that we chiefly have to reckon.[1] Here the situation is complex. Hegel rejected Kant's doctrine of radical evil, though not of the reality or seriousness of evil. He eventually gave up the Kantian postulate of immortality, having, like Kant, no interest in the resurrection of Christ as an historical event. At the same time, the notion of life dominates his philosophical endeavour, and both the suffering and death of Christ are central to

[1] *Theology of Hope*, p. 211, and *The Crucified God*, pp. 253 f. For criticism of Hegel's Christology see *ibid.*, p. 92.

his idea of essential Being reconciling itself with itself.[1] Hegel's is not, therefore, a simple continuation of the Western tradition. The position seems rather that although he correctly redresses the balance to consider the problem of death as well as that of sin, his structural re-interpretation of theism has placed the whole of soteriology in a new context. Thus, although much of the original diversity and subtlety of the Christian tradition has re-entered the picture, making Hegel's work an exceedingly fruitful subject for theological study, what has changed is the original conception of the distance between God and man, which gave both to man's acts and to his mortal weakness its ultimate seriousness.[2]

Moltmann's presentation of his topic has themes which derive both from the Western tradition as mediated by Luther and interpreted by Kant and Hegel. For Moltmann, as in Luther, the problem-context for all speech about God is the righteousness of God. The man who does not stand under the cross has no *locus standi* for himself or his utterances. This epistemological principle is developed as a powerful moral criticism of 'wisdom, religion and power politics' (p. 24), and content of salvation given as freedom, interpreted both psychologically and politically. All this is consistent with the basic Western tradition focusing on the evil circumstances which constitute man's slavery to sin. At the same time Moltmann offers strong criticism of the Kantian and Ritschlian moralizing of dogma as an 'unbalanced regression' (p. 30). Consistent with Hegel's response to Kant are, likewise, the strong plea for a doctrine of the Trinity, the criticism of the hope of immortality in the context of a 'life' philosophy (interpreted as the freedom of the Spirit), and the acceptance of suffering and death as a means of reconciliation with the human situation. In remarking on Moltmann's use of Hegel one must beware of giving the impression to an audience generally antipathetic to that philosopher's influence that one is seeking to bring in a verdict of guilt by association. Moltmann is far from being a disciple of Hegel, as his specific and emphatic criticism of Hegel's neglect of biblical history shows. The fact is, however, that Moltmann's indifference towards belief in life after death is a characteristic he shares with Hegel, and that the transformation of the idea of eternal life into a philosophy of history, especially one which embodies the 'trinitarian history of God', is a basic Hegelian procedure. Whether Western theology should pursue this line further, or whether neglect of certain important features of the Christian tradition has become altogether too

[1] *Phenomenology of Mind*, London, 1931, pp. 780 f.

[2] Cf. Werner Schultz, 'Die Transformierung der *Theologia Crucis* bei Hegel und Schleiermacher', *Neue Zeitschrift für systematische Theologie und Religionsphilosophie*, Bd. 6, Berlin, 1964, pp. 290–317, reprinted in *Theologie und Wirklichkeit*, Kiel, 1969, cf. esp. p. 95.

marked to be supportable will only emerge if it is possible to produce, even if only in barest outline, some coherent kind of alternative. To this attempt we now turn.

III

We must start with the significance of death. All death is separation; but it is more, if it is final. It stamps as irreconcilable the oppositions, failures, sicknesses, misunderstandings, fears and hatreds of human relations. The memory of these may be all but overwhelming for the surviving party. And if it were true that there was a survival of death without any assurance of reconciliation and forgiveness, the thought of survival would be intolerable.

The threefold victory of Jesus shows us initially that our natural fear and abhorrence of death is a wholly rational reaction. Nothing occurs more frequently in criticism of the Christian's belief in life after death than that it attempts to conceal the unpleasant reality of death.[1] But we should distinguish between dying and death. It is a perennial human, and not merely Christian temptation to romanticize dying, which for some is the hardest work of their lives and may also be hard for the living to endure. The Christian who contemplates the death of Christ has perhaps less reason to fall into this trap than others, though it is understandable if he does. Concerning death, however, there are no grounds for charging Christians with concealing the truth. Only if it could be known for certain that there was no hope of resurrection would Christian faith in this respect be fraudulent. But it is not so known, and I fail to see the justice for claiming greater 'realism' or 'honesty' in the alternative view that death is final. There is no loss of realism in the Christian's view of the death of Jesus. For his own death *was* a defeat of love in powerlessness; his dedication to men was eventually surrounded and overwhelmed by their fear, their cynicism and their tragic weakness. None the less it was a death which was embraced. Jesus turned his face steadfastly to go up to Jerusalem, and as the certainty of his fate became apparent he turned his own powerlessness into an active force. In embracing death, his goodness of will, his character, turned the suffering into a triumph, the cross into a royal throne.

The grip of death, its stamping with finality the failures, incom-

[1] Cf. Alex Comfort, *Nature and Human Nature*, Pelican edn., London, 1969, pp. 168 f. A more restrained version of the same theme occurs in Iris Murdoch, *The Sovereignty of Good*, London, 1970, pp. 79 and 87. Thus Iris Murdoch allows a consoling function to the idea of 'a beauty which teaches that nothing in life is of any value except the attempt to be virtuous'. Austere though this is, one can without much difficulty imagine the kind of argument which would purport to show the fictional character of such consolation and its capacity to protect the psyche from the pain of purposelessness.

pleteness and likely impermanence of Jesus' own influence was broken by the resurrection. The fear that his mission would fail was turned, in Palestine, into a joyful assurance that there was more to do and to say in the future. But it is in the exaltation and the sending of the Spirit that the possibility of the permanent significance of Jesus for all humanity, past, present and future is announced. The exaltation expresses the conviction that Jesus' significance is not confined to his own time and such limited areas of the globe as might feel his influence subsequently. Without the victory of the exaltation the resurrection would be either the resuscitation of a corpse or the appearance of an embodied spirit—an interesting phenomenon, no doubt, providing evidence for some kind of death-survival claim, but not necessarily of central significance for mankind.

The exaltation, however, transforms for the Christian his whole notion of life. The physico-chemical, the organic and the psycho-social aspects of human evolution will be seen by him as consummated in the realization of communion with God, its originator. This communion with God is continuous with the highest love of which man is capable. Love is a force which *may* transform his social relations at every stage from infancy and the turmoil of adolescence, into life-long marriage and the necessary resignations of old age. I say 'may' because there are many expressions and forms of love, some of which are indeed destructive and most are tinged with selfishness. Transformed love is love which has gone to school with the character of Christ, and learnt, in company with the countless diversity of other disciples, the persistent goodness of will which is the intention of Christ's God and Father. Man's endemic and self-destructive irrationality is not, therefore, soluble until he learns to fashion his social loves so as to conform them to that love which is continuous with communion with God.

What is this process of conformity? It is essentially a creative, individual matter which rejoices in and maintains the remarkable diversity of humanity. Its instrument is experience of the reality of forgiveness. A man who has offered himself for forgiveness is one who is both aware that he is judged and is also capable of an act in which he, no more than momentarily perhaps, places someone other than himself at the centre of his own existence. One can be aware of judgment and not make this displacement of self, which issues in a morbid and ultimately self-indulgent condition; or one can displace oneself and not be aware of judgment, which issues in a form of moral passivity. To do both, however, to be aware of judgment *and* to displace self is to offer oneself for forgiveness; and this experience is, in human relations, continuous with one of the most treasured experiences spoken of by Christians, the discovery of divine forgiveness, itself the sole grounds for the hope of fulness of life.

The Christian claims to know, through the teaching of Christ, the reality of divine judgment upon himself and the hope of divine forgiveness. He claims that his life is held even now in communion with God, by the humanity of the ascended Christ at God's right hand. He claims that throughout each of life's stages he can live in confidence that his powerlessness fully to realize the presence of God is not the last word on his existence. And he claims that he is empowered, here and now, to achieve both in his innermost awareness and in his actions things to which he would never dare to aspire, left to his own devices. So much he may claim through his dependence upon his ascended Lord and through his gift of the Holy Spirit.

But what of all humanity? Is the Christian's confidence achieved at the expense of all the rest of the human race? I cannot believe that it is.

If the Christian hopes that he will be raised to life through the victories of the humanity of Christ, there can be no grounds for his not at least *hoping* that the same may be true for all others. He believes, likewise, that he will face the judgment of God in which his own attempts at discrimination will be enlightened, and there can be no grounds for his not believing that the same may be true for all others. That at least will persuade him of the rationality of a resurrection to judgment. What, then, beyond this? Here what needs to be asked are the major questions concerning judgment, forgiveness and reconciliation. If all have fallen short of the goodness of God, all stand in need of the true judgment and forgiveness of God himself. We do not judge others, nor do men judge themselves because their own judgment is fallible. If then God is alone judge it follows that all we can say is that we believe the way of forgiveness and reconciliation is open. For if it is open to *us*, I fail to see by what right we can believe that any particular individual is destined to a future of perpetual exclusion from God. I say this of any individual case which may be known to us; and this is neither to affirm or to deny the thesis of universalism, which rests upon considerations of a general nature. What we have good grounds to fear and to hope for ourselves, we have grounds to fear and to hope for others. A Christian who is capable of believing that 'God will save him' no matter what he does, is capable, no doubt, of believing the same of all men. And, likewise, one who fears that he himself may ultimately fail must fear the same for others. But who is so confident of his powers of self-knowledge that he would envisage the course and consequence of judgment on himself? Similarly it would be more, not less, absurd for one to enact in imagination the passing of divine judgment on others.[1]

1 Thus Karl Rahner makes the important observation that 'the eschatology of salvation and of loss are not on the same plane' and asks why we should know more about others than about ourselves, 'others for whom we are to have as

Is this view any better placed *vis-à-vis* the criteria offered above, and in particular those whose deaths provide theodicy with such bitter urgency? The answer to this question returns us to the initial problem noted in Moltmann's treatment of the topic, the relation between doctrine on the one hand, and attitudes and practice on the other. It is possible, as the history of Christian theology abundantly confirms, to profess a set of doctrines and at the same time to nourish attitudes and indulge in practices derived from wholly different sources. There is no automatic protection from this, any more than there is from the accidental or unconscious entertainment of contradictory beliefs. If, however, we persist in entertaining the hope that all men will rise to the perfect judgment of God, important perspectives are opened up on the human situation, with potentially profound effects for our attitudes and actions towards others.

For the judgment of God is a universal judgment, in which men of an inconceivable variety of types, reflecting the myriad divisions of time, place, culture and social class stand before one judgment seat. There will take place a true discriminatory perception on all that has been thought, believed, aspired after and done in the name of truth. The significance of this belief for the Christian is that it is the quality of this true judgment which must shed its light on his own present attitudes and conduct, for which his limited experience does not provide the necessary basis. To aspire to judge others with a true judgment implies a different attitude from the self-confident passing of judgment referred to above. This aspiration has no room for the belief that one already possesses all the necessary criteria (the phenomenon of sectarian intolerance) or for a total lack of interest in the possibility of universal criteria (the phenomenon of indifferent agnosticism). The Christian is forced into the position of having to make the effort of aspiring to know others as God will know them, and of seeing himself in the context of this knowledge. Two practical results stem from such a transformed and enlarged outlook. In the first place, it becomes at once a more complex and a more urgent task that modes of communication be found by means of which the gospel is rendered intelligible and vivid beyond the relatively uniform assumptions of our personal environments. And, secondly, it becomes possible to question our own dependence upon the stability and continuity of our personal circumstances. Only if a theologian is personally willing to immerse himself in something of the fantastic variety of the actual experiences of living and dying will his theology be delivered from the deadly parochialism of his own immediate

---

much hope as for ourselves, and whose destiny cannot be more indifferent to us than our own', 'The Hermeneutics of Eschatological Assertions', *Theological Investigations*, Vol. IV, London, 1966, pp. 338 f.

circle, and bear some traces of the universality intended in the Christian gospel.

In the second place, it is a consequence of entertaining belief in life after death that we begin to wrestle with the idea that the realization of that communion with God implies a notion of 'life' surpassing the limits of our all too lazy imaginations.[1] The possibility arises of an experience of life and of an awareness of a potential for growth at once conditioned by, yet independent of, the constraints of heredity and environment, or of the limitation of our probable future time. Many of the Greek fathers saw no reason to suppose that an individual attained limitless perfection at once in the kingdom of God; the process of exploration of the field of God's love would reveal, they believed, an unlimited area. There is a twofold significance in this. In the first place this is a belief which addresses itself to the problem of genuine late conversion, when the limits of personality and of mortal time prevent an active realization of the power of the love of God. The Christian hope for the remaking of man cannot surely depend on the relative adaptability of the life-style of younger persons. Old age imposes severe limitations, and the onset of death may begin with the destruction of possibilities previously open to the personality.[2] If dying, however, does not rob us of time in our relation as creatures to God, the possibility is open that one who responds to the love of God late in his mortal span may yet correctly perceive that there is in himself a potential beyond the probable future of his personality. And in the second place, reflection upon heaven ceases to be a futile or even dangerously misleading activity. For what is involved is a perception of oneself as being formed by

[1] Cf. Stewart R. Sutherland, 'What Happens After Death?', *Scottish Journal of Theology*, Dec. 1969, Vol. 22, pp. 404–18. This essay makes two important points; (i) that all talk of life after death commits one to speaking of endless life continuous with this life and (ii) that part of what the Christian wishes to affirm in speaking of eternal life intimately concerns what he holds to be of ultimate value here and now. The concern of the writer is to pursue the latter point, as the really important part of the Christian tradition, without affirming or denying belief in endless life. My purpose in the present essay is to affirm the coherence both of believing in life after death, as endless life continuous with this life, and in holding that such life is the 'true life' of 'true discernment' here and now. Cf. also the same writer's, 'Insight and Belief; Edwin Muir on Immortality', *Human World*, No. 2, Feb. 1971, pp. 47–56, for an exploration of an example of the integration of ethical self-knowledge and belief in immortality.

[2] Kant's references to death-bed repentances, in *Religion within the Limits of Reason Alone*, are rather remarkable. He is obliged to suppose that the clergyman must either (a) pronounce the man's case hopeless, or (b) that he must undertake to transform the man on the spot (p. 63), or (c) that he must exacerbate the dying man's guilty conscience, to get him to perform acts of reparation (p. 72)—only the last being a worthy, or possible course of action. Having, as Kant believes, no more time a dying man without the capacity or wherewithall to make reparation is in a truly desperate situation.

the attractive power of the love of God. Human friendship not surprisingly is the source of this analogy—the enigma of an individual's identity may slowly unravel itself as he sees himself reflected in the love of a friend. Friendship of such a quality is, for the befriended, a person-forming environment, in which the self takes on its true character and receives the power to carry out its responsibilities with greater consistency and integrity. By means of this analogy we may begin to formulate to ourselves what it would mean for us and for others to live in the field of the creative love of God, each starting from the point we really occupy. Nor should we, as 'aristocrats of the mind', be tempted to scorn the suggestion that new heavens and a new earth will bear a relationship to the physical environment of our present life.[1] Heaven, in short, becomes in our imagination the future of that in us and in our interaction with the world which is of ultimate worth; that, in other words, which has become part of the completion of the will of God in time, and which may not, therefore, be allowed 'to slip away from Him into futility or nothingness' (*ibid.*, p. 250).

[1] Thus W. A. Whitehouse in 'New Heavens and a New Earth?', in G. B. Caird *et al.*, *The Christian Hope*, London, 1970, pp. 93 ff.

19 The Problem of Defining a Theology of Culture with Reference to the Theology of Paul Tillich

by JOHN HEYWOOD THOMAS

In his introduction to the volume of Barth's papers entitled 'Theology and Church' Professor Torrance makes the illuminating comment that Barth's intention was to create a *diastasis*, 'a radical separation between theology and culture, which he felt to be eminently necessary if we were to think clearly again about God, and about man, and of their reconciliation in Jesus Christ'.[1] The intention of the *Romans* was 'by no means an attack on culture as such, but rather the opposite, upon a bogus mystification of culture which required to be disenchanted of its secret divinity before it really could be called human culture'.[2] While the thinking of Paul Tillich concerning the relation of theology and culture does not need such words of justification it nevertheless does need some explanation. It is true that of all the labels and descriptive phrases which Tillich's theology drew to itself none is more apt than the phrase 'theology of culture' which indeed was a phrase he himself used in order to describe his work.[3] Our task in this paper is not simply that of expounding the various discussions of a theology of culture which Tillich left us in his work but more particularly that of understanding how to define this theology. Tillich's great virtue, as is so clear from his delightful memoir, *On the Boundary*, was that like the Latin poet he would boast *humani nil a me alienum puto*. For a generation of theologians becoming increasingly concerned with problems of politics and of ecology this is a wholly admirable emphasis. Yet the problem with which we are here concerned arises when someone with a theological innocence analogous to the boy who declared the emperor to be without any clothes says, 'But, I thought that theology was about God'. That Tillich is right in insisting that the theologian must have something to say about culture nobody wants to deny, but if this

[1] *Theology and Church*, London, 1962, p. 22.

[2] *ibid.*

[3] *The Theology of Paul Tillich*, ed. Kegley and Bretall, New York, 1951, p. 13; cf. *On the Boundary*, London, 1966, pp. 68 ff. and Leibrecht's introduction to the *Festschrift* for Tillich, *Religion and Culture*, pp. 3–27.

argument and this comment are theological then some clarification of the method of theology is needed.

The reference to Professor Torrance's description of Barth's early work will remove the temptation to adopt the phrase 'theology of culture' as a term to be contrasted with 'kerygmatic theology'. Whatever the differences between Barth and Tillich (and there clearly were fundamental differences of outlook and method) there is no warrant for such an easy opposition as this. Not only is there a real sense in which Tillich's work is a kerygmatic theology,[1] but there is the same concern for the essential worth of human culture. Never an opponent of culture Barth could with justice be said to have thrown out with an abandon so characteristic of genius some *jeux d'esprit*, like his great essay on Mozart, which are significant contributions to the theology of culture. Thus what can indeed be the object of idolatrous worship becomes for the mind of faith the means to achieve a service of God. Barth's aim, no less than Tillich's, was to expound the claims of God known by faith as the Father of our Lord Jesus Christ upon the whole of life—including culture. In this both theologians are true to their Reformation heritage. If one may adopt Tillich's favourite terms heteronomous and autonomous to characterize Luther's critique of both medieval and Renaissance moralism we can say that the former was rejected by Luther as heteronomous while the latter was rejected by him as autonomous, and both views of morality were rejected as moralistic. For him the good was something made available as a gift of the Holy One in the forgiveness of sins. If it were necessary to argue further for the impossibility of using the term 'theology of culture' as a contrast with Barth's 'kerygmatic theology' we need only consider the basic definition of the nature of theology given by Tillich in *Systematic Theology*, volume 1. There we are told that the function of the theologian is to be faithful to the traditional message while attempting to do justice also to the other pole of theology, namely its contemporary situation. Clearly then it is no use regarding the phrase as a simple contrast to 'kerygmatic theology'.

The idea of a theology of culture was the subject of a famous lecture Tillich gave to the Berlin section of the Kant Society soon after World War I. Exactly forty years later he wrote in the preface to *Theology of Culture* (a volume which sadly did not contain the Berlin lecture so that this did not appear in an English translation until 1969): 'It is a source of great satisfaction to me that after the passing of forty years I can take the title from this volume from my first important public speech.'[2] Not only does he indicate the im-

[1] Cf. Kelsey, *Fabric of Tillich's Theology*, New Haven, 1967, p. 1; Petit, *La Philosophie de Religion de Paul Tillich*, Montreal, 1974, p. 27.

[2] *Theology of Culture*, New York, 1959, p. v.

portance of the lecture but he emphasizes the fact that the relation between religion and culture has always been a central problem in his thinking.[1] The date of that first lecture is important; for, as Professor Jean-Paul Petit has recently pointed out,[2] the sense of desolation which was the aftermath of World War I, the conviction that it had left 'the whole house in ruins', was the decisive influence on all Tillich's reading and thinking for years to come. It left on his theology the indelible mark of a tragic sense of life. In a very important sense, then, the idea of a theology of culture is a response to this sense of desolation. His very first article had expressed the same revulsion towards the compromising attitude of the Church as Barth had felt. It was wrong for the Church to join forces with the exploiting powers and the young theologian begins what seems a Marxist gospel as he pleads for a positive stance towards socialism.[3] However, that it is not a Marxist revision of Christianity is evident from the way in which the theology of culture is related to the traditional moral theology and also from the accounts of his own development given in *On the Boundary* and *The Theology of Paul Tillich*. First, he made very plain in the lecture on the theology of culture that it was no longer possible to do traditional moral theology; for in the extra-ecclesial situation that had been produced by the First World War it was essential to attack something more fundamental, *viz.* the very cultural framework of modern life. There could no longer be any question of a theological system of ethics. 'What was essentially intended in the theological system of ethics can only be realized by means of a theology of culture applying not only to ethics but to all functions of culture. Not a theological system of ethics, but a theology of culture.'[4] If there is this continuity of purpose between the traditional theological system of ethics and the theology of culture then we cannot argue that Tillich has seen his aim to be a revision of the purpose of theology which it must be if this is a Marxist version of Christianity. The issue is not whether Marxism contains an ethic (for it is abundantly clear that it does) but whether it provides the same kind of justification of ethics. The necessity of abandoning the traditional method of theological ethics was borne in on Tillich by the secularism of the post-war world. Such a situation, he thought, demanded the more fundamental approach of a theology of culture. Secondly, Tillich's autobiographical memoirs afford us ample evidence for saying that this idea

[1] Cf. 'Lessing und die Idee einer Erziehung des Menschengeschlects', *Gesammelte Werke*, XII, pp. 97–111; *Protestant Era*, pp. xvi, 55 f.; *Systematic Theology*, Vol. III, pp. 4–5.

[2] *op. cit.*, pp. 23–4.

[3] 'Christentum und Sozialismus, 1919', *Gesammelte Werke*, II, pp. 21–8.

[4] *What is Religion?*, New York, 1969, p. 160.

of a theology of culture not only ante-dated any Marxist influence but derives from entirely different influences. The autobiographical sketch in *The Theology of Paul Tillich* recalls the importance of the father's influence on the young intellectual, in particular a series of conversations which enabled young Tillich to grasp the key to the whole notion, the possibility of a synthesis between an autonomous culture and a living faith.[1] Similarly it is well known that his experience as an army chaplain was profoundly significant for him as a theologian struggling to attain a clarity of personal vision. He realized for the first time that there was a great divide between official Lutheranism and the mass of the working-classes; and though this led him to a socialist position in politics that may be very close to Marxism that was itself no more than an expression of the fundamental position which was a *religious* socialism. Again, his discovery of painting and his cultivation of knowledge and appreciation of art —all this is too well-known a story to need retelling. What does need to be emphasized is that this interest in art and art-history was a formative influence on the development of his theology and obviously on the development of a theology of culture.[2] The lecture on the theology of culture begins by distinguishing between the situation of the empirical sciences and that of the cultural sciences. In the former the thinker's own standpoint is something to be overcome whereas in the latter it is of the essence of the project. Having identified his task as itself in that sense, then, a cultural one Tillich launches on his argument which is composed of five steps. First, amongst the distinctions it is important to make none is more so than that between theology and philosophy of religion, 'Theology is the concrete and normative science of religion'.[3] As such theology has nothing to do with either a particular object called God or a special complex of revelation. The essential connection with the concrete standpoint of an individual confession distinguishes theology from philosophy of religion. However, it is based on the categories of philosophy and indeed there is a relation between philosophy and theology that is in one sense reciprocal.[4] Tillich sees this distinction as the rejection of an 'authoritarian limitation upon individual standpoint', and its clearly Hegelian inspiration is something to which we shall return later. The second step in the argument, however, is the rejection of the tradition of a theological ethics in favour of a theology of culture. This necessitates an analysis of the relation between religion and culture. Religion is not a particular area of human activity as with

[1] *op. cit.*, p. 8.

[2] *On the Boundary*, pp. 26–30, 46–7, 85–90. Cf. *The Theology of Paul Tillich*, pp. 64 ff.

[3] *What is Religion?*, p. 157.

[4] *ibid.*, p. 158.

Kant, Hegel or Schleiermacher.[1] The religious potency is to be distinguished from its expression in a religious act. Religion is nothing other than the experience of unconditioned absolute reality 'which is above all beings which at the same time is the absolute Nothing and the absolute Something'.[2] The relation between science and religion which will thus be exemplified in theology is the paradoxical transformation of autonomy in a theonomy which does not destroy it. It is at this point that Tillich offers a hypothesis which is decisive for the formula that sums up his theology of culture. The hypothesis is that the autonomy of cultural functions is grounded in their form whereas theonomy is grounded in their substance.[3] The task of a theology of culture is to survey the whole of culture from the standpoint of substance in an attempt to reveal its spiritual import. It will produce 'a general religious analysis of all cultural creations', 'a historical-philosophical and typological classification' of cultural history and a 'concrete religious systematization of culture'. Illustrations of a cultural-theological analysis are given to explain and develop this understanding of a theology of culture and their most important feature is the concentration on the relation of form and substance. The final question is what now happens to the specifically religious culture. There are three possible answers to this problem of the relation of a theology of culture and dogmatic ecclesiological theology. They are: the Catholic position, the traditional Protestant position and a position adumbrated by the Aufklärung. Theology of culture is oriented towards the internal dynamism of historical process and seeks to rediscover the absolute in the relative.[4] Tillich's closing words echo Hegel—'religion is the beginning and the end of all things, and also the centre, giving life and soul and spirit to all things'.[5]

Before following Tillich's development of these ideas in his other papers of this period it will be useful to look at the philosophical sources of this idea of a theology of culture. We saw that the development of a theology of culture was Tillich's answer to the problem posed for theology by the non-ecclesial or secular character of the world to which he spoke after World War I. If there is any theme that can be said to be central to Hegel's philosophy of religion it is that of God and secularity. The 'early theological writings' show Hegel the young revolutionary thinker arguing for religious liberty[6];

[1] *ibid.*, p. 160.
[2] *ibid.*, p. 162.
[3] *ibid.*, p. 164.
[4] *ibid.*, pp. 177 ff.
[5] *ibid.*, p. 181.
[6] *Hegel's Early Theological Writings*, ed. Knox and Kroner, Harper Torchbook, pp. 104–29. Cf. Nauen, *Revolution, Idealism and Human Freedom*, The Hague, 1971.

but most significant is the conclusion of the essay 'The Spirit of Christianity' where Hegel bemoans the fact that the Church had oscillated between two extremes.[1] From 1800 until his death in 1831 Hegel was concerned with this problem which informs the whole of his philosophical effort.[2] It is not only the thoroughness with which Tillich sought to build a system of thought that earns for him the comparison with Hegel but also a parallel development in his own thinking. Both men seem to me to have moved away from the practical political concerns which were the inspiration of their early thought to a more abstract concern. Again, the essentially theistic nature of the question is what both stressed—the problem of the secular is fundamentally a problem about the nature of God. Here they both protest against the two extremes represented by a one-sided belief and a one-sided secularism, and indeed the very way in which Tillich describes the oscillation between these extremes as a tragic cycle is reminiscent of Hegel.[3] Further, like Hegel Tillich sees the answer to the conflict of extremes to lie in a third way. Neither autonomy nor heteronomy has the final word but theonomy: culture cannot be in essential conflict with religion because religion is the substance of culture. In this connection the Hegelian source of Tillich's thinking is an important factor in his argument; for crucial to that is the typically Hegelian move of saying that what is 'overcome' is nevertheless 'preserved'. Finally, both thinkers could with some justice be said to have transposed theism from its traditional 'key' of God's existence. That is, neither of them was concerned about the debate between theism and atheism. While Hegel often spoke of the death of God Tillich indulges in the paradox that the only atheism is the assertion of God's existence. In both cases their 'atheism' could be defended as a particular philosophical theory of God's existence. Yet another source was the profoundly influential romantic movement which could be said to have moulded the young Hegel but which in any case had a strong attraction for the young Tillich. In particular we know that the philosophical expression of romanticism in the thought of Boehme and Schelling exerted a profound influence on the development of Tillich's thought.[4] This romantic heritage is seen in the rather mystical interpretation of religious and secular reality in the lecture on the theology of culture.

Although Tillich's articles published in the years following 1919 develop the themes of the first published articles and notably those of the lecture on the theology of culture there is very little that is

[1] *ibid.*, p. 301.

[2] Cf. Claude Bruaire, *Logique et religion chrétienne dans la philosophie de Hegel*, Paris, 1964.

[3] Cf. *The Phenomenology of Mind*, pp. 462–99.

[4] *On the Boundary*, pp. 47, 51–2, 54; *The Theology of Paul Tillich*, p. 5.

relevant to the problem of defining the theology of culture. In fact few things were published by him between 1919 and 1922; but the articles on the problem of mass[1] are important as showing the concrete grounding of the 1919 insights. The task of the 1922 article was the enlargement of his perspective on culture and the establishment of it on a firmer basis. However, the article is mainly concerned with a critique of the concept of religion and the demonstration that the concept must and can be overcome. It is in the publication *The System of the Sciences* (1923) that Tillich returns to the problem of theology. Here he rejects the more or less traditional classification of science as Naturwissenschaften and Geisteswissenschaften in favour of a threefold classification: Denkwissenschaften, Seinswissenschaften and Geisteswissenschaften. This threefold classification reflects Tillich's understanding of the principles of knowledge—thinking, being and spirit which are connected with form, content and substance or import (Gehalt) respectively.[2] He gives an account of their relationship which he calls his three propositions of absolute thought (Being is that which determines thinking), absolute being (Being is the contradiction of thought) and spirit (Thinking is being itself). By means of this threefold classification Tillich is able to offer a more comprehensive and also a more detailed analysis of the sciences; and the most important achievement is the dialectical synthesis of being and its contradiction, thought. That synthesis is the fulfilment of meaning. Substance, then, rather than form is where this fulfilment of meaning is to be grasped. If a culture is merely formal it is unfulfilled; for the function of culture is to express being through conditioned forms. The basis for his theology of culture in epistemology Tillich has thus provided with this rather Hegelian account of thinking and the correlated account of the 'system' of sciences.

It is as a science of culture (Geisteswissenschaft) that he classifies theology. Tillich's system of sciences is not an empirical description of sciences but is intended to be some logical account of the variety of sciences and their methods.[3] There is a sense in which the system is indeed metaphysical—the sense in which the metaphysical is 'the living power, the meaning and the blood of the system'.[4] The sciences of culture are also called normative sciences in the system.[5] Already in both 'On the Idea of a Theology of Culture' and 'The Conquest of the Concept of Religion in the Philosophy of Religion'[6] Tillich had tended to speak of theology as an element in a science of culture

[1] 'Masse und Persönlichkeit' (1920) and 'Masse und Religion' (1921) which were included in *Masse und Geist*, 1922: *vide Gesammelte Werke*, II, pp. 35–90.

[2] *Gesammelte Werke*, I, pp. 109–293, esp. pp. 117 ff.

[3] *ibid.*, I, p. 113.

[4] *ibid.*, p. 117.

[5] *ibid.*, p. 220.

[6] Cf. *What is Religion?*, pp. 155–181, 122–154.

rather than a separate science—whether of a particular object or of a special complex of revelation. In *The System of the Sciences* he speaks of a theonomous metaphysic but strangely enough he calls this not theology but dogmatics. It seems to me that he did not succeed in clarifying two positions which he was then adopting. One was that of Schelling who wanted to overcome the opposition of dogmatic theology and philosophy in a new theosophy. The other was the more methodological point about the dependence of theology on other disciplines. Though there are traces of these separate lines of thought in his later work I believe that Tillich resolved his problem by identifying dogmatics and theology. Also it is clear from his later reflections that Tillich tended to regard his early attempts to combat the destruction of theonomy in the post 1919 situation as over-optimistic. He had sought to create a theonomous analysis of culture but the culture he sought to analyse was not theonomous. It did not 'express in its creation an ultimate concern and a transcending meaning not as something strange but as its own spiritual ground'.[1] From this account it is clear that, though Tillich persisted in regarding a theology of culture as one of the tasks of theology he did not offer any real further clarification of what he had proposed as such in the 1919 lecture. We return then to that lecture to attempt a clarification.

Perhaps a word of criticism is appropriate at the outset of this clarification. I have shown how the Hegelian reconciliation of God and secularity is probably the most significant influence on Tillich's theology of culture. This is an unfortunate influence—for two reasons. The first is a doctrinal matter; for it seems to me undeniable that throughout his writing and particularly in his last work, *Lectures on the Proof of the Existence of God* (1829), Hegel developed what may be called a pantheistic doctrine of God. Dealing with the cosmological proof he says that its truth is Spinoza's doctrine of Absolute Substance. The real point of interest in the proof is the mediation of the Infinite through the finite. God and the world are to be put in a thoroughly reciprocal relation and we must move in our thinking about God towards an identity of the two terms. Though Tillich is able to escape the charge of pantheism in his explicit doctrine of God in *Systematic Theology* the charge could be pressed here on the ground that he does not dissociate himself from his Hegelian inspiration. Secondly, Hegel's argument against the traditional doctrine of God on transcendence is that it leads to a cultural manicheism which he regarded as outmoded. Thus, as Fackenheim remarks, the Hegelian philosophy presupposes the ultimacy of 'the modern bourgeois Protestant world', which is taken as 'in principle final and indestructible', as the seminal form of the Kingdom of

[1] 'Religion and Secular Culture', *Journal of Religion*, 1946, p. 80.

God.[1] Of all philosophical sources then this is the least appropriate for Tillich; for we have seen very clearly that the motivation to produce a theology of culture was the profound dissatisfaction Tillich felt for his Protestant background. Whatever Tillich was he was no bourgeois intellectual; so far was he from being wedded to the outlook of modern bourgeois Protestantism that he emerged as a theologian by denouncing that ideology and prophetically condemning the temptation to identify that Protestant world with an incipient Kingdom of God. This is clear enough from what we have said about the very close links between his theology and Marxism. Despite the fact, then, that much of the Hegelian legacy in Tillich's theology of culture is a deliberate attempt by Tillich to construct an epistemology and a philosophy of science that would be almost tailor-made solutions to the problems such as theology raises it can also be said that he has created for himself unnecessary difficulties. Therefore it seems to me that any useful discussion of his thought must ignore these elements and ask how exactly we are to define this vision of a theology of culture.

If there is one thing clear about the idea of a theology of culture it is that theology is a discipline with a reference that is as wide as culture. The reason for saying this is not that theology is itself a cultural phenomenon but that its subject-matter relates to the very basis of culture in meaning. As itself a form of culture theology does indeed exemplify a very special form of the problem which a theology of culture recognizes as central, *viz*, how the various kinds of meaning which make up our culture are related to that meaning which is revealed in religion as the meaning of life or the meaning of the world. It also shows how a theology of culture is unavoidable in that the theologian finds in his own person a problem which he might otherwise be tempted to reject as unimportant or even non-existent. Let us begin from this point which it is fairly easy to grasp. Just as other forms of thought and art reflect the thinking of their day so quite clearly does theology. The work of G. Wilson Knight is a very interesting example of this two-way traffic. Though stoutly rejecting any tendency to moralize he has shown the 'Christian affinity' of Shakespeare and also how his plays represent an advance.[2] Furthermore, it is perhaps not sufficiently understood by theologians how far they are utilizing the skills and insights gained in other disciplines. Tillich never tired of saying how he had early grasped the truth that theology advanced by incorporating within itself a method which was scientific. This means that in doing theology we are often obliged to avail ourselves of the insights of the physicist, the biochemist, the

[1] Fackenheim, *The Religious Dimension in Hegel's Thought*, Bloomington, 1967, p. 224.

[2] See especially G. Wilson Knight, *Shakespeare and Religion*.

psychologist and the anthropologist. In this way the issue of the relation of theology to culture is an easy one to resolve; for in so far as his task is cultural it is quite simply impossible for the theologian to fulfil his task without any relation to culture. That this does not answer any problem about the status of that relation in the methodology of theology is also equally clear. Tillich is an example of a theologian who deliberately sought to do theology from within the cultural struggle and effort of his period. With the notable exception of his refusal to take note of linguistic philosophy the whole complex of his cultural situation is reflected in his work. He gives an inspiring example of that prophetic practice of sitting where the people sit. By so doing he shows not only that he understood the situation of the theologian but also the way in which his task is relevant to his situation. The cultural origin of theology is less important than its cultural relevance. This is a necessary characteristic of theology because it is concerned with the meaning of life. Now there is a certain confusion in the use made by Tillich of this concept of meaning both in relation to the sphere of cognitive meaning and that of the philosophy of meaning. The importance of the latter can be dissociated from his particular schematism of meaning and thought. The problem of the meaning of life as a philosophical problem is concerned with what can or cannot be said to be the case such that this is a significant assertion about the way I ought to live. Though Wittgenstein says 'The world of the happy man is a different one from that of the unhappy one'[1] we generally assume that this question is about a common world and that what I decide about my life is on the basis of the answer to that question. Ever since Moore it has been fashionable to distinguish between ethics and metaphysics and to reject the view that there is any metaphysical or theological basis for ethics. It is not necessary for us to argue that moral statements are based on some theological judgment in order to say that a theological judgment does have moral implications. What Tillich would insist—quite rightly—is that it is impossible to avoid giving an answer which is more metaphysical than moral to the question whether life has meaning. That answer is one which sees Wittgenstein's point about the unity of man and his world but rejects his attenuation of the meaning of 'world'. Man is one with his world because man is the relation of himself and the world. More and more Tillich sought to expound the significance of this anthropology (for which he was indebted to Kant, Dilthey and Heidegger) for the theologian in his concrete situation. The notion of world contains that of culture and thus we are led from the concern of theology with the meaning of life to the concern of all culture. To follow Tillich's argument through

[1] *Tractatus Logico-Philosophicus*, 6.43.

its neo-Kantian analysis of thinking and form is to lose the vision.

If the vision of a theology of culture can be separated from the discussion of thinking and form we must be able to give the notion of a 'cultural-theological analysis' content in a different way from Tillich's. In the section of 'On the Idea of a Theology of Culture' dealing with this theme[1] he employs a method that was to be very characteristic of his work: he takes only examples that can with justice be called tailor-made and his exposition of the analysis is scanty. Expressionism and neo-Kantian philosophy are clear examples of an art and a philosophy where the notion of form is both all important and yet subsidiary to the main concern of the creation. In *On the Boundary*[2] Tillich speaks of the importance for his thinking of his discovery of art and in particular expressionist art. It seems to me that he is here guilty of arguing from what is true in a specific instance to a general rule. His preference for expressionist art as a religiously significant art springs very largely from his predilection for the dynamic models for thinking of the ultimate reality which is the object of religious faith. We know that his favourite descriptions were 'ground of being' and 'the abyss of being', expressions which can be traced back through mystical literature to a Plotinian source. The idea of a power that erupts like a volcano clearly fits both the mystical situation and the struggle of the expressionist artist. Indeed Tillich explicitly says[3] that he chooses the expressionist school of art because it seems to him 'to offer a particularly impressive example' of the above-mentioned relation between form and substance; 'and because these definitions were worked out partly under its influence'. The preoccupation of expressionism with broken forms, broken objects and the broken and reconstructed features of things is thus a tailor-made example of a theory of the relation of culture to religion as form to substance, especially when this is to some extent derived from the consideration of this artistic school. It seems to me that what Tillich wants to say here is that what gives a painting its religious significance is the honesty or authenticity with which the artist expresses his encounter with ultimate reality rather than the particular form of the painting both in the sense of its style and its subject.[4] This is what he regards as the real import of the painting and consequently why he distinguished it both from the form in the sense of style and also from the content which is the subject. Neo-Kantianism is a philosophy in which 'form rules absolutely' which 'had forged for itself a new form, which in the name of intuition opposed the autonomous forms of

[1] *What is Religion?*, pp. 168 ff.

[2] Cf. pp. 28 ff.

[3] *What is Religion?*, p. 169.

[4] Cf. 'Existentialist Aspects of Modern Art', in Michalson, *Christianity and the Existentialists*, New York, 1956.

knowledge'.[1] This second example is meant to show how philosophical advance can only be achieved by the substance breaking the form so that unlike the first it is not already a theonomous situation. Nevertheless, my criticism holds inasmuch as the validity of Tillich's analysis depends entirely on the Janus-character of this philosophy rather than any general conflict or tension between form and substance. What I mean is that in neo-Kantianism the 'two faces of the Critique' of Pure Reason, to use Strawson's phrase,[2] continue. A contributory factor is Kant's unquestioning belief in Euclidean geometry, Newtonian physics and Aristotelian logic. Strawson points out that Kant's theory of geometry is not defensible as a whole but does contain valuable insights and in any case is easily detached from the main argument of the Critique. The important doctrine of the Analogies of Experience is however obscured by the anxiety to establish a priori principles of natural science. 'As for the effect of Kant's uncritical acceptance, and unconstrained manipulation, of the forms and classifications of traditional logic, this . . . may be held in part responsible for his boundless faith in a certain structural framework, elaborate and symmetrical, which he adapts freely from formal logic as he understands it and determinedly imposes on the whole range of his material. Over and over again the same pattern of divisions, distinctions and connections is reproduced in different departments of the work. The artificial and elaborate symmetry of this imposed structure has a character which, if anything in philosophy deserves the title of baroque, deserves that title. But this is a feature which . . . we can in the end discount without anxiety.'[3] Thus Tillich's second example does no more than illustrate his argument and certainly does not help to establish it.

The problem that I have raised is how we give content to the notion of a theological analysis of culture. It seems to me that Tillich's discussion of this in the 1919 lecture is less helpful than his more general discussion of 'the dialectic of autonomy' elsewhere.[4] The problem is simply put by saying that the difficulty of the concept is that there seems to be no way in which the analysis can be controlled. It will be hardly analysis if it turns out to be an imposition of a theology on the material to be analysed. A very good example of what I have in mind is the mordant criticism made by F. R. Leavis of Brother George Every. In a characteristically incisive and abrasive piece entitled 'The Logic of Christian Discernment'[5] F. R. Leavis offers a concrete exposition of his thesis that Christian Discernment

[1] *ibid.*, p. 170.
[2] *Bounds of Sense*, London, 1966, p. 15.
[3] *ibid.*, pp. 23–4.
[4] Cf. *What is Religion?*, pp. 149 ff., *Systematic Theology passim.*
[5] *The Common Pursuit*, Peregrine edition, pp. 248 ff.

is 'a decidedly bad thing'. He castigates Brother George Every as an illustration of this; for Every's little book *Poetry and Personal Responsibility* seems to Leavis defiantly to justify the unfavourable conclusion he had already reached about Christian Discernment. Every did not 'try to be a critic'. The pieces of verse he quotes 'get no critical examination and don't as a rule support the implicit assumption that the author matters as a poet'. 'He can glide with perfect aplomb, in a paragraph, from *Little Gidding* to Miss Anne Ridler and Sidney Keyes without a hint of any perception on his part that, for any serious treatment of his theme, something of a change of level has occurred and that he cannot still be dealing with significance of the same order.'[1] For Leavis Christian Discernment is what is here invoked by Every as a sort of *deus ex machina* to absolve himself from the literary critic's kind of discrimination. The fact that this is nothing more and nothing less than the appeal to the natural man's dislike of any suggestion that there are matters calling for certain qualifications which can only be gained by discipline and experience makes Leavis all the more determined to resist this and to show the absurd consequences of the logic of such discernment. What is perhaps even more significant than the slaughter of Brother George is the suggestion made by Leavis at the end of his piece that Every was doing the cause of religion a great deal of harm.[2] I have no intention—nor indeed have I the requisite knowledge for such an intention—of assessing the justice of Leavis' criticism of Every's book. It does, however, seem to me to highlight the peculiar difficulty of the Christian theologian in this second half of the Twentieth Century. What Dr Leavis shows is not only the ridiculous lengths to which the logic of a certain kind of Christian Discernment will lead us but also the dangers inherent therein for our very understanding of the nature of theology itself. His chief criticism of Every, we recall, was that he did not try to become a critic. The difficulty of doing theology at the moment is that we must equip ourselves with certain skills before we can begin to do our distinctively theological work; and this is as true of our work on the boundary with art as it is of work on the boundary with science.

A related problem concerning the theology of culture is that we seem to be misled by the facility with which a comparison is made with established and intelligible disciplines like philosophy of art. It is, as we have already seen, part of Tillich's argument that a theology of culture is a second-order study like philosophy of art. I want to suggest that there is a sense in which the analogy is merely verbal. We are tempted to think that in exactly the same way as the philosopher turns his attention to the various fields and thus engages in or

[1] *op. cit.*, p. 249.
[2] *op. cit.*, p. 253.

perhaps even creates a discipline which is nevertheless still philosophical so does the theologian engage in a theology of culture. Here, then, the culture analysed and discussed is like the mathematics, science or art analysed and discussed by the philosopher in a philosophy of mathematics or of science or of art. In the only book which has been devoted to the subject of Tillich's theology of culture M. Gabus seems to me to accept this analogy despite his critical comments on Tillich's vagueness and his very definite reservations about the place given to philosophy.[1] The temptation to adopt this analogy has a strong foundation in our language. We speak of a history of art and indeed of the physics of music as well as of a philosophy of art. It might seem natural then to talk of the theology of culture in just the same way. However, there is no way in which theology can analyse concepts or discuss problems of meaning in a distinctively theological way that is strictly analogous to the philosophy of art. We could say this only if it were true that in theology, as in Wittgenstein's view of philosophy, we do not change anything. That is to say, if theology were a neutral or a methodological study we could imagine the theologian performing various operations on cultural material which would be exercises in clarification or the resolution of puzzles. However, theology can never become this kind of neutral study, as Tillich himself appreciated well enough. If it has a fixed criterion and operates within a theological circle as he says[2] then there is no relevant sense in which theology is neutral.

One other reason why there is a temptation to think of an analogy with philosophy of art is worth mentioning because it reveals a mistaken view of philosophy of art. This is the assumption that there is some kind of artistic essence which it is the task of the philosopher of art to lay bare. We do not need to follow the ways in which this apparently simple assertion changes its character in the different expositions given of it by philosophers; but we can note that it is as often a doctrine not of an essence of art but of the way in which we view art and consequently that it becomes a psychological or an epistemological doctrine rather than a metaphysical one. Whichever form it takes it is clearly not an adequate or perhaps even helpful definition of philosophy of art. It cannot be maintained that the philosopher's task is the definition of a particular essence when it is by no means clear that the presence of this would be a sufficient

[1] Jean-Paul Gabus, *Introduction à la théologie de la culture de Paul Tillich*, Paris, 1965, pp. 33 ff., 216–20, 227–9, 233–7. The great weakness of this book is that it is too much concerned with Tillich's theology in general and too little concerned with the problem of a theology of culture. Also M. Gabus does not seem to me to have grappled adequately with the way in which Tillich's theology is hampered by a philosophical heritage but is nevertheless a demonstration of the philosophical character of theology.

[2] See *Systematic Theology*, 1, pp. 14 ff.

condition for calling something a piece of art. Furthermore one of Wittgenstein's most important lessons was that we must not imagine that the use of a general term means that there is a property which is common to all things which can be classified by this general term. It is precisely this kind of idea to which we are so easily led by Tillich's talk of the substance of culture. As I have already said, it is a fatal mistake to argue from the meanings which are the concern of various sciences or various pieces of art to that meaning of life which is properly the concern of theology. Let me make it quite clear that I am neither ascribing a Berkleyan theory of general terms to Tillich nor am I denying that it was Tillich's strength as a theologian of culture that he was alive to what he could learn about the meaning of life from art. What I am saying is that it will not do to say simply that theology of culture is like philosophy of art as if there were in both cases some kind of essence which was to be uncovered and defined.

What we are led to in this argument is the problem of how it is that theology of culture can both allow the autonomy of the material it treats and also be a normative discipline. Some advance can be made towards solving the problem by returning to the issue raised by Leavis. I accepted his point of general criticism that no theological evaluation of poetry could flout the canons of literary criticism. However it does not follow from this that we ought never to pass moral and political, philosophical or even theological judgments about art. Lionel Trilling makes some very relevant and illuminating comments in talking of poems and novels. 'Criticism, we know, must always be concerned with the poem itself. But a poem does not always exist only in itself: sometimes it has a very lively existence in its false or partial appearances.'[1] When he proceeds to show how the traditional estimate of Wordsworth's Immortality Ode has misconstrued the poem he is concerned with certain epistemological and historical considerations. Similarly in his assessment of the recent American novel he appeals to psychology and social sciences when he writes 'It is questionable whether any American novel since *Babbitt* has told us anything new about our social life. In psychology the novel relies either on a mechanical or classical use of psychiatry or on the insights that were established by the novelists of fifty years ago.'[2] So whatever the purist may say, the fact of the matter is that there are a host of non-aesthetic criteria that are relevant to art-criticism. It is therefore as appropriate to bring theological considerations as any other to the task of evaluating a creation. How this is done will vary in exactly the same way as the task of the theologian varies in relation to the different areas of life to which theology is applied.

[1] *The Liberal Imagination*, New York, 1950, p. 129.
[2] *ibid.*, p. 263.

That is, it will be a matter of theological anthropology when we are dealing with something like Francis Bacon's horrifying pictures of faces and bodies or Iris Murdoch's novel *The Unicorn* and it will be a theology of society which will be relevant to our evaluation of Picasso's *Guernica* and so on. This suggests that the theology of culture is indeed less concerned with the form of culture than its content and substance, as Tillich had actually argued. My contention is that the point can be put more simply and clearly by saying that theology must be concerned with culture because it is not merely concerned with some isolated event but with the historical event of Jesus Christ. A christian theology is a theology of creation as much as a theology of redemption. Therefore one of its main tasks is the illumination of the presence of Jesus Christ in the history of the world. The difficulty and importance of this notion of presence are well illustrated by Professor Mackinnon in his Gifford lectures.[1] Let me say simply that I do not introduce the notion here in order to say something vaguely pious but innocuously fanciful. It is to say that Christ is truly present but under the conditions of the time when he is not present bodily. There can be a theology of culture as some clarification of a sign of Christ's presence only when we can show the necessary tendency of that material to elicit the response of faith. However, if we are able to argue that there is a continued presence of the Triune God in His world then culture can equally be criticized by appeal to this norm. The confession that we have the mind of Christ is not only the revelation of the world's sacramental quality: it is the stimulus to a prophetic judgment.

[1] *The Problem of Metaphysics*, Cambridge, 1974, pp. 196 ff.

20 All in One Place or All of One Sort?

On Unity and Diversity in the Church

by *LESSLIE NEWBIGIN*

Among the many fields in which Professor Torrance has borne his witness to the Gospel, the quest for Christian unity is not the least important. If, in these later years, his mind has been chiefly given to other issues, I do not believe that this implies any weakening of that deep commitment which led him to take such a notable part in the work of the Faith and Order Commission and in the labours for the unity of the Church in Scotland a quarter of a century ago. I hope, therefore, that it is not unfitting to include in a volume written in his honour, some reflections on the present state of the discussion of unity among the Churches, and not too optimistic to hope that he may even now be willing to turn his mind again to issues to which at one time he devoted so much of his great gift of analysis and argument. I say this because his theology is—it seems to me—essentially a missionary theology, because a true concern for Christian unity can only be nourished in the context of the missionary passion, and because the contemporary state of the discussion of Christian unity in the country prompts serious questions about our commitment to mission.

I

It is commonly accepted that the movements which led to the formation of the World Council of Churches were powered by a concern for the fulfilment of the Church's obligation to the world. The central thrust came from the experience of the mission fields. It was here that the conviction was born that disunity among the Churches is not merely unfortunate but intolerable. It was here that deep mutual trust was born, leading on to a vast amount of practical co-operation. The movement for Faith and Order was a direct product of this, because it became obvious that trust withers and co-operation is frustrated if the underlying issues of division are not tackled. The Movement for Christian Life and Work had separate roots, but it too grew out of a concern that the Church should fulfil its duty to the world by working for justice and peace.

When these two latter movements joined to form the W.C.C. in 1948, there were very different and indeed mutually contradictory ideas about the nature of the unity which was the goal of the whole effort. To some it was sufficient to work for a spiritual unity, and precision about organizational goals was unimportant. For some it was axiomatic that unity could only mean the re-integration of all Christians into the unbroken unity of apostolic faith and order which has existed since Pentecost. For some the goal was 'organic union' into which all the riches of the different Churches would be brought. For some the picture was rather of a federation of churches organized in confessional families on a global scale. In 1948 it had not yet become necessary to ask for more precision than was provided by the basis—'a fellowship of Churches which confess Jesus Christ as God and Saviour'.

It was inevitable that, almost as soon as the founding assembly was over, the member Churches began to ask—What exactly have we committed ourselves to by becoming members of the Council? Are we committed to some particular model of unity? Or, on the other hand, by the very absence of commitment have we relativized our ecclesiology, implying (in default of a clear statement to the contrary) that our view of the essential nature of the Church is no longer binding on us? When the Central Committee met at Toronto (1950) an effort was made to answer these questions. In its famous statement the Committee said, in effect, that membership in the Council implied a commitment to unity but not to any particular form of unity. The Council was to be the place where different concepts of unity would meet in open dialogue, and in which the Churches must seek to find the form of unity which is agreeable to God's will.

This declaration of neutrality—necessary at the time—could not be more than provisional. It could not take the place of a serious effort to define the goal. The World Council of Churches cannot be permanently uncommitted about the form of unity which God wills for the Church, because it is itself a form of unity. Obviously it is not and does not claim to be more than a transitional form—a camp-site on the road towards the real goal. But if those in charge of a camp-site do not agree about the road, the camp-site becomes a shanty-town, and eventually a slum. The question of the nature of the unity we seek is not a timeless question which can be taken up or postponed at our pleasure. There is a time limit after which the options do not remain open. To remain permanently uncommitted about the goal of unity would have meant to accept the present conciliar form of collaboration as the permanent force of Christian unity. And it does not need to be repeated that—by the standard of any reputable ecclesiology—this is the wrong form.

It was therefore proper that the decade following the Toronto Statement saw a strenuous attempt to define more precisely the unity which the Churches should seek. The fruit of the quest was the statement adopted at the 3rd Assembly of the W.C.C. in New Delhi, as follows:

> We believe that the unity which is both God's will and his gift to his Church is being made visible as all in each place who are baptised into Jesus Christ and confess him as Lord and Saviour are brought by the Holy Spirit into one fully committed fellowship, holding the one apostolic faith, preaching the one Gospel, breaking the one bread, joining in common prayer, and having a corporate life reaching out in witness and service to all and who at the same time are united with the whole Christian fellowship in all places and all ages in such wise that ministry and members are accepted by all, and that all can act and speak together as occasion requires for the tasks to which God calls his people.

The statement looks to a fully committed fellowship *in each place* within such an ordering as shall ensure that it is in full unity with the fellowship *in all places*. It is an attempt to spell out in basic terms what has usually been called 'organic union'. It seemed that there was the beginning of a consensus about the road to be taken.

The ensuing decade, however, witnessed a very fundamental change in the situation. When Pope John announced the calling of the Second Vatican Council, and when it was further made clear that observers would be invited from among the 'separated brethren', the question had to be asked: how is the Roman Catholic Church to deal with the vast and confused multitude of many different kinds of bodies which make up non-Roman Christendom? The Roman Catholic Church is organized as a single body throughout the world; non-Roman Churches are not. Few of these extend beyond the boundaries of a single nation. Some of them are organized entirely as independent local congregations. Even to have invited a representative of each of the member churches of the W.C.C. would have been impossible.

It was therefore a reasonable decision that the Vatican should deal with non-Roman Christendom in the main (though not exclusively) through the various world alliances and federations formed by the several confessional families—Lutheran, Reformed, Anglican, Methodist and others. These bodies were therefore invited to appoint observers to the Council, and it was natural that they should play a key role in following up its work. During the subsequent years there has been a large number of bilateral theological conversations between the Roman Catholic Church and the several world confessional bodies. Some of these have produced important doctrinal agreements which have attracted wide public attention—more attention than is given to the multilateral agreements reached by all the Churches which are members in the Faith and Order Commission of the World Council of Churches (including the Roman Catholic Church) and more attention than is given to the numerous unions of Churches which have taken place at the national level.

As a consequence of these developments the vision of unity centred in the unity of 'all in each place' has faded from view. In its place there is a growing tendency to see unity as the friendly co-existence and co-operation of widely dispersed Christian bodies each retaining its distinct identity at the local level. This view has a special attraction at this time because it promises freedom for a great variety of expressions of the one Christian faith. It thus speaks to the contemporary feeling for pluriformity in the life of society. This vision has been adumbrated in eloquent words by Cardinal John Willebrands who leads the Secretariat for Promoting Christian Unity:

> May I invite you to reflect on a notion which, it seems to me, has received much fruitful attention from theologians recently? It is that of the *typos*, in its sense of 'general form of character', and of a plurality of *typoi* within the communion of the one and only Church of Christ.
>
> When I speak here of a *typos* of the Church, I do not mean to describe the local or the particular Church in the sense the Vatican Council has given it . . . The notion which I submit to your attention, that of a *typos* of a Church, does not primarily designate a diocese or a national Church (although in some cases it may more or less coincide with a national Church). It is a notion which has its own phenomenological aspects, with their particular theological meaning.
>
> In the Decree on Ecumenism we read: 'For many centuries the Churches of East and West went their own ways, though a brotherly communion of faith and sacramental life bound them together.' The theological element which must always be present and presupposed is the full 'communion of faith and sacramental life'. But the words 'went their own ways' point in the direction of the notion which I would like to develop a little more . . .
>
> Where there is a long coherent tradition, commanding men's love and loyalty, creating and sustaining a harmonious and organic whole of complementary elements, each of which supports and strengthens the others, you have the reality of a *typos*.
>
> Such complementary elements are many. A characteristic theological method and approach (historical perhaps in emphasis, concrete and mistrustful of abstraction) is one of them. It is one

approach among others to the understanding of the single mystery, the single faith, the single Christ.

A characteristic liturgical expression is another. It has its own psychology; here a people's distinctive experience of the one divine Mystery will be manifest—in sobriety or in splendour, inclining to tradition or eager for experiment, national or supranational in flavour. The liturgical expression is perhaps a more decisive element because 'the liturgy is the summit toward which the activity of the Church is directed; at the same time it is the fountain from which all her power flows'.[1]

II

A rather full development of this line of thought has recently been undertaken by Professor John Macquarrie, Lady Margaret Professor of Divinity in the University of Oxford, in his book *Christian Unity and Christian Diversity*. This is an important contribution to the discussion and calls for critical examination.

The first chapter establishes the fact that diversity has been a mark of the Church from its earliest beginnings and that a proper diversity is not the contrary of unity but its necessary corollary. The second chapter develops this theme of pluralism as a necessary feature of society and of the Church, and claims that Christianity became more vigorous in countries where denominationalism has flourished. The third chapter on 'Practical Ecumenism' calls for co-operation between the Churches in practical service to the world in contrast to 'the type of ecumenism that aims to bring into being national and united Churches in each country'. In the fourth chapter the fundamental problem in ecumenical theology is said to be the 'Catholic-Protestant one', and this is further defined—following Paul Tillich—in terms of the contrast between 'Catholic substance' and 'Protestant principle' (p. 35). The fifth chapter deals with 'Structures of Unity'. The claim is made that 'the best existing model for Christian unity' is to be found in the relation of the Uniat Churches of the East to the Roman Catholic Church. What is envisaged is 'no attempt to set up a unitary or uniform Church, either by absorbing one body into the other, or by trying to work out some sort of hybrid' (p. 43) but that the different traditions continue to be embodied in distinct autonomous organizations in the same geographical areas, but with full mutual recognition and all acknowledged by Rome as the centre. In the conditions of modern society, unlike those of Cyprian's day, one must abandon the idea that there should be in each place one flock and one shepherd (p. 44). The prayer of Jesus 'that they may all be one' 'had nothing to do with "schemes" of organic union' (p. 42).

[1] Cardinal John Willebrands, *One in Christ*, 1971, 1, pp. 118–19.

The sixth chapter is entitled 'Rome the centre of unity'. 'The Roman Catholic Church is, in a unique way, the guardian of catholicity', and Rome will therefore have to be the centre and focus for unity—a unity which would be expressed in a series of uniate relationships with the other Christian bodies. The next five chapters consider the theological issues, which would have to be adjusted before this goal could be achieved. The final chapter—'The Wider Ecumenism: Christianity and other Faiths' looks towards a more comprehensive unity including Christianity and the other world religions. The claim that there is salvation only in Christ is 'fanatical talk', and the hope of the conversion of the nations to the Christian religion was a nineteenth-century dream which is now a thing of the past. It is not only the Christian Church but all the religions of the world which now have the opportunity 'to lead all men into a genuine humanity'.

I confess that I have found it a strange experience to read this book. It is as though one were reading the essay of an astronaut who had left the earth about fifty years ago and had been in orbit ever since. The organic union of two or more Churches to form a single body is referred to as an abstract possibility which would produce either a take-over or a hybrid; the reader would never guess that more than sixty of such unions have taken place in the past fifty years and that millions of Christians are living in such united Churches, daily thanking God for the blessing of unity. The model of unity which is offered is the one which was popular among Protestants of the free-church type half a century ago: the peaceful co-existence of separated bodies each representing particular traditions and a particular style of churchmanship. The work of Faith and Order in the past fifty years is completely ignored.

Whatever be the causes of this apparent amnesia, the splash-down will certainly create a wide circle of ripples. Indeed the concept of unity advocated in this book is likely to be very popular for it offers an invitation to reunion without repentance and without renewal, to a unity in which we are faced with no searching challenge to our existing faith and practice, but can remain as we are. What is to be said of this invitation?

III

(1) I start where Professor Macquarrie ends and where the modern ecumenical movement begins—with the missionary question. If indeed the concern to preach Christ as Lord and Saviour to all nations was a nineteenth-century mistake, then certainly the modern ecumenical movement was a mistake too. It was directly out of the experience of foreign missions that the wider ecumenical movement

was born. For how can one invite all men of every culture to recognize Jesus as their one Lord if the confession of his name comes from people who have not themselves found in him a sufficient centre of unity? How will a Hindu recognize the name of Jesus as supreme above every name, if those who bear this name define their own identity not by reference to it, but by reference to the names which evoke the memory of their special religious and cultural histories?

I do not wish in this place to discuss the proposal which Professor Macquarrie, following W. E. Hocking, puts forward for the reconception of the Church's missionary task, as I have done this elsewhere.[1] My concern here is with the question of Christian unity. In particular I want to say that Professor Macquarrie's closing chapter on 'The Wider Ecumenism' confirms the impression given by the whole book, that he has radically misunderstood the nature of the ecumenical movement. When Bishop George Bell wrote a popular introduction to the Ecumenical Movement he called it 'The Kingship of Christ', and thereby pointed to its real meaning. The movement which—by common consent—looks to the Edinburgh World Missionary Conference of 1910 as its place of birth, has been concerned first and foremost with the claim that Christ is King and that—as part of the claim—we are obliged to bring all our own separate confessional traditions to him in penitence in order to receive correction, and renewal. It has never been concerned simply with unity for the sake of unity. When therefore, Professor Macquarrie offers a scenario in which all the religions of the world have an opportunity to lead men into a genuine humanity, and the mission to make disciples of all nations is abandoned as a relic of nineteenth-century imperialism, he is not offering a wider ecumenism, but a radically different programme which begins by challenging the central conviction from which the ecumenical movement was born.

In the light of this final chapter it is easy to understand the thrust of the book as a whole. It is concerned simply with the problems of unity and diversity as problems of human society and of how to achieve a proper balance and synthesis of both. It is not concerned with the Christian faith as such. It does not speak of the Cross and Resurrection of Jesus, of salvation and of loss, of man's hope and despair. It therefore does not see division among Christians as radically sinful, as a distortion of the Church's true nature. It calls for minor mutual adjustments rather than for radical change. It offers a model for ecclesiastical co-existence, for co-habitation without commitment, for reconciliation without repentance or renewal. It

[1] *A Faith for this One World?*, London, 1961, pp. 46–53. Hocking's idea of 'reconception' has been much more fully discussed in *Religious Truth and the Relations Between Religions*, D. G. Moses, Madras, 1950, pp. 123–42.

would be impossible to bring such a title as 'The Kingship of Christ' into the argument of the book. The realities on which Professor Macquarrie takes his bearings are sociological rather than theological. It is, he says, 'within the context of the general search for a pluralist society that the problem of ecumenism is to be understood' (p. 11). Here we are in a different universe of discourse from that of the ecumenical pioneers. We may well agree that the *context* of the discussion must include the contemporary currents in society, but the *principles* of action, the criteria for decision, the direction in which the Church should move must be sought in a fundamental discussion of the nature and purpose of the Church itself. Such a discussion is absent from this book.

(2) The basic question which the book sets out to answer is the form of unity which is compatible with the desirable measure of diversity in the life of the Church. Very rightly Professor Macquarrie insists that to attempt to coerce or cajole all Christians into one mould would be futile. He reminds us that the whole created world gives evidence of its Creator's delight in variety, and that the New Testament contains within itself a rich variety of styles—both of teaching and of practice. Clearly the Church must have room for a vast variety of ways of expressing the Christian faith and living the Christian life. And yet—it is agreed—we must recognize that there are limits to variety. Or, to put it another way, there has to be *some* kind of unity, and the question 'What kind?' can only be answered by reference to some basic understanding of the nature and purpose of the Church itself.

The Church can only be defined in terms of Jesus Christ and his mission. Jesus announced the reign of God, and called those whom he chose to follow him, to be with him and to be sent out with the same announcement. Though the initial call is to Israel, the announcement concerns all nations, for God's reign is the reality for all. The promise is that all nations will be gathered to the messianic feast, and this promise will be fulfilled through his atoning death. Of this his resurrection is the assurance and the Spirit given to the community of those whom he has called is the witness. At the heart of this community is the eucharist feast which is both a sacramental participation in his atoning death, and a foretaste of the messianic banquet. In one of the earliest references we have to the eucharistic feast Paul writes: 'We who are many are one body for we all partake of the same loaf'; he goes on to a severe rebuke to those who are not willing to share the same loaf and the same cup; and he concludes with the statement that 'as often as you eat this bread, and drink this cup, you proclaim the Lord's death until he comes' (1 Cor. 10:17, 11:26).

Clearly the Church is here seen as a company of people who are bound together in a recognizable unity, centred in the person and work of Jesus and looking towards a universal consummation of which the manifest kingship of Christ will be the centre. The same letter emphasizes the great variety of gifts with which different members of the company are furnished, and calls for freedom in their exercise. But it defines a limit to variety in terms of the need to serve the whole body in its unity.

The letter to the Galatians—perhaps the earliest of Paul's letters—records the sharp conflict that arose between Peter and Paul on this issue of visible unity in sharing the same table fellowship. In Antioch, Christians of two different 'types' found themselves together in one place. Certainly neither denied that the others were Christians. There were obviously overwhelming arguments of prudence and expediency to support the proposal that the Christians from Jerusalem should retain their distinct identity. But Paul thought that the whole truth of the Gospel was involved in resisting the proposal. To break the fellowship at the one table would be to deny the central reality of the Gospel.

Behind the division in the Corinthian Church lay the celebration of rival names—'I am of Paul', 'I am of Apollos', 'I am of Cephas' and 'I am of Christ'. These differing names presumably reflect not only personal loyalties, but also differing ways of stating the Christian message, differing styles of teaching and practice, differing 'types'. We have already noted that the canon of the New Testament itself is witness to the great variety of styles which were accepted as authentic within the primitive Church. And yet Paul severely rebukes those who identify themselves by these different names, accuses them in fact of 'carnality' (1 Cor. 3:1–4). Behind this accusation is the solemn recalling of them to the Cross of Jesus Christ as the centre of the Gospel, and to the baptism in which they had been incorporated into Christ. There is only one name which can define their identity as those whom God has called, from whatever cultural or religious background (see 1:24) and that is the name of Jesus Christ. To define themselves by other names is to fall from the realm of the Spirit into that of the flesh. However great may be the variety of gifts and 'styles' within the Church (and later chapters suggest a great variety—especially chapters 12 and 14) the one name of Christ, the name of the one who died and rose again for the salvation of the world, is the one name by which they can be called. They are defined as those who are 'in Christ', and this means to be incorporated in a visible and recognizable company of people who break bread together and in this act are made participants in his life.

Now it is of course true that unity is something personal and spiritual and that it is never—short of the end—perfect and complete. In this sense—I quote Macquarrie—'the unity of the Church is, like its sanctity, something that in history is always coming to be' (p. 41); but it does not follow from this, as Macquarrie states on the same page, that 'it is really absurd to say that the Churches became united by such and such a date, or will become united by such and such a date'. On the same page Macquarrie uses marriage as an illustration of the way in which the unity of the Church is to be understood in personal terms and not in organic ones, as something which allows both for 'an element of *rapprochement* and an element of distancing'. Indeed a man and woman within marriage must always be growing into unity and can—alas—also grow apart from one another. Their unity is never perfect. And yet it is not absurd to say that on such and such a day they were married and on such and such a day they were divorced. There is a curious docetism about the argument of this book, the suggestion that, because unity has an aspect that is inward and spiritual, it follows that the visible and historical forms which unity must take can be dismissed from consideration, or can be discussed on merely sociological, as distinct from theological grounds. We are not discarnate spirits. We are human beings who can only express our love for and responsibility to one another in visible and recognizable forms. The true unity of the Church will be that form of enduring mutual commitment which recognizably expresses that relation to one another in which we are placed by Christ's calling of us into the fellowship of his cross and resurrection, a relationship of unconditional and total mutual reconciliation. When Macquarrie, following Bultmann, says that our Lord's prayer for his disciples that they might be one has 'nothing to do with what nowadays are called "schemes" of organic union' he reveals once again the falsehood of that existentialist interpretation of the Gospel which would divorce it from contact with the real history of which we are a part.

(3) In decisively rejecting organic unity as a model for the Church, Professor Macquarrie advocates as a model the relation between the Roman Catholic Church and the Uniat Churches of the East. He is apparently unaware of the violent reaction which even the suggestion of such a model would provoke among orthodox Christians. He seems to be almost unconscious of the existence of Eastern Christendom as a reality to be taken account of in discussing Christian unity. The Church, for practical purposes, is taken to mean Western Christendom. Indeed, one may add, the Churches of Asia and Africa seem also to be beyond the horizon of his consciousness.

The uniat model as here suggested would imply that the present denominational and confessional families would exist side by side in each geographical area, each with its separate hierarchy and with its distinct doctrines, customs and rules, all related in some undefined way to the See of Rome, a relation which would include intercommunion with Rome and with one another. I leave for later discussion the place of Rome in this scenario, and discuss this now only as a model of unity in each place.

What is proposed is that Christians in each place will be organized separately under separate hierarchies. They will be distinguished from each other not (as are the Uniat Churches of the East) by different languages and ethnic origins, but by different confessional and denominational traditions. Though organized under separate and autonomous jurisdictions they will practice inter-communion and will in other ways mutually recognize one another. And they will co-operate in common tasks for the service of the world around them.

On this model I have five comments.

(a) Professor Macquarrie praises very highly the kind of ecumenism which brings Christians together to work at common tasks for the world around them and which is entirely unconcerned about denominational labels. 'The time has come', he says, 'for the churches to look out upon the world. It might be surprising how much unity would develop unconsciously through a common response to the challenges of contemporary society.' 'The unity which is so elusive when churchmen talk to each other may begin to burgeon when they are able to engage in common practical concerns' (p. 23). We must forgive our astronaut that he has hardly had time to get his bearings! This is exactly the slogan of the early 1920's: 'Doctrine divides but practice unites'. This is what one may call the primeval stage of ecumenism. It was reached in India in the mid-nineteenth century and in Europe fifty years later. Co-operation in practical tasks is a vital necessity, but the experience of the past 50 years shows that it is not enough. The enormous development of practical co-operation among the churches in the past 50 years, deeply significant as it is, becomes self-frustrating when it stops short of the basic issues concerning the life of the Church itself. This is the burden of the recent messages of the Ecumenical and Moscow Patriarchates to the World Council of Churches. Professor Macquarrie seems to be offering as the agenda for the future precisely that formula whose inadequacy the past 50 years have so sharply demonstrated. The profound question of the nature of the Church itself cannot be permanently left on one side. The Church is not just (though it should always be) a body that serves society. It is the body sent into the world to be the bearer of peace—peace with God and with men, the sign and first-fruit of God's new humanity. It cannot permanently evade the question: where is that fellowship in which I can become and permanently remain truly a member of God's family at peace with him and with my neighbours?

(b) Professor Macquarrie extols the values of denominational diversity and quotes the vigour of Church life in the United States as an example. I am writing these words during a visit to the United

States where I am surrounded by evidence of the massive collapse of the denominational boom of the 1950's. It would be foolish to make sweeping judgments on American Church life either in the 50's or in the 70's. But can anyone believe that the intention of Jesus, as we know him through the New Testament, is reflected in the kind of inter-denominational competition that has marked much of American Church life? One can certainly agree with Macquarrie that the monochrome Church orders of Spain or Sweden are not what we are seeking, but what is the kind of 'vigour' that we look for? Is this jungle of rival organizations all competing for support on the basis of some appeal other than the one they have in common (namely the call of Jesus Christ himself), really a sign of the kingdom? Is the Church intended to be 'successful' by the standards which are inevitably used to measure success when one gets into this kind of competition? Is this really the authentic fruit of the true Vine? Does this kind of success provide a standard by which churches are to be compared?

I venture here to refer to one piece of personal experience which is relevant because it permits a comparison of like with like. From 1936 to 1947 I was a missionary working in the Madras area of India, and for most of this time I was somewhat familiar with the Churches in Madras city. In 1947 there occurred the event which Professor Macquarrie regards as 'absurd' but which nevertheless happened: the Anglican, Methodist and Reformed Churches in South India became one Church. In 1965, after an absence of eighteen years, I returned to Madras as bishop to serve the same Churches which I had known two decades earlier as competing congregations. I did not find that they had become uniform: on the contrary I found a rich variety of styles in worship and practice. What I found was congregations less concerned about their own affairs and more ready to think in terms of God's will for the life of the city as a whole, less like competing clubs each trying to enlarge itself and a little more recognizable as sign and foretaste of God's kingdom.

(c) Professor Macquarrie defines 'the fundamental dialectic in ecclesiology' as the Catholic-Protestant one and (following Tillich) elucidates this in terms of 'Catholic substance and Protestant principle'. He goes on to say, therefore: 'Protestantism and Catholicism need each other. They belong together and neither can absorb the other' (pp. 34–6). I do not accept this description of the ecclesiological situation and I shall discuss it later. But if it were true it would surely invalidate the model which Macquarrie is offering. If these two things 'belong together' why should they be organized as separate, parallel and competing jurisdictions? Will not the whole substance of life in the Church be corrupted by this separation? Can there be a true 'comprehension' (p. 36) of the two in the practical life of the Church if the ordinary Christian has to choose between adhering in his own neighbourhood to the substance or to the principle? If Macquarrie is right *can* they continue to exist as separately organized jurisdictions?

This *argumentum ad hominem* leads to a more general statement. Professor Macquarrie is rightly eager to safeguard a theological comprehensiveness which allows for continuing argument, for the freedom which enables differences to be developed, for an openness 'in which the truth is ever coming to be in a dialectical way' (p. 36). He is writing (understandably) as a professor and not as a pastor. 'The truth is not found in a consensus in which all can rest' (p. 34). If such a consensus were to occur there would be nothing more for professors of theology to do! A university faculty of divinity would indeed be a sad place if this were to happen! But the Church is not an academy. It exists as a society in virtue of a common faith directed towards God known in Jesus Christ through the Spirit. It exists moreover, to bear witness to the faith among all men as the truth of the human situation, to command this faith among competing beliefs and ideologies and to manifest in its own life the reality and power of the living Jesus as the true friend, Lord and Saviour of all men. It is vitally important that this faith should be stated in such a way as to leave large (though not unlimited) freedom for theologians to explore its meaning and to engage in the dialectic without which thought is impossible. But from the proper statement that theology must be free from premature and imposed consensus formulae which exclude questions that need to be asked, one cannot move—as Macquarrie seems to do—to the conclusion that *churches* should be organized as separate jurisdictions upon the basis of different theological perspectives. This is not the way to preserve real freedom of theological debate, but rather the way to confuse and corrupt it by issues extraneous to the heart of theology. A truly comprehensive theology will be one which has its exercise in a Church which holds people of every different, and even sharply contradicting types within one fellowship of love and service. Certainly this can lead to agonizing tensions, but it is precisely in these tensions that the test is provided both for the adequacy of the theology and for the depth of commitment to Christ and to one another.

(d) Professor Macquarrie's model envisages a series of separate and parallel ecclesiastical bodies, each having its own autonomy, but practising inter-communion. Here again we are offered a model which was popular 50 years ago. The English Free Churches at that time often pointed with satisfaction to the fact that they practised open communion towards each other and contrasted this with what appeared to be the intransigence of the Anglicans who insisted that communion and unity cannot be separated. Nothing has surprised me more about this book than to find Professor Macquarrie reverting to this ancient model. I was brought up in that tradition and shared the resentment that the Anglican attitude created. I have come to respect and to share the fundamental conviction (though not necessarily every expression of it) which lies behind that Anglican attitude. To share in the communion of the Body and Blood of Christ is to enter into the most solemn and binding of all possible obligations to him, and through him to those with whom we share in the communion. I find this incompatible with anything less than a full commitment to maintain, or to seek, full fellowship with them. I think that such inter-communion is right as a part of a serious commitment to unity. I do not think it is right as a merely occasional act between those who accept no binding commitment to one another. As promiscuity devalues marriage, so—I am bound to confess—I think that the inevitable effect of this would be to erode the meaning of churchmanship.

(e) Professor Macquarrie is concerned with Christian unity and Christian diversity. He is rightly concerned that unity should not inhibit diversity. But the model he offers contradicts his intention. When men see the Church they see it in the place where they are. In Professor Macquarrie's scenario what they will see will be a group of societies manifesting a variety of styles and types, but together bearing witness to the fact that Christ is *not* a sufficient centre of unity to enable their differing types to live together as one family. It will be evident that the name of Jesus does *not* stand for a reality which transcends the very real and precious diversity of human types and which can therefore create a fellowship in which they can mutually enrich one another. It will make little difference that these separated groups are represented at some world gathering by persons who meet together for an annual conference. What will be clear will be that these separate groups define their identity not by the name of Jesus, not by the Gospel, not by the mighty realities which we confess in the ecumenical creeds, but by the various names which each of them have inherited from their separate histories. The differences which can so greatly enrich the unity (as the experience of a united church shows) become instead the grounds of division.

(4) The scenario which Professor Macquarrie offers has the See of Rome as its centre. 'Rome the Centre of Unity' is the title of the chapter in which he gives his vision for the future. 'The Roman Catholic Church is, in a unique way, the guardian of catholicity.' Therefore the next question to be asked is: 'What form of catholicity would the separated churches need to manifest so that Rome could take them into a unifying fellowship?' (pp. 51, 53).

One rubs one's eyes at these almost unbelievable remarks! Has Professor Macquarrie offered this proposal to any Orthodox churchman? He must surely know that in Orthodox eyes Rome has lost the fullness of catholicity and only in the Orthodox churches has full catholicity been maintained. Leaving aside the matter of the Uniat Churches (which represent in Orthodox eyes the most shocking of the Roman violations of catholicity) Orthodox Churches will certainly not accept the claim that Rome is the unique guardian of catholicity. It would be difficult to imagine a more totally futile starting point for a discussion of unity from an Orthodox point of view.

If it was ever pardonable to think of unity in terms primarily of the western churches, it is surely unpardonable now. The Orthodox churches in Russia and Eastern Europe are occupying one of the most important positions in the world from the point of view of the future of Christianity in the twenty-first century, for it is they who are on the vital frontier where Christendom must come to terms with Marxism, and where that style of Christian thought and life has to be worked out which will show that the Church has learnt the lessons which Marxism has to teach. At this moment of history to ignore Eastern Christendom would be unpardonable shortsightedness.

Underlying his view that Rome is the centre of unity is Professor Macquarrie's thesis that 'the fundamental dialectic . . . is the Catholic-Protestant one'. This was accepted in the 1920's and governed the findings of the Amsterdam Assembly of 1948. It is more difficult to defend it now. In a book (*The Household of God*, S.C.M. Press, 1952) written almost a quarter of a century ago I argued on purely biblical grounds that it was impossible to arrive at a satisfactory doctrine of the Church in terms of this twofold scheme, and that one could do justice to the biblical evidence only by speaking also of the pentecostal element in a true doctrine of the Church. At that time I was not thinking mainly of the Christian groups called Pentecostalists with whom I had, at that time, little contact, but rather of a necessary dimension of the life of the Church in all times and places. Since then, as is well known, the Pentecostal Churches have undergone enormous growth and are, without any rival, the most rapidly growing groups in Christendom. Professor Macquarrie does not suggest that he is aware of their existence. Yet talk of Christian unity (and still more of Christian diversity) is futile if it ignores this. The Pentecostals will rightly insist that their witness cannot be properly understood if it is to be interpreted in terms of a Catholic-Protestant schema. It can only be understood on the basis of a theology of the Church which is biblically grounded.

And, finally, no serious Protestant theologians will accept the view that the difference between Roman Catholicism and Protestantism is the difference between 'the substance, the concrete embodiment of the spiritual presence' on the one hand and 'a critical principle which seeks to relativise every claim to theological finality or absolute authority' on the other (p. 35). It is difficult to believe that this caricature of the reality is meant to be taken seriously. It would certainly disqualify Karl Barth from being recognized as a Protestant —to say nothing of the multitudes of simple (or not so simple) 'Bible Christians'. There is of course a grain of truth in this statement (as in all caricatures) but it cannot be accepted as a serious description of what divides Catholics from Protestants. This concerns difficult questions about what 'the substance' is, about how 'the concrete embodiment of the spiritual presence' is recognized. The scheme proposed here does not help us to get to grips with these real differences. In fact the chapters in which Professor Macquarrie discusses five theological issues which would have to be adjusted before Rome could accept the 'separated churches' into a uniate relation simply illustrate the barrenness of this proposal. There is no sign here of real dialogue, of a real mutual questioning and correction at a deep level of theological seriousness. Such real theological work is to be found in the reports of the Faith and Order Commission, of which the Roman Catholics are full members, but to these there is no reference, unless perhaps his contemptuous remark about the 'ecumenical jet set' (p. 19) is intended to refer to this work.

(5) Professor Macquarrie reserves his most severe reprobation for the effort to create united churches within the several nations. This effort 'smacks too much of the old "cuius regio eius religio" formula' (p. 12). It is 'quite misguided' and is 'the last thing the world needs' (p. 26). Such unions, if Rome is not included, 'can hardly be more than denominational realignments' (p. 51). Unions, in particular, based on the Chicago-Lambeth Quadrilateral (Scripture, Creeds, Sacraments, Ministry) are working with 'an abstract idea of the framework of unity' whereas the proposal of Professor Macquarrie would be 'the living visible unity of the churches themselves' (p. 49). The reasoning is difficult to follow here. I must say that I have found the Church of South India to be a living and visible unity and not an abstract idea! But the main question is that of the propriety or otherwise of seeking unity at the national level.

There are certainly points to be carefully considered here. The coming of Rome into the ecumenical conversation called in question the models of union developed in the years following the Lambeth Conference of 1920. This model was shaped by the experience of the churches which were heirs of the Reformation. They had inherited the medieval concept of a single society with both civil and ecclesiastical aspects, a concept which—after the break with Rome—could be expressed only in the form of national Churches. They had also lived through the experiences of the following centuries when 'free' churches developed which broke with the traditional concept of a single civil-ecclesiastical society but still operated within the bounds of the nation-state. The massive entry of the Roman Catholic Church into the ecumenical movement raises radical questions for both of these models: it calls in question the traditional free-church attitude to the State and it also demands the consideration of supranational models of unity. We have here some of the important items for the agenda of the coming years.

Nevertheless the quest for unity at the national level is not to be by-passed, and to dismiss it as 'misguided' shows a failure to grasp the real issues. The Church must always take a form which is relevant to the forms of human society in which it lives. This is because the Church does not exist for itself but for God, and for all men, because it is not a club for those who care to belong to it, but the company of those whom God has chosen and called to be 'a kind of first-fruit of his creatures' (James 1:18), a sacrament of the unity of mankind (*Lumen Gentium*) a sign and foretaste of his purpose to reconcile all things to himself in Jesus Christ. In the words of André Dumas, summarizing the teaching of Dietrich Bonhoeffer: 'The Church is the world as it is meant to be in Jesus Christ, the space where the world is structured according to its own centre'.[1] For this reason the structures of the world can never be irrelevant to the structures of the Church. The Church—in the New Testament—is always the Church of a place. It is the place where the given structure of human neighbourhood is re-created as brotherhood.

Of course this has its dangers. The Church is always in danger of becoming conformed to this world, and when this happens a national Church can become a mere mouthpiece of the unredeemed sectional desires of the nation. But there can be a truly national Church which is the Church *for* that nation in a sense analogous to the sense in which Jesus is *for* mankind, and to seek for a truly national Church in that sense is not misguided. Nor is there any evidence that churches of a 'free-church' type organized in world confessional families are, by that kind of structure, better able to speak God's word to the nations than are nationally organized Churches.

Certainly the discussion of unity cannot stop at national level. In particular the question of primacy is one that must be taken very seriously in all discussion of the form of visible unity. But this in no way invalidates the efforts of those who are seeking unity at the national level. Rather the present development in the Roman Catholic Church of more effective organs of government at the national level underlines the need for and the propriety of a quest for unity in each nation.

1 *Dietrich Bonhoeffer: Theologian of Reality*, p. 82.

IV

In his chapter on 'Practical Ecumenism' Professor Macquarrie speaks of the development of a 'secular ecumenism' which he recommends as 'giving priority to the unity of mankind over ecclesiastical unity' (p. 26). Perhaps this phrase brings us to the crux of the matter. It implies, as does much of the argument, that the unity of mankind is something which can be pursued as an alternative to the unity of the Church. My belief is that the Church is put into the world as sign and foretaste and instrument of the unity of mankind. I do not believe that there is any other centre around which all men can be reconciled and made one family except Jesus Christ who in his incarnation, and victorious passion has reconciled men to God. Every proposal for human unity depends upon some concept—implied or expressed—of the basis upon which men can be reconciled to one another. There is no proposal for unity which does not imply some basis. The nature of that basis may not be obvious to me because I take it for granted, but to the man of some other culture or faith or ideology it is obvious—and foreign. Thus my programme for human unity appears to him as a threat to his freedom, and his equally as a threat of mine. If we are serious about the unity of mankind we have to be explicit about the basis on which we conceive of such a unity. That means that we have to be explicit about our vision of the ultimate meaning and purpose of human life.

I find no place in all human history except Jesus Christ and him crucified, risen and regnant, at which I can believe it possible for all men to meet in mutual forgiveness. I find in the Church, drawing into its fellowship peoples of every kind and culture, a credible sign and foretaste of that unity.

The question is this: What form of Church unity will correspond to the proper character of the Church as a sign of human unity? Clearly that form must include both local and global expressions. The New Delhi statement on the nature of the unity we seek, looks to a form of unity which is both local and global. The model of unity advocated by Professor Macquarrie envisages a form of global unity centred in the See of Rome, but does not envisage a local unity in which all in each place who hear the name of Christ form one fully committed fellowship. His basic argument at this point is that such a local unity would be destructive of the diversity which is proper to the nature of the Church.

We are bound to agree that it is unthinkable that all Christians in each place could be obliged to belong to one of the divided 'denominations' as we now know them. That needs no argument. For indeed these 'denominations' are but distorted fragments of the Church. None of them can be recognized as simply 'the world as it is meant to be in Jesus Christ, the space where the world is structured according to its true centre'.

I think also that we must agree that these separated and distorted fragments cannot adequately fulfil their role as signs of the unity of mankind either by limited co-operation, or by affiliation to a world body. 'Areas of ecumenical experiment' at the local level quickly reach the point of frustration because each of the participating denominations has its own distinct forms and rules. Attendance at world assemblies once in five years can be valuable but it is not a substitute for commitment to the neighbours with whom one is in contact every day of the week.

The crucial question is this: can there be a manifestation of the life of the Church in each place which is—on the one hand—so open, so free, so welcoming of variety and even contradiction, that men and women of every kind can be at home in it; and—on the other hand—so deeply rooted in the saving work of Christ crucified and risen that its members can accept one another, forgive one another, love one another, belong to one another? Can there be a visible and recognizable and therefore local expression of the fact that what God has done in Jesus Christ is nothing less than the destruction of all the powers that separate men from God and from one another, or must this be only a truth that remains in the mind, above involvement in space and time? Can there be a Eucharist in every place on every Lord's Day where *all* who confess Christ as Lord and Saviour can meet—with all the vast diversities and contradictions that belong to our human condition, and share the same loaf and the same cup, give thanks to the same God, and go out to continue his mission in the world?

Such a unity implies the death of all our denominations as we know them. It implies the surrender of every name, every claim to identity, so that the name of Jesus alone may be on our lips, and so that we may find our identity only in the fact that we belong to him. It is nothing abstract or theoretical. It is immensely costly. It involves long and patient work to reach the mutual understanding without which there cannot be such a mutual commitment. It rejects the false spirituality which imagines that the High Priestly prayer of Jesus has nothing to do with the long and costly and even agonizing wrestlings that are needed before such understanding and such commitment are possible. It is not ashamed to be deeply involved in the hard and difficult and even trivial details of a plan of union. It is ready for long disappointment and for the discipline of prayer that seems for long to be unanswered.

Is such unity possible? Can there be in each place such a shared common life in Christ as can be a credible sign of the unity of all mankind? God knows. But to give up the quest of such unity is to settle for something less than the Gospel.

Bibliography of the Published Writings of Thomas F. Torrance (1941–75)

Compiled by BRYAN GRAY

NOTE CONCERNING ABBREVIATIONS

The system of abbreviations adopted in this bibliography is that recommended by Siegfried Schwertner in his *International Glossary of Abbreviations for Theology and for Related Subjects*, Berlin: Walter de Gruyter, 1974.

1941

The Modern Theological Debate, issued for private circulation by the Theological Students' Prayer Union of the Inter-Varsity Fellowship of Evangelical Unions, London, 1941.

'Predestination in Christ', *EvQ*, **13** (1941), pp. 108–41.

'The Importance of Fences in Religion', *The British Weekly*, Jan. 30, 1941, pp. 179–80.

'We Need a Decisive Theology before we can Restate the Creed', *The British Weekly*, Nov. 20, 1941, p. 79.

Review of N. Kemp Smith, 'The Philosophy of David Hume', *The British Weekly*, May 15, 1941, p. 48.

Review of 'Thomas Reid's Essays on the Intellectual Powers of Man', *The British Weekly*, Dec. 18, 1941, p. 142.

1942

'Reason in Christian Theology', *EvQ*, **14** (1942), pp. 22–41.

1943

'Kierkegaard on the Knowledge of God', *The Presbyter*, n.s.1 (1943), 3:4–7.

Review of Leonard Hodgson, 'Towards a Christian Philosophy', *EvQ*, **15** (1943), pp. 237–9.

1945

'In Hoc Signo Vinces', *The Presbyter*, **3** (1945), 11:13–20.

1946

'The Doctrine of Grace in the Apostolic Fathers', D.Th. thesis, University of Basle, 1946.

Published as *The Doctrine of Grace in the Apostolic Fathers*, Edinburgh: Oliver & Boyd, 1948; Grand Rapids: Eerdmans, 1959.

Excerpts in Edmund J. Fortman, *The Theology of Man and Grace: Commentary*, Milwaukee: Bruce, 1966.

1947

'The Word of God and the Nature of Man', in F. Camfield, ed., *Reformation Old and New; Festschrift for Karl Barth*, London: Lutterworth, 1947, pp. 121–41.

Reprinted in *Theology in Reconstruction*, pp. 99–116.

Review of C. Van Til, 'The New Modernism: an Appraisal of the Theology of Barth and Brunner', *EvQ*, **19** (1947), pp. 144–9.

1948

'The Doctrine of Grace in the Old Testament', *SJTh*, **1** (1948), pp. 55–65.

Review of K. E. Kirk, ed., 'The Apostolic Ministry; Essays on the History and Doctrine of the Episcopacy', *SJTh*, **1** (1948), pp. 190–201. Reprinted in *Conflict and Agreement*, 1:212–14.

Review of T. H. L. Parker, 'The Oracles of God: an Introduction to the Preaching of John Calvin', *SJTh*, **1** (1948), pp. 212–14.

Edited with J. K. S. Reid: *Scottish Journal of Theology*, **1** (1948–), Edinburgh: Oliver & Boyd, 1948–69; London: Cambridge University Press, 1970–4; Edinburgh: Scottish Academic Press, 1974– .

1949

Calvin's Doctrine of Man, London: Lutterworth, 1949; Grand Rapids: Eerdmans, 1957.

German edition, *Cakvins Lehre vom Menschen*, trans. F. Keienberg. Zurich: Evangelischer Verlag, 1951.

Japanese edition, trans. Sakae Izumeda, Tokio, 1957.

'Faith and Philosophy', *HibJ*, **45** (1948–9), pp. 237–46.

'Universalism or Election?', *SJTh*, **2** (1949), pp. 310–18.

'Concerning Amsterdam.' I. The Nature and Mission of the Church; a discussion of volumes I and II of the Preparatory Studies', *SJTh*, **2** (1949), pp. 241–70.

Reprinted in *Conflict and Agreement*, 1:195–225.

Review of the Report of a Church of England Study Group, 'Catholicity, a study in the Conflict of the Christian Traditions in the West', *SJTh*, **2** (1949), pp. 85–93.

Reprinted in *Conflict and Agreement*, 1:48–57.

Review of Rudolf Pfister, ed., 'Zwingli Hauptschriften, Bd. XI:3 Zwingli der Theologe', *SJTh*, **2** (1949), pp. 441–4.

Review of Johannes Klevinghaus, 'Die Theologische Stellung der Apostolischen Väter zur altestamentlichen Offenbarung', *EvQ*, **21** (1949), pp. 153–5.

1950

'A Study in New Testament Communication', *SJTh*, **3** (1950), pp. 298–313. Reprinted in *Conflict and Agreement*, 2:58–74.

'Salvation is of the Jews', *EvQ*, **22** (1950), pp. 164–73.

1951
'Answer to God', *BibTh*, **2** (1951), pp. 3–16.
'History and Reformation', *SJTh*, **4** (1951), pp. 279–91.
Review of A. E. J. Rawlinson, 'Problems of Reunion', *SJTh*, **4** (1951), pp. 427–33.
Reprinted in *Conflict and Agreement*, 1:69–75.
Review of Edmund Schlink, ed., 'Evangelisches Gutachten zur Dogmatisierung der lieblichen Himmelfahrt Mariens', *SJTh*, **4** (1951), pp. 90–6.
Reprinted in *Conflict and Agreement*, 1:156–62.
Review of William Robertson, 'The Biblical Doctrine of the Church', *SJTh*, **4** (1951), pp. 433–7.

1952
'Eschatology and Eucharist', in D. M. Baillie and J. Marsh, eds., *Intercommunion*, London: SCM 1952, pp. 303–50.
Reprinted in *Conflict and Agreement*, 2:154–202.
'The Eschatology of the Reformation', in W. Manson, G. W. H. Lampe, T. F. Torrance and W. A. Whitehouse, *Eschatology: four occasional papers read to the Society for the Study of Theology*, *SJTh.OP*, **2**, pp. 30–62.
French version, *Les Reformateurs et le fin des Temps*, trans. Roger Brandt, Neuchâtel: Delachaux et Niestlé, 1955.
German version in *EvTh*, **14** (1954), pp. 334–58, trans. by H. Quistorp.
Review of a Report of a Church of England Study Group, 'The Fulness of Christ: the Church's Growth into Catholicity', *SJTh*, **5** (1952), pp. 90–100.
Reprinted in *Conflict and Agreement*, 1:57–68.
Review of Oscar Cullmann, 'The Earliest Christian Confessions', *SJTh*, **5** (1952), pp. 85–7.
Review of Heinrich Heppe, 'Reformed Dogmatics, set out and illustrated from the Sources', *SJTh*, **5** (1952), pp. 81–5.
Review of C. R. B. Shapland, ed., 'The Letters of St Athanasius concerning the Holy Spirit', *SJTh*, **5** (1952), pp. 205–8.
Review of Adolf Hamel, 'Kirche bei Hippolyt von Rom', *SJTh*, **5** (1952), pp. 208–11.
Review of J. S. McEwen, 'Why we are Christians', *SJTh*, **5** (1952), pp. 316–19.
Review of William Manson, 'The Epistle to the Hebrews', *SJTh*, **5** (1952), pp. 309–13.
Review of Alan Richardson, ed., 'A Theological Word Book of the Bible,' *SJTh*, **5** (1952), pp. 319–20.
Review of L. Nixon, ed., 'Calvin's Sermons: vol. 1: The Mystery of Godliness, and other selected Sermons: vol. 2: The Deity of Christ and other Sermons', *SJTh*, **5** (1952), pp. 424–7.
Review of Gordon Rupp, 'Luther's Progress to the Diet of Worms', *SJTh*, **5** (1952), pp. 427–8.
Edited with J. K. S. Reid: *Scottish Journal of Theology Occasional Papers*, **1**– , Edinburgh: Oliver & Boyd, 1952–69; London: Cambridge University Press, 1970–4; Edinburgh: Scottish Academic Press, 1975– .

1. G. A. F. Knight, 'The Biblical Approach to the Doctrine of the Trinity', 1953.
2. W. Manson, G. W. H. Lampe, T. F. Torrance and W. A. Whitehouse, 'Eschatology: four occasional papers read to the Society for the Study of Theology', 1952.
3. Thomas F. Torrance, 'Royal Priesthood', 1955.
4. John K. S. Reid, 'The Biblical Doctrine of Ministry', 1955.
5. Karl Barth, 'Christ and Adam: man and humanity in Romans 5', trans. T. A. Smail, 1956.
6. N. Q. Hamilton, 'The Holy Spirit and Eschatology in Paul', 1957.
7. Arnold Ehrhardt, 'The Apostolic Ministry', 1958.
8. Karl Barth, 'God, Grace and Gospel', trans. James S. McNabb, 1959.
9. Markus Barth, 'Was Christ's Death a Sacrifice?', 1961.
10. John D. Godsey, ed., and trans., 'Karl Barth's Table Talk', 1963.
11. Paul Ramsey, 'Deeds and Rules in Christian Ethics', 1965.
12. C. E. B. Cranfield, 'A Commentary on Romans 12–3', 1965.
13. Emmanuel Amand de Mendieta, 'Apostolic Traditions in Basil of Caesarea', 1965.
14. James D. Hester, 'Paul's Concept of Inheritance', 1968.
15. A. J. B. Higgins, 'The Tradition about Jesus', 1969.

1953

'The Christian Doctrine of Marriage', *Theol.*, **56** (1953), pp. 162–7.

'Where do we go from Lund?', *SJTh*, **6** (1953), pp. 53–64.
Reprinted in *Conflict and Agreement*, 1:226–37.
German version in *EvTh*, **12** (1952–3), pp. 499–508.

'The Modern Eschatological Debate', *EvQ*, **25** (1953), pp. 45–54, 94–106, 167–78, 224–33.

'Our Witness through Doctrine', *PresW*, **22** (1953), pp. 314–26.
Reprinted in *Conflict and Agreement*, 1:89–103.
French version in *VC*, **8** (1954), pp. 110–20.

Review of F. L. Cross, 'St. Cyril's Lectures on the Christian Sacraments', *SJTh*, **6** (1953), pp. 90–2.

Review of J. Robert Nelson, 'The Realm of Redemption', *SJTh*, **6** (1953), pp. 320–25.

Review of Otto A. Dillenschneider, 'Das Christliche Weltbild', *SJTh*, **6** (1953), pp. 435–6.

Review of LeRoy Edwin Fromm, 'The Prophetic Faith of our Fathers: The Historical Development of Prophetic Interpretation', 3 vols., *SJTh*, **6** (1953), pp. 207–12.

1954

'The Atonement and the Oneness of the Church', *SJTh*, **7** (1954), pp. 245–269.
Reprinted in *Conflict and Agreement*, 1:238–62.
German version in *EvTh*, **15** (1954), pp. 1–22.

'Proselyte Baptism', *NTS*, **1** (1954), pp. 150–4.

'Liturgy and Apocalypse', *Church Service Society Annual*, **24** (1954), pp. 1–18.

French version in *VC*, **11** (1957), pp. 28–40.

'The Way of Reunion', *CCen*, **71** (1954), pp. 204–5.

Review of Tiburtius Gallus, 'Interpretatio mariologica Protoevangelii posttridentina usque ad Definitionem Dogmaticam Immaculatae Conceptionis, pars prior', *SJTh*, **7** (1954), pp. 97–9.

Review of B. B. Warfield, 'The Inspiration and Authority of the Bible', *SJTh*, **7** (1954), pp. 104–8.

Review of P. Barth and D. Scheuner, eds., 'Calvini Opera selecta, vol. 2', *SJTh*, **7** (1954), pp. 320–1.

Review of T. Stupperish, ed., 'Melanchthons Werke, vol. 1', *SJTh*, **7** (1954), pp. 319–20.

1955

Royal Priesthood, SJTh.OP, **3**, Edinburgh: Oliver & Boyd, 1954.

French version in *VC*, **12** (1958), pp. 233–328.

'Karl Barth', *ET*, **66** (1955), pp. 205–9.

'Kingdom and Church in the Thought of Martin Butzer', *JEH*, **6** (1955), pp. 48–59.

Reprinted in *Kingdom and Church*, pp. 73–89.

Review of F. L. Cross, '1 Peter, a Paschal Liturgy', *SJTh*, **8** (1955), pp. 101–2.

Church of Scotland Interim Reports of the Special Commission on Baptism —a series of brochures prepared in the name of the Commission by T. F. Torrance (convener) and published annually, May 1955–May 1962 inclusive. For private circulation only.

1956

Kingdom and Church—A Study in the Theology of The Reformation, Edinburgh: Oliver & Boyd, 1956.

'Karl Barth', *USQR*, **2** (1956), pp. 21–31.

'The Place of Christology in Biblical and Dogmatic Theology', in T. H. L. Parker, ed., *Essays in Christology for Karl Barth*, London: Lutterworth, 1956, pp. 13–37.

Reprinted in *Theology in Reconstruction*, pp. 128–49.

'A Sermon on the Trinity', *BibTh*, **6** (1956), pp. 40–4.

'Ein vernachlässigter Gesichtspunkt der Tauflehre', *EvTh*, **16** (1956), pp. 433–57, 481–92.

'Israel and the Incarnation', *Interp.*, **10** (1956), pp. 3–10.

Reprinted in *Jud.*, **13** (1957), pp. 1–18.

Reprinted in *Conflict and Agreement*, 1:285–303.

'Karl Barth. In honour of his Seventieth Birthday', *ET*, **67** (1956), pp. 261–3.

'Le Mystère du Royaume', *VC*, **10** (1956), pp. 1–10.

'The Place of the Humanity of Christ in the Sacramental Life of the Church', *Church Service Society Annual*, **26** (1956), pp. 1–10.

"The Meaning of Baptism', *CJT*, **2** (1956), pp. 129–34.

Reprinted in *Conflict and Agreement*, 2:125–32.

Review of Ronald Selby Wright, ed., 'Asking Them Questions', *SJTh*, **9** (1956), p. 112.

Review of Ernst Staehlin, 'Die Verkündigung des Reiches Gottes in der Kirche Jesu Christi. Zeugnisse aus allen Jahrhunderten und allen Konfessionem', Vol. 1–2, *SJTh*, **9** (1956), pp. 90–2; 3–4, *SJTh*, **13** (1960), pp. 219–20; 6, *SJTh*, **19** (1966), pp. 227–9.

Review of F. C. Schmitt, ed., 'S. Anselmi Opera omnia', *SJTh*, **9** (1956), pp. 88–90.

Edited with G. W. Bromiley, Karl Barth's *Church Dogmatics*, 13 vols. Edinburgh: T. & T. Clark, 1956–75.

I.1. The Doctrine of the Word of God. Prolegomena, Part 1, trans. G. W. Bromiley, 1975.

I.2. The Doctrine of the Word of God. Prolegomena, Part 2, trans. G. T. Thomson and H. Knight, 1956.

II.1. The Doctrine of God, Part 1, trans. T. H. L. Parker, W. B. Johnston, H. Knight, J. L. M. Haire, 1957.

II.2. The Doctrine of God, Part 2, trans. G. W. Bromiley, J. C. Campbell, I. Wilson, J. Strathearn McNab, H. Knight, R. A. Stewart, 1957.

III.1. The Doctrine of Creation, Part 1, trans. J. W. Edwards, O. Bussey, H. Knight, 1958.

III.2. The Doctrine of Creation, Part 2, trans. H. Knight, J. K. S. Reid, G. W. Bromiley, R. H. Fuller, 1960.

III.3. The Doctrine of Creation, Part 3, trans. G. W. Bromiley, H. Ehrlich, 1960.

III.4. The Doctrine of Creation, Part 4, trans. A. T. Mackay, T. H. L. Parker, H. Knight, H. A. Kennedy, J. Marks, 1961.

IV.1. The Doctrine of Reconciliation, Part 1, trans. G. W. Bromiley, 1956.

IV.2. The Doctrine of Reconciliation, Part 2, trans. G. W. Bromiley, 1958.

IV.3. The Doctrine of Reconciliation, Part 3, vols. i and ii, trans. G. W. Bromiley, 1961–2.

IV.4. (fragment) The Doctrine of Reconciliation, Part 4, trans. G. W. Bromiley, 1969.

1957

When Christ Comes and Comes Again, London: Hodder & Stoughton, 1957; Grand Rapids, Eerdmans, 1957.

'Abendsmahlsgemeinschaft und Vereinigung der Kirchen', *KuD*, **3** (1957), pp. 240–50.

English version in *Conflict and Agreement*, 1:122–34.

'One Aspect of the Biblical Conception of Faith', *ET*, **68** (1957), pp. 111–114, 221–2.

Reprinted in *Conflict and Agreement*, 2:74–82.

'A New Approach—Presbyterian and Anglican Conversations', *The Presbyterian Record* (Toronto), July–Aug. 1957, pp. 19, 36–7.

Reprinted in *BibTh*, **8** (1957), pp. 26–36.

Reprinted in *Conflict and Agreement*, 1:134–45.

1958
'The Mission of Anglicanism', in D. M. Paton, ed., *Anglican Self-Criticism*, London: SCM, 1958, pp. 194–208.
'Karl Barth', in G. L. Hunt, ed., *Ten Makers of Modern Protestant Thought*, New York: Association Press, 1958, pp. 58–68; rev. ed., 1971, pp. 47–54.
'The Origins of Baptism', *SJTh*, **9** (1958), pp. 158–71.
Reprinted in *Conflict and Agreement*, 2:93–106.
'Aspects of Baptism in the New Testament', *ThZ*, **14** (1958), pp. 241–60.
Reprinted in *Conflict and Agreement*, 2:106–25.
'Consecration and Ordination', *SJTh*, **9** (1958), pp. 225–52.
Reprinted in *Conflict and Agreement*, 1:134–45.
'What is the Church?', *ER*, **11** (1958), pp. 6–21.
Reprinted in *Conflict and Agreement*, 1:104–22.
'La Doctrine de l'Ordre', *RHPhR*, **38** (1958), pp. 129–42.
English version, 'The Meaning of Order', *CQR*, **160** (1959), pp. 21–36.
Reprinted in *Conflict and Agreement*, 2:13–30.
Review of F. L. Cross, ed., 'The Oxford Dictionary of the Christian Church', *SJTh*, **11** (1958), pp. 320–1.
Review of K. E. Skydsgaard, 'One in Christ', *SJTh*, **11** (1958), pp. 330–3.
Review of Kurt Galling, ed., 'Die Religion in Geschichte und Gegenwart', Vol. 1, *SJTh*, **11** (1958), pp. 322–3; 2–3, *SJTh*, **13** (1960), pp. 217–19; 4–5, *SJTh*, **15** (1962), pp. 84–5.
Translated and edited, *The Mystery of the Lord's Supper: Sermons on the Sacrament preached in the Kirk of Edinburgh in A.D. 1589 by Robert Bruce*, London: James Clark, 1958.
Introduction and historical notes to *Tracts and Treatises on the Reformation* by John Calvin, trans. H. Beveridge, 3 vols., Edinburgh: Oliver & Boyd, 1958; Grand Rapids: Eerdmans, 1958.

1959
Conflict and Agreement in the Church. Volume 1: Order and Disorder, London: Lutterworth, 1959.
The Apocalypse Today, Grand Rapids: Eerdmans, 1959; London: James Clark, 1960.
'Uppfattningen om försoningen i urkyrkan. Kristi ämbete (Conceptions of Atonement in the Early Church. Christ's Office)', trans. L. G. Rignell, *SvTK*, **35** (1959), pp. 73–100.
'What is the Reformed Church?', *BibTh*, **9** (1959), pp. 51–62.
'Calvins Lehre von der Taufe', in Jürgen Moltmann, ed., *Calvinstudien*, 1959, Neukirchen: Neukirchener Verlag, 1959, pp. 95–129.
French version in *RThPh*, **2** (1959), pp. 141–52.
Review of Joachim Beckmann, 'Quellen zur Geschichte des christliche Gottesdienstes', *SJTh*, **12** (1959), pp. 108–9.
Review of Paul F. Palmer, 'Sacraments and Worship', *SJTh*, **12** (1959), pp. 109–10.
Review of M. F. Toal, ed., 'The Sunday Sermons of the Great Fathers', *SJTh*, **12** (1959), pp. 109–11.
Translated and edited with an Introduction, *The School of Faith: the*

Catechisms of the Reformed Church, London: James Clark, 1959; New York: Harper, 1959.
Edited with David W. Torrance, *Calvin's Commentaries*, 12 vols., Edinburgh: Oliver & Boyd, 1959–65; Edinburgh: The St Andrew Press, 1972; Grand Rapids: Eerdmans, 1959–72.
The Gospel according to St John 1–10, trans. T. H. L. Parker, 1959.
The Gospel according to St John 11–21 and the First Epistle of John, trans. T. H. L. Parker, 1961.
The Acts of the Apostles 1–13, trans. W. M. G. McDonald and J. W. Fraser, 1965.
The Acts of the Apostles 14–28, trans. J. W. Fraser, 1966.
The Epistles of Paul the Apostle to the Romans and to the Thessalonians, trans. R. Mackenzie.
The First Epistle of Paul the Apostle to the Corinthians, trans. J. W. Fraser, 1960.
The Second Epistle of Paul the Apostle to the Corinthians; and the Epistles to Timothy, Titus and Philemon, trans. T. A. Smail, 1964.
The Epistles of Paul the Apostle to the Galatians, Ephesians, Philippians and Colossians, trans. T. H. L. Parker, 1965.
The Epistle of Paul the Apostle to the Hebrews; and the First and Second Epistles of St. Peter, trans. W. B. Johnstone, 1963.
A Harmony of the Gospels: Matthew, Mark and Luke, 3 vols. Volumes I and III trans. A. W. Morrison; volume II trans. T. H. L. Parker, 1972.

1960
Conflict and Agreement in the Church. Volume 2: The Ministry and the Sacraments of the Gospel, London: Lutterworth, 1960.
'The Ministry of Men and Women in the Kirk. Brief Theses', *Manse Mail*, May 1960, pp. 11–13.
'Justification. Its Radical Nature and Place in Reformed Doctrine and Life', *SJTh*, **13** (1960), pp. 225–46.
Reprinted in *Theology in Reconstruction*, pp. 150–68.
Reprinted in D. J. Callahan, H. O. Oberman and D. J. O'Hanlon, eds., *Christianity Divided*, London: Sheed & Ward, 1962, pp. 283–304.
Reprinted in *idem., Catholiques et Protestants, Confrontations théologiques*, Paris: Le Seuil, 1963, pp. 261–87.
'Die Arnoldshainer Abendmahlthesen', *OeR*, **9** (1960), pp. 133–50.
English version in *SJTh*, **15** (1962), pp. 283–304.
Review of Otto Karrer, ed., 'Neues Testament', *SJTh*, **13** (1960), p. 222.
Revised and edited with Ronald Selby Wright, *A Manual of Church Doctrine according to the Church of Scotland*, by H. J. Wotherspoon and J. M. Kirkpatrick, London: Oxford U.P., 1960. Reprinted with corrections, 1965.

1961
'Karl Barth', *ET*, **71** (1961), pp. 261–3.
'A Living Sacrifice: In Memoriam John Baillie, 1886–1960', *RelLife*, **30** (1961), pp. 329–33.

'Reconciliation in Christ and in His Church', *BibTh*, **12** (1961), pp. 26–35.
'Catholicity in the Reformed Tradition', *BDT*, **2** (1961), pp. 4–8.

1962

Karl Barth: an Introduction to his Early Theology, 1910–1931, London: SCM, 1962; New York: Harper, 1962.
'Die Wahrheit, Wie Sie in Jesus ist', in Kurt Scharf, ed., *Vom Herrengeheimnis der Wahrheit. Festschrift für Heinrich Vogel*, Berlin: Lettner, 1962, pp. 254–76.
'Le Problème des relations entre Anglicans et Presbytériens en Grande-Bretagne', *Eet*, **75** (1962), pp. 15–39.
'The Kirk and the Church of Rome', *The Scotsman*, April 2, 1962, p. 6, cols. 3–5.
'Scientific Hermeneutics according to St Thomas Aquinas', *JThS*, **13** (1962), pp. 259–89.
'Gnade und Natur; der Einfluss der reformatorischen Theologie auf die Entwicklung der wissenschaftlichen Method', *ThZ*, **19** (1962), pp. 341–56.
English version in *Dialog*, **2** (1963), pp. 40–9.
Reprinted in *Theology in Reconstruction*, pp. 62–75.
Review of John Alexander Lamb, ed., 'Fasti Ecclesiae Scoticanae. The Succession of Ministers in the Church of Scotland from the Reformation', *SJTh*, **15** (1962), pp. 91–2.
Review of John Calvin, 'Concerning the Eternal Predestination of God', trans. J. K. S. Reid, *SJTh*, **15** (1962), pp. 108–10.
Introduction to *Theology and Church, Shorter Writings 1920–1928*, by Karl Barth, trans. Louise Pettibone Smith, London: SCM, 1962, pp. 7–54.

1963

'La portée de la doctrine du Saint-Esprit pour la théologie oecumenique', *VC*, **17** (1963), pp. 166–76.
German version in *OeR*, **12** (1963), pp. 122–31.
English version in *Theology in Reconstruction*, pp. 229–39.
'The Foundation of the Church', *SJTh*, **16** (1963), pp. 113–31.
Reprinted in *Theology in Reconstruction*, pp. 192–208.
'Jesus the Servant Today', in A. Reeves, ed., *Christ's Call to Service Now*.
Report of the Student Christian Conference, Bristol, 1963, London: SCM, 1963, pp. 11–21.
'Das Problem der theologischen Aussage heute', *ThZ*, **19** (1963), pp. 318–337.
English version in *Theology in Reconstruction*, pp. 46–61.
Shortened version, 'The Scientific Character of Theological Statements', *Dialog*, **4** (1965), pp. 112–17.
'Anglican-Methodist Reconciliation', *British Weekly*, Feb. 28, 1963, p. 7.
Review of Bernard Lambert, 'Le Problème Oecumenique', *SJTh*, **16** (1963), pp. 101–5.
Review of Heinrich Scholz, 'Mathesis Universalis. Abhandlungen zur Philosophie als strenger Wissenschaft', *SJTh*, **16** (1963), pp. 212–14.

Review of Y. H. Krikorian and A. Edel, eds., 'Contemporary Philosophic Problems. Selected Readings', *SJTh*, **16** (1963), pp. 302–3.
Review of G. A. Abernethy and T. A. Langford, eds., 'Philosophy of Religion. A Book of Readings', *SJTh*, **16** (1963), pp. 302–3.
Introduction to *A Calvin Treasury—Selections from The Institutes of the Christian Religion*, trans. F. L. Battles, ed. William F. Keeseck, London: SCM, 1963.
Foreword to *Heirs of the Reformation* by Jacques de Senarclens, trans. G. W. Bromiley, London: SCM, 1963.

1964
'Changed Outlook of Christians on Unity', *The Scotsman*, Jan. 29, 1964, p. 8, cols. 3–5.
'Theology and Science. Dogmatics the Key to Church Unity', *The Scotsman*, Feb. 10, 1964, p. 6, cols. 3–5.
'Science, Theology, Unity', *ThTo*, **21** (1964), pp. 149–54.
'The Ministry of Men and Woman in the Kirk. Brief Theses. Second Series', *Manse Mail*, Feb. 1964, pp. 17–20.
'Women in the Ministry. Reply to Dr Lillie', *Manse Mail*, May 1964, pp. 9–11.
'Sermon on Exodus 20:1–14', *Monkton Combe Society*, April 1964, pp. 13–18.
'Theological Education Today', *New College Bulletin*, **1** (1964), pp. 18–30. Reprinted in *Theology in Reconstruction*, pp. 13–29.
'Knowledge of God and Speech about Him according to John Calvin', *RHPhR*, **44** (1964), pp. 402–22.
  Reprinted in *CCen*, **81** (1964), pp. 696–9.
  Reprinted in *Theology in Reconstruction*, pp. 76–98.
'A Comment on the New Morality', *Common Factor*, **2** (1964), pp. 17–20.
'John Calvin's Values for Today', *Common Factor*, **2** (1964), pp. 24–5.
'A New Reformation?', *LQHR*, **189** (1964), pp. 275–94.
  Reprinted in *Theology in Reconstruction*, pp. 259–83.
'The Roman Doctrine of Grace from the Point of View of Reformed Theology', *ECQ*, **16** (1964), pp. 290–312.
  Reprinted in *Theology in Reconstruction*, pp. 169–94.
  Reprinted in Piet Fransen, *Intelligent Theology*, London: Darton, Longman & Todd, 1969, 3:46–77.
Review of J. B. Phillips, 'Good News for Modern Man', *SJTh*, **17** (1964), pp. 351–3.
Review of W. A. Whitehouse, e.a., 'A Declaration of Faith', *British Weekly*, June 18, 1964, p. 4.
Edited *New College Bulletin*, vol. 1–3, 1964–6.

1965
Theology in Reconstruction, London: SCM, 1965.
'The Epistemological Relevance of the Holy Spirit', in R. Schippers, e.a., *Ex Auditu Verbi: Theologische Opstellen Aangeboden aan Prof. Dr. G. C. Berkhouwer*, Kampen: Kok, 1965.
  Reprinted in *God and Rationality*, pp. 165–92.

'Viens, Esprit Createur, pour le renouveau du culte et du témoinage', *RHPhR*, **45** (1965), pp. 193–211.
German version in *ThZ*, **21** (1965), pp. 116–36.
English version in *Theology in Reconstruction*, pp. 240–58.
'A Tribute to Dr. John Alexander Lamb', *New College Bulletin*, **2** (1965), pp. 5–6.
Obituary notice to Dr. Albert Schweitzer, O.M., *The Times* (London), Sept. 6, 1965, p. 10, cols. 4–5.

1966
'Service in Jesus Christ', in J. I. McCord and T. H. L. Parker, eds., *Service in Christ: Essays presented to Karl Barth on his 80th Birthday*, London: Epworth, 1966, pp. 1–16.
'The Mission of the Church', *SJTh*, **19** (1966), pp. 129–43.
French version in *VC*, **20** (1966), pp. 1–16.
'Bonhoeffer's Christology', *The Scotsman*, May 28, 1966, p. 3, cols. 1–8.
'Queries to the Assembly on Church Union', *The Scotsman*, May 27, 1966, p. 10, cols. 3–6.
'The Christian Doctrine of Marriage', in J. M. Morrison, *Honesty and God*, Edinburgh: The St Andrew Press, 1966, pp. 155–62.
Review of Heinz Brunotte and Otto Weber, eds., 'Evangelisches Kirchenlexicon, Kirchlich-theologisches Handwörterbuch', *SJTh*, **19** (1966), pp. 226–7.
Review of Willis A. Shotwell, 'The Biblical Exegesis of Justin Martyr', *SJTh*, **19** (1966), pp. 229–31.

1967
'The Implications of Oikonomia for Knowledge and Speech of God in Early Christian Theology', in Felix Christ, ed., *Oikonomia: Heilsgeschichte als Thema der Theologie. Oscar Cullmann zum 65 Geburtstag gewidmet*, Hamburg: Herbert Reich, 1967, pp. 223–38.
Greek version in *Ekklesiastikos Pharos*, **51** (1969), pp. 32–48, 186–200.
'Thomas Ayton's "The Original Constitution of the Christian Church" ', in David Shaw, ed., *Reformation and Revolution. Essays presented to the Very Rev. Hugh Watt*, Edinburgh: The St Andrew Press, 1967, pp. 273–97.
'Diakonia in Jesus Christus', *IMis*, **56** (1967), pp. 201–15.
'The Eclipse of God', *BQ*, **22** (1967), pp. 194–214.
Reprinted in *God and Rationality*, pp. 29–55.
'Reformed Dogmatics not Dogmatism', *Theol.*, **70** (1967), pp. 152–6.
Edited and provided the Introduction to *Jesus and the Christian*, by William Manson, London: James Clark, 1967; Grand Rapids: Eerdmans, 1967.

1968
'Intuitive and Abstractive Knowledge from Duns Scotus to John Calvin', in *De doctrina Ioannis Duns Scoti. Acta tertii Congressus Scotistici Internationalis. Studia Scholastico-Scotistica*, **5**, Rome: Societas Int. Scotistica, 1972, pp. 291–305.

'Theological Persuasion', *Common Factor*, **5** (1968), pp. 47–57.
Reprinted in J. McDowell Richards, ed., *Soli Deo Gloria*, Richmond, Va.: John Knox Press, 1968, pp. 125–36.
Reprinted in *God and Rationality*, pp. 195–206.
'Cheap and Costly Grace', *BQ*, **22** (1968), pp. 290–311.
Reprinted in *God and Rationality*, pp. 56–85.
'The Ethical Implications of Anselm's De Veritate', *ThZ*, **24** (1968), pp. 309–19.
'Hermeneutics according to Schleiermacher', *SJTh*, **21** (1968), pp. 257–67.
Obituary notice for Karl Barth, *The Times* (London), Dec. 11, 1968, p. 10, cols. 6–9.
Review of Edward Schillebeeckx, 'Revelation and Theology', *NBl*, **49** (1968), pp. 490–92.

1969
Theological Science, London: Oxford University Press, 1969.
Space, Time and Incarnation, London: Oxford University Press, 1969.
'Karl Barth', *SJTh*, **22** (1969), pp. 1–9.
'La Mission de l'Eglise', in S. Dockx, ed., *L'Esprit Saint et L'Église. Catholiques, orthodoxes et protestants de divers pays confrontent leur science, leur foi et leur tradition: l'avenir de l'Église et de l'oecumenisme*, Paris: Fayard, 1969, pp. 275–94.
'Ecumenism and Science', *Oec.*, 1969, pp. 321–38.
Reprinted in *God and Rationality*, pp. 112–34.
'Karl Barth: in Hommage', *High Point College Review of Theology and Philosophy*, April 1969, pp. 5–12.
'Spiritus Creator', in Lukas Vischer, ed., *Le Traité sur le Saint-Esprit de Saint Basile*, Taizé: Presses de Taize, 1969.
Reprinted in *VC*, **23** (1969), pp. 63–85.
'La Philosophie et la Théologie de Jean Mair ou Major (1469–1550), i. Notitia et Dialectica', *ArPh*, **32** (1969), pp. 531–47; 'ii. Theologica', *ibid.*, **33** (1970), pp. 261–94.
'La teologia nell'eta della scienza', *Renovatio*, **4** (1969), pp. 545–64.
English version in *God and Rationality*, pp. 89–111.
'The Word of God and the Response of Man', *Bijdragen*, **30** (1969), pp. 172–83.
Reprinted in *God and Rationality*, pp. 137–64.
Review of Carlo Balić, ed., 'John Duns Scotus Opera omnia', vols. 1–6, 14–17, *SJTh*, **22** (1969), pp. 479–81.
Review of Karl Rahner, e.a., 'Sacramentum Mundi', vols. 1–3, *SJTh*, **22** (1969), pp. 481–4; 4, *ibid.*, **23** (1970), p. 94.

1970
'Theological Rationality', in E. Descamps, ed., *Ecclesia a Spiritu Sancto edocta, Lumen Gentium, Mélanges théologiques. Hommage à Mgr. G. Philips*. Gembloux: Duculot, 1970, pp. 455–73.
Reprinted in *God and Rationality*, pp. 3–25.
'The Hermeneutics of St Athanasius', *Ekklesiastikos Pharos*, **52** (1970), pp. 446–68; 89–106; 237–49; **53** (1971), pp. 133–49.

'The Problem of Natural Theology in the Thought of Karl Barth', *RelSt*, **6** (1970), pp. 121–35.
'Professor Daniel L. Deegan', *New College Bulletin*, **5** (1970), pp. 121–35.
'Alexandrian Theology', *Ekklesiastikos Pharos*, **52** (1970), pp. 185–9.
'Sermon on Acts 2:41–47', *Ekklesiastikos Pharos*, **52** (1970), pp. 191–9.
Reprinted in John B. Logan, ed., *The Relevance of Orthodoxy*, Stirling; Drummond Press, 1971.
Review of E. D. Willis, 'Calvin's Catholic Christology', in *SJTh*, **23** (1970), pp. 92–4.
Foreword to '*Secular Christianity*' *and God Who Acts*, by Robert J. Blaikie, London: Hodder & Stoughton, 1970.

1971

God and Rationality, London: Oxford University Press, 1971.
'The Place of Word and Truth in Theological Inquiry according to St. Anselm', in P. Zavalloni, ed., *Studia medievalia et mariologica, P. Carolo Balić OFM septuagesimum explenti annum dicata*, Rome: Editrice Antonianum, 1971, pp. 131–60.
'The Breaking of Bread', *Liturgical Studies*, **1** (1971), pp. 18–26.
'Die eine Taufe, die Christus und seiner Kirche gemeinsam ist', *KuD*, **17** (1971), pp. 188–208.
English version in *Theology in Reconciliation*, pp. 82–105.
'Newton, Einstein and Scientific Theology', Eighth Annual Keese Lecture, The University of Tennessee at Chattanooga, 1971. Reprinted in *RelSt*, **8** (1972), pp. 233–50.

1972

'Doctrine', a bibliographical contribution to *A Theological Book List 1971*, ed., A. Marcus Ward, London: Theological Education Fund, 1972, pp. 20–3.
'Where is God?', in Ronald Selby Wright, ed., *Asking Them Questions*, London: Oxford U.P., 1972. 1:17–26.
'Truth and Authority: Theses on Truth', *IThQ*, **39** (1972), pp. 215–42.
Partial French translation (theses only), *Ist.*, **18** (1973), pp. 44–7.
Review of Alistair McKinnon, 'Falsification and Belief', *SJTh*, **25** (1972), pp. 437–55.
Review of S. Brown and G. Gall, eds., 'William of Ockham. Opera philosophica et theologica. Opera theologica 2', *SJTh*, **25** (1972), pp. 456–8.
Review of G. Etzkorn and I Brady, eds., 'Roger Marston. Quodlibeta quattuour ad fidem codicum nunc primum edita', *SJTh*, **25** (1972), pp. 458–9.
Edited with J. K. S. Reid, *Monograph Supplements to the Scottish Journal of Theology*, 1972– , London: Cambridge University Press, 1972–4; Edinburgh: Scottish Academic Press, 1975– .
No. 1. H. Martin Rumscheidt, 'Revelation and Theology. An Analysis of the Barth-Harnack Correspondence of 1923', 1972.
2. Horton Harris, 'David Friedrich Strauss and his Theology', 1974.

3. Robin H. S. Boyd, 'India and the Latin Captivity of the Church', 1974.
4. Eberhard Jüngel, 'The Trinity: God's Being in Becoming', trans. Horton Harris, 1975.

1973

'The Church in an Era of Scientific Change', *Month* (1973), pp. 136–42, pp. 176–80.
Reprinted in *New College Bulletin*, **7** (1973), pp. 19–31.
Reprinted in *Theology in Reconciliation*, pp. 267–93.

'The Relation of the Incarnation to Space in Nicene Theology', in Andrew Blane, ed., *The Ecumenical World of Orthodox Civilisation. III. Russia and Orthodoxy. Essays in honor of Georges Florovsky*, The Hague: Mouton, 1973, pp. 43–70.

'The Integration of Form in Natural and Theological Science', *Science, Medicine and Man*, **1** (1973), pp. 143–72.

Review of J. B. Bauer, ed., 'Bauer Encyclopaedia of Biblical Theology', *SJTh*, **26** (1973), pp. 229–31.

Review of M. Schmaus, A. Grillmeier and L. Scheffczyk, eds., 'Handbuch der Dogmengeschichte', *SJTh*, **26** (1973), pp. 100–2.

Review of Alistair McKinnon, ed., 'The Kierkegaard Indices', vol. 2, *SJTh*, **26** (1973), pp. 106–8.

Review of Thomas Aquinas, 'Opera omnia iussu Leonis XII P.M. edita', vols. 40 and 48, *SJTh*, **26** (1973), pp. 350–2.

Review of Peter Lombard, 'Sententiae in IV Libris Distinctae. Editio tertia. Ad Fidem Codicum Antiquiorum restituta', Vols. 1 and 2, parts 1 and 2, ed., Fathers of the College of St Bonaventure, *SJTh*, **26** (1973), pp. 488–90.

1974

'The Evangelical Significance of the Homoousion. Sermon on John 5:17', *Abba Salama*, **5** (1974), pp. 165–8.

'Science and Philosophy in an Era of Cosmological Revolution', *Abba Salama*, **5** (1974), pp. 168–70.

'Athanasius: a Reassessment of his Theology', *Abba Salama*, **5** (1974), pp. 171–87.
Revised version in *Theology in Reconciliation*, pp. 215–66.

'The Contribution of the Greek Community in Alexandria to the Intelligent Understanding of the Christian Gospel and its Communication in the World of Science and Culture', *Abba Salama*, **5** (1974), pp. 188–92.

'Une contribution aux recherches de Foi et Constitution sur le ministère ordonné', *Ist.*, **21** (1974), pp. 429–34.

1975

Theology in Reconciliation: Essays towards Evangelical and Catholic Unity in East and West, London: Geoffrey Chapman, 1975.

'The Function of Inner and Outer Word in Lonergan's Theological Method', in Patrick Corcoran, ed., *Looking at Lonergan's Method*, Dublin: Talbot Press, 1975, pp. 101–26.

'Hermeneutics, or the Interpretation of Biblical and Theological Statements, according to Hilary of Poitiers', *Abba Salama*, **6** (1975), pp. 37–69.
Article: 'Ecumenismo' in *Encyclopedia del Novecento come lessico dei massimi problemi*, Rome: Ricordi, 1975.
Enlarged English version in *Theology in Reconciliation*, pp. 15–81.
'Towards an Ecumenical Consensus on the Trinity,' *ThZ*, **31** (1975), pp. 337–50.